# THE
# RESCUE

A True Story of Courage and Survival
in World War II

STEVEN TRENT SMITH

JOHN WILEY & SONS, INC.

New York • Chichester • Weinheim • Brisbane • Singapore • Toronto

*To Geoffrey and Martha, for their encouragement and support,*
*and Al Dempster, for his unstinting assistance*

Published by John Wiley & Sons, Inc.
Published simultaneously in Canada

Design and production by Navta Associates, Inc.

**Library of Congress Cataloging-in-Publication Data:**
Smith, Steven Trent, 1947–
   The rescue : a true story of courage and survival in World War II / Steven Trent Smith.
     p. cm.
   Includes bibliographical references and index.
   ISBN 0-471-41291-0 (cloth : alk. paper)
   1. Crevalle (Submarine) 2. World War, 1939–1945—Naval operations— Submarine. 3. World War, 1939–1945—Naval operations, American. 4. United States. Navy—Search and rescue operations—Philippines—Negros Island. 5. World War, 1939–1945—Underground movements—Philippines—Negros. 6. Negros Island (Philippines)—History. 7. Philippines—History—Japanese occupation, 1942–1945. I. Title

D783.5.C74 S63   2001
940.54'5973—dc21                                                              00-043856

# CONTENTS

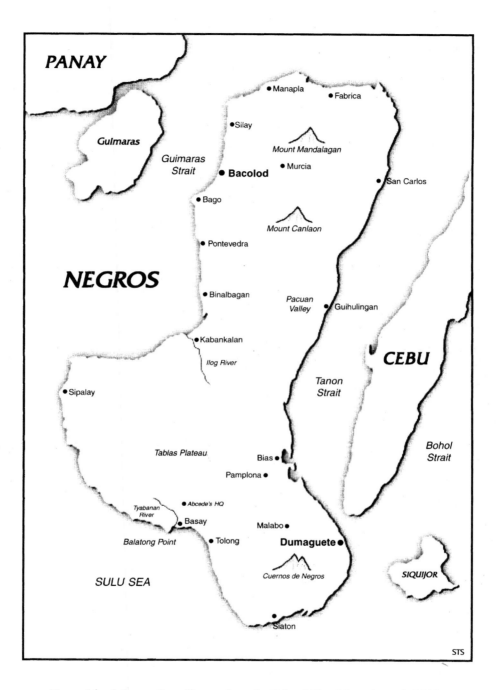

Negros Island. *Source:* Guerrilla map drawn by Colonel Abcede's engineers in 1943.

# AUTHOR'S NOTE

I HAVE BEEN IN THE THRALL of the Pacific for as long as I can remember. Its sway over me is inexplicable. Growing up near San Francisco, a visit to The City always meant a stop at the Golden Gate Bridge to watch the ships coming and going. I still recall the thrill of seeing a giant aircraft carrier glide beneath the span. My mother often read to me about the Pacific: about tramp steamers plying their trade, about divers seeking rare black pearls, about China Clippers on the sea and in the air. I spent hours curled up beneath the tall windows of the Redwood City Library, poring through dog-eared *National Geographics*, looking for pictures, stories, anything about the Pacific. I longed to travel to the fabled places on those pages: Hawaii and Hong Kong; Palau and Pohnpei; Auckland, Adelaide, Manila, and Nadi. After working as a photojournalist for a quarter of a century I can say with immense satisfaction that I did visit all those places, and each lived up to my imaginative expectations.

The roots of *The Rescue* lie in this love for the Pacific, which was manifested as a lifelong interest in all things Pacifica and especially in World War II as it was fought in that gargantuan arena. And they lie, too, in a more recent curiosity spawned by a computer game, a simulation of submarine warfare given to me by my son Geoffrey. That sparked an interest in reading every book I could find about the U.S. Navy's submarine campaign. That led, in turn, to a realization that no one had written a thorough history of the nearly three hundred "special missions" conducted by U.S. submarines during the war. Here was a worthy project, to write a scholarly study of those patrols. After a few months of research, however, I kept coming back to the story of the USS *Crevalle*'s rescue mission of forty Americans stranded in the Philippines. It beckoned seductively, tugged at me vigorously. Further delving revealed that her mission in May 1944 was twofold, that she also picked up captured Japanese war plans. The discovery in the National Archives of reports concerning some of those forty passengers clinched the project, for it gave me a solid basis upon which to begin writing not just about the events but, more important, about the people.

In the ensuing months I was able to track down the fates of all but one of the rescued Americans. *Crevalle*'s chief yeoman, Al Dempster, put me in touch with the former refugees he had located. And over the course of a year my own researches turned up others. For months there was no news about the Macasa and Jaboneta families, or of Miss Modesta Hughes. I had a standard question for everyone I spoke with: "Do you know . . . ?" And always the answer was "No." But one day somebody finally said, "Maybe." Dorothy Dowlen said I should call Donald Bell. He led me to Constantino Bernardez, who pointed to Christian Malahay, who led to Carmen Park, who led to Nana Aicodan, who had a number for Ricardo Macasa in Arizona. When I finally reached Dick, he was thrilled to hear about my interest in his family and their tale of escape. He in turn pointed me toward Ernie Jaboneta, who wrote casually in a letter, "By the way, I recently met another *Crevalle* passenger. She lives right here in San Francisco and her name is Modesta Hughes." What a thrill to find the elusive Miss Hughes. I have interviewed most of those still living, tapping fading memories of a great adventure more than a half century ago. I especially want to thank Earl Ossorio, Russ Snell, Howard Chrisco, the Real family, Joan and Jean Fleischer, Rodger Winn, Dean Lindholm, Ernie Jaboneta, and Dick Macasa for putting up with my frequent calls for still more information. Dempster also put me in touch with his *Crevalle* crewmates. Their stories about that harrowing mission enhance the narrative. Many others gave generously of their time—people often peripheral to the story, but whose recollections nevertheless helped fill it out.

Archival sources included the obvious: the National Archives, the Naval Historical Center, the Military History Institute at Carlisle Barracks, and the MacArthur Memorial (archivist James W. Zobel was especially helpful). But the more obscure archives, such as the American Historical Collection in Manila and that of the Presbyterian Historical Society in Philadelphia (just seventeen blocks from my house), turned out to possess materials that could only be described as *treasures*.

I owe special thanks to my agent, Rita Rosenkranz, for her patience and perseverance; and to Stephen S. Power at John Wiley & Sons, Inc., for his enthusiasm, wit, and ability to smooth out the rough bits. And the output was read, over and over again, by Martha, whose comments were always incisive. To her goes my gratitude and my love.

The following conventions are used in this book: Japanese personal names are written in the word order preferred in Japan, with the family name first; geographic place-names follow 1944 usage; times are local (unless otherwise noted).

While there have been published accounts of the rescue and of the secret papers, this is the first time the two tales have been linked. I have sought to re-create the events depicted as accurately and vividly as possible. Every incident portrayed is a matter of record. Where personal stories conflict, I have made an educated guess about which might have been the most likely version— not always choosing the most dramatic. Some quotations have been shortened for clarity (particularly radio messages and decrypts). The "subspeak" quotes are derived from ships' logs and war patrol reports. The narrative dialogue comes from interviews or from published and unpublished sources, including letters and diaries. I am deeply indebted to Viola Winn, Paul Lindholm, and Manuel Segura. Without their rich personal accounts of events, my story would not have been complete.

# Prologue

CLOUDS SHROUDED MOUNT MANDALAGAN as dawn broke above Negros. To the west, along the coast, the remaining residents of Bacolod woke to an uneasy silence. White flags hung limply from houses and shops. The American flag was absent altogether. Those few who ventured into the streets were greeted by a calm punctuated only by the occasional burst of an exploding shell. Four miles to the north they could see black smoke towering above the gasoline tanks at Banago Wharf. And halfway across Guimaras Strait they could see four ships steaming slowly toward the shore. One was obviously a warship, the others apparently transports. It seemed prudent to return home to await developments. It was Thursday, 21 May 1942. The Japanese had finally come calling.

For five months, since the second Monday in December, the Japanese had waged war in the Philippines. They quickly took Manila and northern Luzon, Davao and southern Mindanao. Afterward their tentacles spread slowly, patiently awaiting surrender. American and Filipino defenders had fought bravely throughout the winter. But mounting losses, dwindling supplies, and sickness had reduced their numbers, their effectiveness, and their ability to hold their ground. On 11 March General Douglas MacArthur fled the islands on orders from President Franklin Delano Roosevelt, promising he would return. With no reinforcements on the way, defeat was inevitable.

Bataan Peninsula on Manila Bay was overrun on 9 April 1942. A hundred thousand defenders fell into enemy hands. Many died on the Death March to prison camps in central Luzon. The Japanese then turned their attention to the reduction of Corregidor, the island fortress at the very mouth of the bay. For nearly four weeks incessant shelling made the island a living hell. Finally, mercifully, the siege ended on 6 May when MacArthur's successor, General Jonathan Wainwright, unconditionally surrendered the remaining eleven thousand American and Filipino troops on the island and throughout the rest of the Philippines.

Following the surrender the Japanese moved rapidly to consolidate their gains. And so it was that on 21 May a tiny invasion force lay off Bacolod, ready to occupy the island of Negros. Its commander, Colonel Kumataro Ota, a China veteran, sent in the first wave of boats at ten-thirty that morning. The lead landing craft carried six American prisoners of war, a demonstration to the Filipinos that Americans were not invincible. The occupation went smoothly. Within a few weeks Ota had control of the entire island. Or so he thought.

The Philippine archipelago embraces seven thousand islands. Most are mere spits of sand barely able to stay afloat at high tide. Others, such as Luzon and Mindanao, are massive. Slung between the two largest is a group of islands called the Visayas, and in the center of the Visayas lies Negros. Wedged like a boot between Panay on the west and Cebu on the east, Negros is the country's fourth-largest island—one hundred forty miles in length, twenty to fifty miles in width. The island's only cities, both of them small and quaint, sit catty-corner from one another: Bacolod, a sugar town, on the northwestern coast; Dumaguete, a college town, on the southeastern coast. The coastal plains of Negros extend like a horseshoe around the northern half, covered with sugar-cane fields that stretch at times for miles. Sugar brought misery to many on Negros, wealth and political power to a few. But it was sugar that put Negros on the map. Before the war the island supplied the majority of the country's sugar and exported vast amounts around the world, especially to the United States.

Running nearly from its top to its toe, a hulking mountain range forms the spine of Negros, punctuated by four mile-high peaks. In the north sits Mount Mandalagan; in the center the majestic volcano Mount Canlaon; in the south *Cuernos de Negros*—the Horns of Negros. Surrounding this *Cordillera Centrale* dense jungles and hardwood forests blanket vast areas. It was here that many residents of Negros had fled following the outbreak of war. When the Japanese finally came, nearly a third of the population was living in the mountains.

Among those in hiding were hundreds of American citizens. Some were missionaries. Some were teachers. There were growers and planters and lumbermen; miners, engineers, and businessmen. All were wanted by the Japanese.

It was in the mountain fastness that the guerrilla movement first sparked to life. Men willing to fight for freedom and die for the Philippines, organized at first into small bands and, as time passed, into larger and larger units until they counted their numbers in the tens of thousands. Always ill equipped and underarmed, the resistance on Negros, led by men such as Salvador Abcede and Ernesto Mata, nevertheless kept the Japanese off-balance with lightning raids meant to harass and confuse.

On neighboring Cebu, under the inspired leadership of a former mining engineer, James M. Cushing, the rebels grew rapidly in strength, fighting pitched battles against their enemy. Cushing excelled under the pressures of war. A man of few accomplishments before the war (and after), during the conflict he rose to genuine greatness, becoming a beloved hero to the beleaguered Cebuanos.

Gradually the extent of the burgeoning resistance movement revealed itself to MacArthur's Southwest Pacific Area (SWPA) headquarters in Brisbane, Australia. In late 1942 GHQ sent to Negros a reconnaissance party led by Filipino war hero Jesus Villamor. Back came the news: A full-fledged guerrilla organization exists and desperately requires the general's personal support. And so MacArthur began a program of blessing, then supplying, the guerrillas not just on Negros, but also throughout the Philippines. He managed to persuade the navy to provide submarines to deliver clandestine cargos of weapons, medicines, radios, and food. At ninety tons a load it was only a token, but it tangibly proved to the Filipinos that MacArthur would honor his pledge.

In November 1943 the Japanese issued an edict to the Americans hiding in the hills: Give yourself up or we will hunt you down and kill you ruthlessly. No one took up the enemy's offer. The enemy ratcheted up the pressure. Within a few months raiding parties had captured nearly a dozen families. MacArthur was alarmed. He decided to evacuate, by submarine, as many people as he could. Through the end of the year and well into 1944 the guerrillas contacted all remaining Americans on Negros, hustling them to the remote southwestern coast of the island. There they waited sometimes weeks for a submarine to pick them up. Once at sea the refugees faced a fifteen-hundred-mile voyage through waters infested with enemy patrols. If they were lucky—if they made it to Australia—freedom would be theirs.

# CHAPTER 1

---

# *Special Mission*

LIEUTENANT COMMANDER FRANK WALKER was not averse to hollering orders through the open hatch. "Mr. Mazzone, bring us to periscope depth!" The Navy Department would surely disapprove of his method, but in the cramped confines of a submarine it was a method that worked quite well. "Sixty-four feet, Captain," came the response from below. Walker turned to his executive officer, Lieutenant William J. Ruhe. When Walker gave a slight nod, Ruhe gave a firm tug on the control handle. The shiny periscope slid silently, smoothly upward. Crouching on the conning tower deck, Walker caught the scope's levers as it rose. "Hold it there." Ruhe shifted the lever. With his right eye glued to the optics, Walker quickly crabbed in a full circle. He first checked the horizon, then the sky. "All clear. Take it up." The tube rose again, and with it the captain, his back slightly hunched as he squinted at the world above him. Clicking in the six-times magnifier for a telescopic view, he carefully, slowly panned left, then right, then left again. "I see the beach, but no signals. Range. Mark." "Three thousand double-oh," came the response. "Down scope."[1] Ruhe tugged the pickle-shaped handle again. The scope dropped quickly, leaving the bare metal tube glistening in the dimness of the conning tower.

Walker turned to his yeoman, Al Dempster. "Yeo, what's that security signal again?" Dempster pulled the flimsy from his clipboard and reread the radio message: "Two white panels fifty yards apart, Skipper." [2]

The captain took a few minutes to sip a cup of coffee, brought hot and fresh from the officers' pantry by his chief steward. He called again for the scope. As he swept the horizon he spotted a white speck to the north. In high magnification he could make out a sailboat headed along the coast. He watched it carefully, for Frank Walker had developed an aversion to small boats. Just two nights before, while transiting Balabac Strait—a heavily patrolled passage between northern Borneo and the west-southwestern tip of the Philippines—

USS *Crevalle* (SS291), a Balao-class fleet submarine, taken after the war.
(U.S. Navy Photo from the National Archives)

the crew of the most innocent of outriggers shot flares into the sky as the submarine passed, attempting to alert the Japanese to his presence. He had vowed that night to blast out of the water any boats that got in his way.[3]

Walker turned his attention to the beach. He scanned the shore from north to south and back again. As the periscope plunged into its well, he told his crew there was nothing yet to see. No people. No flags. Nothing. "Mr. Ruhe, post a watch on both scopes and maintain course zero-five-zero." The captain disappeared down the control room hatch. It was nearing eight-thirty on Thursday morning, 11 May 1944, as the USS *Crevalle* crept silently beneath the dark waters of the Sulu Sea, two miles off the coast of Negros.[4]

When the call for volunteers to man the periscopes squawked over the intercom, Motor Machinist's Mate John Maille jumped at the chance to get away from the tedium of tending the engines and motors. After he climbed up into the cylindrical steel capsule that was the conning tower, he asked Bill Ruhe what they were looking for. Ruhe described the security signal. Maille leaned into the eyepiece of the scope to begin his watch.

Below in his tiny cabin, Francis David Walker Jr. reviewed the orders that three days before had terminated his war patrol, sending him a thousand miles to the north, into the middle of the Visayas. A frown creased his pudgy face as he read:

TOP SECRET. PROCEED TO BALATONG POINT, POSITION NORTH OF
BASAY, NEGROS ISLAND (LAT. 9-24 N. LONG. 122-36-36 E.). AT
SUNSET 11 MAY OBSERVE SECURITY SIGNAL, SURFACE, AND RECEIVE
FROM BOAT FLYING U.S. COLORS TWENTY-FIVE PASSENGERS AND
IMPORTANT DOCUMENTS.[5]

"Rescue mission," he muttered to himself. Frank Walker would have preferred to shoot his remaining torpedoes at some meaty target, return to Australia for more, and get on with the job of waging unrestricted war against the
enemy.

The thirty-one-year-old Annapolis graduate was a vastly experienced submariner. His war had begun in these very waters, as executive officer on the
Manila-based *Searaven*. With her he had made six desultory war patrols,
including his first special mission, delivering fifteen hundred rounds of three-
inch antiaircraft shells through the Japanese blockade to the beleaguered garrison at Bataan. But when Bataan fell on 9 April 1942, *Searaven* was told to
dump the ammunition and forget the Philippines. Her crew must have been
heartbroken at the lost opportunity to aid American forces. Two days later
*Searaven*'s patrol was again terminated when orders came through for a second special mission: rescue thirty-three Australian aviators from West Timor.

*Crevalle*'s officers for her third war patrol (left to right, back row: Dick Bowe, Howard
Geer, Jim Blind, Executive Officer Bill Ruhe, Captain Frank Walker; front row:
George Morin, Walt Mazzone, Luke Bowdler). (U.S. Navy Photo via Al Dempster)

Though successful, the pickup took five difficult, dangerous days, and on the way down to Fremantle a fire in one of the engineering compartments disabled the submarine. For more than twelve hours *Searaven* drifted helplessly in the Timor Sea. Another submarine came to her rescue and towed the wounded sub into port.[6] For Frank Walker that patrol was not an auspicious introduction to special missions.

After leaving *Searaven*, Walker was rotated back to the States to help put *Crevalle* into commission in June 1943. He made two very successful runs as her exec under the daring Lieutenant Commander Henry Glass Munson. Now the boat was Walker's.

Walker had good reason to feel optimistic about *Crevalle*'s third run. The crew had responded well under his direction. His superiors in Australia would surely approve of his aggressive leadership. Hadn't he already fired eighteen of his twenty-four torpedoes, sinking or damaging three Japanese *marus*, merchantmen like that monstrous oil tanker? For that there might be a Navy Cross in the offing. But Walker would rather forget the shellacking his boat had taken after putting down the big maru, sixty-one bone-rattling depth charges in a sustained attack that nearly destroyed *Crevalle*. He must have shuddered when he thought how close to oblivion he had taken his first command. When the special orders ditted and dahed out of the ether, Walker had been preparing to turn his ship homeward, back toward Fremantle in Western Australia. Perhaps en route he would have found some unwary convoy to attack. Perhaps he would have been able to fire his remaining five torpedoes and chalk up another ship. *Crevalle* was a fighting machine, not a bus. But with receipt of these new orders Frank Walker had reluctantly resigned himself to play bus driver.

His bus was one of ten dozen Balao-class fleet submarines built for the navy during World War II.[7] Each a tad longer than a football field, the fifteen-hundred-ton ships were the successful culmination of forty years of American submarine design and experience. Named after a particularly fierce variety of saltwater jack, *Crevalle* was a product of the Portsmouth Navy Yard in New Hampshire.[8] Into her cramped interior spaces she packed a crew of eight officers and seventy-two enlisted men, most of them hardened veterans of undersea warfare, all of them volunteers. She carried six torpedoes in her forward tubes, four in her aft tubes, and fourteen reloads. She could dive well below four hundred feet, cruise more than eleven thousand miles without refueling. On the surface her diesel-electric drive could push twenty-one knots. Submerged, running off her batteries, she could sprint at nine knots for an hour, or slug along at two knots for nearly two days.[9] Unlike the aging *Nautilus* and *Narwhal*, big cruiser subs now fully dedicated to Philippine cargo runs, *Crevalle* was a modern fleet submarine. She was not designed to carry passengers; her builders intended for her to sink ships. And *Crevalle* had already proved she was up to that task. After just three patrols she took credit for sending eight vessels to the bottom. A bus indeed.

Up in the conning tower, motormac John Maille continued his periscope sweeps, scanning the shore for white panels. The seaman had not been told that two dozen American refugees were to gather on the beach at sundown, hoping for deliverance. The captain would withhold that information from his crew at least until those signals appeared, and those people appeared, and a rescue seemed imminent. If no one showed up that evening, Walker was prepared to make another attempt the following night. Then he would leave the refugees to fend for themselves. After all, he thought, what could be so special about these people—and those papers?

# CHAPTER 2

## *The Missionaries*

IT WAS THE DEAD OF WINTER in 1941 when missionaries Paul and Clara Lindholm first laid eyes on Negros. They emerged from their cabin at dawn as the Manila steamer *Panay* cruised down Tañon Strait, the brown hills of Cebu to port, the green mountains of Negros to starboard. The couple watched with fascination when Dumaguete City hove into view. Surveying the tranquil scene, they wondered what this little jewel held for them. Just a month before, they had been serving God in China. But the threat of war overtook their lives as the Japanese Army advanced across that nation's eastern provinces. The family heeded the advice of their consulate and that of their employer, the Presbyterian Board of Foreign Missions, and evacuated. Paul quickly accepted another Far East assignment, a position teaching and evangelizing in the Philippines.

This was a very different world from the one the Lindholms had left behind. Even at sunup the heat was oppressive, as the cold had been in China. Vibrant colors replaced gray monotones. And above all, it was a peaceful place. When the ship sidled alongside the long stone jetty that Saturday morning in February, Paul and Clara felt more than a tinge of excitement.[1] From afar this little town seemed paradisiacal: warm and friendly, a proper place to raise children, a fitting place to serve the Lord.

Dumaguete lies at the toe of Negros, at the confluence of Tañon Strait, Bohol Strait, and the Mindanao Sea. For that reason it has for centuries been the most important town on the eastern side of the island, and more recently the provincial capital of Oriental Negros. To its back, barely eight miles inland, rise the steep umber peaks of Cuernos de Negros. In the early 1940s Dumaguete was a busy market town and interisland port with a thousand-foot quay often crowded with bancas, schooners, ferries, and the odd freighter picking up a load of copra or hemp. To those who arrived by sea, as most people did, the town seemed from a distance rather small and quaint. The faint, sweet aroma of drying coconut filled the air. Pastel houses glowed in the early morning sun. Shops hung with floral fabrics waving in the gentle offshore breeze faced the bay along a curving beachfront esplanade. Rising above myriad palms, the stately coral-block watchtower hinted at the city's Spanish origins. But those palms hid much of Dumaguete from view, hid the fact that it was an education center of some national prominence.

As lines were pulled taut around black iron bollards and the teak gangway dropped into place, *Panay*'s whistle blew a deep-throated note. In response, the dock suddenly came alive. People streamed onto the jetty, anxious to meet a loved one or a business partner. Food stands selling fresh slices of pungent durian and sugary cane treats appeared from nowhere. A long line of carts pulled by the ubiquitous *carabao*—the water buffalo—threaded its way through the mass. Passengers laden with cheap suitcases and woven abaca bags crowded the narrow ramp as they made their way down into the horde. Families and hawkers intermingled on the pier and there, amid the crowd, stood a gray-haired man dressed in a linen suit, his head covered by a neat Panama. At his side a woman, her pearl-white face shaded by a parasol, squinted upward, scanning the deck. When the family of five reached the brow at deck's edge the woman on the dock pointed, then waved, joined by her companion.

"Dayon!" the man shouted welcome in Visayan when the Lindholms reached the quayside. The couple approached, introducing themselves as Dr. and Mrs. Arthur L. Carson. He was president of Silliman University. It was he to whom Paul had written about working in the College of Theology, he who had persuaded the Board of Foreign Missions to assign the family to Negros after their disappointment in China. Paul introduced his family: wife, Clara; daughter, Beverly; and sons, Dean and Jamie.

Following the pleasantries, the little group turned to walk up the long jetty. Where the pier widened at the midpoint, Dr. Carson led them to a waiting college car.

The vehicle wound through the throng, passed open sheds piled high with pallets of hemp, turned onto Rizal Avenue's gentle arc. Immediately to their right were two of the school's most imposing buildings, and between them stood four stone block pillars. "The Gates of Opportunity," Dr. Carson pointed out. At the next turning the car pulled onto Silliman Avenue, and after making another right, onto Hibbard Avenue, came upon the verdant quadrangle. The second term was already half completed; the greensward separating the classroom blocks was alive with students. He proudly told them the school had more than twelve hundred that semester.

Just a little farther on, the vehicle pulled up to a stout house sitting among rows of equally stout houses, all freshly whitewashed and standing upon pilings, all surrounded by lush gardens and trees burdened with colorful fruit. Broad steps rose from the lawn to reach the front door, a full story off the ground. Lattice surrounded the undercroft, insulating the house from the humid heat. Dean exclaimed to his mother that the roof was made of straw. He had never seen anything like it.[2] Indeed, the steep, peaked roof was thatched with fronds of nipa palm, giving the residence a decidedly tropical countenance.

The interior was simply furnished with locally made pieces and a few leftovers from previous Western tenants. The floor was polished hardwood. The walls were more like plaited room dividers than solid bulkheads. The high ceiling, woven from split bamboo stalks, allowed air to circulate freely. The windows were many, but none had glass. A cloth awning held in place by a bamboo pole was suspended above each window. When the weather turned wet, closing a window required nothing more than unhooking the pole to let the cloth cover the opening. It was simple and effective, the Philippine way.

The Lindholms quickly adapted to their new life. Beverly, then eight, and Dean, three months short of six, were enrolled as the only non-Filipinos at the local public school, but would not start until the new term began in June. Both were relieved when they learned that their classes would be taught in English, a common practice of the day. In lieu of school those first months, the siblings used their long break to make friends and explore Dumaguete and its environs. Jamie, properly James Milton, was just nine months old when the family arrived in the Philippines. Born in Suchow, China, he happily stayed home with his nannies, Foni and Dulia, while Clara taught English and music at the university.[3] Paul threw himself into his new job with his usual zeal. Though he taught some classes at the university, he got the most pleasure from being out among the Negrenses, learning their language (Cebuano on this side of the island), organizing church conferences, and most of all spreading the word of God. In those early days he traveled extensively around Negros and throughout the Visayas, over to Leyte and Bohol and Cebu. He wowed his Filipino audiences when he showed them a colorful lantern slide program depicting the life of Jesus Christ, then led the congregation in song with his vibrant baritone voice.[4]

Arthur and Edith Carson returned to the Dumaguete jetty three months

The Lindholm Family (left to right, James, Beverly, Paul, Janet, Clara, Dean).
(Dean Lindholm)

after the Lindholms arrived, to welcome another family of refugee missionaries. Gardner and Viola Winn had come down from Peking, after a short working layover on Luzon, with two small children in tow and a third due that summer. Gardner, a second-generation Presbyterian missionary, was to teach English and Bible studies for the university, while his wife would teach the Scriptures at Silliman High School.

The Winns moved into their own whitewashed house along the row of faculty homes. Gardner, always a missionary at heart, fell into the unaccustomed role of teacher. He understood the practicality of wearing light-colored clothing in the tropics, but chafed at having to wear a necktie every day. Rodger, four, and two-year old Norman remained at home under the care of their young Filipina minder, Victoria.[5] A sister joined them two months after their arrival; in July Viola gave birth in the mission hospital to Elinor Joyce. The university's family grew by one.

SILLIMAN WAS AN ANOMALY in the Philippines, a four-year, Protestant-run university offering degrees in several disciplines. The school was founded in 1901 as the Silliman Institute with a substantial donation from retired businessman Horace Brinsmade Silliman.[6] Two years earlier the Christian philanthropist had offered the Presbyterian Board of Foreign Missions in New York City ten thousand dollars to found a school in the Philippine Islands, recently acquired by the United States from Spain after their brief conflict in 1898. The board desperately wanted Silliman's money, but a school in the Philippines was the last thing they wanted to spend it on. The church already had productive missions in a dozen other countries, and the board wanted to use the grant to support these programs. Horace Silliman was adamant. If they did not build in the Philippines, they might as well forget it. The board caved. After several more delays, Dr. David Sutherland Hibbard and his wife, Laura, who ran a school on the neighboring island of Panay, were hired to open the institute. Fifteen high school students were enrolled for the 1901 term.

Silliman grew rapidly. Girls were admitted in 1912. A two-year college program was begun in 1915. In 1921 the Silliman Bible School was organized, with help from the Congregational Churches of the United States. And in 1938 the school became a fully accredited university.

Though the school was American-founded and for the most part American-run, only a handful of the faculty were U.S. citizens. The longest tenure was held by Charles Glunz, a German American who was head of the university's Industrial Department. Glunz came to the Philippines in 1898 with the U.S. Army and had stayed on ever since, joining Silliman in its infancy. In his sixties, the tall, heavyset Glunz spoke with a slight accent and possessed the vigor of a man half his age. It was widely believed that Glunz could build anything—he had designed and supervised the construction of most of the university's buildings. But his real genius was taking bits, pieces, scraps, and refuse, and turning them into something useful or needed. Once the director of a school play told Glunz she needed a "Creation." "Capital letter or ordinary?" he asked. "Oh, big capital, *à la* Genesis," she replied. "Okay," said Glunz with a shrug. And so it came to pass. His *Big Capital Creation*, electrically controlled, thrilled and awed audiences.[7]

Dr. James W. Chapman, a world-renowned entomologist and head of the Zoology Department, arrived with his wife, Ethel, before World War I. Chapman delighted in searching the tropical jungles of Negros for new species of insects (ants in particular), some of which he named after Silliman friends. Henry Roy Bell and his wife, Edna, came to the institute as newlyweds in 1921. Roy started in the History Department, then moved on to Physics; Edna taught home economics.

Reverend James F. McKinley arrived at Silliman in 1930 with his wife, Virginia. Short and stocky, the Congregationalist minister helped found the

School of Theology. Robert Benton Silliman (no relation to Horace) taught history and directed the university press. He lived in town with his wife, Metta, and her bookish sister, Abby R. Jacobs. The sisters both taught English. Indeed, they were considered the "backbone of the English Department."[8] Jacobs also taught journalism, and supervised the publication of the school's weekly newspaper, the *Sillimanian*. The remainder of the faculty and admin-istration (as well as the entire staff at the affiliated Mission Hospital in Dumaguete) were Filipinos. Among them were Assistant Professor of English Benjamin Nisce Viloria and the commandant of the university's ROTC pro-gram, Captain Salvador Abcede.

The president of Silliman University was Dr. Arthur L. Carson, appointed in 1939. Carson was an old Asia hand, having spent two decades as a mis-sionary and educator in northern China. A farm boy from Pennsylvania, Car-son had felt a religious calling early in life. A dedicated scholar, he mastered Latin, Chinese, and, later, Japanese. His arrival at Silliman, heralded by a mid-night torch parade from the docks to the school, signaled what was to have been a new era for the university. Carson quickly won the admiration and respect of his students and his faculty and made ambitious plans to expand the school. He plunged ahead with his designs despite the deepening crises in Asia and Europe.

Crises indeed. The late 1930s brought four belligerent countries to the world stage: Mussolini's Italy, Stalin's Soviet Union, Hitler's Germany, and Hirohito's Japan. Benito Mussolini sent his army into the deserts of Ethiopia in 1936. Stalin invaded Finland in 1938, the same year Hitler annexed Austria and Czechoslovakia. And on Friday, 1 September 1939, Germany entered Poland. That Sunday England and France declared war on Germany, marking the beginning of World War II. The United States was reluctant to join the fray, so on the fifth of September President Franklin Delano Roosevelt declared America's neutrality. Perhaps seeing "the writing on the wall," he also author-ized the first of many increases in the size of America's military forces.

On the Asian front, the Japanese had conquered Manchuria in 1931 and had attacked China proper in 1937. By the time the Nazis invaded Poland, Japan controlled vast amounts of eastern China, from Manchuria in the north to Shanghai in the south, and inland for a hundred miles or more. It seemed apparent to Roosevelt and his military planners that eventually Japan would attempt to expand its empire into Southeast Asia, even perhaps into the Philippines.

The U.S. Navy had been keeping a wary eye on Japan since the Russo-Japanese War in 1905, in which the czar's naval forces were crushed. Nippon gained vast territory in the western Pacific during World War I when Japan, then a Western ally, grabbed Germany's Micronesian possessions. Following the war the League of Nations awarded the territories to Japan as a mandate under league guidance. The decision was opposed by American planners, for it gave Japan a strategic foothold in the Pacific upon which imperial forces could build a network of military bases to control millions of square miles of ocean. So that it might patrol and defend its new territory, the island nation embarked upon an ambitious naval building program ultimately designed to put it on a par with the United States and Britain. A series of arms control agreements limiting the number and size of warships were negotiated and signed in the two decades following the end of the war, but Japan never particularly adhered to them. It seemed to some observers that by the 1930s Japan and the United States were plunging headlong into a battle for control of the Pacific.

The war in Europe escalated dramatically during the spring of 1940. In April, Germany invaded Denmark and Norway. In the following month Germany overran Belgium, the Netherlands, and Luxembourg. The *coup de grâce* came in June, with the fall of France. The heart of Europe was now in Adolf Hitler's hands. While headlines blared and diplomats complained about German aggression, Stalin occupied Estonia and Latvia. During that month President Roosevelt declared a state of national emergency.

With the Germans now pulling French strings, the northern part of French-controlled Indochina (Vietnam, Laos, and Cambodia) was opened to a Japanese "military mission."[9] In the next few months France made more concessions to the Japanese, giving them the right to occupy ports, air bases, and railways in Southeast Asia. In direct response, Roosevelt imposed a pair of trade embargoes on Japan. The first, laid down on 5 July 1940, prohibited the exportation of strategic raw materials and machine parts. The second came three weeks later, with a ban on the shipment of iron and steel and, most critically to Japan, aviation gasoline. The nation was heavily dependent upon the United States for petroleum. With no natural supply of its own, the embargo pushed Japan to war. The emperor's government turned its attention and its designs southward, toward the rich oil fields of the Netherlands East Indies (now Indonesia).

As the situation in Asia worsened, in July 1941 President Roosevelt recalled

General Douglas MacArthur to active duty as commander of United States Army Forces in the Far East (USAFFE). The general knew he had a tough job ahead. His American forces were meager in number and ill equipped. And the Philippine Army he had been training since 1936 was weak, badly organized, and poorly led.

These momentous events had little immediate effect upon the people of Negros. In quiet Dumaguete war fears, though widespread, were subdued. MacArthur's arrival directly benefited Silliman's ROTC program. The cadet corps finally received a small shipment of 1903 Springfield rifles. Now his cadets could train with real weapons instead of bamboo sticks. Throughout the summer and fall young Captain Abcede kept up a frantic training schedule as the Philippines attempted to move to a war footing. Other than the ROTC, there were no military units of any consequence, no outward signs of war preparations, American or Filipino, anywhere on the island.

Unbeknownst to the Sillimanians, Thanksgiving 1941 was to be the last opportunity for the nineteen American adults and their thirteen children to celebrate a holiday in peace. In early November Clara Lindholm sent out her annual Christmas letter. "Dear Friends," she wrote. "This will be our first Christmas in the tropics. The poinsettia hedges that stand higher than our heads are already preparing for their part in the festivities. It will seem to us who are used to Minnesota white Christmases like having Christmas in July." She closed, "Christmas will bring you all close to us despite the distances and the uncertainties of the world today."[10] As the families began to prepare for— to look forward to—that most Christian of holidays, their world was about to change with drama and swiftness.

IN THE PHILIPPINES, 7 December 1941 was a Sunday just like any other. The Winns, the Carsons, and the Bells attended Sunday services on the campus at Dumaguete, followed by ample dinners, short strolls, lazy siestas, and light suppers. Sunday evenings in the Winn household were spent in song and prayer, as they usually were down the block at the Lindholms'. But this particular Sunday was unusual for Paul and Clara. He was on Cebu, returning from a church conference in Bohol. She was abed at the mission hospital, feeling the first contractions of her labor with what would very soon be her fourth child. Beverly, Dean, and Jamie stayed with friends. That Paul ventured to take a journey at such a precarious time was nothing new to the family. They knew he often put church business ahead of their needs—a fact they reluctantly accepted.

In Dumaguete, time would not come to a standstill until dawn on Monday, the eighth. It, too, began like any ordinary day. People rose, performed their toilet, prepared breakfast, made plans for the week. But about seven that morning radios crackled with stunning news that quickly passed from house to house, block to block, waterfront to foothills.

Gardner Winn was at the breakfast table preparing for his 8:00 Bible class. Viola joined him there; the couple shared a pot of coffee. Outside, beyond the house, they could hear an indistinct noise, at first a low murmur of excited voices, shortly becoming a roar. Viola stepped to the dining room window. She could see knots of excited students on the edge of the campus. Suddenly their maid Guillerma burst into the house. Racing to Gardner, she cried, "Sir, the Japanese have bombed Pearl Harbor!"[11]

The attack caught U.S. forces unaware and unprepared. By midmorning the main firepower of the Pacific Fleet was sunk or damaged: eighteen men-of-war, including eight battleships, and nearly two hundred aircraft. Casualties were shocking: twenty-three hundred men killed or missing, twelve hundred more wounded.[12] The United States had finally been drawn into the war.

Winn took the bulletin calmly, asking if the young Filipina had heard anything else. "They have bombed Clark Field, too." The news alarmed Viola. Her husband did what he could to soothe her fears, assuring her that things might not be as bad as they first sounded. While Gardner crossed over to Silliman to learn what he could, Viola went out to the corner market to stock up on extra food in case the emergency was real.

Seventy miles to the north, across Tañon Strait on Cebu, Paul Lindholm had just reached the house of missionary friends Bill and Grace Smith following an all-night crossing from Bohol. No sooner had they sat down to breakfast than a radio announcer from Manila broke into the morning program with his startling report. Paul's first thought was how to get home to his wife and children on Negros. He had begun to pack his things when a telegram arrived announcing the birth of Janet Claire Lindholm at five twenty-five on Monday morning. "ALL WELL MUCH LOVE CLARA."[13]

Lindholm walked down to Cebu City's usually busy, now tumultuous, waterfront, there to seek passage to Dumaguete. It took him hours to find a vessel willing to make the voyage, but by first light on Tuesday he was walking up the long stone jetty, heading straight for the mission hospital to see his family.

All across the campus, all across the city, people milled about, shock and sometimes fear radiating from their faces. Classes met, but teachers were unable to keep students focused on their studies. As more news came in that morning—that Davao in Mindanao had been bombed, that northern Luzon had been bombed—anxiety among faculty and students rose proportionally. At 10:00 A.M. regular Monday chapel was held in the packed assembly hall. Dr. Arthur Carson introduced the governor of Oriental Negros, Guillermo Villanueva, who told the audience that the Philippines were now in a state of national emergency. Major Robert H. Vesey, commander of USAFFE forces in the province, tried to calm the gathering by saying that Dumaguete would not soon be attacked, and that in any case he was confident the United States would eventually emerge victorious. Dr. Carson was the last speaker. He tried to convince his students to stay at Silliman for the final six weeks of the semester. He reminded them that MacArthur was in charge now; surely the Japanese had met their match. The president concluded by saying that classes would continue, at least until the situation was clearer.[14]

As students and faculty filed out of the steamy hall, thoughts raced through their minds. The situation was not at all clear this first day of war, but, they reasoned, it was a fact that the Japanese had attacked American forces on at least two fronts and it made sense that sooner or later Negros and Dumaguete would be targets. By late Monday afternoon the school was being inundated with phone calls and telegrams from anxious parents throughout the islands, directing their children to come home as quickly as possible. As the sun dipped behind Cuernos de Negros the roads had become jammed with cars and trucks and buses, all headed away from the city. The quay, too, was crowded with evacuees, waiting for the arrival from Mindanao of the steamer *Panay*. She would take her passengers north—home for some, an ill-conceived refuge for others. Many students were looking for southbound passage, among them Modesta Hughes. The nineteen-year-old sophomore, a U.S. citizen through her American father, was trying futilely to get home to Davao.

On 13 December Dr. Carson made the painful decision to close the school. His message was couched in language suggesting that the move was merely an early Christmas vacation. But in their hearts everyone knew it meant the end of the school year. An odd feeling of optimism pervaded the Philippines in those first few weeks of the war. People could not bring themselves to believe that the fighting would continue for more than two or three months. The United States, they truly believed, was not about to lose the Philippines to the invaders. They thought it only a matter of time, a short time, before the Japanese were driven from their shores and life would return to normal. Very few people were prescient enough to foresee that the war might drag on in the Philippines for more than three years.

That morning Viola Winn carried home two armloads of food from the Chinese market, then sent her maids Victoria and Guillerma back to pick up the remainder of her order. When Gardner returned from the campus, he brought good news. He told his family that until the situation became clearer, they had been invited by Jim and Virginia McKinley to buckwheat with them to their summer house high on the slopes of the big mountain. "Buckwheat?" Gardner explained that it meant "clear out" in the local dialect, that it was a corruption of the word "evacuate."[15] It was a comfort to Viola that her family had somewhere to buckwheat to. Except for a brief visit to Clara and Janet at the mission hospital, packing continued throughout the day. Gardner wanted his books to go, Rodger his toy chest. Just a handful of volumes and a few most precious toys made the cut. Viola left her favorite tropical-weight frocks on the hanger, choosing instead practical, durable, but ugly seersucker dresses. The next morning the family waited by their meager assemblage of belongings for a truck to pick them up and take them to the mountains. But the truck was rather late in coming—two days late.[16]

Life was a whirlwind for the Lindholms, too. While his wife and newborn daughter remained in the hospital, Paul arranged to have the entire family

The Winn Family (left to right, Rodger, Viola, Gardner, Norman, Elinor (Rodger Winn)

evacuate to Jim and Ethel Chapman's house in the mountains. To keep himself busy he erected a sturdy bomb shelter in his backyard. He decided to pattern its design after the snow forts he had built as a child on the plains of Minnesota. Working alone in the sweltering heat, Paul first laboriously dug a deep, rectangular hole. Using thick logs, he built a solid roof, which he then covered with tin sheeting. Dozens of bags of sand completed the haven. He was quite proud when his shelter was voted the best in Dumaguete. Before the month was out, Lindholm spent a morning burying a stash of Silliman University records, sealed in tin cans, beneath his house. More precisely, he deposited them: from the northeastern corner, 1 meter south and 5.5 meters west.[17]

On the eleventh the Winn family buckwheated to Camp Lookout.

This little barrio of summer cottages owned by Silliman faculty sat astride a big peak, at an elevation of sixteen hundred feet, where the air was cool and the views of Dumaguete and Tañon Strait and south to the Sulu Sea were nothing less than spectacular. A road had been built in 1935 that very nearly reached the Chapmans' small cottage. Mountain Rest, the McKinleys' house, was another few hundred yards up the hill. On that first Thursday of the war, Jim McKinley had driven the school's Chevrolet station wagon, full of Winns and their things, until the road petered out. The family then made the strenuous half-hour climb to the bungalow on foot. It was their first taste of trekking through the mountains of Negros.

*Cargadores* carried the Winns' possessions up the slope on their backs. Rodger and Norman received a great thrill—they got to ride upon the shoulders of two of the Filipino carriers. The maid Victoria carried five-month-old Elinor. The steep trail was overgrown; the lead carrier had to hack his way through with a huge bolo knife. After crossing a frigid stream, the party came to a level glade. There, before them, stood Mountain Rest. It was a modest cottage, built in the Visayan style, surrounded by flowering bushes including, most poignantly of all, tall poinsettias covered in brilliant red and pink blossoms. They reminded Viola, sadly, of the Christmas fast approaching.[18]

The following Wednesday, the Lindholm family arrived at Camp Lookout, settling in at the Chapman house.

The Chapmans had built their cottage in 1917. Begun as a small bamboo hut with a thatched roof, over the years it had grown into a multiroom house of good size. The structure was sturdy, the floor was split bamboo, the roof had nipa-palm shingles. The rather basic kitchen sat ten feet behind the house, with an enclosed lattice connecting the two. The dwelling had two porches:

one with a view of Dumaguete, the other looking down on the adjacent three-hundred-foot ravine and up toward the mountain summits. The couple had put considerable work into their property during almost a quarter century of ownership. An iron pipe brought fresh water down from the hills, providing for a shower and even a flush toilet. They built an extensive garden, planting banana trees, pineapples, avocados, and coffee plants.[19] It was an idyll to which they had loved to retreat to escape the incessant coastal heat and the bustle of town life.

After staying at the Chapmans' for a few days, Paul Lindholm decided to move his family into a nearby hut used as a clinic by the Filipinos. With the help of some local men he increased the floor space of the one-room shanty. The Lindholms' two maids, Foni and Dulia, helped weave nipa-leaf walls, and in a few days' time the hut became a home.

Each morning the faculty men would drive back down to Dumaguete in McKinley's Chevy, there to assist in any way they could. McKinley, Chapman, Silliman, and Lindholm were all active in the weeks following Pearl Harbor: guarding the town from looters, distributing food equitably on behalf of the provincial government, handling civil affairs for the USAFFE unit that had suddenly appeared from the sea one night. Only Gardner Winn stayed behind. A lifelong pacifist, Winn believed that to perform any task to aid the war effort, no matter how insignificant, was against his principles. He had written to friends earlier that year, "Would to God our energies were turned to the building of true economic as well as political democracy, rather than to increasing the instruments of war."[20] While some of the Sillimanians thought Winn an ideological purist, and many disagreed outright with his position, they nevertheless respected him for the depth of his convictions.[21]

For Viola Winn the unrest was an especially trying ordeal. Three times since the beginning of the year her family had been uprooted. The moves had brought too much disruption into the otherwise orderly life of a woman now forty years old and set in her ways. At nights, lying awake while Gardner slept peacefully at her side, Viola imagined terrible things happening to her family, imagined the war as a long, endless "black tunnel." Her depression was especially acute on Christmas Day. How she longed "for one of those joyous snowy Christmases at home."[22]

The poinsettias that surrounded the properties at Camp Lookout added a festive holiday cheer, quite unlike anything the Winns or the Lindholms had ever experienced. To add a further touch, Virginia McKinley and her girls brought out of the forest a small tree that all the children then helped decorate with paper chains. In the pitch darkness of Christmas Eve—a strict blackout was in effect—the families gathered around to sing carols and share prayers. Filipino highlanders joined the Americans, bringing guitars and more good cheer. The sharing buoyed everyone's spirits.

A Christmas service was held the next day on the hillside overlooking Dumaguete. Hymns and carols were sung, and Paul Lindholm gave a short message in English and in Cebuano. Ethel Chapman and Metta Silliman made sure each of the children got some sort of present, such as candy or a home-made toy. Rodger Winn gave Dean a baby bird he had found in the woods a few days earlier. The Filipinos brought gifts of fruit and precious fresh eggs. Abby Jacobs and Bob Silliman brought food up from town, making an otherwise somber observance into a quite festive day on the slopes of Cuernos de Negros.[23]

FOR THE FOLLOWING TWO WEEKS, normal life continued its abeyance. The news from the fronts was not good. The day after Christmas, General MacArthur abandoned Manila, declaring it an open city, and retreated to the narrow confines of Bataan Peninsula at the mouth of Manila Bay. Throughout Asia the Japanese continued their relentless assault, attacking Hong Kong, Guam, Wake Island, Singapore. Almost like dominoes these places and more fell, and the British, Dutch, Chinese, and Americans were powerless to stop the juggernaut.

By late December, USAFFE forces had taken over the Silliman campus. As many young men as could be found were impressed into the ROTC training program. All the while, work proceeded apace on the construction of the school's new church. Charles Glunz supervised Filipino crews in the pouring of a huge vault beneath the structure. Here Dr. Carson planned to hide the bulk of the school library, science equipment, athletic trophies, class pictures, treasurer's reports, and manifold other items, all carefully cataloged. Across campus Abby Jacobs produced a one-sheet *Daily Sillimanian,* which became the only newspaper in town. She filled it with reports from the radio, with military communiqués, and with helpful hints on how to survive the crisis. Her brother-in-law, Bob Silliman, supervised the university's press, printing everything from army requisition forms to emergency money.[24] For safety's sake, the mission hospital moved twenty miles north, to Pamplona.

By the second week of January 1942, it seemed clear that a second exodus was in the offing. Dr. Carson sent a search committee led by Jim McKinley to Malabo, a plateau in the mountains west of Dumaguete. The object was to find a place suitable as an evacuation center for the Silliman Americans. From the end of the Palimpinon road, an hour and a half's hike inland, the committee found what appeared to be an ideal refuge. There was abundant fresh water, fertile land for gardening, and plentiful groves of coconut trees. Above all else, Malabo was well hidden and hard to find. On the eighth of January Edith Carson and Edna Bell, accompanied by their four children, moved to Malabo to begin setting up the camp. They were soon joined by the stranded student from Davao, Modesta Hughes. The old Silliman crowd was beginning to disperse into the jungles.[25]

Just the day before, the Lindholms and the Winns had departed from Camp Lookout, bound for Guihulngan, a little coastal town halfway up the island. During his evangelizing missions, Paul Lindholm had become friendly with the leading pastor in the area, Eugenio Malahay. After the war began the Filipino had asked the missionary to come work with church leaders in his area. Lindholm knew that his Cebu friends Bill and Grace Smith had a cottage in the hills behind Guihulngan; they offered to let the Lindholms use the house as a hideaway. It seemed an ideal setup, especially for Paul, who was anxious to resume his proselytizing. He talked Gardner and Viola Winn into joining his family on the trek north. On a sunny Wednesday the families set off in a borrowed truck and a college station wagon driven by Theology Department colleague Alvin Scaff. As he bid farewell to friends at Mountain Rest, Gardner Winn turned to Ethel Chapman and said, "See you in concentration camp!" At the time she thought the idea absurd.[26]

FROM SIATON IN THE SOUTH to Toboso in the north, the coast of Oriental Negros was never more than a mile or two from the foothills of the Cordillera Centrales, except near Tanjay and Bais, where a flat plain extended nearly ten miles inland. Cebu loomed a dark hulk across the narrow Tañon Strait. A ribbon of road ran the length of the island, often but not always coral-paved, and usually in disrepair. This coastal highway passed fishing villages and cane fields, salt ponds and rice paddies. On any other occasion it was a drive to be enjoyed, scenery to be awed by, a pleasurable adventure. Even that day in January, as the Winns and the Lindholms rode north, their trip seemed at times like a Sunday drive in the country; it was so easy to forget that there was a war on, that men were fighting and dying on the islands to the north. Viola Winn was the only one in the party apprehensive about their journey. As they passed a group of Filipino refugees standing on a beach awaiting a boat, she was seized by panic. Viola suddenly wanted to be off this road, out of this truck, hiding safely in a house far away. In a few moments the tranquillity of her surroundings, the happiness on the faces of her children, the serene visage of her husband, soothed her. She felt calmer by the time the little convoy pulled into the sugar town of Bais for refreshments—hot banana fritters and *calamansi* limeade. Late in the day the families arrived at the sprawling Malahay home on the outskirts of Guihulngan. Eugenio, his wife, and their many children all made their guests feel welcome.

After a leisurely and filling breakfast the next morning, the Americans prepared to buckwheat farther into the hills. Malahay had organized cargadores with bamboo sleds, carabaos to pull them, and horses for all. The children were thrilled at the thought of getting to ride real horses. Clara rode a sled, clinging to tiny Janet all the while. Viola declined a ride, preferring to go on foot. Bags and packages were tied down to the bamboo with thin twists of vine. By noon the group was ready to move out, led by Christian Malahay, a student of Clara Lindholm's at Silliman. At times the going was rough. Once, Clara tumbled out of the sled, the baby in her arms. Fortunately, no one was hurt. By midafternoon the two families had covered the six miles from town and had reached their destination, the ramshackle house that had served as a summer home for the Smiths.[27]

The house at Tinayunan Hill was not exactly as advertised, due to the presence of a large colony of termites. These hungry creatures had managed to reduce parts of the cottage to the consistency of newsprint. However flimsy, though, the place was home.

The two families were warmly welcomed by members of the church, who came bearing gifts of food. But quickly, with fifteen mouths to feed, food became a major source of worry. Every day the four maids foraged in the nearby barrio markets. Coconuts were easily purchased or bartered for and were versatile nutriments. The family helpers bought them four dozen at a time, carrying them to the house on the hill upon the back of a carabao (which also, conveniently, provided fresh milk). This new life took some getting used to.[28] There had been amenities at Camp Lookout—limited amenities by Western standards, but amenities nonetheless. Here on the hill, life was flat basic. But the families perceived that they were a good deal safer here than overlooking Dumaguete.

Their security was always of paramount importance. One day shortly after arriving, Paul and Gardner were down in the barrio when a man ran into the cluster of homes shouting that Japanese soldiers were coming up the path. This was fearsome news to Filipinos and Americans alike. In a flash the square cleared, residents barricading themselves in their houses. As fast as they could, the two missionaries headed straight back toward Tinayunan, meeting young Norman and his mother coming down. As the men explained their rush, a Filipino called out to say that the scare had been a false alarm. The missionaries were astonished to learn that a local person had mistaken them, dressed as they were in khakis and bronzed from the sun, for enemy soldiers and, in a panic, had spread the alarm. Such were the jitters on Negros that spring.[29]

When his family felt settled at Tinayunan Hill, the Reverend Lindholm threw himself back into evangelizing. Up in the hills he began to assist local pastors and deacons in the rural churches, organizing leadership training institutes and occasionally leading services. The man loved what he did, loved to spread the gospel, and was very good at it. In the eyes of the Presbyterian Board of Foreign Missions, he was the consummate missionary.

PAUL LINDHOLM WAS THEN thirty-eight years old. Of middling height, gaunt and serious, he was the youngest of fourteen children born to Peter and Jenny Lindholm in Ortonville, a small farming community near the shores of Big Stone Lake in far western Minnesota. Peter, a Swede, came to the United States in the 1880s and, like so many thousands of other Scandinavians, sought his fortune on the flat, fertile plains of the upper Midwest.

Paul grew up in a deeply religious household, where Bible reading and prayer were part of the family's everyday life. As a child he loved to listen to the stories of faraway lands and mysterious peoples told by visiting missionaries. He would sit quietly in wide-eyed rapture as guests told tales of exotic places like China and Persia and the jungles of Guatemala. Their adventures sparked an interest in the boy, a kind of wanderlust that would propel him throughout life.

After graduating from high school, Paul was invited to join two Bible students on a gospel campaign through the Northwest. He would be responsible for the music. That summer he traveled to a dozen states, conducting hymns, singing, getting a taste of life beyond the Plains. It was from this experience that Lindholm began to think he had found his true calling. For the first time he seriously considered making a career of the ministry.

Upon completion of the tour, and after much thought and prayer, Paul enrolled at Minneapolis's Northwest Bible and Missionary Training School. There he met fellow student and local girl Clara Jane Malbon. Clara was a few inches shorter than Paul, with dark wavy hair, rather thick eyebrows, high cheekbones, and a faint smile always upon her lips. She was raised in the nearby suburb of Robbinsdale, the eldest of four children born to Perez and Sadie Malbon. When her father died—Clara was only eight—the family found itself in dire straits. Because Sadie had no financial acumen, she asked a family friend to manage her husband's estate. He invested badly and dishonestly; it did not take long for the cash to vanish. But somehow Sadie managed to keep the family together, and though they never had much money, the Malbon children were raised in a loving and spiritual household. Seeking fellowship, the widow had joined the undenominational Emmaus Church. It was not long before Sadie became a voracious reader of the Bible. Sometimes when Clara came home from school she found her mother still at the breakfast table, still dressed only in her robe, reading the Good Book. Mrs. Malbon had found the Lord and began sharing her discovery with her children.

Paul Lindholm's relationship with Clara flourished. She said later that she had fallen in love with his beautiful voice.[30] Just a year after meeting, the couple was engaged to be married. It was an engagement that would last six years.

It was always evident to Clara that her fiancé had his heart set upon becoming a missionary. In April 1931 the couple made a plan for their future. They announced they would wed in August. And then they made application to the Board of Foreign Missions. They carefully studied the brochures sent by the church, then filled out the lengthy forms. Six weeks later, just before Paul was ordained a minister in the Presbyterian Church, the betrothed were assigned to the China Council.

Their wedding took place on a warm Friday, 14 August 1931, at the Emmaus Church in Robbinsdale.[31] Before they cut the multitiered cake, they removed a small ceramic figure of Cupid standing in the buttercream frosting on the top layer, tucking it away as a keepsake. Their "working honeymoon" was a cruise from Vancouver to Shanghai, compliments of the Board of Foreign Missions. There were strings attached, of course: the term of enlistment. Paul and Clara were expected to live and work in China for six years before return passage would be forthcoming. When they arrived, the newlyweds were given a brief orientation to the missionary community in the city's South Gate district, then caught the train for a two-hour ride inland to the ancient city of Suchow.

The city thrilled them. It was crisscrossed with canals, and upon those narrow waterways junks plied their trade. It was a city of silk—China's main producer of the luxurious cloth. It was a city unlike any the Lindholms had ever experienced. As they walked down the narrow streets, their senses were assaulted. Oh, the sights! Tiny women wrapped in rich silks hobbled about on bound feet. Chicken claws and pig snouts toasted on sooty charcoal braziers. Stands sold eels and snakes and edible puppies. And the sounds! A cacophony of alien voices pierced the air. Shrill flutes noisily played strange and wonderful harmonies. Alien Asian bells rang across the temple squares. And the smells! Market stalls were fragrant with exotic herbs and spices, which stabbed at their nostrils. The air was perfumed by the aroma of humanity, of half a million people crowded behind the city's ancient stone battlements. And the tastes! There was thick congee rice gruel with pieces of pork and chilies; roast duck slathered in honey glaze and mixed with rice noodles; and to finish, treacly-sweet steamed red bean buns.

They weren't in Ortonville anymore.

Paul and Clara spent twelve happy months in Suchow. At the start of their second year the couple moved to Shanghai, back to the mission compound at South Gate. Paul had already caught the notice of China Council leaders. They sent him into the field, to undertake rural evangelism. It was an assignment he relished By now, by the autumn of 1932, Clara was pregnant with their first child. Beverly Jean Lindholm was born in Shanghai on 16 January 1933.

Paul's work required building relationships with lay and pastoral leaders of rural churches. One of his most memorable experiences in China was a journey to a leadership congress in a town a hundred miles to the west. So that he might get a better feel for life in the countryside, he and three companions pedaled across the hills and plains, stopping each night in a small village, meeting the residents, sharing their food, enjoying their hospitality. When the forum was over, the four cycled back to Shanghai via a different route, visiting different villages. The experience had such an effect on Lindholm that he asked to be reassigned from the cushy compound in South Gate to a rural village.[32]

The Lindholms packed carefully and practically, taking a bed, a stove, books, warm clothing, Western food, and the baby's playpen. In the spring of 1934 Paul, Clara, and baby Bev boarded a boat on the Whangpo and set out for Zau Ka Loo Keu, two hours north of the great city. Their home was three rooms, with log ceilings and roughly hewn floors, at the back of the village chapel. The furnishings were few. An old pulpit served as a cupboard, a school desk as a washstand. There was little space and there were few comforts, but Clara did what she could to cheer the place up, adding pictures and dried flowers and colorful pillows. In the first few days the villagers were so curious about the people from "outside the kingdom" that they crowded around the windows at dinnertime to watch the strangers eat their meal.[33]

Paul dedicated himself to his labors with customary passion, thriving under the new responsibilities given him. Reverend Lindholm held evangelistic meetings and Bible classes, opened a Christian reading room, and organized boys' and girls' clubs. And it was in this little village that he first began to show his lantern slides depicting the life of Christ. It became his biggest attraction.

He sometimes set up the show in a church or a courtyard, but most often under a large tent he carried with him. While his assistants hung a faded sheet as a screen, Paul pulled out of its black box the ungainly wooden and brass projection apparatus. A felt-lined case held the several dozen three-by-four-inch hand-colored glass transparencies portraying Jesus from His birth in the manger through His crucifixion. Word spread quickly around the village that an entertainment was in the offing. By the time Lindholm was ready to raise the curtain, he often had an audience numbering several dozen. After a brief introduction, shimmering images appeared, one after another, upon the screen. Paul narrated the story in fractured (but ever improving) Chinese, exhorting his audiences to sing along with him at appropriate places, or at least to hum along. He brought the curtain down with an invitation to learn more about the church and the Christian God. Wherever he went the show was a big hit, an ice breaker, a successful evangelistic tool.

Clara, however, did not enjoy the rural experience. She found it difficult to live under such primitive conditions. Each morning she went with her helpers to the nearby canal to fetch water. The stream was not a pretty sight. Indeed, it was a health disaster waiting to happen, but it happened to be the only source for the entire village. Sometimes as she stood on the muddy banks, the young American watched in disgust as local women washed their chamber pots in the trough. As a missionary's wife, Clara was expected to put up with the inconveniences that being "on the field" brought. Still, she pined for the comforts of South Gate and the companionship of other westerners.[34]

As a bitter winter gave way to the warming winds of spring, Paul could be proud of his accomplishments in the village. He had spread the word of God. He had picked up a few converts. He had helped illiterates learn to read. The missionary believed he had made a real and positive impact upon the lives of the people in his district. His commitment to his congregation impressed the elders at South Gate, but it was time to return to Shanghai. Clara was again with child, and she wanted to give birth in the secure surroundings of the city's modern foreign hospital. Shortly after the family had resettled, she gave birth to Dean Malbon Lindholm, on 12 May 1935.

The family's first term of enlistment ended in 1937, bringing with it a welcome year of home leave. When they returned to Shanghai the following September, what they found shocked them. While the Lindholms had been steaming toward America the previous year, the Japanese had invaded the city. Desperate fighting had devastated vast tracts of the metropolis, including the missionary compound at South Gate and the Lindholms' tidy brick house. Everything had been reduced to a pile of rubble—all the furnishings, the library, family heirlooms—everything except the little Cupid that had adorned Paul and Clara's wedding cake. To the family, that ceramic figure became an icon of love's power to conquer adversity.[35]

In September 1939, just three weeks after Germany invaded Poland, the Lindholms were again assigned to Suchow. As they settled in, Clara learned she was expecting her third child. Paul was so busy, so committed to the church, that he barely spent any time with his wife and children that Christmas. In his absence the family made the best of the holidays, trimming the tree and constructing a miniature manger. With the dawn of the new year, the Lindholms found themselves in the middle of a rapidly deteriorating political crisis. Bands of guerrillas attacked Japanese troop trains, even attacked their enemy's garrisons in numerous small towns. For Paul, working in the field became a hazardous undertaking. One day, while the missionary was performing a baptism, a Japanese soldier burst into the church and marched up to the font, demanding to see the American's passport. The tense moment passed without incident, but the experience shook the missionary.

James Milton Lindholm entered the world at Suchow on Tuesday, 21 May 1940, the same day German troops reached the English Channel coast of France, encircling a vast and fleeing Allied army in a move that would quickly focus the world spotlight upon a small French resort town called Dunkirk.[36]

Throughout that year the Japanese Army continued to battle Chiang Kai-shek's Nationalist forces for control of East China. The Lindholms came to feel that life in China was becoming untenable. When the U.S. consulate in Shanghai issued its recommendation that families evacuate, Paul decided to act. He wrote to his old missionary friend Dr. Arthur Carson at Silliman

University about the possibility of a position there. Carson liked the idea. He wired his request for the Lindholms' transfer to INCULCATE NEW YORK, the cable address of the Board of Foreign Missions. A telegram arrived in Suchow at about Christmas, directing the family to depart early in the New Year for Dumaguete.

Now, in the spring of 1942 and on the run from the Japanese in the hills above Guilhulngan, the Lindholms' earlier China adventure seemed a dim and distant memory.

THINGS REMAINED RELATIVELY QUIET in the Visayas until late spring. Except for an occasional strafing or bombing, the enemy paid scant attention to Negros. On Cebu, just across the strait, things were not so quiet.

Cebu City was the second largest in the Philippines, and its port was the second most important. After the war began the American presence there grew; it became a major waypoint for the transshipment of men and goods north and for the evacuation of civilians and wounded troops south.

In the first days of the conflict most of Cebu City's population buckwheated into the hills surrounding the city. In the winter months, when the enemy showed no interest in the island, many people returned to their homes, trying to return to normal lives. But toward the end of March the Japanese began in earnest to lay siege upon Cebu, seemingly intent upon taking the island. By the first week of April the city was a ghost town patrolled by Filipino and American soldiers. Among them was Captain James M. Cushing, a mining engineer who had lived for many years in the Philippines. Because of his background, Cushing had been assigned to the Corps of Engineers. To a man who hungered for action, he found his duties mind-numbing, the stupidity of the U.S. Army overwhelming. He thought the service had become a "paperwork and country club crowd."[37] As the situation on the island began to disintegrate, Cushing noticed that the men around him—officers mostly—were disintegrating, too.

An American lieutenant, near panic, came to the miner one day with a plea: "I have an hour to truck some dynamite down to the harbor. Can you help?" Cushing said, "Sure. Where's the dynamite?" The officer said he had no idea. He had asked around, but no one seemed to know. Cushing questioned a couple of shopkeepers and quickly learned where the explosives were stored. The young officer then whimpered, "I don't know what I'm going to do! I only brought eight men. I don't see how they're going to carry the dynamite down from that hill and get it loaded in time."

Cushing looked the lieutenant squarely in the eye and said irritably, "Look around you. There are dozens of residents who are itching to help in any way they can." The man's response stunned the miner. "I am not authorized to hire help for the U.S. Government." Here Cebu City—the whole of the Philippines, in fact—was on the verge of collapse, and this young man was worried about breaking the rules. Cushing spun on his heels, rounded up a hundred men, and, forming a human chain, moved the dynamite down the hill and into the waiting truck. Now all he had to do was get the percussion caps that would ignite the explosives.

He went to another shed and found the door padlocked. As he prepared to break the lock the officer shrieked, "You can't do that! It wouldn't be right!" Cushing gave the man a withering look, smashed the lock anyway, and liberated the percussion caps. This was not the first time he had seen an American officer crumble at a critical moment, and it disgusted him.[38]

Jim Cushing had reluctantly joined the army when war broke out. He had never pictured himself as a military man, had no military training, but was given a temporary commission by Brigadier General Bradford Grethen Chynoweth, commander of the Visaya Force. Cushing was assigned to plan and rig the demolition of strategic facilities in and around Cebu City. It was just the sort of meaty duty he sought. That April, as the Japanese closed in on Cebu, Cushing pushed the plungers. He was especially proud of the destruction of an oil tank farm on the offshore island of Mactan. With the help of some Filipino soldiers, he placed dynamite under each of the dozen storage tanks. The showman in James Cushing was evident when he decided to blow the farm at night, to make the fireworks even more spectacular. The huge explosion turned night into day. Of this he wrote, "[O]ne might think that this was wanton destruction, however it was entirely necessary. There was no means at the time to transfer this valuable fuel elsewhere."[39] Cushing continued his rampage, destroying bridges, wharves, any facilities that might have military use. The work he performed was so dangerous, but performed with such zeal, that he earned the nickname "Suicide Cushing."[40]

When the Japanese overran the city, Chynoweth pulled his forces back into the interior. To the general, finding food for the troops was the most urgent requirement. One day an agitated Cushing paid a visit to headquarters. The temporary captain made it clear to the general that he was not interested in scrounging for food, instead asking permission to dynamite the quarters of the enemy commander. Chynoweth refused. Cushing was crushed. Soon after, the miner headed south to Mindanao, where there was still promise of fighting. The general later said of Jim Cushing: "[He was] a fighter. He wanted to accomplish great things immediately. He had no fear whatsoever, he was young and aggressive. [But] we were too slow for him. He craved action."[41]

There was little for Cushing to do in Mindanao. When an American defeat seemed inevitable, he headed back to Cebu. There he would soon establish one of the most effective guerrilla organizations in the islands—an assemblage of patriots who, in one fleeting moment of luck and determination, would pull off an intelligence coup of such import that it would influence the outcome of the war.

AMERICAN AND FILIPINO FORCES were on the run throughout the Philippines; every battle they fought was a rout. Bataan Peninsula fell on 9 April: Cebu Island was invaded the next day. Organized resistance there ended in weeks. Corregidor surrendered the first week of May, and with it, the entire archipelago. On 21 May 1942, the Japanese Army finally occupied Bacolod in northern Negros, encountering no opposition. Five days later they landed troops in the south, on the long stone jetty at Dumaguete. Even before the capitulation of USAFFE forces, the Lindholms had moved farther into the island's interior.

Some weeks before, Eugenio Malahay's teenage son Christian had approached Clara, his former English teacher, with this plea: "You led me through the jungles of infinitives and gerunds; now let me lead you through the jungles of Negros to a place of greater safety."[42] He had in mind Pacuan Valley, over the Calatcat Mountains from Guihulngan. The Malahay family owned a house there; Christian offered the Lindholms the adjacent Sunday school building as their new home. On May Day the family mounted horses and ponies for the daylong journey inland. After stopping twice for refreshments provided by loyal churchgoers, the party reached Pacuan Valley shortly after dark. Christian's uncle Enrique greeted them warmly and invited them in for a fine dinner of chicken and rice washed down with fresh cocoa.

Despite the worsening situation in the Philippines, May proved a peaceful respite for the family, especially for the children. Rudolfo Bernardez, son of Silliman High School's principal and one of their mountain guides, sold them a small, spirited pony that provided hours of amusement for Beverly and Dean. Neighbors made toys for the children. Dean was delighted with a mahogany yo-yo he was given. The dry, packed soil around their house was ideal for challenging the Malahay kids to a round of marbles.[43] So that the children might keep up their studies, Clara, using an old desk borrowed from Enrique, opened a school under the shade of a banyan tree for all the hill children. She taught math and reading, while friends taught the two American students native crafts: spinning cotton on a hand-operated gin, weaving baskets, and making rope from hemp fibers. On 12 May the family celebrated Dean's seventh birthday, and a week later, Jamie's second.[44]

Before the Lindholms left Tinayunan they had asked the Winns to join them in the isolated valley. Gardner turned down the invitation, to his wife's dismay, on the grounds that a single large group would be easier for the Japanese to find than two smaller ones. Paul believed there was another reason. He believed that Gardner, who had lived under the Japanese in Korea, was not much concerned about being overtaken by the enemy. Winn had shown a similar sangfroid a few days earlier, after mysterious visitors turned up at the hill. Viola, apprehensive by nature, felt deeply uneasy about the strangers. When she shared her concerns with her husband he shrugged them off, telling her he was sure his family would be all right no matter what happened. There was nothing, he believed, to be gained by worrying.[45] His words, usually reassuring, were small comfort this time.

Instead of going to Pacuan with the Lindholms, the Winns set out some days later for a barrio called Balogo in a valley a few hours' hike southwest. There, overlooking the slow-moving Hinubaan River, its banks lined with palms and poinsettias, they moved into a stilt hut owned by Mateo Malahay, a nephew of Reverend Eugenio's.

Life at Balogo was idyllic. Gardner and the children spent hours sitting along the banks of the stream, beneath the shade of great mahogany trees, reading, loafing, swimming in the clear, soothing waters. It was, for the moment, an altogether pleasant existence. But there was one aspect of buckwheat life that Viola particularly despised: being shoeless. The children, not surprisingly, loved it. And Gardner, of course, did not mind one way or the other. To Viola, being unshod was a loathsome fact of their new existence, one she never got used to even after thirty months in the jungles.[46]

The two missionary families stayed in close touch throughout June, visiting one another at least once a week. While the children played together, the adults swapped news. There was always information to share. Once the Japanese had landed on Negros they began a concerted search for stray American soldiers and civilians. In Dumaguete enemy intelligence officers had learned that many Silliman faculty had fled into the mountains. Over the subsequent weeks search parties, large and small, scoured the coastal towns and the foothill barrios for the evacuees.

On 24 June 1942 the Lindholms had their first serious fright of the war.

Paul was working in the family garden when Grace Malahay scurried up the slope shouting that the Japanese were in her village. "Run! Hide!" she cried.[47] Lindholm gathered his family and sent them racing up the hill to a decrepit hut they had earlier decided to use as a hideout. He ran into the Sunday school house and began to fling telltale belongings out the back window into the high cogon grass. Paul wanted the enemy to find nothing that would give away the presence of foreigners. He tossed out clothes, books, and his army issue shoes, then headed quickly up the hill, barefoot.

It was a tight squeeze in the tiny house for the four Lindholms and their two helpers. Then another family joined them there. All night they sat huddled in the heat, sweat pouring from their bodies; sat huddled but absolutely silent for fear they would be discovered. When morning came, Paul asked Enrique Malahay about the Japanese visitors. The old man chuckled as he related the story: "I told them that not long ago fifteen men took the American family through the forest, to the other side of the island, where there was an American ship that took them to Australia." He said, "They even made me get all the men around here to carry all their things! Even a big piano! Over the mountain, to that ship!"[48] It was now clear to Paul that their Sunday school home at Pacuan was not safe.

On the last day of June the Lindholms packed their few belongings and marched deeper into the valley, farther up into the hills, to the small barrio of Busilak. They moved into Deacon Osias Mondejar's newly completed stilt house. The good deacon had planned to live there himself, but readily gave it over to the missionaries. Like so many other of the Americans' Filipino friends, Mondejar was more than willing to sacrifice his own comfort for theirs. The one-room dwelling sat on the side of a gentle hill, with views of the mountains to the southeast. Clara dubbed it the "giant wicker basket."[49] It seemed a tranquil sanctuary from the ills of the world.

But those ills were never far away. One evening a messenger hurried up to the Lindholms' new home with bad news: "Gardner Winn has turned himself in to the Japanese." Paul and Clara were stunned.

# CHAPTER 3

## *Separation*

ONE AFTERNOON IN THE FIRST WEEK of July, Christian Malahay dashed into the Winns' camp at Balogo with a message from his father. Viola unfolded the note he gave her. It was short, to the point: "The Japanese will be here soon. Hide as well as you can. E. Malahay." The teenager added breathlessly, "The Japanese are in Pacuan now. They know you live here."[1]

Viola led the boy to Gardner. He scanned the letter, then asked Christian how many Japanese were coming. "Just one," the boy replied. "Don't worry then," the missionary said. "We'll serve him coffee." Both Viola and Christian were shocked by Gardner's response. The situation seemed very serious; the Winns were in grave danger. Malahay did what he could to impress upon the man the need to vacate their house immediately, before the Japanese arrived.[2] Finally, perhaps swayed by reason and by the fearful look on his wife's face, Gardner agreed.

Viola ordered the two maids to pack whatever they could. She grabbed a sheet, threw it on the floor, threw clothing into the center, then wrapped it into an easily carried bundle. Rodger and Norman helped by adding a few toys. Within a few minutes the family was ready to depart. After a quick sweep to make sure no sign of their having lived in this house remained, one by one the Winns climbed down the narrow steps at the front. They would head to a vacant hut they had discovered on the other side of the hill. The track was muddy, the going was rough and steep. After several minutes the family had gone only a few hundred yards, only reaching the home of their neighbor Benito, the waterman. They were still within sight of their own house.

The old man came to their rescue. Guiding them up the slope to a small shed, a lean-to really, partially hidden by bushes, Benito promised to distract the Japanese should they show interest in the shack. He then returned to his house to wait.

The wait was only a few minutes but seemed interminable. Gardner, watching his stilt house through a hole in the hut's wall, whispered about the arrival of two men, "I can see them. There are two horses tied up there."[3] One of the men, called Vicente, was a Filipino businessman—the owner of a dry goods store—who was a longtime resident of Guihulngan.[4] The other was an officer of the Philippine Bureau of Constabulary. Both worked for the enemy. Gardner watched as the pair entered his house. Turning, the missionary could see Benito sitting on his own porch, calmly sharpening tools. When the Japanese collaborators had finished searching the Winns', instead of climbing toward the old man's, they rode down the slope and across the river, headed for the far ridge. In time they disappeared from view.[5]

Gardner and Viola decided it was unwise to return to their home. Two loyal neighbors volunteered to lead them through the jungle to another hut, where the family spent a restless night. In the morning a stranger appeared at their door, momentarily frightening everyone until he broke into a broad smile and handed over two pots full of rice and vegetables and chicken. The Winns, who had had nothing to eat since their escape except a can of cold peas, fell upon the food ravenously.

Walter Malahay, the eldest son of Eugenio, and Bernardo Sumcad, a Silliman student, arrived to guide the Winns to a safer hiding place. Before the party could leave, Mateo Malahay, whose stilt house the family had abandoned just the day before, shuffled into their camp. As he approached Gardner, the gaunt Filipino trembled in fear, his hands tugging at the tails of his blue shirt. He began to speak. He began with an apology. "I'm sorry, sir." "Sorry about what, Mateo?" the missionary asked. "About the Japanese, sir."[6]

Gardner gazed at the man quizzically. Slowly, in a quiet, quivering voice, the landlord related his trouble. Yesterday the Japanese had paid him a visit, down in Guihulngan. They told him they had visited the house at Balogo. They told him they had expected to find the renegade American missionary there. But, they said, the house was vacant, though it showed signs of recent habitation. They told Mateo they had a proposition for him. Gardner listened intently.

"The Japanese said I must bring you back or they would shoot me."[7]

Everyone was shocked, except Gardner. He calmly pushed his thick glasses up onto the bridge of his nose, stroked his chin with his hand, stared briefly at the ground, and then said resolutely in his resonant voice, "Of course I'll go with you."[8]

Of course I'll go with you? The words rang in Viola's ears. She wanted to scream. What do you mean, go with him? Gardner turned to his wife, expecting her to say she would gladly go, too. She looked into his eyes. They were bright, unblinking, tranquil. Gardner Winn had just made the most momentous decision of his life. He was obviously committed to this course, he would not be swayed. But the words he wanted to hear from her were not forthcoming. She could not bear to lose him, but what about herself, what about the children? Perhaps, he suggested, Guillerma and Victoria would take care of the children, then she would be free to join him. The thought horrified her. "I'm sorry, I'm so sorry. I love you so much. But let me stay," she implored.[9] Anguish briefly filled her husband's eyes. Gardner could see that she would remain with the children. He took her hands in his, bowed his head, and said a short prayer. He kissed Rodger and Norman and Elinor in turn, then kissed Viola. He thanked the maids. Then turning to the still shaking Mateo, he said he was ready. The pair walked away down the path, never looking back.[10]

Viola slumped onto a log, trying to fight off panic, trying to make sense of the dreamy events that had unfolded so swiftly in so few minutes. She had awakened that morning with her husband at her side and every reason to believe that her family would continue to stay free in the jungles. And now, her mind ajumble, it began to sink in that Gardner was gone. Of his own volition, his own beliefs, he was gone. He had left his family behind and was gone. Just like that. Viola could rationalize his decision. She had lived with him long enough, knew him well enough to understand how and why he could do this. But emotionally . . . that was another thing entirely. She felt drained and helpless.

The missionary's wife looked up to see Rodger and Norman standing nearby, Rodger fighting back tears. She reached out to squeeze his hand. It was at times like this when Viola turned to prayer. Since the beginning of the war she had frequently said little prayers to herself to help her through days filled with the unknown and the fears such suspense brings. When she was young Viola had expected to experience some supernatural phenomenon that would tell her she would be "saved." She had wanted something like Charles Glunz's *Big Capital Creation,* a spectacular sign from the Lord that lit up the sky with colored lights and smoke, some form of *deus ex machina* that would transform her life, revealing to her the real God in all His power and glory. Over the years such an experience never came, but in her daily life Viola came to see the Lord's work in many, often tiny, sometimes nearly imperceptible ways. In time, Viola Winn had come to believe that God had helped her weather the numerous hardships she had encountered. In time, she came to feel at peace with her faith.

Now facing the biggest challenge of her life, she discovered her faith was rock-solid. It was what gave her the strength to go on. She finished her prayer, rose from the log, turned to the others in her party, and said quietly, "Let's go."[11]

Gardner and Mateo hiked down to Balogo, where they surrendered to the Filipino constabulary. They were taken to the Japanese garrison at Guihulngan. After questioning, Mateo was released unharmed. A few days later Reverend Winn was sent on to Dumaguete. That first morning of separation, while he sat imprisoned at the one-room schoolhouse at Guihulngan, Gardner penned a note to his wife. I am well, he assured her, you needn't worry. He closed with a simple prayer.

GARDNER LEWIS WINN WAS BORN to missionary parents in Fusan, Korea, on 23 February 1911. His father, Rodger Earl Winn, had been assigned to the field by the Board of Foreign Missions just two years earlier. Korea was torn by strife when Reverend Winn arrived at the mission in the southern city of Andong. Japan had recently annexed the ancient nation, changed its name to Chosen, and ruled it with an iron fist. It was during this repressive period that Rodger Winn carried on the work of his mission and into which his three children were born.[12]

Despite the turmoil, Gardner considered his childhood in Korea a happy one, in which his whole life revolved around religion: daily family prayers, Bible readings, Sunday school, and endless church-related activities. His father's evangelistic work made a deep impression upon the boy. Most Sundays Rodger Winn preached at the simple timber-and-stucco City Church, its roof of galvanized iron paid for by contributions from Presbyterian parishioners in faraway Lake Forest, Illinois. Winn's itinerate work, spreading the Christian word, often took him out into the field, so that he was home rarely. The children looked forward to their father's return, for if they behaved well during his absence, it meant a special treat: two persimmons each. The kids eagerly lopped off the top of the fruit and with a spoon dug out the soft, peach-like pulp. The delicacy became one of Gardner's lifelong favorites.

Through contact with Korean church friends and through his own eyes, young Winn became aware of the people's unrest; aware, too, of Japan's brutality toward the Koreans. For his own part, Gardner learned to get along with the Japanese, whose soldiers he often encountered and whose language he attempted to learn. But what he heard, what he witnessed in Korea during those tumultuous days stirred deep feelings of compassion and of compromise that would guide him throughout his life.

Just a week before Christmas 1922, the fabric of the family's life was shredded by the sudden death of Rodger Earl Winn.

The sanitary conditions of Korea in the early 1920s were primitive; disease spread rapidly, in the water, in the air, from human to human. When an epidemic of dysentery swept through the villages around Andong, the missionary was called to provide aid and comfort. Thousands of Koreans succumbed to the pestilence. The Reverend Winn, with meager medical resources, eventually helped stem the onslaught, but soon he, too, succumbed. The family's neighbor Dr. Roy Smith did what he could. Even the eminent Dr. Fletcher came down from the church hospital at Taiku, but it was too late. Rodger's family watched helplessly as he grew weaker, racked by fever, vomiting, and incessant, dehydrating diarrhea. The infection spread from his digestive tract to his vital organs, bringing with it shock and, finally, death. He was only forty.

Gardner was traumatized. The tragedy made him forever fearful that the same fate might befall him. But his father's death also served to intensify the son's determination to join the missionary corps; indeed, to become a medical missionary, so that he might prevent similar tragedies from happening to others.

There were still three years left on the Winns' term of enlistment. The Board of Foreign Missions would not reimburse the family for their expenses if they left the country sooner, despite the death of missionary Winn. Catherine had little choice but to stay on in Korea. To make ends meet, she took a teaching job in the North, at the Pyongyang Foreign School. Finally, in 1925, she was free to leave, to go home to Emporia with her three children.

Back in Kansas, while Catherine Winn supported the family by teaching, her eldest son completed his secondary studies at Emporia High School, graduating with honors in 1927. Following in his father's footsteps, the young man entered the College of Emporia on a scholarship, majoring in psychology, with a minor in German. In his junior year, Gardner got his first job in the church— as a janitor at twenty dollars a month. He also received, unbeknownst to him, his first evaluation by the Board of Foreign Missions. In November 1930, missionary recruiter Gilbert Lovell submitted a report to the Board noting that "Winn, Gardner Lewis" was interested in pursuing a career as an evangelistic missionary. Lovell wrote, "This fellow has stuff and should make a good missionary with more maturity and experience."[13] Gardner graduated the following June, ranked in the middle of his class of forty-eight. Like his father,

Gardner then enrolled at McCormick Theological Seminary in Chicago.

By now Gardener's resolve to become a missionary had strengthened further, though he had given up the idea of pursuing a medical degree. Entering the foreign service was a choice, he later said, that was "the most natural thing in the world."[14] He believed his calling in life was the ministry, and in that capacity he felt he would be happier, more productive. While attending the seminary, Winn began to gain experience as a preacher. As a sophomore he got a job preaching in Rockford, Illinois, a position he kept until graduating in May 1934. The pastoral work helped him solidify his own Christian beliefs and provided him with growing confidence in his abilities as an evangelist. With his booming bass voice and his gift for crafting ringing, moving sermons touched with humor, Gardner became a popular preacher.

At the seminary Winn became involved with a pacifist group, the Fellowship of Reconciliation (FOR). The organization was founded in Cambridge, England, at the beginning of World War I, the inspiration of an English Quaker and a German Lutheran. The U.S. chapter, formed in 1915, helped organize what have since become the American Civil Liberties Union and the National Conference of Christians and Jews. As World War II approached, the FOR actively encouraged nonviolent resistance, helping to support conscientious objectors. What attracted Winn to the fellowship was its stated purpose: "To explore the power of love and truth for resolving human conflict" through nonviolent activism. Gardner responded especially to the principle of refusing "to participate in any war or to sanction military preparations."[15] The precepts of the fellowship struck a deep chord within the young Bible student. Over the years his convictions in favor of nonviolence grew stronger, even though he was frequently at odds with friends and family, for his position was not popular in an era of rising prowar sentiments.

After his ordination, Winn took a position at a small parish in northern New Jersey. On his days off he took classes at Drew University in Madison, classes he hoped would lead to a doctoral degree. This small Methodist-affiliated theological school offered a Ph.D. in rural sociology, which Winn thought would be helpful in his missionary career.

It was at Drew that Gardner met Viola Ida Schuldt, the daughter of a minister in the German Methodist Church. Viola was also studying for her Ph.D., having earned her B.A. at Western Union College in 1924 and her master's at Northwestern in 1927. When they met, Gardner was twenty-two, Viola a decade older. Despite the difference in ages, the pastor found his fellow student attractive. She was well educated, smart, and independent. He liked that. Her family and religious background were very similar to his own. He liked that. And though he did not consider her beautiful, he did admire her ample body. In later years he would say she was "nicely built."[16] He liked that, too. Viola Schuldt brought to Gardner Winn's life a kind of stability and maturity that had been missing. On 21 November 1935, the couple was married in Parsippany, New Jersey.

Earlier that year Gardner had carefully answered the sixty-six questions on the Personal Information Blank appended to the Application for Missionary Service and sent it to the Board of Foreign Missions in New York. He added that because of his background and training he would prefer to be assigned to Korea, evangelizing in the villages. The Board approached Winn's application leisurely. They took no action for more than two years.

The Winns were not shoo-ins. The Board took a dim view of the ten-year age difference between husband and wife; they were not comfortable with the wife being the older of the two. Secretary Speer noted, with an exclamation point, that when Gardner was seventy, Viola would be eighty! Four others had reservations about the disparity in ages, though one was so impressed by Viola's résumé that he wrote he would welcome her to the "rural field in China."[17] What swayed the group in the end was an impassioned testimonial in support of Viola Winn from Reverend Ralph Felton, professor of religion at Drew University. He noted her fine Christian spirit, her strong character, and her ability to adjust to difficult situations.

In May 1937 the Board of Foreign Missions voted to accept Gardner and Viola Winn into the missionary service, assigning them to Shantung Province under the auspices of the China Council. Now joined by baby Rodger Lewis, the family finally sailed for China on 3 September 1938. For Gardner Winn it was the fulfillment of a lifelong aspiration.

Upon their arrival in China the family moved into the Presbyterian Mission at Peking, there to spend the first year learning the language. Winn had traveled extensively in the Far East as a child—the sights and sounds and smells of Asia were not new to him, but certainly brought back long-forgotten, and dear, memories. For Gardner, it was, in a way, a homecoming. Viola found herself overwhelmed by China and its great, crowded, dusty capital. For her, the mission offered a quiet sanctuary, with familiar voices and American accouterments. In mid-1939, following completion of his language studies, the Winns were due to be relocated to the Presbyterian station at Yihsien, on the border of Shantung and Kiangsu provinces, but complications with her second pregnancy—Viola was now thirty-eight years old—delayed the family's move until after the birth of Norman Lorentz.

The mission at Shantung was the Presbyterian Church's largest and most important in China. The mission had been established in 1872, rather later than most of the church's stations in this vast nation. The role of the missions was multifold, not just limited to preaching the gospel of Christ. They established hospitals and clinics, schools and colleges, even institutes for the insane and for the blind—activities beyond the inclination of the Chinese government.[18] In Yihsien alone, the church had built primary and secondary schools, a girls' middle school, an agricultural high school, and a thirty-bed hospital. The station also coordinated seven local churches and many Christian groups. American personnel included a registered nurse, an education specialist, an evangelist, and now, at the beginning of 1940, the Reverend Gardner Lewis Winn.

But by the end of 1940 Gardner's career as a China missionary ground to a halt. That autumn the U.S. government sent word that Americans who were not urgently needed should evacuate as quickly as possible. In November a letter arrived from the China Council suggesting the Winns put in for transfer to the Philippines. Gardner fired off a telegram to Arthur Carson at Silliman University. An arrangement was made and the family sailed from Shanghai on 13 December for "temporary duty" to Dumaguete, Negros Oriental.[19] In May 1941, after two brief assignments on Luzon, Gardner and his family finally arrived at the long stone jetty at Dumaguete, met there by the Carsons. Winn was to teach at the university's Theological School, his wife at Silliman High School.

The Philippines seemed an eminently peaceful place in an increasingly contentious world, certainly a far cry from the turmoil in northern China. The Winns quickly assimilated into university life, enjoying their new station immensely. On 24 July, Viola gave birth to Elinor Joyce at the mission hospital. She now felt she had the "perfect trio": two boys and a girl. That month, in a letter home, she wrote how much she loved the Philippines. In China Viola had been simply a "missionary's wife." Here she felt as though she had something to contribute by teaching, by directing plays, by training student volunteers for Sunday school work. Gardner may have been disappointed at leaving China. His wife most decidedly was not.

A YEAR LATER, IN THE SUMMER of 1942, Viola Winn found herself alone and on her own. The war was barely eight months old when Gardner left her in the hills above Guihulngan. That same day she and the children were led away from Balogo, north toward Pacuan Valley. Norman got a ride on Walter Malahay's shoulders, while Bernardo Sumcad looked after Rodger. Year-old Elinor was in the care of the two maids, Guillerma and Victoria. That left Viola to carry a basket of food and a mind full of burdens, real and imagined. The events of the morning troubled her, but she felt she had to push on. As darkness fell, the party kept climbing higher and higher, at times over very rugged terrain with nothing but faint moonlight to illuminate the path. When they reached Pacuan they were introduced to their new guide, Zosimo Paglinawan, treasurer of the Pacuan church and another Malahay cousin. Mr. Paglinawan told Viola they were in much danger, that the Japanese were in the area. After bidding Walter and Bernardo farewell, the Winn family started off into the night once more.

Mr. Paglinawan led the family to his house in the village of Hulba, where he lived with his aunt and uncle. The couple seemed unhappy at the arrival of the Americans, and the Winns were cautioned to stay inside during daylight so they would not be seen by passersby on the busy trail that fronted the house. Three days after their arrival, the treasurer warned the Winns of a Japanese patrol a dozen miles away, suggesting the family leave Hulba for a more secure sanctuary. Viola distributed various unneeded belongings for safekeeping, including seven beautiful hand-embroidered dresses made especially for infant Elinor. She was deeply saddened to leave these behind, for the dresses represented to her a peaceful and normal life. In times of stress she had often opened the tied bundle of newspapers that protected the clothes, pulled them out to look at them, hold them, gain solace from the dreams they embodied.[20]

Their host took the Winns to a bark house hunkering amid a stunted cornfield. Viola was repelled when she gazed into the hovel full of chickens and their filthy soil. She knew she could not let her family stay in this wretched hovel. Reluctantly, for she did not want to offend her benefactor, Viola made it clear to Mr. Paglinawan that she and the children would rather join Gardner in prison than live out the war in that miserable bark hut. She asked if he could get a message to the Lindholms, for she felt she needed their counsel. He agreed to find a courier, then suggested that the family could stay in a cave he knew of in the jungle near Matakay. The thought was scarcely more appealing than the hole they now stood beside, but she knew it would prove a safer haven until Paul and Clara were able to respond. Once again, the little caravan took to foot. For the first time Viola and the children entered the forest that covered the interior of Negros. They followed cautiously as Mr. Paglinawan and his helper Tino cut a slight trail through the dense jungle. It was rough going, but by noon they came upon the cave.

A small slit in the hillside covered with liana vines opened into a dark, damp chamber. Their guide told Viola that her family would be safe in the cave. "We can't live here," Viola responded. Mr. Paglinawan had a pained look on his face. She did not mean to cause trouble, but her mind was made up. Her family would set up a shelter outside the cave, within sight of the path. She was willing to take the risk that they might be seen. Mr. Paglinawan's anguished expression did not diminish, but he realized Mrs. Winn was adamant. He offered to return with some men to help build a proper camp.[21]

As the men were working, a group of guerrilla soldiers came out of the forest. Their leader was Walter Malahay, carrying a message from his father. Viola unfolded the note, reading it silently. Pastor Malahay's words were not comforting. He had declined to deliver her letter to the Lindholms, citing the safety of all concerned. He closed by promising to visit her later that day. Just before sundown Eugenio and Maria came up the trail, she dressed in a beautiful, billowing piña cloth blouse. The elder Malahays had brought fresh food with them: tiny *calamansi,* from which a refreshing limeade could be squeezed, and *bulad,* tasty forest pigeon. The two families sat down that night to a fine feast.

Later, when the Winns and their maids settled in to bed, Viola read aloud a favorite psalm, the Twenty-third: "The Lord is my shepherd; I shall not want. He maketh me to lie down in green pastures; he leadeth me beside the still waters." After reciting the fifth stanza of this psalm of David's confidence in the grace of God, the missionary's wife stopped. "Thou preparest a table before me in the presence of mine enemies." A warmth suddenly enrobed her. She repeated the line. "Thou preparest a table before me in the presence of mine enemies." That was exactly her predicament that very evening. And pausing over the psalm was, Viola believed, a sign from God, a sign that He would lead her through the valley of the shadow of death. She felt her fears dissipate, and the warmth filled her.[22]

FOUR NIGHTS LATER, Gardner returned.

Victoria was the first to spot him, as he walked up the trail by the spring where she had filled a bamboo tube with fresh water. The family helper ran ahead, shouting. The news stunned Viola, who hastily gave up Elinor to the

maid and raced down to greet her husband. He looked terrible as he struggled
up the steep path. He looked, too, like he was carrying a great emotional burden, so great it stopped Viola in her tracks. Feelings gave way to rational thinking. Why, she thought, has he returned? As they approached one another the
answer flashed in her mind. Her first words to Gardner were abrupt: "Whom
did you come for—the Lindholms or me?"[23]

"You," he answered. The word stung her. She thought this had all been
resolved weeks before. She had resigned herself to his loss, to her living in the
jungles with the children until the family could be reunited. She knew, too, that
this was not the time for that reunion.

"Did you escape?"

"No. They told me to bring you and the children down. They've treated me
well so far. If I don't return, they'll kill Mateo."[24] It was the same story, the same
dilemma. She yearned for Gardner, but she knew in her heart that she could
not return with him. After lunch, while he played with his daughter and sons,
Viola suggested they visit Paul and Clara Lindholm to seek their counsel.
That evening, Christian Malahay guided the couple through the jungle. It was
a moonless night but of course they could not use flashlights or torches. With
the teenager leading the way, the trio stumbled blind and barefoot over unseen
terrain, an occasional "Ouch!" punctuating the forest stillness. After six hours
of this torture they reached their destination, near Busilak.[25]

IT WAS DAWN WHEN THE WINNS walked up to the bugang grass thicket that hid
the cave entrance. They called the Lindholms by name. A sleepy head peered
out from the cave entrance. "My Lord, it's Gardner!" Roused from the miserable
hole they called home, Paul and Clara offered their old friends a meager breakfast. "We're so glad to see you!"[26] Viola was shocked when she ducked inside
the cave. "Be careful where you walk," warned Clara; the ceiling was only three
feet high, requiring adults to stoop when moving about. Stalactites ceaselessly
dripped water—finding a dry place to roll out a sleeping mat was impossible.
Unable to build a fire in the cave lest someone see the smoke, the Lindholms
depended upon loyal church families to bring them food each day. To make matters worse, the six Lindholms shared the grotto with three other families.

The couples ate breakfast in the dank dimness of the cavern. When they had
finished, Viola suggested they go outside to talk. Joined by Christian Malahay,
the group sat in a small clearing of bugang, safe from prying eyes. The sun beat
down. Insects buzzed the air. Monkeys frolicked in the trees above. The dis-

cussion turned serious. Clara told the Winns that she and Paul had very nearly surrendered after they heard that Gardner turned himself in. "We were just waiting for confirmation you had gone, too," Paul said to Viola. Christian Malahay spoke up. "We do not want you to go down. My family will do all that we can to keep you safe. As God provides for us, we will share whatever bounties He will bless us with. Please know that I am speaking on behalf of my parents and my brothers and sisters."[27] For a long moment no one said a word. The generosity of Christian's words, of his offer, was overwhelming. Paul turned to Clara, then back to the Winns: "We'll stay." Viola felt a chill. "What do you think we should do?"[28] she said. Should Viola and the children go with Gardner, or should he return to the Japanese alone?

Paul Lindholm framed his response carefully. "If you all go down, your lives will be endangered, especially the lives of the children. But Gardner, if you don't go back, the lives of all of us up here will be endangered." Winn mulled over his friend's words. "If I do go back alone, what can I tell the Japanese when they ask about my family?" He could not bring himself to lie. Again, Malahay took the lead: "We are in a state of war. The ethics of speaking the truth should not be seriously considered. Personal safety should be the main issue."[29] Gardner was visibly uncomfortable with Christian's line of thinking. Lying went against every grain in his body. Paul thought he saw a way around the problem: "Say to the Japanese you don't know where your family's hiding. That'll certainly be true by the time you return to town." It was an awkward solution, but in the end it was the one Gardner chose. He turned to Viola: "If you want to stay, I'll go back alone. I'll trust God and the Filipino people to take care of you."[30] And so it was settled. Before parting, the two couples joined in singing hymns. The final song was Gardner's favorite: "Guide Me, O Thou Great Jehovah."

That afternoon Christian Malahay guided Gardner back to Guihulngan. Viola walked with her husband, hand in hand, until they reached Pacuan Barrio. Gardner spoke a short prayer, "May the Lord watch between us until we meet again." "Amen," they said in harmony.[31] Gardner disappeared down the trail with Christian. Viola, led by another Malahay, returned to her children. Within hours the family was on the move again, to a new hideout deeper in the hills.

At Guihulngan, the Japanese commander was disappointed to see Reverend Winn come in alone. He asked where his family was. Gardner could now honestly answer that he did not know. And then he could honestly say that his wife had run off with another man, a Filipino. The officer laughed.

"Who needs a woman like that?" Gardner smiled wanly. He was soon returned to Dumaguete, still later taken to Bacolod, then on to internment at Santo Tomas in Manila, there joining several thousand American civilian prisoners.

GARDNER KNEW IN HIS HEART that he really did need Viola Ida Schuldt. What did it matter that the love of his life was ten years his senior? She was strong, independent, and smart. Viola's father, Frank Henry Schuldt, had emigrated from his native Mecklenburg, Germany, in the mid-1880s, working as a minister in the German Methodist Church. He met and married Mary Lorenz, an Ohioan. Viola was born in her father's parish, Lansing, Iowa, on 19 August 1901, the last of eight children.

Her childhood was punctuated by frequent moves as her father was reassigned to churches throughout the Midwest. When Mary Schuldt took ill with a serious bronchial condition in 1915, the family moved to Lorange, Louisiana. Viola spent that first year at home, caring for her mother. The following term she finally enrolled in high school, completing the course in just three years. The young woman earned a teaching certificate, and taught elementary classes in Lorange for two terms before matriculating at Morningside College in Sioux City, Iowa. The beginning of her college career was an experience Viola did not enjoy, but one in which she discovered God.

It was important to the young woman to be a member of a college sorority. But when her application was rejected, it was a devastating blow. Viola's insecurities overwhelmed her; she felt completely worthless and turned to religion for reassurance. She was disappointed that her efforts at prayer and Bible reading and meditation did not reveal the Lord's presence. Her efforts turned to the overt—Viola attended a revival meeting, expecting some sign that God had come to her. Others in the crowd were so moved, but the Lord did not come to Viola Schuldt that evening. With the passing of time, what Viola did feel was greater self-confidence, increasing independence, and the barest hint that there was a caring, loving God. This confidence, she eventually came to believe, was the work of the Lord. And in that small revelation Viola Schuldt discovered how God might live and work within her. In her junior year Viola transferred to Western Union College in nearby La Mars. There she thrived. She won a place as a class officer, became a leader of the YWCA, and was on the college debating team, an activity she enjoyed and that earned her a third-degree key in the Pi Kappa Delta Forensic Society.

Upon graduating, Viola taught high school English in Williamsfield, Illinois, for two years. But memories of her college debating successes drew her back to academia. In 1926 she enrolled simultaneously at Northwestern University and at Garrett Biblical Institute, both in Evanston, Illinois, to pursue her master's degree in Christian education. Upon completing her studies, Viola took a job with the Methodist Home Missions Council in central New York, organizing church schools and camps in rural parishes. In 1933 she moved to northern New Jersey to assume similar duties in Dover. The following year thirty-two-year-old Viola Schuldt met twenty-two-year-old Gardner Winn while attending classes at nearby Drew University. She was quite taken by the small, bookish man with the deep bass voice. She especially enjoyed his wry, quiet sense of humor, a funny story often prefaced by a chuckling "huh, huh, huh."

When Viola Winn had submitted her application to the Presbyterian Board of Foreign Missions, it was evident she did not relish the prospect of living and working in some far-off place. In answer to a question about her motives, she wrote that her husband was most anxious to become a missionary, adding tentatively that she supposed her own interest was due only to Gardner's yearning to work overseas. Nevertheless, the secretaries gave Mrs. Winn high marks for leadership, ability to win friends, and an above-average outlook on life.[32]

FOLLOWING GARDNER WINN'S VISIT and concerned about their own security, the Lindholms moved to a safer, larger cave. They called the place *Ziph,* a name taken from the Scriptures, for the wilderness of Ziph was one of the hideouts David used when being pursued by King Saul. In the Bible, 1 Samuel was an especially appropriate selection by Reverend Lindholm. David fled from Ziph when he learned that collaborators had betrayed him: "And Saul went on this side of the mountain, and David and his men on that side of the mountain: and David made haste to get away for fear of Saul; for Saul and his men compassed David and his men round about to take them. But there came a messenger unto Saul saying, 'Haste thee, and come; for the Philistines have invaded the land.' Wherefore Saul returned from pursuing after David, and went against the Philistines." To the Lindholms, Ziph not only represented a refuge, but also a hope that soon the Americans would invade the land and vanquish their pursuers.

The entrance to Ziph was well hidden by tall grass, which gave the family a secluded "front porch" where the children could play in the sun. The cavern had no level ground for sleeping, so friends made a raised bamboo floor, a sort of interior silt house complete with a thatched roof, where bedding could be rolled out, away from the ever-present moisture. For further protection from creepies and crawlies the family slept under mosquito nets.

Clara kept the children busy, playing games and teaching Beverly and Dean from the Bible and from hymnals they had on hand. In the evening the group read by the dim light of a coconut oil lamp. And at bedtime they all joined to sing hymns and say prayers.

After a month at Ziph the two youngest children, Jamie and Janet, became ill, most likely from living in the perpetually damp grotto. Paul consulted with the local churchmen who were protecting the family. The next day the Lindholms abandoned their molelike existence to return to the brightness and warmth of Deacon Mondejar's house at Busilak in Pacuan Valley. The children quickly recovered their health. Busilak would remain their home for the next year.

It was now the end of August 1942. The growing guerrilla movement provided the Lindholms with some sense of security. At the very least, they would be warned in time to flee back to their subterranean sanctuary. It was a unique warning system. "Bolo Battalions" of farmers and mountain men, organized by the Reverend Eugenio Malahay, kept a watch on the Japanese and their quislings. At the slightest hint of an enemy expedition a warning was sounded, the bolo-men pounding on bamboo tubes or blowing into large conch shells called *budyong* to raise the alarm. In this simple, primitive manner the signal was relayed quickly into the remote hills by the network of loyal patriots.[33]

About the same time that the Lindholms moved aboveground, Viola Winn, with Rodger, Norman, and Elinor, moved away from their clearing by the cave to a stilt house on the edge of the forest not far from Hulba. Their guardian, Mr. Paglinawan, was not pleased with Mrs. Winn's decision to relocate, though he had little choice, given the woman's strong will. The new house was barely a dozen feet square, but Viola was especially happy that it had a real front door that provided, she felt, some measure of privacy and security. At this place the Winns' flight ended.[34]

While war raged throughout Asia and the Pacific, for both families, life in Pacuan Valley was relatively quiet, their lives almost normal, their basic needs met.

Food was scarce but always available. Both families had small stores of canned goods, mostly fruit and vegetables, which they had carried throughout their flight. These precious cans were strictly rationed. Coconuts were plentiful and cheap and were put to myriad uses. The nut's water was drunk. Its meat was eaten raw or dried or cooked, or even pressed to produce a serviceable lamp oil. The husks and the shells were turned into cooking and eating implements. Corn became a staple food, most often used in ground form. Foni and Dulia milled their own maize beneath the Lindholms' raised house, crushing the maize beneath two small millstones loaned by a churchman. Pigweed, a local leafy plant, made a reasonable substitute for spinach. The bud of the forest palm was a tasty, nutritious green. Camotes served as sweet potatoes. Bread and cakes could be made from cassava flour. Bananas, common along the coast, less so in the mountains, were considered treats when they could be obtained. Sugar was another treat. It came in small sacks, bought or bartered from itinerant traders. The maids taught Clara and Viola how to make candies from the unrefined brown sugar. The Winns kept a few laying hens, which supplied eggs. From time to time the families were able to purchase chickens from a traveling, pathside market; they roasted the chickens on a spit. But meat was generally unobtainable in any other form, save an occasional monkey. And, of course, the children thrived on fresh carabao milk—to the amusement of the Filipinos, who considered the beasts too dirty to milk.[35]

Health was always a concern in the hills, for medical care was nonexistent. The nearest friendly doctor was sixty miles to the south. The Winns and the Lindholms were thankful to God for maintaining their well-being under such trying conditions. All around them Negrenses were falling prey to malaria. By taking precautions against the anopheles mosquito, carrier of the disease, both families were able to avoid the sickness. Everyone was careful to use netting over their bedding at night. They also used a locally produced antimalarial; quinine had long been unavailable. An ingenious chemist at Silliman had discovered the quinine qualities of a local tree, the dita. A powder was ground from the bark, and when brewed into a bitter soup and drunk in sufficient quantities, dita staved off the worst of malaria's symptoms.[36]

During the typhoon season in the fall of 1943, Dean Lindholm came down with bacillary dysentery. Within hours of developing a high fever, his heart began to race, he vomited all his food, and his stools were ridden with blood. His parents feared their elder son was dying. They felt completely helpless, completely at the mercy of God, to whom they prayed continuously. Clara remembered that she still had a bottle of "miracle medicine"—sulfanilamide tablets—acquired years before in China. This pioneer antibiotic had revolutionized the treatment of bacterial disease. Paul and Clara hoped it would knock out Dean's dysentery. But how much to give the eight-year-old child? They had been told that the drug's side effects might be dangerous. In desperation they cut the remaining tablets in half, giving them to their son at fifteen-minute intervals. By the next morning, as Dean's symptoms eased, he fell asleep for the first time in twenty-four hours. His exhausted parents were filled with relief. The sulfa had indeed performed a miracle. Within another day, the young patient was on the mend. Doctors were later to say that the true miracle was Dean Lindholm's luck in surviving both the dysentery and an overdose of the powerful drug.[37]

Cleanliness was a never-ending challenge. Nearby streams provided running water in which to bathe; a natural bathtub was formed where the water slowed and pooled. A fresh palm leaf made a convenient bathmat. The families scrubbed themselves clean with locally made soap—crude, smelly, but effective. Every day the maids would take a load of laundry down to the stream. Using the same soap, they lathered up the soiled clothes, pounded the dirt out with rocks upon rocks, rinsed them in the clear riffles, and hung them to dry on the forest's edge. Repeated washings broke down the fibers, wearing out the cloth rapidly, requiring repeated mending and patching.

And so, to keep their families clothed, Clara and Viola became expert seamstresses. Out of sheer necessity both quickly graduated from making simple repairs to manufacturing new clothing. Viola took the big tent Gardner had bought at Guihulngan, cut it into pieces, and sewed a fantastic array of pants and shirts and skirts for herself and the children. Linens could be cut down as well, or traded for cloth, finished goods, straw hats, or rattan sandals. Both Viola and Clara learned to make their own thread. Winn planted a patch of cotton, from which she and her maids spun a coarse but usable filament. Sewing needles were worth ten times their weight in gold. Viola once dropped her last one through the slatted floor of the bark house. The girls combed the undercroft but could not find the needle. Winn was disconsolate until Guillerma acquired a new one by trading some precious cans of beans.[38]

Continuing the children's education became a primary focus. Clara donned her teaching cap, instructing Beverly and Dean from elementary textbooks hidden by church friends before the Japanese had a chance to destroy them. Viola, a former grade-school teacher herself, taught reading and writing and arithmetic to Rodger, then age six. For both families the Bible was, and always had been, more than a spiritual guide and constant inspiration. It was a primary source of reading material as well.

Throughout the Lindholms' travails, Paul continued his rural evangelism. He conducted one-day revival meetings for the mountain people. And he baptized newcomers to Christianity—more than three hundred during the course of the war. One of his favorite activities was directing the Pacuan Drama Cavalcade, a youth theatrical troupe that gave performances throughout the hill country. Riding Whitey, his sturdy pony, the missionary traveled widely throughout Oriental Negros. He presided at weddings and funerals. There were always workers to train, churches to organize, conferences to attend. As the resistance movement took hold, Lindholm began to act as unofficial chaplain to many of the small guerrilla bands that roamed the mountains.[39] When he heard that some soldiers were taking advantage of Filipino women, he tried to stop the abuse. On more than one occasion the pastor personally counseled soldiers accused of immoral acts. All his efforts meant much to the mountain people. To Christian Malahay, Lindholm was the reincarnation of Paul the Apostle: strong physically, mentally, and spiritually.[40] Thanks in no small part to Paul Lindholm, the church was remarkably alive and well on Negros during even the darkest days of World War II.

Throughout the remainder of 1942 and into 1943 the missionary families stayed in the lush valley above Guihulngan. That summer the Lindholms moved to a new house just minutes down the trail from Viola. For the first time in nearly two years the children had friends to play with.

December 1943 brought the families their third Christmas in hiding. They celebrated by sharing dinner at the Lindholms'. Paul conducted a simple service in the morning—a ceremony Viola did not attend. Gardner's absence preyed on her emotions, and an emotional day like Christmas . . . well, she knew she would not be able to control the tears once they began to flow. It was better if she stayed away, better if she sent the children instead. The day was happier for Viola after the service. Clara had prepared a wonderful, if frugal, feast. After the simple meal the families exchanged gifts. Viola gave Clara lingerie she had sewn herself. It was not frilly, just sensible, serviceable wear made from worn-out clothing. In return, she was given a fine piece of cloth. Paul got a new razor blade Viola had kept squirreled away since the beginning of the war. Janet and Elinor received Raggedy Ann dolls. It was a day of simple gifts and significant blessings. It was also a day full of holiday cheer, bringing back memories of happier, more peaceful Christmases. The families ended the evening with a round of carols.[41]

WITH THE COMING OF THE NEW YEAR, hopes were raised that the war might soon end. Neighbors had rigged a radio, around which everyone gathered each evening to hear the news. And the news was often good. In November U.S. forces had landed on Tarawa in the Gilbert Islands, and in December, on New Britain. In January American and British troops invaded Anzio in central Italy. The tide was turning against the Axis.

In the Philippines, the guerrilla movement was growing in strength. General MacArthur had begun officially recognizing resistance units throughout the archipelago and especially in the Visayas. He appointed district commanders on each of the big islands: Ingeniero on Bohol, Kangleon on Leyte, Peralta on Panay, Cushing on Cebu, Abcede on Negros. Each of these leaders had been carefully vetted to ensure his loyalty to the United States and his determination to drive the Japanese from their homeland. Unbeknownst to the Winns and the Lindholms, in January 1943 MacArthur had begun sending submarines loaded with supplies from Australia to the guerrillas in the Philippines. At first these missions were undertaken by fleet submarines diverted from their war patrols. But in October of that year a special supply unit was organized to regularly provision the resistance fighters and to evacuate Americans trapped in the islands.[42]

Late in February 1944, Paul Lindholm was visited by Captain Rustico "Rusty" Paralejas, once a Silliman student, now a guerrilla officer. He was carrying a brand-new but odd-looking rifle. "It's a carbine," said Rusty. "There are thirty-eight of them at headquarters." When Paul inquired where he got it the man said, "By submarine, from Australia."[43] Lindholm was astonished by the news. Even more thrilling was a report from Christian Malahay, now a lieutenant with the resistance, that Lindholm's university colleagues the Carsons, the McKinleys, the Bells, the Sillimans, Abby Jacobs, and a dozen others had left the island on the same submarine bound for Australia and freedom.

Paul desperately wanted to believe this news. Rumors reverberated in the mountains of Negros—the hills were rife with apocryphal stories—and the missionary worried that this might be just another of those. But if it was true, and if another submarine came to Negros, it might mean that his own family could finally escape from the Philippines. That very thought posed to Paul a dilemma of Solomonic proportions: Would he go with them, or would he stay behind on Negros to continue his mission? Lindholm kept his concerns to himself, at least until he could confirm the wild stories.

The next day the minister from Minnesota became a true believer.

One of their helpers had gone into the barrio in search of food. She returned with two dozen coconuts. She also carried proof positive that the submarine had indeed paid a visit. In one hand she held out small bars of chocolate wrapped in gold foil imprinted with the words "I Shall Return—MacArthur." In the other she clutched a shiny new 1944 calendar, emblazoned with the famous slogan at the top and featuring a photograph of General MacArthur himself. There he stood, corncob pipe in his mouth, four stars gleaming on his collar, his crumpled cap heavy with brass insignia sitting squarely on his balding pate. On the back of the calendar was printed a map of the southwest Pacific.[44]

The Lindholm household was ecstatic. Within minutes the Winn children came running across the ridge with chocolate-smeared faces. The question on everyone's mind was "When can we go to Australia?"

But amid all the wonderful news there was bad news, too. The families learned that Charles and Hettie Glunz (he of the *Big Capital Creation*), Alvin and Marilee Scaff, and Jim and Ethel Chapman had all been captured by the Japanese and removed to a concentration camp in Manila. Bad news, too, for Viola Winn. There continued to be no word about the fate of Gardner.

Two weeks after the departure of the submarine *Narwhal* and her Silliman passengers, Salvador Abcede, now a colonel, dispatched his adjutant, Major Ben Viloria, to locate and contact the three remaining American families hiding in the Negros hills: the Fleischers, the Winns, and the Lindholms. It took the guerrilla officer forty-eight days to reach Pacuan Valley. His patrol was delayed four times by skirmishes with Japanese Army units, during which two of his men were wounded. On the afternoon of 9 April 1944, while en route to Guihulngan, Viloria chanced to encounter Paul Lindholm on the trail.[45] They returned together to the Lindholms' house, where the Filipino asked the Americans if they would like to go home. There was joy in Hulba that night.

Now Paul Lindholm finally faced the dilemma that had been rolling around in his mind for six weeks. He deeply believed he should remain on Negros. He had always borne in mind the paramount duty of every missionary: to make Jesus Christ known as Savior, Lord, and Master. That put God before country, even put God before family, and that is exactly what Paul Lindholm had done for the thirteen years he had been in the field. He had missed Christmases with his family to be with his congregants. He had missed the birth of his daughter for church business. He had sometimes let them fend for themselves in the hills above Guihulngan while he rode the circuit from parish to parish. For the family's part, they had grown accustomed to his long absences—it was just a normal part of life in the Lindholm household.[46] But now it would no longer be a matter of watching husband and father ride over the hill to Busilak. It would be a matter of several thousand miles, of separation for the duration of the war and the concomitant uncertainties such circumstances bring. It was a matter that would weigh heavily upon Paul Lindholm's heart and soul until he could see his family safely off the island. He broached the subject with his wife and children. They seemed, to him, supportive. They seemed, to him, agreeable to the idea. The missionary decided he would make the trek to the sea with them. If the submarine came, he would go out to it. And if, once aboard, he felt the family was in safe hands, then and only then would he leave them. It seemed, to him, a reasonable solution to a vexing problem.

THE JOURNEY WOULD BE an arduous one. From Pacuan Valley in the highlands of Oriental Negros, the Winns and the Lindholms would have to march across the ridges that skirted the Cordillera Central. En route they would encounter dense jungles and hardwood forests, swift and dangerous rivers, vast fields of needle-sharp cogon grass. Where the mountains turned to the southeast, they would turn westward, out onto the rolling plains of the Cabadiangan Plateau. At the edge of the highlands one last, long defile would take them down to the narrow strip that defined the southwestern coast of the island. When they reached the Sulu Sea their journey would be complete.

In the early morning darkness of Wednesday, 19 April 1944, the refugees began their march south. The leader of the convoy, Rusty Paralejas, was a loyal Sillimanian. The night before, he had urged secrecy upon the families, cautioning them to tell no one about the trip, not even their closest friends.[47]

The caravan was large, numbering three dozen. Besides the six Lindholms, four Winns, and four maids, there was an armed guard of ten guerrilla soldiers led by Captain Paralejas. Two other former students, Lieutenant Constantino Bernardez and Melchor Siao, also accompanied the group. Melchor was a Chinese Filipino from Cebu City who often made the journey across the Tañon Strait to Negros, smuggling small requisites such as sewing needles and writing ink, both impossible to find in the mountains. On this trip Melchor brought exciting news from his island: Colonel Cushing's guerrillas had captured ten Japanese prisoners, including an admiral and secret documents, from a seaplane that crashed off the coast of Cebu at the beginning of April. None of the refugees suspected that within two weeks they would share a ride south with those very papers.

The troupe's train consisted of sixteen cargadores and a handful of pack-

American refugees trekking through waist-high cogon grass near the end of
their ten-day journey. Captain Rustico Paralejas is leading the column.
(Frame from an 8mm home movie via Rodger Winn)

horses. The bearers struggled with their loads, an amazing variety of packages,
from fifty-pound sacks of rice to woven-rattan suitcases to bamboo boxes filled
with cookware. Some men transported their burdens atop their heads. Some
jauntily tucked their loads under their arms. At the rear of the pack two cargadores carried heavy supplies hung from a bamboo pole slung between their
shoulders.

Food for the journey was supplied by Eugenio Malahay's family, Mr. Paglinawan, and other members of the church. They had provided rations for two
weeks, mostly corn, rice, and white beans. As a treat, Clara had made candy
balls from roasted ground cacao beans and melted sugar.

On that first day the party was buzzed several times by passing enemy
planes. Whenever Captain Paralejas spotted one he ordered his wards to disperse to whatever natural cover was handy. When the party marched through
fields of cogon grass, where sanctuary was nonexistent, they were directed to
lie flat until the officer gave the all-clear. The only untoward incident of the day
occurred when a leech was found on Janet Lindholm's eye. Removing the
slimy creature required a dash of salt on the end of a stick, poking the leech
until it withered and fell to the ground. Except for a brief bit of panic and some
mild stinging, eighteen-month-old Janet was none the worse for the experience. At the end of the day the evacuees stopped at a guerrilla camp, sharing a
freshly killed goat for a festive meal.[48] They had walked nearly ten miles that
day, a good pace.

Though Paralejas had picked six horses, including the Lindholms' Whitey and the Winns' Jack, most of the group marched on foot. At times the children delighted in walking, often dashing far ahead of the pack, then waiting for them to catch up. But at other times the children, too fatigued or too cranky to walk, hitched a ride on one of the horses. Clara usually rode Whitey, Janet clutched in her arms, another child sitting behind her. The Winns' helpers shared responsibility for carrying Elinor, a heavy burden as she approached her second birthday.

At times progress was slow. One morning the party encountered a jumble of large trees cut down to clear space for a cornfield. Logs were strewn about like pick-up sticks, and the horses could not get through. While cargadores took another, more difficult path with the horses in tow, the rest of the group climbed over and around the fallen trees. The following day was even rougher when the trail became especially steep. Some slopes required crawling on all fours, grasping for handgrips among trailing vines. It took two men to move each horse up the banks. One pulled from the front, the other pushed from the rear. One of the packhorses collapsed during the march. His load was transferred to another. The collapsed pony was barely breathing. He was covered in leaves and left behind to fend for himself.[49] The party was far off the regular trail now; local guides were hired to lead them.

At the end of each day Captain Paralejas tried to find houses in which the families could stay. They once stopped at a remote plantation. The gracious owner invited the group to spend the night; foreign visitors were a welcome novelty. The man's two daughters turned out to be avid chess players; they spent the evening engaged in a series of challenging matches with Rusty Paralejas, another aficionado.[50]

The middle of the trek was the most arduous, filled with steep climbs and slippery descents. In the first of several such incidents, the Lindholms' Whitey stumbled with Beverly while trying to cross a ditch, throwing the eleven-year-old to the ground. Though scared, she was otherwise unharmed.

Tragedy nearly struck on the following morning. The caravan was making its way slowly down the trail, which wound precipitously along a narrow shelf on an otherwise sheer cliff. The views of the valley below were spectacular. Viola was eager to reach the bottom, for then lunch would be served alongside the cool stream she had been watching from above. A few paces behind her, Clara and Dean were sharing Whitey's wooden saddle. The horse picked his way through the loose shale, placing his hooves carefully so as not to lose his footing. He stopped at a particularly large rock, and when Clara went to dismount, a swarm of hornets dived out of a crevice in the cliff face and attacked. The huge insects—each nearly two inches long—first went after the horse, stinging his mouth repeatedly until he reared into the air, nearly throwing the riders as he twisted away from his tormentors. The hornets then went for the humans, stinging Clara and her son and one of the soldiers who had run over to help. Their fury spent, the hornets sped away. But the damage was done. In minutes the faces and limbs of the victims swelled out of proportion. And the pain was unrelenting. Cool, soothing mud was fetched from the banks of the stream and applied to faces and arms. But the effect was only temporary. Throughout the day and into the night Clara and Dean suffered soreness and swelling that persisted until the following day.[51]

Then the next morning a scare was in store for Paul, Jamie, and Janet. While riding Whitey across a shallow ford, the horse slipped on a scummy rock, lost his footing, and went down on his side. Paul managed to stay in the saddle, clutching Janet tightly, barely keeping her head above water until help arrived. Meanwhile, Jamie climbed out from beneath the tangle of the horse's rear legs, drenched but not hurt.

The penultimate day on the trail was unremarkable, which pleased everyone. By now the group had left the central mountains and descended into the vast, undulating Cabadiangan Plateau. No longer was there a jungle canopy to hide their movements from air patrols. All day the party marched cautiously, nervously, across plains barely covered with grass. The only incident was an encounter with a herd of wild carabao. Unlike the predictably placid domesticated creatures, the wild variety were given to mean streaks, manifested by unprovoked attacks.[52] The refugees gingerly circumvented the carabao, hacking a new path through the cogon.

Anticipation was high on the tenth day, for the end was quite literally in sight. As the troupe neared the coast, the forests returned. The surefooted Whitey had one more adventure up his fetlocks. Clara, Jamie, and Janet were in the saddle. As the horse felt his way around gnarly tree roots, he overreached with one leg once too often. The strain on his belly burst the saddle cinch, tossing the three Lindholms into the arms of a surprised cargadore. Paul, standing a dozen yards away, captured the entire scene on Viola Winn's 8mm movie camera.[53] The caravan stopped for lunch at Candalaga, where the guerrillas had set up a troop school. Here Ben Viloria, Rustico Paralejas, and Constantino Bernardez left the party. Here, too, Guillerma and Victoria, Foni

Clara Lindholm nearly falls off her horse during the arduous trip through the jungles of
Negros. (Frame from an 8mm home movie via Rodger Winn)

and Dulia departed. For security reasons Abcede forbade the maids to go any
farther; he sent them home to their families.

For three years and at great personal sacrifice, the girls had remained with
the Winns and the Lindholms. Their loyalty, tested often, had never been in
question. Clara and the children hugged their helpers and bade them an emotional farewell. The loss seemed especially hard on Viola. As she well knew, the
Filipinas had saved the lives of her family not just once, but time and again.
Tears streaking the dust on her cheeks, Viola waved to the girls as they were
led down the path by a soldier. She never saw them again.

Arriving in the camp, Paul received news that the day after the families left
Pacuan the Japanese had raided the valley. More than a hundred heavily armed
troops swept into Hulba, burning huts and homes and even the new chapel
that had been built there. The enemy soldiers had come to capture the renegade American missionary. Only by luck and the grace of God was Paul Lindholm already on the trail headed south.

Following their lunch, the group, with new escorts, continued down the
track. That afternoon they caught their first glimpse of the Sulu Sea. It was a
thrill to see blue water again. The troupe descended toward the coast, passing
cornfields and coconut plantations—signs that civilization was near. As the sun
was setting, the caravan reached their destination, the isolated barrio of Basay.
The Winns and the Lindholms had walked nearly a hundred miles in ten
days. When she turned in that night, Viola said a little prayer: "Thank you,
Lord, for the safe journey. Thank you, Lord, that it is now over."[54]

# CHAPTER 4

## *The Sugar Families*

FROM TEN THOUSAND FEET, distant Negros looked to Earl Kenneth Ossorio like an emerald isle surrounded by sparkling turquoise and cerulean seas. The lofty peak of Sicaba Diutay was swathed in cottony clouds stretching southward as far as the eye could see. As the Ford Trimotor lumbered across Guimaras Strait, the twelve-year-old boy watched in fascination as the plane's shadow blinked over fishing bancas and interisland steamers. Nearing the coast, Kenneth could see bright white beaches lined with coconut palms and tiny barrios full of multi-colored dots that were people at work and at play and that appeared to move in slow motion from such a great height. To his right he could barely make out the town of Bago, with its church spires reaching high above the trees, its shiny tin-roofed houses glowing in the tropical sun. Ahead, beyond the two pilots in the cockpit, he could see towering Mount Canlaon rising defiantly above the clouds, smoke drifting lazily from its barren brown cone.

In August 1940 Ossorio was returning home to Negros after a nine-month visit to the States. His father, George, sitting just across the aisle watching the vistas as intently as the boy, was chief engineer for the North Negros Sugar Company near Manapla. Kenneth's mother, Loretta, sitting in the seat behind, thought how beautiful these Visayan Islands looked, how much different they were from her native Louisiana. She thought, too, about the son they had left behind there, with her parents in Baton Rouge. Schooling on Negros left something to be desired. George Jr. would be better off in an American high school. A tinge of guilt swept

Kenneth Ossorio, 1945.
(E. K. Ossorio via Al Dempster)

Loretta Ossorio.
(E. K. Ossorio via Al Dempster)

through her. He'll be all right, she consoled herself, and he'll come to visit in 1942.[1]

The drone of the engines changed pitch as the Ford made a gentle turn to the north. The Trimotor began a long, slow descent toward the provincial capital and the island's largest, richest city. Kenneth, his face practically glued to the window, watched the ground grow closer, the trees taller, until with a sudden *whump* the plane's wheels touched the verdant grass of the airfield. A brief, bumpy taxi brought the plane to the spare, wooden terminal. Perched on the roof, a small sign proclaimed in fading letters "BACOLOD, ELEV 20." A larger sign barked, "Iloilo-Negros Air Express Co., Inc."

An airline man in khaki pants and shirt opened the plane's door. The rush of hot, humid air into the all-metal chamber snatched the breaths from the dozen passengers as they fumbled for their hats, their purses, their papers and cases. They quietly walked down the now-sloped aisle, out the small oval door onto terra firma. A fresh sea breeze kissed them pleasantly as they ambled toward the shade of the terminal.

The Ossorios heard their name called, and turned to see a small man wearing a white *barong* moving quickly toward them. The family recognized him as the driver from the sugar company. He showed them to the car, then collected their things. Minutes later, baggage loaded, people settled, the hour-long journey up to Manapla began.

On the coast road the natty station wagon, North Negros Sugar Company stenciled on the front doors, made good time to the first town, Talisay. The car slowed to a crawl near the square; it was market day, the crowds were thick. Kenneth spotted a coconut vendor. The driver pulled over while the elder Ossorio bought four drinking nuts. In the tropics there is nothing more refreshing than the cool nectar of a coconut. Thirsts

George Ossorio.
(E. K. Ossorio)

quenched, driver and passengers continued north through the countryside. To their left was the sea, and ten miles across it the island of Panay. To their right was the cane, unending tracts of sugarcane swaying in the late afternoon sun.

Before war came to the Philippines, sugarcane fields stretched for miles across the broad, flat alluvial plains of northern Negros. Ten feet tall at harvest time, more than a million acres of the dense, sweet reeds grew in rich volcanic soil from the coast right to the foothills, as prominent a geographic feature as the mountains of the Cordillera Central. Cane had been cultivated in the Philippines for hundreds of years, long before the arrival of the Spanish in 1521. With the completion of the Suez Canal in 1869, sugar growers on Negros saw new markets open to them in Europe and America. Fresh capital poured in. Production rose quickly. By 1940 the Philippines was the fifth-largest supplier in the world and sugar was by several times the nation's principal export.[2] It was a massive industry that brought great wealth and power to Negros or, more accurately, to a small handful of Negrenses families, the *hacienderos.* In contrast, the *sacadas*-the quarter million Filipino sugar workers who did the hard and dirty work—barely eked out a living.

As the family passed through Silay, Kenneth caught glimpses of the sumptuous homes built there by the sugar rich. Hidden behind one formidable wall lay Balay Negrense, the elegant residence created by Yves Leopold Germain Gaston, the Frenchman who in 1846 first planted cane commercially and whose shrewd vision brought prosperity to both himself and Negros. On the far side of town, as the station wagon picked up speed again, the boy could see lavish portals and grand iron gates imperiously guarding narrow lanes that disappeared into the cane fields. These paths, he imagined, meandered through vast haciendas, leading eventually to palatial mansions set beneath swaying palms. There were Ossorios who lived like that. But his father was only a "poor" cousin, living in a company house at the sugar mill. With four servants to assist, life at Manapla was a far cry from the wretched poverty in the sacada barrios. Still, to a young boy, thoughts of possessing the vast wealth of the hacienderos was an enticing fantasy.

As the car approached Victorias, the smoke of a mill could be seen in the distance. More than two hundred bustling sugar mills—the sugar centrals—dotted the Negros countryside. Some were small operations, capable of producing just a few dozen tons of raw sugar each day. Others, such as the Victorias Milling Company, could process two thousand tons or more a day.

A central was like a small town—a company town. There were barrios to house the full-time workers. There was a tree-lined street with fine homes for the executives. There were medical clinics, churches, sometimes even schools and shops. The mills themselves were conglomerations of tin buildings large and small, surrounded by tall brick chimneys that belched smoke and steam into the otherwise pure Visayan air.

Thousands of workers harvested the cane. Swathed from head to foot in thick protective clothing, sacadas swung large bolos to fell the sweet stalks. Others loaded the reeds onto carabao-drawn carts for transport to the railheads. From Binalbagan on the south to Cadiz on the north, the cane-covered plain was crisscrossed by narrow-gauge railways—a thousand miles of tracks, on which dinky trains carried cane out of the fields down to the bustling centrals.

At the mill, hundreds more workers processed the sugar. Cars of cane were rapidly unloaded by giant steel claws feeding a continuous moving belt. The conveyor carried the cane through rolling knives, cutting the stalks into short pieces. The cane was pressed seven times to extract every drop of its precious sweet juice. Impurities were removed in liming tanks and settling tanks. Evaporators thickened the juice, reducing it to syrup. Centrifuges separated the pure crystals from the molasses.[3] Finally, those crystals of brown sugar were dried and packed into hundred-twenty-five-pound sacks. Tens of thousands were stored in rows of red-roofed bodegas. When the time came, the little trains carried the laden sacks back across now-barren sugarfields to the coast, there to be loaded onto ships consigned to Carquinez and Philadelphia, Bristol, Le Havre, and a score more ports of entry.

The shadows grew deep across the countryside as the afternoon sun waned. An hour out of Bacolod the car reached Manapla and continued still farther up the coast highway. A few miles beyond the town the driver swung on to a well-oiled road, skirting a sign reading North Negros Sugar Company, Inc. For ten minutes more the car slid past sheer walls of cane stalks until, after one last tight bend in the road, it came upon the central's main compound. Straight ahead was the mill itself, but the car turned right, down the tree-lined street. It passed neat pastel houses sitting high on pilings until it pulled up in front of one quite recently painted. The Ossorios were home after a nine-month absence. They had left about the time Germany invaded Poland. They returned shortly after the conquest of France. Such was the state of the world.

THE NEXT MORNING GEORGE OSSORIO went down to the administration building for a briefing with the general manager, his cousin Louis Ossorio.

The North Negros Sugar Company was founded by Louis's father shortly before World War I. Because it bypassed Asia, that war made the Ossorios very rich. By 1940 the company was one of the largest centrals in all the Philippines, producing more than three thousand tons a day. The two men had much to talk about. They conferred about the progress of the harvest begun that May, now one-third complete. They discussed the condition of the sugar business and, of course, that led to talk about the political situation. Japan had been at war in China for several years. The effect upon Far Eastern sugar markets had fortunately proved minimal. Europe had been at war for ten months, a conflict the cousins knew would soon adversely impact Negros. Their real fear, though, was war between the United States and an increasingly belligerent Japan. Such an eventuality would be catastrophic for the company; most of its product was shipped to America. When the meeting ended, George returned to his office, there to plow through months of paperwork left by his staff for him alone to deal with.

Though George's parents were European—his father Spanish, his mother English—he himself was Asian born and raised. He was, at five-foot-seven, short and stocky. His skin was very fair, his eyes a penetrating gray. From age eighteen he had worked at Manapla, where he soon showed his aptitude as a sugar man. In 1922 the family sent him to America to learn all he could about modern production methods. He enrolled at Louisiana State University in Baton Rouge, majoring in sugar technology. During his second year at LSU George met a local girl, Loretta Ferrara, a dark-haired teenage beauty of Italian heritage. Their relationship blossomed and grew; the pair were married on 8 May 1924. Ten months later Loretta gave birth to their first child, George Jr.[4]

When George Ossorio completed his degree in 1926 he fully expected to go back to the Philippines, to a job at the sugar central. But a family feud intervened. Desperate for a way to support his own family, he took a job as a mechanical engineer with Allis-Chalmers in Milwaukee, Wisconsin. There, on 21 March 1928, Earl Kenneth was born. There, too, George applied for and won American citizenship. The following year, family problems ironed out, he returned with his wife and children to Manapla as the chief engineer of the North Negros Sugar Company.

AFTER THEIR NINE MONTHS AWAY from Manapla in 1940, the Ossorios quickly fell back into the routine of life at the sugar central. George plunged into this job with renewed vigor, eager to try out new techniques recently learned in the

States. Loretta spent the mornings giving lessons to Kenneth. Though the Filipinos were justifiably proud of the progress made toward the creation of a free public school system—America's greatest legacy in the islands—Loretta felt that the local schools could not provide her son with the education she wanted for him. But she also hesitated to send him away to a boarding school. So, like American expatriate mothers around the world, Loretta Ossorio fell back on home schooling, specifically the popular Calvert System. Created by Baltimore's famous Calvert School, the teaching program provided a comprehensive curriculum for grades kindergarten through eight. An annual subscription included a detailed lesson manual, pertinent books, and appropriate supplies. Upon the family's return to the Philippines, Loretta and Kenneth entered grade six. The plan was most thorough: reading children's classics, vocabulary, sentence diagraming, mathematic ratios, proportion and percent, graphing, science of life forms, memorizing poetry, geography of Asia and Africa, ancient history. Periodically Kenneth submitted to a written examination, which was sent on to Baltimore for review and comment. As the school's brochure proclaimed, "The essence of a Calvert education is a solid grounding in the basics."[5] Loretta was there to ensure that Kenneth was so grounded.

THE OSSORIOS' NEXT-DOOR neighbors on the tree-lined street were also Americans, Samuel W. Real and his family. Real was of mixed blood—a mestizo. His father, William, a soldier from Iowa, had come to the islands during the War of Philippine Independence in 1900. After the uprising was quelled, William stayed on, marrying a young Filipina, Bernadina Navales. The couple made their home on Cebu, there raising eight children. Sam, the only son, was born in 1904. After finishing grammar school, the boy went to the States to study electrical engineering at the Westinghouse School in Pittsburgh. In 1930, at age twenty-six, Sam Real returned to the Philippines, technical school certificate in hand, promptly securing a job with the Manila Electric Company.

In the spring of that year the young electrician caught an interisland steamer for Negros. He stopped to visit his family, then went on down to Dumaguete to see his sisters Grace and Felicidad at Silliman University. One night Sam invited the girls to dinner. They insisted they bring their roommate Rose Vail, a vivacious nineteen-year-old mestiza from Lucena in southern Luzon. Rose insisted that she bring along her boyfriend. The five found an inexpensive eatery in the small college town. The chemistry between Sam and Rose must have been very special, for the boyfriend was relegated to one corner of the

The Real family
(left to right, Rose, Bill,
Sam, Nancy, John,
Hermann [Fritz], Berna).
(Rose Real via Al
Dempster)

table and soon was gone from Rose's life entirely. She found herself falling deeply in love with Sam Real. And he, in turn, was quite taken by the twinkle in her eyes and her lovely, warm smile.

During the school holidays Sam went home with Rose to meet her parents. Her father, Edmund Alonzo Vail, was a tough civil engineer born and raised in New York. He was surprised and pleased when he realized that he and Sam's father had fought side by side in the war at the turn of the century. He regaled the table with tales of battles in the jungle. Like William Real, Edmund Vail had stayed on in the islands. He built railways and bridges, married a Filipina, Albina Militar from the tiny island of Romblon, and raised a family. He had lived and worked throughout the Philippines in the ensuing three decades, at the time calling the small Negros coastal town of Pulupandan home. Edmund was quite impressed with Rose's new boyfriend. Like himself, Sam had an engineering bent; the two could talk for hours about things mechanical. A paternal blessing was not long in coming.[6] The couple were married at Pulupandan on 25 October 1931.

Shortly after the wedding, Sam quit his job with the Manila Electric Company. Wanting to be closer to both his own family on Cebu and to Rose's, he took a position with the Insular Lumber Company as an electrician at its giant mill complex near Fabrica in northern Negros. A year later son William Edmund was born, named after the two grandfathers. John Frederich and Berna Rose followed. In 1937 Real accepted a better job at the North Negros Sugar Company, as chief electrician. Two more children were born at Manapla: Hermann George (nicknamed Fritz) in 1938, and in January 1940, Nancy.[7]

To Sam and Rose, life at the sugar central was the "good life." They lived in a nice home. They had servants to look after them. They went to monthly parties hosted by the company at the clubhouse. Rose enjoyed working in her tropical garden. The children were happy and healthy. Billy had inherited from his grandfather and father an abiding interest in mechanics—in what made things work. He loved to help his father on projects around the central, crawling under machinery, learning how the complex mill functioned. For fun, he sometimes hopped a sugar sack for a ride down the mile-long conveyor from mill to warehouse. To brothers John and Fritz, the central was one grand playground. They spent hours in the bodegas, defending sack forts from imagined attacks. And the sugar trains made ready props for games of cowboys and Indians. A favorite, if dangerous, pastime was crossing the railway trestles, hoping a train would come along, for if one did, the kids would hang over the side of the narrow wooden bridge, sometimes dangling a hundred feet in the air. Concerns about the children's education pervaded the Real household as they had the Ossorios'. Rose and Sam chose to send Billy and John to a missionary boarding school in Capiz in northeastern Panay and Berna to a convent school in nearby Bacolod.[8]

During the summer holidays the Reals often visited the family coffee farm in the shadow of Mount Canlaon in central Negros. Rose's father had bought the property some years before, mainly as an investment. Her mother, Albina, had supervised the tenant farmers who grew coffee in the highlands, rice in the lowlands, corn in between. They stayed at the comfortable plantation house on the edge of the dense forest. There were streams for the children to swim in, horses for them to ride, jungle trails to explore. As a child, Rose had reveled in the isolation the farm provided. At age sixteen she had climbed the volcano—a two-day trek. She had never forgotten how wonderful the views of the Visayas were from the ten-thousand-foot peak. In the trying years ahead the place the family called "the ranch" would serve as a safe haven for Rose and her family.

K ENNETH O SSORIO WAS AWAKENED by his father's gentle shaking at the break of dawn on Monday, 8 December 1941. "The Japanese bombed Pearl Harbor! We're at war!" The teenager was shocked.[9]

Sam Real came running up from the mill, barely able to contain himself. He dashed up the front steps, shouting to his wife about the news he had just heard on the radio. Rose's first thoughts were of her children. Bill and John were at school on another island. They must be terrified, she thought.

At the Capiz Baptist Home School on Panay, the Real brothers awoke that morning to utter confusion. Teachers ran from building to building, many of them crying. In first period an announcement was made that war had broken out with Japan, that the school was closing, that all children must return home. With no way to contact their family, the brothers felt lost and alone. They resigned themselves to wait, in hopes that Rose or Sam would come, soon, to retrieve them.[10]

Rose arranged passage to Panay within a day. Though less than sixty miles as the crow flies, Capiz was a long trip. It began with the drive down to Bacolod. Then there was the steamer from Banago Wharf across the Guimaras Strait to Iloilo. Then the slow, dusty train ride through the ricefields to Capiz town. Finally, the taxi ride to the school. Bill and John were thrilled to see their mother. Many schoolmates had already left. But many more were still waiting for parents, for family, for someone, to take them home.

Relations between the United States and Japan had been deteriorating throughout 1941. But when war actually came, the shock around the sugar central was palpable. Americans and Filipinos feared for the days ahead. In the tentative period following Pearl Harbor, while enemy aircraft pounded bases on Luzon and Mindanao, the Ossorios somehow believed the Japanese would never invade the Philippines. At first, the worst they could imagine was being cut off from America for several months. Like so many others, they presumed that reinforcements for the beleaguered garrisons would surely arrive soon. But when the enemy landed in force at Lingayan Gulf, Luzon, on 22 December, their fears grew exponentially. It was a somber, joyless Christmas at Manapla. The good life had come to an end.

Once the children were safely back home, Sam and Rose made plans for the immediate future. Mother and children would head for the Vail family rice plantation near La Castellana; Sam would continue at the sugar central as long as he could. Rose took down the curtains from the house on the tree-lined street and packed them for the journey. Not knowing if they would be gone for six months or six years, she packed everything she could: clothing, medicine, linens, books, cookware, cans of Boston baked beans and Vienna sausages. The children climbed into the family car, joined by their mongrels, Thunderbolt and Lightning. They headed south down the coastal highway, encountering little traffic along the way. The towns they drove through seemed much too quiet. The peacefulness was eerie. An hour below Bacolod, at San Enrique, Sam pointed the car inland. Passing through canefields and rice paddies, the Reals soon reached La Castellana and, a little ways beyond, the farm. It was another of Edmund Vail's properties, a rather small place nestled among bamboo thickets and leafy trees where the lowland plains butted against the foothills. Ricefields, carefully irrigated by planters under the watchful eye of Rose's older brother Louis Vail, dotted the property. He and his wife, Trinidad, lived comfortably in the two-story farmhouse. It felt cramped when Rose and her five children moved in.

Within weeks the central was virtually deserted. Most of the workers, from harvesters to managers, buckwheated to the foothills east of the mill, uncertain how long it would take the Japanese to reach Negros. In late January 1942 George Ossorio had his men build an escape house for his family in the hills near Sicaba Diutay, three hours' hike beyond the railhead. Before the family could occupy their new home, Loretta was hurt in a car accident. George, who was unaccustomed to driving, was at the wheel of a company car when it failed to negotiate a sharp bend in the road. The station wagon shot off the edge, rolling into a narrow gully, crashing to a sudden halt. The others escaped harm, but Loretta's back was badly injured. After getting some sugar workers to help extricate her, George rushed his wife to the Bacolod hospital. Her injuries were extensive, her recovery agonizingly slow. She passed the weeks by reading, knitting, and listening to the radio. And it was from her hospital bed that Loretta learned over the air of General MacArthur's flight from the Philippines on 11 March, of the fall of Bataan on 9 April, and, finally, of the collapse of resistance on Corregidor on 6 May. The next day George came to evacuate her to the mountains. At Manapla the family boarded a sugar train with as many belongings and supplies as they could carry. At the end of the line, cargadores shouldered the bulky packages for the trek up the heavily wooded slopes. Still unable to walk, Loretta was carried the entire way, flat on her back, a nurse constantly at her side.[11]

George had persuaded three of his fellow engineers to accompany him to the hideout. Louisianan Larry Acoin fled the central with his wife, Adele, and their four children. Tony Sanz, who was Spanish, brought Lena and their two kids. Juan Compos, a Filipino with six little children, joined them. Life at the foothills camp was rustic but, at the time, safe. The days passed slowly for Loretta and Kenneth at Sicaba Diutay. Confined to the camp by George, their main activity was reading. They quickly went through the deep pile of magazines they had brought with them, then turned to the classics, thoughtfully provided by the Calvert School.

After he got his family settled at the plantation, Sam linked up with George, and the pair returned to the central. They wanted to make sure the plant and its people were all right. War had come just as the harvest season was ending. The fields were nearly bare, the bodegas were piled high with sugar sacks that would never reach market. So that the Japanese could not capture a functioning sugar mill, the managers decided to destroy it. Sam assisted the company's chemist, Courtland Ashton, in the sad task of placing demolition charges at strategic points around the plant.[12] When he was satisfied there was nothing more he could do at Manapla, Sam Real performed his duty as an able-bodied citizen of the United States by joining the U.S. Army on 5 February 1942.

At the time the military situation on Negros was a bit muddled. There were few troops defending the island from an enemy who had, in those early days of war, no interest in invading it. Most of the Japanese Army's resources in the Philippines were concentrated upon the reduction of Bataan Peninsula and Corregidor Island—tasks proving far more difficult than the enemy anticipated. The Japanese were also busy consolidating their positions in northern and southern Luzon and southern Mindanao. For the most part, the rest of the archipelago remained in American hands. The troops on Negros, mostly ill-trained Filipino conscripts, had little to defend and little to defend with.

Sam and his brother-in-law Louis Vail were assigned to the Signal Corps. The pair were kept busy working on telephone and radio installations around the island. After Bataan fell to the Japanese, Real was given a commission as first lieutenant. Fighting on Luzon continued into early May, but organized resistance ended following the collapse of Corregidor. On 15 May all U.S. forces in the Philippines were ordered by General Jonathon Wainwright to surrender. While some Philippine Army units melted back into the jungles to fight another day, most American soldiers, Sam Real and Louis Vail included, became prisoners. They were taken to a military prison camp at Bacolod, there presumably to sit out the war.

IN THEIR HIDEOUTS, the families kept up with world news each night by tuning in to station KGEI, broadcasting its shortwave signal from a powerful transmitter near San Francisco, California. After a long winter of grim reports from the fronts, of loss after loss, the news began to improve in the spring, to grow almost encouraging. In May U.S. naval forces turned back the Japanese Navy at the Battle of the Coral Sea. A month later, at the Battle of Midway, the Americans defeated their enemy, sinking four precious aircraft carriers. This victory was a turning point in the war. But with the defeat of the American garrison on Corregidor Island, all of the Philippines had slipped into Japanese hands. It would take more than three years to wrench the islands from the enemy's grip. While perhaps a ray of sun shone upon Midway that June, in the hills of northern Negros the world of those in hiding grew only darker.

IT WAS NOT UNTIL 21 MAY 1942 that Japanese soldiers occupied the island. Within days army forces fanned out around the countryside, setting up garrisons and outposts and looking for stray Americans. It did not take them long to reach Manapla. Local sympathizers, among them former sugar central carpenter José Okamoto, were quick to tell the Japanese about the Americans hiding in the hills. Runners were sent to the several hideouts with a curt message from the enemy commander: Surrender or face death!

George Ossorio and the sugar men discussed their options. Ossorio was adamantly opposed to surrendering. The other three failed to see his logic. They gathered their families, gathered their things, and hiked back down the hills to give themselves up. Because they were Americans, the Acoins spent the war interned at Santo Tomas University in Manila. Filipinos Sanz and Compos went to work for the Japanese.

That June, as the three families descended, the Ossorios ascended. With great foresight George had built another house a few hours farther up the mountain. Some weeks later a Japanese Army patrol came searching for the family. This was led by Edward Weber, a forty-five-year-old German married to a local mestiza and a longtime resident of Bacolod. When the Japanese took over, Weber took to marching around the city with a pistol in hand, arresting civilians he suspected of working for the guerrillas. As Weber piloted the patrol up the slopes they came across a local man, Mercades Urbano. The German asked the Filipino to guide them to the Americans. Urbano refused, telling Weber he did not know where they were hiding. The Japanese soldiers applied some persuasion: They tied his thumbs with wire and hung him from a tree. The pain was intense; Urbano withstood the torture as long as he could. He finally cried to be cut down, telling the men he would show them the way. And that he did—leading them to the original hillside campsite, now empty. Weber and the soldiers were furious at the Filipino. They beat him mercilessly for his treachery. The patrol moved on, pulling the hapless guide behind them. Later that day Urbano redeemed himself in the eyes of the enemy when he unwittingly led the patrol to the hiding place of an American priest, Father LaSage. Weber thrashed the priest when he tried to escape. The soldiers then took him to headquarters at Bacolod for interrogation. The bruised and bloody Urbano was given his freedom as a reward for his assistance. And the Ossorios remained safely hidden.[13]

ONE DAY, NOT LONG AFTER the surrender, the Japanese paid a visit to Rose Real at La Castellana. There was a polite knock at the farmhouse door. When Rose answered, she was surprised to see a lone Japanese officer standing on the porch. He told her he had come to ask a few questions. Rose nervously invited the man into her home.

She took the officer into the kitchen, invited him to sit down, offered him tea and cookies. In between sips the lieutenant posed his questions. "How long have you been at this place?" "Who is here with you?" "Is it true Samuel Real is American?"[14]

This last query startled Rose. While she struggled for an answer that would sound convincing—be convincing—two-year-old Nancy toddled into the kitchen. She went straight for the man in the neat green uniform, crawled up on his lap, and began hugging him. The officer was disarmed by Nan's affections. He smiled at the playful girl, telling her she was a sweet child. The distraction was only momentary. "About your husband . . ." "Oh, no, he is Spanish," Rose answered persuasively. "He was born in Cebu, of Spanish parents."[15]

"Do you have any guns here?" Rose knew her brother Louis had several cached around the property. In her sweetest voice she answered, "No, my family never kept guns, but you are free to look if you like." She hoped he would not, for she also knew her brother had a powerful Hallicrafters short-wave radio hidden upstairs.[16] "I could show you around."

Regarding the woman carefully, the lieutenant set down his steaming cup. Rising from the chair, he grabbed his cap from the table and turned to Rose. He bowed his head slightly, smiled, and thanked her for her help and for her tea and sweets. As he left the farmhouse he gave Nancy a friendly pat on the head. Rose and her daughter watched him walk up the path to the road. As the officer reached the first thicket of bamboo a squad of armed soldiers, bayonets at the ready, tumbled out behind him. Rose crossed herself. She looked down at her youngest daughter. "Honey, that was close."[17]

That evening the family decided it was time to buckwheat to the ranch deep in the mountains below Mount Canlaon. They packed what they could and departed the next morning. The overburdened car wound its way up into the foothills toward the central massif. There the forest was thick and dank. Log bridges crossed and recrossed roaring rivers. After a strenuous climb in low gear, a few miles south of the great volcano the car pulled off the highway. From here there were no roads, just rutted paths. It was a slow, bumpy trip. The car became mired more than once. The party climbed still higher into the mountains. By day's end, as the shadows grew long, the Reals reached the sanctuary of their ranch house.

A few months later, in late September 1942, while George Ossorio was out foraging for food, Loretta and Kenneth had an unsettling encounter at their second hideout. One day several dirty, disheveled, and heavily armed men appeared at their doorstep. They told mother and son that they were looking for George Ossorio. The pair were at first unnerved, but when the leader of the band introduced himself as Captain Smith, United States Armed Forces in the Far East, they felt much relieved. It was the first time either Ossorio had met guerrillas. The insurgents, led by Captain Charles Henry Smith, former Bacolod branch manager for the International Harvester Company, were part of a larger force living in the hills, striking Japanese truck convoys in the lowlands. When George returned he was pleased to see the guardians. The soldiers spent a few days with the family, entertaining them with tales of their exploits against the Japanese. At the end of the visit Captain Smith invited George and Kenneth to come see the guerrilla camp in the mountains above Cadiz. They all left together for the five-hour hike east. There father and son met Major Fidel Soliven Jr., former police chief of Bacolod and now commander of a growing band of guerrillas.

In December 1942 George Ossorio moved his family to Soliven's headquarters. There they would be safer. On the hike across the mountains Japanese planes flew low across the trail, menacing the party. Loretta began sobbing, sure they had been found out. George comforted her, explaining that the pilots would not have seen anything at the speeds at which they were flying. At the New Year the family moved in to their third house of refuge. Once they were settled, George joined the guerrillas. This he did with enthusiasm; he believed his skills could be of use to the insurgents. He was commissioned as a first lieutenant in the Corps of Engineers, 72nd Division, Subsector G.

IN THAT FIRST SPRING and summer of war Rose Real carried on as best she could. Her brother Edmund took charge of running the highland ranch. Rose took over the marketing. It was no easy task, shopping in the mountains. On market day she rose early, had a quick cup of coffee freshly brewed from farm-grown beans, then set off barefoot with a ranch hand. The hike to the little town was both beautiful and treacherous. The climb down was steep. Numerous streams, cold and swift, had to be carefully forded. But by noon Rose was in the barrio, buying goods the family could not grow for themselves—canned food, onions, garlic, root vegetables. Rose used the excursion to listen for local news: accounts of food shortages, tales of enemy atrocities, gossip about the guerrillas. Every vendor had a different story to tell, a different slant on Philippine affairs. She always left feeling more in touch with, less isolated from, her compatriots. Shopping completed, the ranch hand tied the bulky purchases to a long pole, swung it up to his shoulder to spread the weight, and turned toward the mountain trail. They left the market at midafternoon, arriving back at the ranch at dusk.[18]

In the quiet of the night Rose worried terribly about Sam. She knew he was a prisoner in Bacolod—some friends had seen him there before she moved up to the highlands. There were rumors that the camp would be closed, the captives transferred to bigger camps on Luzon. And there were rumors that those camps were horrible places, where men died every day of disease, starvation, or torture. She feared the worst for her beloved.

But the ever-resourceful brothers-in-law were not content with captivity. They kept their eyes open for a chance to escape. Opportunity knocked one day while Sam and Lou were working in a sugarfield. A station wagon driven by a Japanese sergeant stalled down the road. Sam ambled over to offer his assistance. He told the enemy soldier he could fix it. Raising the hood, Sam began to tinker with the engine. A few minutes later the sergeant left, headed back toward the prison camp. Sam stopped tinkering and began a diligent search for the cause of the trouble. Within moments he was able to get the engine running again. He called to Lou, who came at a trot, jumping into the car as Sam accelerated down the road. Driving along the coast highway toward Bago, they knew they would not get far. After a few miles Sam turned up a narrow dirt path. They ditched the car and headed for the cover of the canefields. After a two-day walk Samuel and Louis reached the Vails' lowlands rice plantation. A farmhand filled them in about the Japanese officer's visit and the family's consequent speedy retreat to the highlands. Though disappointed at not finding Rose and the children, Sam was grateful that they were safe. Another day's walk brought them to the ranch and a joyful reunion.

Some weeks later, Sam Real and Louis Vail joined the guerrillas. They linked up with former Silliman University physics professor Henry Roy Bell. Bell was trying to rebuild a radio set to contact the outside world. Sam and

Lou, who was a whiz with radios, assisted. Bell and Vail cobbled together a radio transmitter from parts gathered throughout the province, while Real scrounged for a way to power the device. For months and months the men tried to send a signal. Just as they were about to give up, in January 1943 they made contact with station KFS in San Francisco.[19] Theirs was the first message from Negros to span the seas, to tell the world that resistance to the Japanese occupation was alive and well. It was a jubilant night in the jungle when the response from America crackled back out of the ether. When MacArthur and his staff at GHQ in Brisbane learned of the connection, they, too, were jubilant. For more than a year they had had no concrete, current information about the situation on the island. For the first time they could get up-to-date reports on Philippine affairs. Other islands began to check in with Brisbane. Contact brought new hope to the insurgent forces, revitalizing the resistance, especially on Negros. There was now anticipation that MacArthur's long-awaited help truly was coming.

UP NORTH, LIEUTENANT GEORGE OSSORIO was lighting up the jungle. There was no electrical power within twenty miles of Soliven's camp. Light at night came from coconut oil lanterns. Power for the radios was provided by a soldier furiously pedaling a stationary bicycle hooked up to a small generator.

Swift streams were abundant in the mountains. That was the engineer's inspiration, for Ossorio knew he could harness the kinetic energy of flowing water. He designed a simple wooden waterwheel that would do the job of sixty cycling soldiers. He directed workers to dig a trench parallel to the creek. While others began to build the wheel, Ossorio sent some men down to Manapla to liberate an electric generator from the sugar central's powerhouse. It required great effort and many days to move the heavy dynamo up the slopes. Meanwhile, the wheel began to take shape. Its spokes and troughs were made from hardwood, abundant in the forests of northern Negros. Seven feet in diameter when completed, it was carefully installed on a trestle above the trench. A wood flume was erected to carry the current from the channel over the top of the wheel. A system of pulleys and belts connected it to the generator shaft. When the stream was diverted, the wheel began to turn. The pulleys creaked. The belts spun. Finally the shaft began to revolve.[20] A small light bulb attached to the generator at first flickered, then dimmed, then went out. But as the water flowed ever faster and the machine turned ever faster, the bulb flickered on, stayed on, got brighter, lit up the jungle—just as George Ossorio said it would. His contraption worked and worked well. It made him famous among the guerrillas. Every commander, every camp, wanted their own waterwheel to power the lights and the radios and, eventually, even the ice cream makers.

The wheel was such a hit in Subsector G, Ossorio was asked to build a second one, farther up the river. His work caught the attention of the Northern Negros Sector commander, Lieutenant Colonel Ernesto S. Mata. Mata maintained his headquarters some miles south of Soliven's Subsector G near Mount Mandalagan, still deeper into the mountains. The twenty-eight-year-old officer had graduated from the prestigious Philippine Military Academy at Baguio. He fought with the Americans on Negros, but refused to surrender his troops when the Japanese occupied the island. At the beginning of 1943 Mata had some five thousand guerrillas under his command covering the entire northern third of Negros.[21]

Mata wanted more from Lieutenant Ossorio than just waterwheels. He put the engineer to work preparing maps of guerrilla-held territory, in particular showing the positions of trails used for communications among the insurgent groups. Ossorio also undertook missions of some risk, destroying roads and bridges in the lowlands with his underequipped engineering troops. His work then caught the attention of the district commander himself. Colonel Abcede promoted George Ossorio to captain in April 1943, and shortly after reassigned him to 7th Military District Headquarters (DHQ) in southern Negros.

All these assignments kept George Ossorio away from his family for weeks at a time. Loretta, hearing about Japanese patrols moving deeper into the jungles, decided to move yet again. She and Kenneth packed what they could for the four-hour trip south. When they arrived, the pair moved in with the deputy governor of Subsector G, Tranquilino Valderrama. Before the war, Valderrama owned a lumber mill at Victorias. The guerrillas burned the complex to the ground to prevent it from falling into Japanese hands. The governor was nonplussed about the tragedy; he filed a claim with the provisional government for eleven million pesos, twenty times the mill's actual value.[22] Nevertheless, Valderrama was a family friend offering aid and comfort at a difficult time. For two months mother and son lived with the Filipino and his family, later moving into their own house within the governor's compound.

Too young to join the guerrillas, Kenneth Ossorio took a job as a filing clerk in the governor's office. He kept regular work hours, attended daily staff meetings, made sure all the i's were dotted and the t's crossed. The main duty of the office was to distribute food supplies equably around the subsector. The exile government had enacted a food tax on the lowland planters, a levy paid not in cash but in food. The plan called for the provincial government-in-hiding to collect 20 percent of each farmer's rice crop to feed the guerrilla army. If there was any left over, each civil employee was paid one year's wages in rice. To the amazement of the hungry army, the number of patronage employees swelled so greatly that there was no food left for the soldiers. The situation created considerable ill will between military and civilian officials. The two parties remained at loggerheads over the issue for months—indeed, for the rest of the war. As a stopgap, Colonel Abcede ordered his rebel units to grow their own food. The measure helped alleviate hunger for the guerrillas, but only somewhat mitigated the friction between the army and the government.[23]

While working as a clerk, Kenneth Ossorio started a collection of war-related ephemera. The guerrillas had organized an extremely efficient postal service throughout the island. It was something like the Pony Express, but on foot through the jungles. Mail couriers were on the move constantly, neither rain nor snakes nor Japanese patrols staying them from their appointed rounds. Everybody had a unique if simple address. A letter to George Ossorio reached him at District Engineer, 7MD. Large quantities of mail and other papers regularly crossed the young American's bamboo desk. One letter in his collection was a 20 February 1943 missive from Tomas Confessor, governor-in-exile of "Free Panay," to Dr. Fermin Caram, Japanese-appointed puppet governor of "Occupied Panay." Confessor argued strongly for a truly independent Philippines:

There is a means to bring about peace even under the present circumstances if Japan is really sincere in her desire to see peace and tranquility here. She should declare the Philippines' neutrality. She should [then] evacuate all her forces from the islands. I am sure that should Japan declare this proposition and formally present the same to the United States, the latter would be compelled to accept it.[24]

For its revelations about internal Philippine politics, this document later piqued the interest of SWPA intelligence, who confiscated it from Ossorio.

Among the teenager's favorite collectibles were items of propaganda—from both sides. A 30 November 1942 notice from Colonel Abcede began, "To the people of Negros: Today is National Day. May it remind us of the days of '96 when our people and our heroes suffered the privations of the revolution." A Japanese proclamation of 23 September 1943 concluded, "We, the Imperial Japanese Army, are so sympathetic that we do not certainly harass or kill you.

But we will promise that we shall not hesitate to kill those who do not surrender. You should join the construction of the New Philippines."[25]

It was only natural for Kenneth to include intelligence documents in his collection—maps, memos, and reports—many original, some painstakingly copied by hand. More than once he swapped one of his comic books for an official paper. One day an American officer, Lieutenant James Halkyard, passed through the camp on a secret mission for Abcede. Halkyard showed the ever-curious Kenneth a highly detailed situation map of Negros, depicting the positions of all the district and subsector command posts and radio stations, as well as the locations of the Japanese garrisons. "Can I have this?" the collector inquired. The officer was taken aback. "Certainly not! This is top-secret stuff." The boy reached under his desk and pulled out an old suitcase half full of papers. He grabbed a handful. "So are these." Halkyard scanned the impressive cache. "Do the guerrillas know you have this stuff?" "No," answered the teenager. "Well, you better be careful. They'd kill you if they knew what you had. Go ahead, keep the map."[26] Kenneth was delighted.[27]

AS THE WAR STRETCHED ON and the guerrilla movement spread, the enemy grew bolder in their attacks upon the Bandit Zone—a boot-shaped area encompassing the heavily forested, mountainous interior of Negros.

When Negros was first occupied in May 1942, nearly two-thirds of the lowland population fled to the hills. The Japanese offered various enticements to lure people back to the towns, plantations, and centrals. By July of that year half of those who left had returned to their homes. In October 1943 the enemy increased pressure upon the denizens of the interior, issuing the Bandit Zone order. By this order, any person found in the Bandit Zone by the Japanese Army was considered an insurgent who could be, and often was, shot on sight. This brought more people down out of the mountains. After that, Japanese raids grew more frequent, more vicious. Special troops augmented the local garrisons on their forays into the zone. The days when Japanese soldiers feared moving deep into the jungle had ended.

On 9 December 1943 a concerned George Ossorio wrote to Governor Valderrama:

The Japs are going to try more mountain campaigns. This was already demonstrated last Oct. And Nov. In this attempt they brought tents and provisions with them and stayed three days. They penetrated deeper into the forests. A thing they didn't dare do last year. The old belief therefore, that if one lived 3 or 4 Kms. inside a forest, it was safe from Jap penetrations, no longer holds true.[28]

The Japanese had built an efficient intelligence network that provided a steady stream of surprisingly accurate information about the guerrillas, based mostly on reports from paid informants. And when they planned a raid, Filipino quislings were employed as guides to lead soldiers to the rebel hideouts. A favorite enemy tactic was to stealthily approach a camp in the darkness before dawn. The troops would fan out around the compound, then pounce suddenly upon the often unsuspecting insurgents in a well-coordinated attack.

In his letter, George Ossorio cited just such a raid. On 28 November the enemy had surprised and captured without a shot a guerrilla officer and his squad of fourteen men in their mountain command post. It was a dark, rainy night—in the past an unusual time for the Japanese to be out in the jungle. George wrote, "This officer did not believe the Japs would come up on such a nite [*sic*]. He relaxed just a little on his watchfulness."[29]

Subsector G strived to remain watchful at all times. Major Soliven had a well-organized spy system in the lowlands. When there was a buildup of soldiers at Fabrica garrison, the guerrillas knew to be on the alert—a raid was in the works. Pickets were placed at strategic points, ready to race their warnings back to headquarters at the first sign of a Japanese patrol. The guerrillas knew they could not hold their position against superior numbers of better-armed troops; the warnings gave them time to evacuate command posts and camps. Sometimes the warnings came a bit late. One dark morning Kenneth Ossorio was rudely awakened by the crack of gunfire. He rousted his mother from her bed and they fled out the back door of their house into the haven of the thick jungle. Bullets whistled through the humid air. Mortars *crrumpped* from out of the forest. By sunup the enemy had retreated. Some weeks later Governor Valderrama took the precaution of building new quarters deeper and higher in the interior—just in the nick of time. Shortly after the district government moved, the enemy made a concerted raid on the old compound. They found it vacant. Before returning to Fabrica they burned it to the ground.

LIKE THE EYE OF A HURRICANE, life at the ranch was peaceful for the Real family. In 1943 the Japanese had yet to penetrate the highlands of central Negros. It was an endless summer for the children. Every day they could go swimming, riding, hunting—pretty much do whatever they wanted. Billy, then eleven, loved to go into the jungle with his dog Thunderbolt. The pair hunted baluds with a small rifle given to the boy by his father. The mongrel helped flush the game, while Bill soon became adept at bringing it down. On the table the birds added variety to the family's diet of fresh vegetables and canned meat. Brother John loved to tag along, playing at hunting with his trusty slingshot. Sometimes Fritz accompanied his brothers, too, always more interested in hunting insects than food for the family.

Rose Real was one tough cookie. Though she missed the amenities of life at Manapla, she managed well in the highlands. She did much of the cooking. An excellent shot, she sometimes went hunting with the boys. Before the horses were slaughtered for food, she often rode the trails close to the house. But occasionally things got the better of her. One day the girls, while playing with their mother's makeup kit, added iodine to her only jar of facial cream. When she discovered the mess she broke down and had a good cry, releasing a flood of emotions she had been holding deep within for months. The children were sad and bewildered by the scene, but it was cathartic for their mother.

To assist her in looking after the children, Rose hired an old mountain woman, Myang, who had a reputation for being a healer. The reputation was not unwarranted. When five-year-old Berna injured her hand, Myang treated it with a remedy made from jungle herbs—about which she possessed great knowledge. Everyone was amazed at how quickly the wound healed.

The only bright spot in Rose's otherwise conventional life was going to the dance. Yes, the dance. Deep in the virgin forest, under the very noses of their enemy, the mountain people held parties. Folks came from miles around to revel in the gaiety. Sam Real was never much of a dancer, but given the chance, Rose could dance the whole night through. On party night the young mother donned her smartest pair of slacks, threw her best shoes around her neck, then set off barefoot through the jungle for the two-hour trek to the gaily decorated social hall where the event was held.[30] Before she entered, she would wipe her feet clean and put on her heels. There Rose had no difficulty finding dance partners among lowland evacuees, provincial officials, and even guerrillas. Filipino bands had the jungle swaying to the sweet rhythms of hundred-year-old waltzes and the latest swing hits from the States. Alcohol was available for a few centavos, usually in the form of *tuba,* a bitter drink made from the coconut palm, or *guhang,* a sticky substance made from the sap of the buri palm. It was probably a good thing that Sam was far to the south, working for Colonel Abcede. A quick-tempered man prone to fits of jealousy, Sam could become unpleasant when his wife was in the arms of another man. Still, the dances made delightful, festive respites from the rigors of war. When she returned, Rose fell easily to sleep in the arms of a waltzing Morpheus.

TOWARD THE MIDDLE OF 1943 life at the ranch suddenly became more serious. One day while playing in the woods, John Real heard gunfire. He knew the sound well enough—he had sometimes gone hunting with his brother. But this was different. There were many distant reports, accompanied by occasional ratta-tat-tats. It sounded somehow ominous to the nine-year-old boy. He raced home to tell his mother.

Rose had heard rumors that the Japanese were finally raiding the Bandit Zone in the highlands. Taking no chances, she moved her family an hour's walk farther into the jungle. It was the first of half a dozen such moves.

With the aid of their servants, the Reals built a lean-to near a swiftly flowing stream. They lashed long branches to the trunk of a big lauan tree, covering them with foliage. The result was a simple shelter that, because of the tree's giant buttresslike roots, was divided into multiple chambers that afforded each family member some privacy. The boys helped dig a well for drinking water, while others gathered wood for the fire. The family cook combed the forest for edibles, returning to camp with a tin full of fresh mushrooms. In succeeding days more supplies were brought up the slope, gradually making the family's new home almost civilized. Here Rose and the children spent the next month.

When word came that the Japanese had slackened their efforts to subdue the Bandit Zone, Rose moved the family back to the ranch. Everyone was pleased to be home again. They found the house in good condition, cared for in their absence by their tenant farmers. The Reals quickly settled into their old routine, though with a sharpened awareness of the dangers surrounding them.

As a security measure, Billy had begun a daily routine of plowing the paths and fields near the house with a carabao, churning the soil to hide evidence of footprints. Early one morning the boy rode the big water buffalo up the hill, as usual. Rounding a thicket of bamboo, he practically stumbled upon a platoon of armed men marching away through the woods. Luckily, none saw him. He turned the awkward beast around and headed home. He shouted to his mother that the Japanese were in the jungle. Rose came running. He told her he had seen sixty or seventy men, dressed like civilian Filipinos, not in uniform. They all had rifles, he said, and he could hear them speaking Japanese.[31] Rose knew it was time to run before the soldiers returned. Again she gathered her family. Again they hiked into the jungle, in a direction away from the enemy. After a couple of hours the party paused near a small river. Rose surveyed the site, then told her family this would be their new home. They all set to work building a hut, gathering firewood, hunting for food. Here they spent another month. And then they returned to the farm.

After repeating the cycle twice more, the Reals returned to find that their farmhouse had been burned to the ground by a Japanese raiding party. There seemed no sense in staying at the plantation any longer. It was too dangerous now. Raids could come at any time, without warning. Rose and the children collected what belongings survived and returned to their last jungle hideout.

But even so deep in the forests, they were alarmed to discover they were not safe. Near their camp some local lumbermen had felled huge trees, which lay helter-skelter upon the ground. While hiking through the tract one day Rose caught a glimpse of movement down the slope. Warily, she made the children hide beneath the giant logs, cautioning them to keep still and quiet. Before long, a line of Japanese soldiers came marching up the very path the family had used just moments before. From the dark shadows beneath the trees, wide eyes followed each marching step—steps so close even a small arm could reach out and touch. It was the closest call yet. And when the family went back to their hut, Rose chose to move again, farther still into the jungle.

By early 1944 finding food had become a problem. The provisions Rose had so carefully packed at Manapla had mostly been consumed. The trips to the market had stopped—it was much too dangerous to be seen in town. Bartering away clothing and linens, Rose had been able to buy food from farmers. She had even traded away the curtains from her house on the tree-lined street. Now she had precious little left. The family resorted to living off the land. Rose learned from the local residents that she could make tasty cakes from cassava flour, and vinegar from fermented bananas.[32] Each day Billy went into the woods to hunt dinner. His usual quarry was monkey. One creature could feed the whole family for a day. Rose would skin the carcass, then cook it on a spit over an open fire. The taste was not to everyone's liking, but to the hungry it was a feast. John contributed to the larder by fishing for eels. Early in the evening he would take a can of giant earthworms to a nearby stream. His wriggling bait was a great attraction to the slippery, snakelike fish. John's catch was a welcome, tasty addition to the Reals' table.

AT THE BEGINNING OF MARCH 1944 Sam Real returned home. From the outside world he brought news and a spanking new Army-issue carbine for Bill, recent copies of American magazines for Rose, and I Shall Return chocolate bars for the girls. He told them the things had come from the submarine that had landed at Basay the previous month. He also told them that more than forty tons of supplies had been unloaded—twelve hundred rifles, a million rounds of ammunition. But Sam saved the best news for last: The Reals were to leave Negros on the next submarine!

The family did not comprehend at first. They looked at one another, slightly perplexed. Sam explained that General MacArthur had ordered all Americans off the island. He explained that they would have to hike down to the coast, a trip that would take a week or two. There, Colonel Abcede would provide a secure hiding place for the family until the next sub came, within a month or two. And when the submarine did arrive, it would take them to Australia, whence a ship would take them to the United States.

As this news sunk in, long-buried emotions began to emerge. Rose and the children had been in such jeopardy for such a long time that the thought of being safe, of being free again, was simply overwhelming. Tears flowed but only briefly, as the reality of their situation overpowered their thoughts of freedom. The situation was all too clear: They lived in a jungle surrounded by their enemy; they faced a two-week march through treacherous territory; the sub, if it arrived at all, had to sail through fifteen hundred miles of Japanese-controlled waters. In reality it seemed as if their chances of making it to Australia were slight. As these thoughts rose within each of them, hopes were not dashed but simply shelved for another day. Right now there were too many preparations for the journey itself to worry about the journey's end.

Sam led his family back down through the forest to the charred ranch house. It was slow going for Billy, recovering from a bout with recurrent malaria. On the way the boy became separated from his family. He wandered, delirious, through the forest alone until it was nearly dark. Rescue came in the form of Thunderbolt, who led the boy back to the main trail and finally to the family house. When Rose heard the dog's familiar bark she rushed out of the house, bursting into tears when she saw her eldest coming down the path. She threw her arms around him in a huge hug, thankful he was safe.[33]

That evening Sam talked to Rose about preparations for the journey. He explained they would need to carry as much food as she could collect. He told her, too, that the Ossorios would be joining them at the farm in a few days. Sam added that he would take care of hiring some cargadores and horses. Using what little money she still had, Rose was able to buy a few bags of rice and dried beans. From an otherwise bare larder she produced several tins of canned food, saved for a special occasion. There was little else she could provide for the journey. The family would have to rely upon the kindness of strangers and nature's own bounty (abetted by Billy's skill as a hunter) as they progressed south.

A WEEK AFTER SAM REAL rejoined his family, Major George Ossorio walked into Governor Valderrama's compound bearing brand-new tommy guns, candy bars, magazines, and hope. Kenneth and his mother were thrilled to see George after six months of separation. He told them about the visit of the submarine *Narwhal* to southern Negros. He told them it was now time for them to leave the island.

The 7 February 1944 call by the cargo sub heralded the growing ability of MacArthur's forces to penetrate deep into enemy-held territory in support of the resistance movement. Both George Ossorio and Sam Real had been closely involved in the premier visit of *Narwhal*. As district engineer reporting directly to Colonel Abcede, Ossorio had supervised preparations for the submarine's arrival. In mid-January Abcede had directed his engineer to dismantle houses along the beach that would become the rendezvous point. "Remove all food—pigs, chickens, etc.," the DCO wrote.[34] Sam Real had worked tirelessly to improve the guerrillas' radio net, so that Abcede could provide at least a modicum of security when the ship came. Both men had noticed the steady stream of American citizens arriving at Tolong for evacuation to Australia, among them Dr. Arthur Carson, Henry Roy Bell, Abby Jacobs, and other Silliman University faculty. That their own families might be able to depart on the next run, due sometime in May, was a point not lost on either man. On 21 February Major Ossorio had been released from duty by Abcede so he could return to the North to reclaim Loretta and Kenneth. Lieutenant Real had left Tolong a few days later, after helping test and distribute the thirty-six new radio transceivers that came in on the submarine.

From Tranquilino Valderrama the Ossorios were able to secure provisions and bearers. From Major Uldarico Baclagon, chief of staff of the 72nd Division, came a promise of protection on the long journey. Loretta convinced her loyal housegirl, Consuelo, to make the trip, both knowing the Filipina would not be able to board the submarine. Kenneth gathered up his documents, now nearly filling two battered suitcases. At the beginning of April 1944 the family and their train left Subsector G for the march to the Sulu Sea. Theirs would be a

significantly longer, more difficult, more dangerous hike than that of the Lindholms and the Winns. What had been a ten-day trek for the others would take
the Ossorios twenty-three days.

GEORGE OSSORIO HAD PLOTTED a course down the island's mountainous
spine using trails by now familiar to him, hoping to cover six miles a day
between dawn and dusk. He planned to move across the open fields and mead-
ows that skirted the forest just above the foothills, avoiding if possible hiking
through the mountains themselves. The caravan he led was relatively small,
numbering at times just twenty people. As the party entered a new subsector,
fresh escorts and cargadores joined the trek. All day they hiked through the stifling tropical heat. Each noon George called a halt while lunch—perhaps dried
fish and rice—was prepared. Then it was back on the trail. Late in the afternoon
the party would stop to secure a campsite for the night—it would be dark by
six. Thanks to the hospitality of the mountain people, the evacuees were often
able to spend the night indoors. When such housing was unavailable, the men
pulled out their big-bladed bolo knives to cut down branches and small trees,
fashioning basic but adequate shelter. Dinner might come from cans Loretta
had carefully hoarded those past thirty months, or might be a freshly killed
monkey or fruit bat. One night they had iguana. "Good chicken," remarked
Kenneth's mother, who had not paid any attention to the cooking of the meal.
"Uh, Mom, it's lizard." "Like I said, good chicken."[35] The guerrilla escorts took
turns standing watch while the others slept. They were so deep in the mountains that Japanese patrols were seldom a concern. Still, runners sometimes
brought news of nearby enemy activity, compelling George to divert from the
main trail until it was safe. Diversions slowed the caravan's progress, sometimes
forcing the marchers to hack their way yard by yard through the dense woods.
At first light, following a breakfast of cooked rice, Ossorio had the party on the
move again. For more than a week this was their routine.

A respite came one-third of the way down the island after George led his
group around Mount Canlaon to the Real family ranch. It was an unceremo-
nious entrance for Kenneth, who rode into the plantation atop a carabao, his
left foot badly infected. The young man's big feet did not comfortably accept
local sandals, so he went barefoot on the trek. At the end of each day he carefully removed the thorns that accumulated in his thick-skinned soles. One
night he missed one. The next day the recalcitrant spike dug deeper into his
foot. By the following day it had become infected. It was a wound that would

have responded well to an antibiotic such as sulfanilamide. Hundreds of bottles of sulfa ointment had come ashore from *Narwhal,* but Kenneth's father had not brought any north. Rose Real went through her now depleted medical kit in search of some substance, some salve that might stanch the infection. She turned up nothing. Then she thought of Myang.

The old mountain healer was delighted at the chance to practice her medicine. She carefully examined Kenneth's foot. After mumbling a few words to herself, she left the wounded boy in the care of his mother and disappeared into the forest. With a worried look, Loretta turned toward her former neighbor on the tree-lined street. Rose, sensing her friend's concern, reassured Loretta that Myang could and would make things better.

The old woman reemerged within the hour, a small basket filled with green leaves and chunks of bark and pieces of fungi dangling from her arm. She spread her condiments on the remains of the front porch and set about making Kenneth's medicine. She put a bit of this and a tad of that into a small clay bowl and ground them with a hardwood pestle. Some leaves she steeped, others she simply chopped. The result was a strong-smelling, nasty-looking pasty concoction. Kenneth winced when the healer spread the gummy mix on his foot. He was then advised to rest. And he was assured that his foot would soon be fine.

The Ossorios remained skeptical about Kenneth's prospects for recovery. But the next morning, when Myang removed the poultice, everybody was surprised to see that the infection had been drawn out by her remedy. When cleaned up, a gaping hole was left in the bottom of Kenneth's left foot, but at least he would be able to walk on it. Myang suggested he stay off his feet, to give the wound a chance to heal. With no fixed date for the arrival of the next sub there never had been any rush to get to Basay; George held the caravan at the Reals' while his son recuperated.[36]

IN A FEW DAYS KENNETH was well enough to travel. The two families bundled up their meager belongings. While Rose passed out a few gifts of prized clothing, the children sadly bade their neighbors good-bye. For the Reals it was a bittersweet departure. Freedom beckoned on the one hand, but to leave their beloved ranch—that was another thing entirely. Billy Real refused to part from Thunderbolt. He was granted permission to take the dog on the trek. He also tucked his pet fighting cock under one arm, unwilling to leave the bird behind either. A little later than George Ossorio preferred, the band of refugees hit the trail.

Now numbering nearly three dozen people, the caravan stretched half the length of a football field. Crossing swift streams was a ponderous, at times dangerous, undertaking. Each of the younger children had to be carried, or passed from arm to arm. Food also received careful handling; the loss of a rice sack would be devastating to the troupe. Traversing roads was similarly cumbersome. Upon an "all clear" signal from George, one by one the travelers crossed. To have come this far only to get caught carelessly crossing a road was a prospect chilling to everyone. Still, the party managed to average six miles a day, even after forfeiting an entire day lost in a leech-infested swamp. When they found shelter in an abandoned house that night the refugees continued to pull the slimy creatures from their limbs. Unfortunately, that house turned out to be a poor choice for a shelter. Shortly after everyone turned in, it became all too apparent that the place was swarming with hungry fleas. An evacuation to the cold, hard ground ensued.

Nerves were frayed when the group started out the next morning, aggravated by a now critical shortage of water. All that morning the band pushed on through the unrelenting heat, searching for the trail from which they had strayed the day before. When the sun was near its zenith a guide excitedly called to George that he had found water. Ossorio hurried through the underbrush to where the man was pointing. What he found profoundly disappointed him. It was nothing more than a tiny brackish brook, barely trickling. While George was deciding how best to draw water from the rivulet, six-year-old Fritz Real accidentally stepped into it, churning up mud and algae, instantly turning the stream murky, the water undrinkable.

Ossorio's temper snapped. Kenneth, standing on the far side, watched as his father yanked the small boy from the spring and began to yell at him. That act in turn incited Sam Real. His face reddened, his eyes narrowed, his teeth clenched. Billy Real watched his father closely, for he knew intimately the nature of the man's horrible anger. While Major Ossorio caterwauled at Fritz, Bill saw Sam shift the carbine he was carrying so that its barrel was now in both hands, as if he were preparing to use the rifle as a club. Kenneth watched nervously as Sam's fingers curled tightly around the hot steel tube.[37] Billy shuddered with expectation as Sam suddenly moved toward the commotion, screaming at Ossorio not to shout at his child. The motion caught Kenneth off guard; he raised the rifle in his own hands, ready to fire if the other man went for his father. The engineer turned his frustration on the electrician. "The water is undrinkable!" In that tense moment thirty thirsty people standing in a wide arc around the fracas waited for the passions to play out. Finally Sam moved forward again, this time toward Fritz. To his youngest son he offered a fatherly hug and a few words of reassurance. George Ossorio, now silently staring at the trickle in the ground, contemplated the group's plight. It was the only spring they had seen all day. He resigned himself to wait until it cleared.[38]

That evening around the campfire one of the cargadores approached Kenneth with a proposition: "Do you want I should kill Mister Sam?"[39] Kenneth was horrified. "No. It's all over. Everybody's friends again."[40] The man disappeared into the darkness. The incident was closed, but relations remained strained for the remainder of the journey.

AS THE CARAVAN CONTINUED SOUTH, the character of the land they crossed gradually changed. The Cordillera Central veered toward the east, toward Dumaguete and the Horns of Negros. After a difficult crossing of the wild Ilog River, the great Cabadiangan Plateau opened at their feet. Rolling hills, mostly barren of significant cover, dominated the uplands. Vast stretches of sharp-bladed cogon grass inhibited travel on foot; roads provided no alternative, for there were no roads. The jungle was confined to narrow strips that followed the course of the many streams and rivers cascading down from the mountains. It was a desolate place.

And it was the very desolation of southwest Negros that made it an attractive base for the guerrillas. The coastal highway running south from Dumaguete ended fourteen miles on, at Zamboanguita. From there a rough, rutted road— dusty in the dry season, a quagmire in the wet—ran around the very tip of the peninsula, passed Siaton, turned north, and terminated twenty miles farther, at Tolong. Telegraph and power lines continued another twelve miles up the shoreline, to Basay. Inland, up in the plateau, there were no towns for hundreds of square miles. The uplands, with an altitude of seven hundred to nine hundred feet, dropped precipitously at water's edge when they collided with the Sulu Sea. A slender coastal plain was dotted with coconut plantations and, increasingly, rice paddies. A 1944 U.S. Army map declared the Cabadiangan "unexplored" (though with help from engineers such as George Ossorio, the mysteries of the barren wilderness were slowly being unraveled and mapped). The only way the Japanese could approach the area was by sea, for they maintained no garrisons between Siaton and Sipalay—a stretch of seventy miles. Across the great plateau, the nearest enemy outpost was forty-five miles from Basay. During the entire war the Japanese raided the area but a dozen times. This isolation is what Colonel Abcede craved, for it gave him a secure space to grow and train his guerrilla forces.

Saturday, 29 April, marked the end of the journey for the Ossorio family when the party reached George's rear command post in the hills behind Tolong, one ridge beyond a tiny settlement called Catumbahan. After a brief rest Sam Real led his family down to the banks of the Bayawan River toward their hideout nearer to Colonel Abcede's headquarters. George penned a quick note to his commander: "Dear Abie, Arrived here at my rear CP today with my family. Will be down tomorrow morning to see you. Good Luck, Geo."[41] While a runner took the message to DHQ, the ever-foresightful engineer took his family two hours' walk back into the foothills, yet another ridge over, to show them their new house, built in an isolated clearing on the edge of a heavily wooded tract. He told them they might have to stay there for some weeks, suggesting they get as comfortable as they could while they waited.

On Monday morning George took Kenneth down to his command post, introducing the boy to his officers and men. Much work had piled up during the district engineer's absence. George attended to his duties while his son thumbed through official documents in search of items for his collection. After spending the night at the CP, father and son hiked down to district headquarters, across the Pagatban below Dayhagen Ridge. Kenneth expected to find a bustling command compound, but Colonel Abcede's DHQ was nothing more than a lone stilt house nestled between coconut palms and the river. While his father went in to confer with Abcede, Kenneth stayed outside. When the meeting broke up, George brought his commanding officer out to meet his son.

The legendary Salvador Abcede seemed rather ordinary to the young man. He was short, dark, and surprisingly youthful. Only thirty, the former army ROTC commander was now responsible for the 7th Military District—the entire island of Negros. Abcede was born in Zambales Province, Luzon, where his father worked as a machinist at the U.S. Navy base on Subic Bay. In 1936 Salvador Abcede graduated from the University of the Philippines with a reserve commission in the Philippine Army. Called up in 1939, Abcede was assigned to the Reserve Officers' Training Corps at Silliman University in Dumaguete. He was a battalion commander when the islands fell in May 1942. Rather than surrender, he took his troops into the hills behind Kabankalan in southwestern Negros. His unit had more than six hundred rifles, and used them that summer to harass the Japanese. After working diligently to unite the fractious guerrillas on Negros (and succeeding), Abcede was promoted over the heads of more senior officers by MacArthur to lead all resistance forces on Negros.[42]

George Ossorio introduced Kenneth to his CO. They shook hands vigorously, exchanged pleasantries, talked about life under the Japanese. And then the military leader of Free Negros retreated into this modest headquarters, there to get on with waging the guerrilla war.[43]

As they walked back toward the hills, George had glum news for his son. Abcede had asked George to stay on Negros. The boy wanted to know what answer his father had given. "I told him I'd stay."[44] They talked little during the remainder of the hike back to the house.

George paid hell for his decision when he broke the news to Loretta. If her husband was going to stay, she would stay. That's not possible, contended George, MacArthur had ordered all American citizens out. While the two argued, Kenneth was deciding what course of action would be best for him alone. Finally the teenager weighed in with his decision. "I'm leaving." He had pulled out his situation map of the Pacific war. He was convinced the Allies would continue to push the Japanese out of other places, that the Philippines would become the final, bloody battleground of the war, and he meant to be far away when that happened. Eventually reason prevailed in the Ossorio household. Loretta agreed to go, and agreed to let George stay behind. The matter was settled.[45]

SAM REAL HAD ARRANGED to shelter his family in a small hut near the mouth of the Bayawan. After they had settled, he returned to duty with Abcede. For the children, romping through the groves and hiking over to the beach soon lost their luster. To pass the time, Billy and John often went down to the *bungsods* that lined the estuary of the broad river. The bungsod was an ancient device for catching fish. Built from bamboo and rattan in the shape of a huge anchor, the fish corral, constructed in waters up to thirty feet deep, could easily be a hundred yards across. Fish would swim into the seaward side of the great contraption, trapped within when the gates were closed tightly.[46] The boys helped the fishermen cast their nets for quarry ranging from small anchovies to large tuna and even swordfish. They were usually rewarded with fresh fish to take home for dinner. On their own, they dived for oysters and crabs. This bounty of fresh seafood was a welcome gift for the table, a welcome change from rice and beans, fruit bat and monkey. Though the period was a quiet, restful lull for the family, they had no idea how long they would have to wait to be rescued by the submarine.

# CHAPTER 5

## The Prisoners of War

In 1940 THE REASONS WHY a man enlisted in the army were many and varied. Jay Russell Snell had two. His job as assistant manager at the Grand Theater in Rochester, New York, felt like a dead end. He was tired of sweeping up everybody's popcorn and Cracker Jacks. He was bored with having to prod young, entangled lovers with his flashlight. Russ Snell wanted more out of life. Then at Christmas, Rose Combatelli, his girlfriend of three years, broke up with him. That clinched it. "Why stick around here?" he thought. And so, on 6 February 1940, Snell enlisted in the U.S. Army and that same day was whisked away to basic training at Fort Slocum, New York. He volunteered for the medical corps. They trained him to be a laboratory technician.

Twelve weeks later, Private Jay Russell Snell found himself aboard an army transport passing through the Panama Canal en route to the Far East. It was a thrilling adventure for this twenty-four-year-old New Yorker who had never traveled far outside his home state. On 21 May 1940 his ship docked at Manila amid great fanfare. Snell went to work in the medical laboratory at the army's Sternberg General Hospital, the most modern, best-equipped hospital in all Asia.[1]

Twenty-eight-year-old Irving Victor Joseph joined for a similar reason. He, too, wanted a better job. Born and raised in Los Angeles, his family moved to San Francisco just as he was starting high school. He graduated in 1930, in the middle of the Depression. Finding and keeping a job was not easy. Joseph floated around the West Coast, trying his hand at various fields. By the time he took his oath on 1 October 1940, Joseph had attended law school, studied photography, and earned a pilot's license, but never found that elusive better job.

When he enlisted, Irving Joseph volunteered for the air corps. After barely three weeks of training he was assigned to the 20th Pursuit Squadron. A week later he was Manila-bound, arriving just before Thanksgiving 1940.[2] His outfit, one of only three interceptor squadrons in the Philippines, was based at Nichols Field outside Manila. The planes they inherited were a great disappointment—ancient Boeing P-26s. These poorly armed, vintage-1934 pursuits poked along at scarcely 200 miles per hour. Back in the States it was relegated to trainer status, but in the islands the P-26 was still the front-line fighter.

For American servicemen, life in the Philippines in 1940 was the "good life," despite the occasional intrusion of global politics. There was always free time to explore the great city of Manila. Nightlife was abundant. The people were friendly. The dollar went a long way—custom-tailored uniforms and handmade shoes were bargains.[3] In a few months Russell Snell and Irving Joseph learned to love the Philippines. Yes, the heat could be stifling, especially to Snell, who hailed from the snow belt of upstate New York. But he liked just about everything else. Liquor was cheap. Women were plentiful. The job was not particularly demanding. Snell originally signed up for a two-year hitch, but soon decided he would not only like to extend his tour but also take his discharge in this island paradise, this land of opportunity.

During the first week of July 1941, Irving Joseph's squadron transferred to Clark Field, sixty miles north of Manila. They moved when Nichols became unusable. The east–west runway was being rebuilt, and the north–south runway was a swamp during the rainy season. Clark was the only first-class airdrome in the Philippines. That meant it had sodded runways solid enough for the big B-17 bombers then arriving from the States. That summer the 20th Pursuit finally received capable aircraft—eighteen snappy Curtiss P-40B Tomahawks. These were the first modern fighters to reach the Philippines. The fact that there was an acute shortage of coolant for the Allison V-12 engines put a crimp in their deployment. Still, the brand-new planes did look spiffy sitting on the flight line.[4]

By mid-1941 the United States was gripped by the need to prepare for war. Huge amounts of money were approved by Congress to build up the armed forces. Industry was turning its production toward national defense. The Selective Service System was drafting thousands of men each month. It looked as if America was finally getting serious about the possibility of war.

In late September the eighteen hundred men of the 200th Coast Artillery arrived in the Philippines. Originally a New Mexico National Guard cavalry regiment, the 200th had been retrained to fight a modern, mechanized war. Considered one of the best artillery units in the country, the 200th was pressed into national service, bringing to Luzon badly needed antiaircraft batteries: a dozen 3-inch, two dozen 37mm, and an equal number of .50-caliber machine guns. Among the men were gun commander Howard Tom Chrisco, a shop-keeper from the Ozarks, and gunner Floyd Calvin Reynolds, a New Mexican farmer.

Howard was the only son of Dan and Laura Chrisco, born in a tiny apart-ment at the back of a storehouse in Timber, Missouri, in 1919. There were four girls in the family—his full sister Irene, and half sisters Mary, Lillian, and Gladys. Their father owned a hundred-acre dairy farm a few miles north of town, near Chrisco Springs. Dan sold milk to loggers in nearby camps for ten cents a quart. Laura churned the butter, selling that for fifty cents a pound. When the family needed more money, Dan took on carpentry work.

The children helped around the farm. Howard always had a full slate of chores, but his real love was hunting and fishing. He would take his .22 into the woods, potting 'coons and squirrels. In the spring and summer he fished Barren Fork Creek, which ran across the farm. The boy forsook hook and line for a long pole with a sharp gig on the end. He mostly gigged perch and suck-ers, and an occasional catfish. Most ended up on the dining room table. There was an abundance of caves in the hills, which Howard and his friends loved to explore. Kerosene lanterns in hand, the boys would venture into the pitch-dark caverns, awed by the huge underground rooms they found. Sometimes the cavers would crawl on hands and knees through narrow passages just to see where they might lead. One cave, nameless like them all, was especially thrilling, for to enter it meant a slide down a fourteen-foot pole through an almost round hole in the ground. It was, Howard liked to say, "entertaining."

Brother and sisters went to Cornell Elementary School in Timber, where Howard was an average student. His high school career was brief. "I quit-uated after a week and two days," he liked to tell folks. The nearest high school was at Rector, nine miles away. In the days before yellow school buses, Howard had to ride a horse to school. Someone figured out that when winter came, Howard's ride would be onerously long and bitterly cold, so they switched him to another school, twenty-five miles down the road, in Eminence. The plan was simple: A local man would convey the boy to school in a van. How-ever, on the first day the driver showed up with a Ford convertible. Into this car piled seven students. Howard Chrisco got to thinking maybe the trip was not worth the effort. The next day the man came with his van, nothing more than a steel shell on a steel frame. The roads were gravel, and dust rolled up into the metal hull. By the time he got to the high school, Howard was covered with dirt. That clinched it. When he got home that night he told his folks, "I'm gonna be a farmer." And so Howard Chrisco's formal education ended.

The young man found work at the local drug store, working eighty hours a week for thirty-five dollars a month. He was expected to be at work at seven in the morning and labor clear through the end of the last show at the local picture house. He worked seven days a week and got one day off *per year:* half a day on Thanksgiving, half a day on Christmas. It was menial work, but in the middle of the Depression it was better than the bread line. When the family moved up the road to Salem in 1938, Howard went to work at Pennett's Mercantile, clerking and making deliveries. After two years he moved on to Stanley Brook's grocery store as assistant manager and butcher. He was working for Brooks when the national emergency intruded into his life. Chrisco could see that he would be drafted soon enough, so he decided to join.[5]

Howard Chrisco was twenty-one when he enlisted. He joined both out of a sense of duty to his country and so he could put his compulsory one year's service behind him and get on with his life. Chrisco took his oath at Jefferson Barracks, Missouri, on 7 March 1941. After basic training he was assigned to the 79th Coast Artillery (AA) at Fort Bliss, Texas. That August, Congress had extended compulsory service to eighteen months. Chrisco, now feeling he had gotten the short end of the stick, applied for but was denied a leave of absence. Frustrated by the ways of the army, he requested transfer to the 200th Coast Artillery, knowing he would go overseas within weeks.[6]

Floyd Calvin Reynolds enlisted with the 200th at Clovis, New Mexico, on 6 January 1941. A thirty-three-year-old farmer, nine years married to Vera, Reynolds met Chrisco when they were both assigned to Battery E at Fort Bliss. There Reynolds was trained as a gunner.

Chrisco and Reynolds and the rest of the 200th were loaded aboard a troop train bound for Oakland, California. It was the first time Howard had crossed the country. Though the desert fascinated him, he would have given up the starkly beautiful landscape in an instant for the green hills of Missouri. When they reached the Coast, the artillery unit was ferried over to Angel Island, smack in the middle of San Francisco Bay. Howard loved the place. First of all, it was verdant. But the views across to San Francisco and the Golden Gate were nothing less than spectacular. In the few days the 200th spent on Angel Island, Chrisco managed to walk its circumference, soaking up the scenery, charmed by the presence of quail (and he without his .22). On 7 September 1941 the men shipped out for the Far East on the USAT *President Coolidge.*[7]

Howard Chrisco
astride a carabao in
late 1941.
(Howard Chrisco)

It was a three-week voyage across the Pacific, with a very short stopover at Honolulu. Chrisco and Reynolds were permitted to disembark for two hours. They plopped themselves down in the shade of a coconut tree, surrounded by flowering orchids. The place seemed like heaven to the two farm boys.

The *Coolidge* arrived at Manila with no fanfare. The 200th was quickly transferred up the broad plain leading north from the capital. The unit's first task upon arrival was to set up AA defenses around Clark Field and nearby Fort Stotsenburg. Colonel Charles G. Sage carefully deployed his men and their weapons around the two bases. Gun pits and interconnecting trenches were dug. Ammunition magazines were constructed. Communication wires were run. It was a first-class installation. When the men began training on the three-inch guns, they discovered there was no target ammunition available anywhere in the islands.

Shortly after he arrived in the Philippines, Howard Chrisco was made a cook. Chrisco protested; he wanted to stay on the guns. But as his CO told him, "Son, I've got plenty of gunners. I need cooks."[8] And that was that.

Robert Lewis Young enlisted at Spokane, Washington, on 26 March 1941, having finished a year of junior college and one semester at Whitworth College. After completing his basic training in California, Bob Young returned to Washington, to Fort Lewis, where he was assigned to field artillery. He spent a month learning radio communications and was then transferred to the 194th Tank Battalion. His unit arrived on 26 September on the same transport as Chrisco and Reynolds.[9]

A month and a day later, Joseph Richard Jenson steamed into Manila. Jenson was just nineteen when he took the oath at Ogden, Utah, on 9 December 1940. Like Snell, he volunteered for the medical corps. At Manila's Sternberg General Hospital, Private Jenson was assigned as an ambulance driver.[10]

James Fred Dyer from Detroit, Alabama, joined the army air corps on 10 October 1940. Thirteen months later, he arrived on the *Coolidge* with the ill-fated 27th Bombardment Group. Though the twelve hundred men and officers of the 27th arrived before hostilities broke, their fifty-two Douglas A-24 dive bombers did not. Their planes were shipped separately on another transport. None ever reached the Philippines.[11]

Private Dyer and his group were first sent to Fort McKinley, just outside Manila, pitching their camp on the parade ground. The commanding officer, Major John H. Davies, felt secure that his A-24s would arrive soon. He made a quick trip to the airfield then under construction at San Marcellino. This barren piece of barely scraped earth just north of Subic Bay was to be the 27th's new home. At least that was the plan. Davies directed a team of engineers to start erecting quarters at San Marcellino.

In the meantime, the major put Dyer and others to work at Manila's Nielson Field fashioning revetments and filling sandbags. His men filled a hundred thousand before they ran out of gunnysacks. To keep his air crews and pilots sharp, Major Davies wangled four virtually obsolete Douglas B-18s for them to train with. The twin-engined B-18, the medium bomber version of the DC-2 transport, was nothing at all like the sleek single-engine, low-wing A-24 dive bomber. But the B-18 was an airplane, and it did fly.

BY LATE AUTUMN WAR CLOUDS were dark and ominous. Negotiations in Washington, D.C., between the United States and Japan had bogged down. In an effort to get the talks moving again, Ambassador Kurusu Saburo flew in from Tokyo on the Pan American Clipper to confer with Secretary of State Cordell Hull. In the Atlantic, German U-boats were attacking and sinking U.S. warships and merchantmen. Throughout the Philippine Islands, training schedules had been ratcheted up. New units were disembarking in increasing numbers; U.S. forces had grown from twenty thousand to thirty thousand in just five months. Thirty-five shiny new Boeing B-17 bombers, fully a third of

America's heavy bomber fleet, arrived at Clark Field to provide a first-strike offensive capability. With all the speed it could muster, the country was moving toward a war footing.

On Sunday, 7 December 1941, the 27th Bombardment Group hosted a splendid party at the posh Manila Hotel. The guest of honor was Major General Louis H. Brereton, MacArthur's air chief. Bands played. Spirits flowed. It was considered the grandest party of the year. And it was to be the last.[12] Across the city Russ Snell, now Sergeant Snell, was out on the town celebrating his twenty-fifth birthday. Thus peace faded into the dawn.

By daybreak on Monday, 8 December 1941, the news had spread like wildfire: Japan has attacked Pearl Harbor! Russ Snell, badly hung over from his weekend binge, was accosted in his bunk by an excited buddy: "We're at war! We're at war!" Snell could not—did not—believe him. "You're nuts!" he told the soldier.[13]

Though all the fighters and bombers at Clark were put quickly into the air that first morning of war, they had no targets. They just circled high over Luzon, vigilantly awaiting the enemy. At one point the 20th Pursuit's Tomahawks sprinted over to Lingayan Gulf to intercept an incoming Japanese strike but found nothing. As they ran low on fuel, the fighters and the bombers began returning to base. Shortly after noon, when the B-17s were lined up on the runway for gassing, while their crews were at lunch, the Japanese struck Clark Field. Fifty-four navy bombers, in two deadly V formations, began dropping their bombs. When they were finished, a second wave, of thirty-four Zero fighters, came in low, strafing the field from all directions. The attack lasted forty-five minutes. To newly promoted Sergeant Irving Joseph, it seemed an eternity.

Sergeant Chrisco was driving a truck full of supplies when the Japanese attacked Clark. When he looked up to see the bombers another soldier said, "Look, it's our navy." Chrisco turned to the man and bellowed, "Our navy, hell!" and ran for his gas mask and rifle. By the time he retrieved them from the mess hall, the earth was turning upside down. These were the most frightening few minutes of his life. Chrisco headed for a far ditch when the pursuits came in to strafe, but flung himself behind a nearer truck. "I sure wish I had half a pint," he said to no one in particular. When the planes passed, he got up and ran again for the ditch. Discovering all the best and safest crannies already occupied, Chrisco ran until he got to a dirt bank. When he found cover, the cook began shooting at the planes with his Springfield rifle, getting off forty-six rounds and hitting nothing.[14]

Over in Battery E's pits, Sergeant Reynolds grimly learned the limitations of his three-inch gun during that Monday midday attack. The gunners pumped thousands of shells into the sky. To their surprise and horror, five out of six were duds. Most of their ammunition dated from World War I. The Japanese bombers avoided the shells that did detonate by simply staying a few thousand feet above the flak. As for the fighters, they came in too low, too fast for the gunners to train on and shoot. The 200th Coast Artillery Regiment's five dozen guns knocked down just five airplanes.

When the enemy bombers and fighters finally departed Clark they left behind terrible devastation. The hangars were ablaze. Lines of planes were wrecked. Hundreds of men were dead or wounded. The 20th Pursuit got only three ships into the air during the attack; five others were destroyed while trying to get aloft. The 3rd Pursuit, another P-40 outfit, lost sixteen of its eighteen fighters and a third of its men. And of the much-vaunted B-17 force? Seventeen of thirty-five bombers were destroyed on the ground that noon. The rest were in the South, safe but useless on Mindanao. In this single attack the Japanese won virtually complete control of the skies over Luzon.[15] It was just the first of many attacks. Day after day the Japanese bombed and strafed the base, until Clark was rendered unusable and untenable.

Down at Nielson Field, Private Jim Dyer's 27th Bombardment Group had no means to fight back. Their planes were still at sea. The 27th's men were relegated to the status of "airdrome troops," tasked with guarding the airfields from fifth columnists. They all felt useless as the bombs fell around them.

Sternberg's operating rooms were filled to capacity by the end of that first day of war. Hundreds of casualties from nearby Nichols Field, and from as far away as Clark, inundated the hospital. As the days passed, those hundreds turned to thousands. The operating rooms ran around the clock; their surgical tables were never empty. Russ Snell and Dick Jenson were exhausted. Snell toiled in his lab almost continuously, typing blood and doing cultures. Jenson made dozens of trips transporting injured soldiers and sailors in his ambulance. But the stream of wounded and dying never let up.

The Japanese sustained the onslaught over the next two weeks. On 10 December their bombers virtually destroyed the naval base at Cavite, sending the main elements of the U.S. Navy's Asiatic Fleet scurrying south, to the Dutch East Indies. On 22 December the Japanese landed in strength at Lingayen Gulf. Two days later they landed in southern Luzon, at Lamon Bay.

Their forces quickly overran weakly defended American and Filipino positions, threatening Manila itself.

ON CHRISTMAS EVE General MacArthur ordered all troops to retreat into Bataan. This thumb-shaped peninsula, fifty miles long, ten miles wide, punctuated by two formidable mountains swathed in dense jungle, formed the western side of the gateway to Manila Bay. Army war plans had long anticipated such a retreat. It was believed that a well-supplied army, controlling the entrance to the bay, could hold out on Bataan until reinforcements were sent from America. MacArthur established his headquarters on the heavily fortified island of Corregidor, five miles offshore. The day after Christmas, MacArthur declared Manila an open city. On 2 January 1942, the city fell.

Bob Young's unit, the I Philippine Corps, hurried down to Bataan from northern Luzon after fighting and losing at Carmen and Guagua.

Irving Joseph's squadron was ordered to redeploy to Cabcaben Airfield, on the eastern end of the peninsula. This small dirt strip, built hurriedly by army engineers, was just big enough to handle the Tomahawks. By this time the entire assets of MacArthur's air force had dwindled from 107 P-40s to just 16; from 52 obsolete P-35s to only 4.[16] Within a month, these, too, were gone.

Jim Dyer got a new commanding officer when Major Davies flew down to Australia to try to find his lost A-24 dive bombers. The 27th's executive officer, Major J. W. Sewel, undertook the thankless task of converting the crack bombing team into an infantry regiment. Along with other air corps units, the 27th was assigned to hold the coastal road between the Pilar and Orion barrios.

A break from the daily routine came for Dick Jenson on 28 December, when he and his surgical team left Manila for Bataan. The doctors and nurses boarded rickety old buses, sitting on facing bench seats for the long, dusty ride around Manila Bay, through the old Spanish town and provincial capital of San Fernando, down Route 7 into the peninsula. Jenson followed behind in his ambulance. They were headed for newly established Base Hospital 1. Located near the barrio of Limay, this facility was nothing like shiny Sternberg, but was nothing more than single-story wooden barracks barely hidden beneath scrubby trees. The operating room had once been a barroom.[17] Equipment was basic. Sterility was a state of mind. But its eight operating tables were kept busy. Indeed, performing a hundred operations a day would not be uncommon; forty would be average.[18]

After just a few weeks at Limay, Base Hospital 1 was moved inland, where the climate was better and the tall eucalyptus trees provided cover from enemy planes. This place became known to all as Little Baguio Hospital because its location in the more temperate foothills reminded some of the cool resort city in northern Luzon.[19] Here Jenson was joined by Russ Snell. The lab facilities at the field hospital were very primitive, but somehow Snell managed. When he could, he pitched in to assist the doctors and nurses at Little Baguio. Dick Jenson was assigned to haul medical supplies, equipment, and the wounded.

Howard Chrisco, Floyd Reynolds, and the men of the 200th Coast Artillery began their retreat the night before Christmas. Three days later, Reynolds went with a small detachment to set up antiaircraft batteries to guard Calumpit Bridge over the Pampanga River. Day and night, men and matériel streamed across this strategically critical span on the main road from Manila. On New Year's Day Reynolds's unit retreated once more into Bataan. Army engineers blew the bridge, and they, too, retreated, sealing a hundred thousand people into the mountainous peninsula.

AT THE END OF JANUARY, Joseph's 20th Pursuit Squadron had no planes left to fly. The men were ordered to join Brigadier General Clyde A. Selleck's 71st Division. Selleck had been given the mission of defending Bataan's south-western coast, commanding what survived of his own division plus a motley mixture of air corps, navy, Philippine, and army personnel. While other units set up beach defenses, Sergeant Joseph's squadron was held in reserve. During February and March, the 20th Pursuit was moved around lower Bataan in an ultimately futile attempt to plug the holes in USAFFE's lines.[20]

Throughout the winter, conditions worsened. Though the American and Filipino soldiers fought bravely, the enemy inexorably gained ground. Food ran short. Disease was on the rise. Worst of all, no relief was in sight. President Roosevelt had decided there was no way the United States could retake, or even reinforce, the Philippines. In March Roosevelt ordered MacArthur to Australia. Lieutenant General Jonathan M. Wainwright took over command of U.S. Forces in the Philippines (USFIP). The "Battling Bastards of Bataan" were left to fend for themselves.

During the first week of April the situation on the peninsula rapidly deteriorated. For two days and nights the Japanese Army rained shells and bombs down upon the defending troops. Ten hit Little Baguio Hospital, killing sixteen patients. The II Corps disintegrated under the relentless enemy drive on the San Vicente line.[21] All reserves were committed to battle. As a last-ditch effort, the 200th Coast Artillery and her sister regiment, the 515th, were pressed into service as ground units. On the afternoon of 8 April the two sections were ordered to hold the enemy near Cabcaben.[22] By this time a mass exodus of soldiers into lower Bataan was in full swing. The scene was absolutely chaotic. Thousands of men tried desperately to cross the channel to Corregidor, thinking it a safe haven. The regiments could not hold the line against the Japanese onslaught of tanks and fresh troops. At seven o'clock that evening Colonel Sage gave the order to destroy all equipment. The 200th's few remaining guns were spiked. The radio height finders were cut into pieces and burned. The huge sixty-inch Sperry searchlights were smashed.

Just before midnight, Major General Edward P. King Jr., commander of forces on Bataan Peninsula, decided to surrender. At 6:00 A.M. on 9 April 1942, King sent a flag of truce to the Japanese commander. After a ninety-three-day siege, seventy-eight thousand American and Filipino troops "passed into captivity."[23]

Howard Chrisco was at the southern end of Cabcaben Airfield when the end came, sitting with Captains Smith and Kneely, sharing a bottle of alcohol one of the officers had snatched from the field hospital. A few sips took the edge off their despair and fear. A few more brought meager comfort to the tragedy that had befallen them. When they heard a tank approach, Captain Smith rose. Pulling off his undershirt, he said to his comrades, "You guys stay here. I'll go out and surrender us." A few minutes later Smith returned, holding his shirt as a white flag and surrounded by Japanese soldiers.[24]

Russell Snell was at Little Baguio Hospital when the enemy came.

Irving Joseph was taken prisoner at Bataan Airfield.

Floyd Reynolds gave himself up at Cabcaben.

Bob Young was taken prisoner at the headquarters of I Philippine Corps.

Dick Jenson was captured in his ambulance by a Japanese soldier.

Jim Dyer surrendered with the rest of the 27th Bombardment Group at their beach defense outpost.

BEFORE THE END OF THE DAY all seven were moved to Mariveles Airfield, near the southern tip of Bataan Peninsula, where the Japanese had established a staging and collection point. Thousands of defeated men—defeated in spirit and body—milled about under the blazing sun. Confusion reigned. The Americans weren't sure what they were supposed to do. Neither were the

Japanese, who had not expected, nor planned for, such a massive number of prisoners. That first day there was nothing to eat, nothing to drink.

Chrisco, the ever-resourceful cook, took matters into his own hands. He talked his guards into letting him go down to a nearby stream to fill his canteen. On the way he solicited donations—handfuls of rice from sympathetic Filipinos. When he reached the creek, he had enough grain to half fill a number-ten can. Then a man gave him a big box of oatmeal. And another gave him a can of bacon. The Missourian cooked up the rice over a hastily built fire, dumped in the oats, dumped in the meat, and when it was done to his satisfaction, shared his feast with another soldier.[25]

In small groups and large, the prisoners of war started up the hot, dusty road to the north. There, on the Pampanga plain, the Japanese were setting up prison camps. The walk was arduous for men ridden with malaria and dysentery, men who had been on half rations for three months. The heat was brutal. The enemy was worse. Men began to fall, and on this march falling was a fatal affliction. Those who did not rise were probably dead before they hit the ground. Those slow to rise were often bayoneted by their captors, left to rot in the heat. They called this the Death March. Ten thousand Americans left Mariveles to walk the sixty miles to the railway junction at San Fernando. One thousand died along the route. A fifth of the forty-five thousand Filipino POWs succumbed.[26]

Snell was on the road for two days. Or was it three? He only remembers coming across a group of army trucks, American-made U.S. Army trucks. A guard grunted at him to climb into one and drive. Snell said no. The guard grunted again—drive, drive. Still Snell said no. Finally the guard stuck his bayonet on Snell's buttocks. "How far? How fast?" said the former assistant manager of the Grand Theater, Rochester, New York.[27]

About fifteen miles up the dusty road from Mariveles, near Balanga, Irving Joseph stopped to assist a companion. The man was desperately ill with malaria. He stumbled, fell, said he could walk no farther. This event may have saved Joseph's life, for just then a truck loaded with Japanese soldiers ground to a halt across the road. The driver, an American serviceman, jumped out and opened the hood. He fumbled around, unable to find the problem.

The troops in the back were getting impatient. Seeing Joseph, the driver called out, "Hey, buddy, do you know anything about these trucks?" Joseph went to the vehicle, crawled under the hood, and after some difficulty traced the problem to a cranky carburetor, which he was able to fix. Both driver and

Japanese applauded his success. They offered Joseph and his malarial companion a ride.[28]

On the tenth, two Japanese officers interrogated Floyd Reynolds. The officers could read and write English but could not speak it, so they interviewed Reynolds in writing. They submitted to him their questions on a sheet of paper. "What happened at Laguna Bay?" "Where are the American nurses hiding?" "Where is the water pipe that crosses from Bataan to Corregidor?" Reynolds wrote that he had no answers to these or any other questions. To his surprise, the Japanese seemed satisfied and, without any threats or mistreatment, allowed him to return to his unit.[29] The next day he started on the Death March.

Howard Chrisco managed to avoid the march altogether. At Cabcaben there was a small motor pool of army trucks. A Japanese soldier ordered him to get into the cab of a U.S. truck and drive it. Like Snell, Chrisco protested. But he got behind the wheel once the guard prodded him in the ribs with his rifle butt. After much mashing of gears, as he tried to figure out how to make the truck move, he got the machine to lurch forward, and off they went. His guard spoke some English, but they communicated mostly by writing notes to one another.[30]

While waiting among the throng at Mariveles, Bob Young was asked if he knew how to drive a truck. When he said he could, the Japanese took him to a church, fed him crackers and catsup, then put him to work.

After a brief interrogation by Japanese officers, the young ambulance driver Dick Jenson was assigned to a quartermaster trucking detail. He witnessed many American soldiers being bayoneted, shot, and run over. One morning a Japanese soldier pushed a Filipino prisoner into the path of his truck. Jenson swerved to avoid the prostrate man, running the truck off the road. Jenson's guard slapped him on the face, reprimanding him for his humanity.[31]

While still in Bataan, Jenson found himself a target of an American artillery barrage from Corregidor, which remained unsurrendered. The Japanese had set up several 75mm guns along the beach at Mariveles Point preparatory to their attack on the island fortress. Army spotters on Corregidor saw the activity. Army guns got busy. In short order the new enemy battery on the beach was blown to bits. The American barrage sent Jenson running for cover. Everybody, captors and captives alike, dived out of the way of the falling shells. Chrisco was up by the motor pool when the shells showered down. He dove under a truck, barely avoiding a flying piece of hot shrapnel eighteen inches long. Some POWs were injured. When General Wainwright learned of the incident he ordered his batteries not to fire into Bataan for three days, lest they injure or kill Americans.[32]

WITHIN A WEEK OF THE SURRENDER the Japanese had rounded up about fifty POWs and taken them to Guagua, a sleepy Spanish town astride Route 7 just south of the rail junction at San Fernando. Here the Japanese Army had established a supply camp. The prisoners were assigned to a trucking detail, driving and maintaining American-made trucks, tasks that had proved difficult for the Japanese. And so the POWs drove captured supplies out of Bataan. They drove men and ammunition up to Subic Bay. They made several trips down to Manila. And they were far, far better off than the men on the roads or in the camps. The drivers were not kept behind wires, but lived in a house on the plaza commandeered from a Filipino family. They had no guards. They ate better than they had on Bataan—three meals a day, cooked by Sergeant Chrisco. They were provided with antimalarial medicines such as quinine and atabrine. The POWs were even compensated for their labors—the princely sum of eighty centavos a day (roughly forty cents, paid in Japanese occupation scrip).[33]

The siege of Corregidor ended on 6 May 1942, when General Wainwright surrendered unconditionally. His message to President Roosevelt was moving: "With broken heart and head bowed in sadness, but not in shame . . . today I must arrange terms for the surrender of the Fortified Islands of Manila Bay . . . my troops and I have accomplished all that is humanly possible."[34]

A few days later Colonel Kumataro Ota arrived at Guagua. A veteran of China and now of Bataan, Ota was to lead the Japanese occupation of the island of Negros with his crack troops, the Ota Butai. He gathered all the American drivers together, chatting with each in near-perfect English. "What city do you come from?" he asked. "What is your favorite sports team?" When he was through, Ota picked ten Americans to accompany him on his expedition. In addition to Snell, Joseph, Chrisco, Reynolds, Young, Jenson, and Dyer, the colonel chose Corporal Joseph Francis Boyland (5th Bomber Command), Private Ramon Corona (200th Coast Artillery), and Private Gavin White (signal corps).

PREPARATIONS FOR THE EXPEDITION to Negros began in earnest. The drivers put in long days moving supplies from Guagua to the port of Olangapo. On 14 May they made their last trip, with trucks full of Japanese soldiers. The vehicles were then winched aboard the decrepit *India Maru*. That evening the little convoy of three transports and a small cruiser steamed out of Subic Bay.

The ten American soldiers were locked into the hold, enclosed in a ten-by-ten animal stall. The heat was stifling, there was no ventilation. The men wore G-strings and nothing more. And all came down with prickly heat. For a week, that was how they lived.[35]

Colonel Ota's objective was Bacolod, the capital. Before Ota could land his troops, he needed to negotiate a surrender with the remaining USFIP units holding out on the island. He first sailed to Iloilo City on neighboring Panay, there to discuss the issue with American officers. On 20 May, Ota met Colonel Carter R. McLennan (representing the commander of Negros, Colonel Roger B. Hilsman) and worked out an agreement to occupy Negros.[36]

At eight o'clock the next morning Ota's fleet steamed off Bacolod. The scene was not reassuring to the Japanese colonel. Sporadic gunfire rang through the air. The wharves were afire. A ten-thousand-gallon gasoline tank burned, cascading billowing black smoke into the sky. Ota waited cautiously. By midmorning the situation seemed more settled. At ten-thirty he sent out the first landing barge. In it were six of the American drivers. They were ordered to stand in the bow, so as the craft approached the shore, Filipinos could see that Americans were not insuperable. The barge hit the beach with virtually no opposition, much to the relief of the drivers.

Unknown to the POWs at the time, they would not have had such an easy landing on Negros if the Philippine Army *had* chosen to fight. Many Filipino units resisted surrender, much to the dismay of Colonel Hilsman and even General Wainwright. A week before the Japanese landing, Hilsman had ordered all units to lay down their arms. Only one battalion, led by Major Pullong Arpa, complied. Several others took to the hills. Hilsman issued another order for surrender. This time Major Fortunato Roque and Major Francisco Gomez led their troops down to wait for the Japanese. Two Filipino battalions, led by Major Salvador Abcede and Major Ernesto S. Mata, refused to give up. They took their soldiers deep into the mountains, there to become the core of the Philippine guerrilla resistance movement on Negros. Before they headed into the jungle, Mata and his men destroyed strategic installations in Bacolod.[37]

Once ashore, the prisoners worked unloading the transports. At day's end they were taken to a former government cottage, which would be their quarters for a few weeks. Though soldiers were housed a few hundred feet away, the POWs again had no guard. They were given white armbands identifying them as laborers attached to the Ota Butai.

At first they hauled troops and supplies to the several outposts the Japanese

Army established throughout Negros Occidental province. The trucks went out to each garrison once or twice a week, taking food, clothing, fuel, and ammunition. The roads connecting the towns were mostly narrow and barely paved. The Fords and Internationals found it slow going.[38]

AS THE JAPANESE SETTLED IN, so, too, did the Americans. The prisoners moved to the Manila Motors Building in Bacolod, just across the street from Colonel Ota's garrison headquarters. This would be home for the next twelve months. There was a large showroom where the trucks were housed, and a shop out back where the prisoners could work on them. The mezzanine housed the army unit to which they were detailed. The Japanese assigned a warrant officer, a sergeant, four corporals, and eleven privates to this quartermaster unit. The prisoners themselves were quartered in an adjoining building, once a pool hall, connected by a door into the garage. Food was shared among captors and captives alike, at least at first. The men quickly grew tired of the Japanese diet of rice and dried fish, so they used their pay to purchase food in Bacolod.

Life for the POWs in Bacolod was never a picnic—their days were very long, often beginning before dawn and ending in darkness—but generally they got on well with their captors. Irving Joseph helped a young Japanese sergeant improve his English. With sugar and peanuts in abundance, the Americans began to make tasty peanut brittle candy, which they gave to the enemy troops. On occasion the two sides got up a game of baseball.

Though they praised the fair treatment they received from Colonel Ota and his young, disciplined soldiers, sometimes even the slightest infraction of the rules resulted in a flesh-opening beating. Once while Joseph was working on a truck in the garage, he was asked by a soldier to assist with another chore. When Joseph asked him to wait a minute the soldier became enraged, picked up a belt, and whipped the POW until welts rose on his back.[39] Such treatment made the prisoners that much more thankful for the few privileges they had.

The ten prisoners did not know how fortunate they were. Their Bataan companions were fairing very badly in the prison camps up on Luzon. At Cabanatuan, a hundred miles north of Manila, thousands of American prisoners were jammed into three camps. Their rations were sparse. Often there was no water. There were no medicines. Men died every day—dozens a day—a total of more than seven hundred in June 1942 alone. A celebration was held among the Cabanatuan POWs on 18 January 1943, the first day no deaths were recorded in the camp.[40]

Joseph Richard Jenson was getting to be a problem for his nine roommates. A hospital incident was just one of many that tried their patience. Worse, Jenson's behavior could be downright dangerous to the group's health and well-being. One afternoon Howard Chrisco discovered a diary Jenson kept, lying open on his bunk. He scanned a few pages, and what he saw raised hackles on his neck. Jenson had been recording all the inconspicuous acts of sabotage the men regularly committed on their trucks, such as damaging parts and dumping gasoline. If their guards ever found and read the journal, the lives of all ten prisoners would be jeopardized. Chrisco read the riot act to the young man.

But it took more than a strong rebuke to keep the lad out of trouble. Jenson once decided he was deeply in love with a beautiful Filipina he met in Bacolod. He planned to propose to her. For this he required a diamond engagement ring. Where to find one in time of war? More to the point, how to pay for one? Jenson convinced a wealthy Bacoleno businessman that the American prisoners needed money to make good their escape. Fervently pro-American, the man donated fifteen hundred pesos to their cause. That was a lot of money— about seven hundred fifty dollars U.S.—enough to buy a most splendid engagement ring. Irving Joseph got wind of the scheme and quickly put an end to it before Jenson could make his purchase.[41]

For much of the time they were in Bacolod Jenson ran a medical practice on the side. He treated Japanese soldiers for venereal disease. At first he liberated the drugs from clinics at the sugar centrals. Later he was able to get medicines through his ever-expanding network of Filipino friends. The rest of the prisoners sternly warned Jenson to quit the business. For a time he did, but his clientele were more persistent. He quietly began practicing again, but was careful to keep it from the others.

WITHIN MONTHS of the Japanese occupation, the Filipino guerrillas grew bold. In the summer of 1942 they began to come down from the mountains to ambush the truck convoys. The daylight raids were more of a harassing tactic than anything else, but the Japanese were worried. The Americans were concerned, too—one of their own might get hurt.

An ambush was usually little more than a squad of guerrillas hiding in the bush, spraying the convoy with the few bullets they had as it passed their location. Sometimes the rebels felled palm trees to block the road. At first this gave the guerrillas a brief advantage over their lightly armed enemy. The toll on the

Japanese could be heavy. One ambush killed twenty soldiers. During another, eighteen of the enemy were killed when guerrillas armed only with bolo knives attacked two trucks, which they then burned to the ground.[42] To Howard Chrisco it seemed as if they were being ambushed two or three times a day. Joseph was once ambushed seven times on one trip. Russ Snell figured their convoys were ambushed more than a hundred times. It could be terrifying, and as they feared, the drivers didn't always get out unscathed. In May Irving Joseph received a painful gunshot wound in the back, the injury requiring hospitalization.[43] On another run, Reynolds was slightly wounded. To Jimmy Dyer, the guerrillas were simply disorganized bandits. The Japanese could not have agreed more.

In hopes of curbing the ambushes, the Japanese tried increasing the number of troops guarding the convoys. They also began using armored cars, which they made the POWs drive. One, called the Cheese Box, was a round tub of double-thick steel punctured strategically with gunports. The other, called The Tanker, had a house-shaped steel enclosure. Both were fitted with armored doors and slitted-steel windshields.[44] The moves failed to reduce the number of attacks. In frustration, the enemy then tried retaliation on innocent civilians. Corporal Joseph Boyland had a particularly horrific experience.

He was behind the wheel of the Cheese Box, protecting a squad of telephone linemen outside Pontevedra. The linemen were hanging a new cable, replacing the miles of precious copper wire the guerrillas had stolen the night before. As Boyland drove into Pontevedra some Filipinos saw the car and began running away. This seemed suspicious to the Japanese. They ordered Boyland to chase after the natives. A gunner in the nose of the armored car began spraying the road with his carbine. He fired down alleys. He fired into windows. When he ran out of ammunition, another rifle was quickly passed to him. After two sweeps through Pontevedra a dozen or more Filipinos lay dead on the ground. It became commonplace after this incident for soldiers to shoot indiscriminately at any civilian they might see along the road.[45]

All the prisoners witnessed similar scenes. Irving Joseph saw soldiers shooting not only people, but gunning down their dogs, pigs, and carabaos as well.[46] Reynolds and Jenson were out one day in the town of Isabela when they saw Japanese troops bayonet a twelve-year-old boy in the churchyard. Locals told them that as many as a hundred bodies had been buried there. They were told that the Japanese executed two or three people a week in Isabela, trying to extract information from them on the guerrillas.[47]

The POWs at Bacolod, Negros, in early 1943 (left to right, back row: Howard Chrisco,
Russell Snell, Jim Dyer, Dick Jenson, Floyd Reynolds; front row: Irving Joseph,
Ramon Corona, Bob Young, Gavin White, Joe Boyland).
(Ramon Corona via Howard Chrisco)

---

Raw brutality failed to win the Filipinos over, so in April 1943 the occupiers tried a new stratagem to rally the civilian population around the Japanese cause, a program called the Peace and Relief Mission.

A town would be chosen for a mission visit. Advance men from the Japanese Propaganda Section, assisted by the local puppet government, came in to organize a festive market day, where rare and expensive commodities could be purchased at favorable rates. They would arrange a concert or a dance, and sometimes pony races complete with prizes. The mission unit, consisting of a brass band, three singers, two nurses, a doctor, ten soldiers, Warrant Officer Miina, and boxes full of goodies, would descend upon the town on the appointed day. While the band played popular tunes, an occasional spirited Sousa march, and sometimes even "God Bless America," the doctor and nurses tended to the town's sick. The soldiers distributed cigarettes and candy, while Miina gave a rousing pro-Japanese speech—in Japanese but translated into Visayan—extolling the virtues of the Greater East Asia Co-Prosperity Sphere. The Japanese meant for the day to foster Pan-Asian solidarity. But to bring people in for a Peace and Relief Mission, soldiers sometimes had to round up Filipinos at bayonetpoint and march them to the town square. Not surprisingly, these tactics proved unpopular with the populace. The Japanese did more harm than good to their cause.[48]

THE LIVES OF THE POWs changed quickly, and for the worse, when the Ota Butai was transferred from Bacolod in November 1942. In its place came a company of older but less experienced soldiers, occupation troops commanded by Colonel Oshiyama. Oshiyama, a forty-five-year-old career officer with clipped hair and a small mustache, was the complete opposite of Ota. Whereas Ota was fair and at times lenient, Oshiyama was harsh and cruel. He took away the prisoners' few privileges. They were no longer permitted to go into town. They could not buy food (though they could accept it as a gift). Their wages were cut from eighty centavos a day to forty. Barbed wire was strung around their quarters. And they were confined to the garage, repairing the trucks but no longer driving them.[49]

The new guards were much rougher on the Americans. Reynolds was beaten several times with a belt buckle for minor infractions. He suffered a permanent and prominent scar on his leg when one of Oshiyama's men threw an iron bar at him. He also had a tooth knocked out by a deftly swung rifle butt. All the POWs were expected to stand at attention while taking this punishment. Any attempt at blocking a slap or a punch simply resulted in more punches and slaps.[50]

To relieve their pain, the POWs began to drink. Alcohol in some form was often available to them in captivity. In the early days it had not been unusual for the men to stop by a tavern when shopping in Bacolod. On occasion they even shared a drink with their captors. Gasoline supplies grew low at about the time the guards' brutality increased. To run their trucks, the Japanese switched to pure alcohol refined from sugarcane. As a fuel, alcohol did not have the same kick as gasoline; it took many more gallons to go the same distance. Consequently, each truck carried a fifty-gallon steel barrel filled with alcohol. This was siphoned into the fuel tank as needed. It was also siphoned off for personal consumption, once the POWs learned the stuff was drinkable (if it was cut prudently with water and a little calamansi juice). Thereafter, some of them stayed slightly sozzled all the time. "It took our minds of our miseries," said Irving Joseph.[51]

To the prisoners' great relief, Colonel Oshiyama was replaced early in the new year by Colonel Yamaguchi. This soldier, a resident of Bacolod, treated the Americans better. He put them back behind the wheel. He restored some, though not all, of their privileges. But he cut their wages to ten centavos a day. As the ration provided by the Japanese grew smaller, and the food available in town scarce and expensive, the POWs felt they might now slowly starve to death.[52]

SINCE THE FIRST DAYS of their captivity, the ten Americans talked often of escape. In Bataan, escape seemed impossible. Where would they escape to? Who would harbor them? But in Bacolod they found they had friends. The POWs were encouraged by what now seemed to be a reasonable chance of success. For months they continued to discuss flight from their captors, but they could never agree on a scheme.

Then, on Wednesday, 21 April 1943, Corporal Joseph Francis Boyland escaped, alone, in the coastal town of Bago.

Just the day before, the air corps corporal became enraged when a Japanese soldier slapped him hard across the face. It was the straw that broke that camel's back. On the twenty-first Boyland was scheduled to take a Peace and Relief Mission down to Bago. Before leaving, he told his companions he would attempt to flee. Surprised, concerned, they nevertheless wished him luck.

At noon on the twenty-first Boyland was sitting in Bago's town square, smoking with his guard. It was market day, the mission was in town. As the band played, vendors haggled with their customers over the price of mangos and mackerel and piña cloth. Children raced around the square chewing sticky *piaya*—sugar pancakes. The scene was festive, noisy, lively. When Boyland's guard ran out of cigarettes he motioned to the POW to stay put, then trotted off across the square to buy another pack. The American took a quick look around, rose to his feet, and sauntered off through the crowd in the opposite direction.

Boyland slipped through the back of the market onto a quieter street. As he walked down the road, he was approached by a Filipino. The American had no idea whether this man was friend or foe. He advanced cautiously. The Filipino called to him, told him "Come with me." Joe Boyland seemed to have no choice. He went with the stranger, down toward the beach, frequently glancing back to see if they were being followed. As they walked, Boyland learned that his guide was a guerrilla soldier. He had been assigned to keep an eye on the Japanese in Bago. The man had seen the prisoners there, too.[53] Boyland asked the man where they were going. To the guerrillas, he said.

They walked quickly among the palms that lined the beach until they were well past the town. The pair then turned inland, toward the hills. They hiked until the sun went down, finding shelter for the night with a sympathetic family. The next morning Joseph Francis Boyland, ex-POW, reached a remote rebel camp, there warmly welcomed by the guerrillas as a free man.

# CHAPTER 6

# *Independence Day*

WHEN WORD REACHED Manila Motors that Joe Boyland had disappeared, Colonel Yamaguchi stormed with rage. He confined the remaining POWs to their quarters until he could devise their punishment. Realizing that he still required their skills to accomplish the mission assigned him, Colonel Yamaguchi decided upon a rather mild course of action. He had the nine men brought before him, then lectured them sternly, his interpreter struggling to keep pace with the angry words spilling from his mouth.[1] He took pains to remind the men that they had been treated very well by the Japanese. From now on, he harangued, he would treat them strictly as prisoners of war. The colonel said he would take away all their privileges—this time for good. Finally, he made the Americans raise their left hands and swear an oath that no one, under any circumstance, would ever attempt to escape. As the men filed out, Howard Chrisco muttered, "I won't *attempt* to escape, I *will* escape!"[2]

The POWs immediately began planning their flight. Irving Joseph argued for crossing Guimaras Strait to neighboring Panay. They could build boats or rafts, or buy them, he suggested, and float the ten miles to the far shore in no time at all. The others were skeptical. Chrisco believed the best route was up into the hills, where the guerrillas might assist them. As before, their debate went on for weeks.

The argument came to a head on Sunday, 4 July 1943. Ramon Corona and Gavin White were on a Peace and Relief Mission down in Murcia, in the foothills below Mount Mandalagan. The seven POWs met over a breakfast of rice and crumbly dried fish. Ironically, they agreed that a group escape was no longer desirable but that each man should now try on his own. After all that bickering, the issue finally seemed resolved. Following the meal, while the others got the day off, Chrisco and Dyer made a resupply run down to Binalbagan, forty-five miles to the south. They arrived back in Bacolod late in the afternoon.[3]

The two drivers pulled their trucks into the Manila Motors showroom to clean and wash them. Things seemed awfully quiet to Chrisco. He knew most of the Japanese quartermaster detail had gone into town on weekend passes. That left only three soldiers at the garage. A quick check revealed that two were out back bathing and the third had gone to do his laundry. Chrisco suddenly realized that the POWs were alone, unguarded. They had been given the perfect opportunity to escape. He told the others, "This is it."[4]

Jenson, Young, and Snell stood lookout while Howard Chrisco climbed the stairs to the mezzanine separating the showroom from the shop. He went straight to the gun rack near the balcony and removed three rifles and seventy-six rounds of ammunition. He quickly descended and threw the weapons into the back of the fastest truck, covering them with a straw mat. Dyer, considered the best driver, climbed into the cab. He started the engine and began to back the big Ford out of the garage. Dark-skinned Irving Joseph grabbed a Japanese Army helmet and jumped in the seat next to Dyer, trying to pass himself off as one of their guards.

Just then Snell spotted two hundred soldiers parading up the road, chanting their victory march. "Yikes!" someone screamed. Dyer jammed on the brakes. The prisoners froze in fear. They could see the whites of the enemy's eyes. They could hear the song clearly, each word crystal clear, getting louder and louder. Hearts raced. Thoughts raced—thoughts of having lost their chance to escape. Irving Joseph uttered a barely audible "Turn, you bastards, turn!"[5] A hundred yards before reaching Manila Motors, the soldiers suddenly whirled down another street.

As the victory march faded, Chrisco cried, "Now!" Dyer eased the truck back again. "Hold it!" shouted Snell. "What's wrong?" an impatient Reynolds wanted to know. Snell said there were BC across the street. Sure enough, a truck of armed Filipino Bureau of Constabulary troops had pulled up in front of garrison headquarters. The BC captain went into the building. While the others anxiously watched the soldiers, Chrisco dropped to his knees and began to pray. Meanwhile, Reynolds went upstairs for another rifle. After an eternity the BC officer reappeared. Seven pairs of eyes followed each step as he slowly, very slowly, walked back to the truck. The truck started. The truck drove off. It disappeared around the corner. "I can't take much more of this," said Joseph with a sigh.[6]

The POWs swung back into action, their attention focused fully on executing their escape. At that moment one of their guards, the one they called

"Blockhead," came in the back door after finishing his bath. "Dear God, it's over now," whispered one of the POWs. "No, it's not," said Dyer with a hiss as he killed the engine, jumped out of the cab, lifted the hood, and began tinkering earnestly. The guard walked through the garage, seeming to take no notice of the men gathered around the truck. When he got to the top of the steps, he noticed rifles missing from the rack. He turned toward the Americans with a puzzled look on his face. Chrisco reached for a steel pipe leaning in the doorway of their quarters, while Joseph and Reynolds approached the young soldier. Both asked for a match. A few feet away Howard Chrisco, ready to clobber the guard if necessary, suppressed a laugh, for neither American smoked. Blockhead seemed befuddled. Chrisco, sensing an opportunity, let go of the pipe and began talking to the Japanese. He told the soldier that the men needed to push the one truck out so they could pull another in. The explanation took some time to explain, then some time to sink in. The enemy soldier finally shrugged and walked down the hall to his quarters.[7]

Tension was high and rising. Sweat from fear, not tropical heat, drenched the prisoners. It was all or nothing now. Looking at each man in turn, Chrisco softly asked if he was in or out. Dick Jenson answered by jumping behind the wheel. Irving Joseph followed him into the cab. Jimmy Dyer pulled the engine hood down. Russ Snell and Floyd Reynolds latched it closed. Bob Young and Howard Chrisco climbed over the tailgate. "Let's get the hell out of here!"[8] Jenson jammed the gears into place. The truck lurched backward, noisily sideswiping the door.

Blockhead suddenly reappeared, on the balcony. "Oh, God," choked Dyer.[9] "What should we do?" Jimmy wanted to know. "Keep going," Chrisco shot back, urging his partners to act as though it were a regular run. The enemy soldier folded his elbows onto the railing, tucked his chin into his hands, and watched the activity impassively. It was a spooky moment, but Jenson kept easing the truck back and back. With a courteous wave and a smile to Blockhead, Jenson drove off as nonchalantly as he could.

Half a block from the garage, the escapees passed their sergeant and warrant officer. Too terrified to do anything else, they saluted the soldiers. To their astonishment, the soldiers saluted back. It was at that moment that an ever so faint glimmer of imminent freedom began to supplant the heavy darkness of impending doom. It was five-thirty in the afternoon, nearing twilight on Independence Day.

When they reached San Sebastian Cathedral, Jenson turned right and sped past the public plaza, still crowded that Sunday evening with Filipinos and Japanese. Suddenly the truck lurched and careened over the sixteen-inch curb with a huge crash. Jenson, startled by a horse cart pulling out of the plaza, had swerved to avoid it. Reynolds and Dyer grabbed for a handrail, fearing the Ford would tip over. Jenson, ambulance driver that he was, managed to keep the truck upright and quickly picked up speed again. In the back, Chrisco tossed a rifle and some ammunition to Snell. "What are these for?" "In case we have to use them," answered Chrisco.[10] They drove in the direction of the provincial capitol building, which would lead them to the beach and the wharves and to the key road out of town. They barreled past the capitol, past a Philippine checkpoint manned by two BC guards. The Filipinos must have thought the truck was on official duty, for they lowered their weapons and waved as it passed by.

Turning on the road toward the sea, the escapees soon reached the Japanese Army outpost at Banago Wharf—the last obstacle to their escape. Chrisco was ready with a loaded rifle, ready to do his duty, to kill the guard if it came to that. But the luck of the seven men held. Minutes before, a Filipino had tried to enter Bacolod through this checkpoint without a pass. That was a serious offense. The Filipino could have been shot on sight. The Japanese guard arrested the man, marched him to a phone box on the wharf, and there reported the violation to his captain. At the very instant the guard was on the phone, the truck weaved through the line of sand-filled steel drums at the unoccupied outpost. It continued unmolested, undiscovered, down the road and out of town.

About three miles north of town, on the highway to Talisay, Jenson turned onto a dirt road heading toward the mountains. After a few more miles, when they got to the hills, they stopped, disabled the truck, and pushed it into a rice paddy. The seven ex–prisoners of war began their hike to freedom.

FOR THREE HOURS THEY TREKKED higher and higher into the mountains, often in drenching rain. Reynolds used a small compass he had stolen from the Japanese to navigate a straight-line course. After encountering increasingly rough terrain, the group decided they needed a guide. When they came upon a small bamboo hut with a dim light burning in the window, Chrisco and Reynolds approached the shack. The Filipino who answered their knock was happily surprised to see armed Americans at the door. "Oh," he said, "the wife and I were talking just today. We were wishing for the Americans to arrive, and here they are!" Then he took a look at the motley crew on his doorstep. He saw only thin, barefoot men dressed in tatters carrying Japanese rifles. The disappointment must have showed on the man's face as Howard Chrisco told him, "I don't think we're the Americans you've been waiting for."[11]

Chrisco then made clear their need for a guide to take them to the guerrillas. The Filipino pointed to another light glowing in the distance. There, they were told, help could be found. And there indeed they found their guide, a young man who turned out to be a guerrilla courier.

After walking all night, all of some thirty or forty miles, the party arrived at a remote guerrilla outpost at about eight in the morning. The main camp was some distance farther on; more marching was in order. But it was apparent that Irving Joseph did not have the strength to keep hiking. His feet were badly swollen from an infection that had taken root some weeks earlier. One of the guides found a carabao for the crippled man. They fashioned a saddle, then tied Joseph to the big water buffalo and set off down the path. By midmorning they reached the main camp, headquarters of B Company, 72nd Infantry Regiment, Lieutenant Villaba commanding.[12]

The guerrillas warmly welcomed the Americans—the first they had seen since the surrender. They were friendly and helpful to the escapees, providing them with a cooked breakfast and secure shelter. This was the first chance the Americans had to relax after their ordeal. Slowly it dawned on them that they were once again free men. Yes, they were still hiding from their enemy, but they were no longer his captives. It was an exuberant feeling, for none had ever been deprived of his freedom before, then regained it (especially in such a dramatic fashion). When a rebel told them they had been very lucky to escape, the group dubbed themselves the Lucky Seven.

After resting for three days, the Seven moved another twenty miles deeper into the interior, to the headquarters of Subsector EF, where they met the commander, Major Marcus V. Ganaban. This location, high in the hills near Mount Silay, was a sort of rest stop for weary travelers on the trails between northern and southern Negros. There were huts there for sleeping, supervised by a former Bacolod hotelier, Second Lieutenant Nicolas "Nick" Rodriguez. One night a Japanese patrol walked right through the guerrillas' picket line, right past sleeping Filipino guards, into the main camp. With bayonets drawn, they crept past Jenson and Dyer asleep on the ground. When they reached the hut where Reynolds, Joseph, and Young were staying, they suddenly kicked down the door. Hell broke loose in the pitch darkness, the enemy as surprised to find people inside as the occupants were to find the Japanese in there with them. The former POWs made haste for the sanctuary of the forest. Young leaped out the back door and landed in a clump of thorny bushes, picking up a nasty crown of deep scratches. The sound of gunfire from both sides punctuated the stillness of the night. Despite the confusion, the Japanese managed to kill Lieutenant Nick, bayonet another man, take a third prisoner, and get away cleanly.[13]

Chrisco and Snell, who had been staying across the river at another camp with the guerrillas' doctor, Lieutenant José H. Yasa, heard the shots. When it was safe, they crossed back to see what had happened. The incident terrified them all, Young in particular. After the skirmish the Americans agreed among themselves to stand watch at night for their own protection.

A messenger arrived in camp one day soon after, with news from Bacolod. Colonel Yamaguchi's troops had turned the city upside down in their search for the missing seven. Hapless Blockhead was beaten to within an inch of his life. The Japanese took into custody Filipinos suspected of aiding the Americans, beating them but not killing them. When Ramon Corona and Gavin White returned to Bacolod, they were put in chains for several days and interrogated closely. Their fates were unknown.[14] The Seven also got word that Joe Boyland was in a neighboring sector, working for Colonel Salvador Abcede.

The free men stayed in Subsector EF for the rest of the summer, mostly recuperating, occasionally going out on patrol. Toward the end of September they reported to Major Uldarico Baclagon at regimental headquarters. Irving Joseph pressed the major for permission for the Americans to stage ambushes. But the Northern Negros Sector commander, Colonel Ernesto S. Mata, had other plans. He did not want the Americans interfering with his guerrilla forces. He ordered Major Baclagon to separate the Americans by assigning each to different areas in the sector. The men were told they were separated for their own safety. That was only partly true. Mata simply did not want any Americans in his way. They repeatedly asked for a meeting with the colonel, but the man never acquiesced. They then asked to be reassigned to the Southern Negros Sector, to live and work under Abcede. That request, too, was denied. The Americans had no choice but to make the best of their new situation. They pitched in where and when they could to assist the resistance.[15]

Within weeks Irving Joseph was chafing at the bit. The unit to which he was assigned gave him nothing to do; his help was not wanted. He quickly tired of loafing around battalion headquarters. The wily sergeant stayed alert for opportunities.

One day in late October opportunity hobbled out of the jungle. Into Joseph's camp near La Castellana came Jim Cushing. He was now Lieutenant Colonel James M. Cushing, now commander of the Cebu Area Command, famed throughout the Visayas for his fearlessness and utter hatred of the Japanese. His exploits were the stuff of legend. Joseph was astonished by the rebel's appearance. He was short, dark, and wore thick glasses and a priest's hooded robe. His frail body was racked by pain, ridden with malaria. Faltering about on a pair of bamboo crutches, Cushing was no longer the vigorous man who had blown up Cebu City eighteen months before.[16]

Cushing had come to Negros to meet with Major Jesus A. Villamor, a renowned hero and fighter in his own right. Villamor achieved international fame in December 1941 by flying his hopelessly obsolete P-26 pursuit against superior Japanese warplanes, shooting one down and surviving. For Villamor's heroism, MacArthur awarded him the Distinguished Service Cross. He was one of the few Filipino officers evacuated to Australia when Bataan capitulated.

When reports began trickling in to GHQ that a nascent guerrilla movement was alive in the Philippines, MacArthur sent Villamor to investigate and report back. His team arrived in southern Negros at the beginning of January 1943 aboard the submarine USS *Gudgeon*. The major proceeded to set up a sophisticated and successful intelligence network, with operatives throughout the Japanese-occupied islands. As MacArthur's personal representative, the thirty-year-old major was charged with the task of qualifying for recognition the guerrilla resistance movements on each island. Official recognition to a guerrilla organization meant a great deal. It meant money. It meant arms. It meant prestige and power. Each group craved recognition by MacArthur. Villamor could not bestow such a prize, but he did make recommendations back to GHQ in Brisbane. The young officer made clear to guerrilla leaders that the true path to recognition from MacArthur required that warring factions quit their infighting; that greedy, egomaniacal officers step down; that intelligence-gathering, not battling the Japanese, was the most important mission.

Lieutenant Colonel James M. Cushing, taken after the war. (Manuel Segura Collection)

Seeking succor, Jim Cushing came calling from Cebu. Though he wanted recognition for his guerrillas, he wanted it on his own terms. He hated the obeisance he had to pay—to Villamor, to MacArthur, to anyone else—when he should have been battling the enemy. He spent many days with Villamor that fall, and many radio messages passed from Negros to Brisbane and back, but to little immediate avail. Cushing won the Filipino officer's respect and sympathy, but even the major was unable to persuade GHQ to proffer anything more than vague allusions of future aid. Cushing parted from Villamor bitterly disappointed.[17]

When Cushing came into the camp that humid autumn day, Irving Joseph saw his chance to get out from under the stifling thumb of Colonel Ernesto Mata. He rounded up Russ Snell and Jimmy Dyer. Suggesting the trio go back to Cebu with Cushing, Joseph said life there could not be any worse than on Negros. They agreed that this was a golden opportunity. Joseph approached Cushing, volunteering the services of the three American soldiers. Cushing was absolutely delighted by their offer. He was, after all, the only American guerrilla on Cebu, maybe even the only American. Having compatriots would make his spartan life more pleasant, and perhaps make the job of killing Japanese easier and more productive. In any case, it would help take his mind off the fact that MacArthur had failed to give the Cebu Area Command the support it desperately needed. On 25 November Cushing led his new recruits over the mountains of Negros, down to the sugarcane plains, across Tañon Strait to Cebu. It would be six months before Snell and Dyer returned to Negros, in the company of two artillery shell casings stuffed with urgently important captured enemy documents.

THE YEAR 1944 DAWNED brightly for the Lucky Seven. They had been free men for six months. They could sense that the war had turned against the Japanese. News from all fronts was encouraging. In the Atlantic, Allied forces were systematically eliminating Germany's U-boat fleet, thanks to timely intelligence from a decoding machine known as Enigma. The invasion of Continental Europe had begun, with a landing in Italy followed by a successful drive up the length of the boot. In the Pacific, U.S. forces had taken the Solomon Islands in a bloody, year-long campaign. In the Southwestern Pacific Area, MacArthur was clawing up through New Guinea. And in a move that would have significance in the lives of the ex-POWs, SWPA had begun a regular submarine supply service to guerrillas throughout the Philippines. Negros benefited quickly. On the seventh of February 1944 the cargo submarine USS *Narwhal* delivered forty-five tons of guns and ammunition, food and clothing, radios and typewriter ribbons to Colonel Abcede at Balatong Point. The submarine returned to Australia with twenty-eight passengers, including Corporal Joseph Francis Boyland. The Seven had good reason to look forward to the new year.

After Russ Snell, Jim Dyer, and Irving Joseph went to Cebu in late 1943, it took several weeks for the four remaining ex-POWs to learn of their friends' flight across the channel. They were not necessarily disappointed at being left behind. All were busy with one job or another. Bob Young moved from subsector to subsector, working on ordnance repair and even doing a little propaganda for the guerrillas. Young avoided going on patrols; he much preferred to stay around the headquarters units, where life was more sedate. At San Carlos Dick Jenson got into the regiment's intelligence section, commanded by Captain B. Z. Beecher, a mestizo. Jenson discovered he enjoyed the thrill of going out on patrol. Floyd Reynolds, by now good buddies with Jenson, stayed around the camp working at the hospital and in the headquarters office, where he was astonished to find that even in these remote jungles the guerrillas had at least as much red tape as the U.S. Army.[18]

Up in Subsector C, Howard Chrisco started going on ambushes with his unit. On Christmas Eve 1943 he and three dozen guerrillas attacked the enemy garrison at Murcia. They struck from all four sides with rifles, a Thompson submachine gun, and two Browning automatic rifles (BARs), while a demolition squad set fire to several houses nearby. The attack was a great spectacle and morale booster but little else. Damage was minimal. There were no casualties on either side.[19]

Three months later, Howard Chrisco was almost killed in a repeat attack.

At dusk on 29 March 1944, guerrillas of C Company came down out of the mountains to execute the attack on the enemy. The plan called for a dozen men, acting as decoys, to sneak into the garrison's fort. At the appointed time, this team would wreak havoc within the compound. The other two squads set up an ambush along the flat, palm-studded Bacolod–Murcia Road. If the decoy worked, the Japanese would send reinforcements from the capital, ten miles distant, and the guerrillas would then do their dirty work.

Chrisco, armed with a brand-new, just-off-the-sub Thompson submachine gun, took the left flank, hiding himself in a roadside ditch. When H hour came he could hear the attack on the fort. Not long after, two trucks full of troops came barreling up the road—on time and as planned. As they passed, the guerrillas on the right flank sprayed the first truck. Chrisco's squad poured lead into the back of the second. The enemy returned fire as the trucks ground to a halt. A fierce firefight followed. When the American saw a dozen armed troops stand up in the truck, he tried to mow down as many as he could. And down they did go. He hesitated for a moment, then watched as three rifle barrels appeared cautiously over the brow of the tailgate. He fired another burst. The barrels disappeared. His tommy gun now empty, he reached for a second magazine. As he tried to snap the new clip in place, Chrisco suddenly heard a noise across the road. He turned in time to see the truck's driver fly into the ditch opposite. A bullet zinged past his left ear. He turned again, and when he did, he caught the second round in his right elbow, severing the nerves. A third followed, creasing his shirt. Howard Chrisco was in dire straits. His arm was bleeding profusely. He was unable to reload. If he wanted to live, he had no choice but to run for it. He threw the tommy gun over his shoulder and bolted for the woods, zigzagging as he went. When he reached the relative safety of a thick coconut grove he stopped to catch his breath. He then dragged himself through rice paddies, twice practically passing out from the pain and loss of blood. The guerrillas finally found him, strapped him to a carabao, and took him into the mountains. The unit's medic fixed him up as best he could with sulfa and Mercurochrome. The next morning they put the wounded American on a pony and led him back to C Company's camp.

The attack on the fort was considered a great success. Only three of thirty-one Japanese soldiers and eight BC troopers on the reinforcement run to Murcia escaped alive.[20] Howard Chrisco knew he was lucky to escape with his own life.

That winter Dick Jenson fell in love. Again.

While he was working for the intelligence section the American met a beautiful young woman, Lydia P. Elizalde. Perhaps just another of his infatuations, Jenson nonetheless fell for her big time. Lydia was the twenty-three-year-old daughter of the acting treasurer of Free Negros, Don Pedro Elizalde Sr. Of Spanish Filipino descent, she was petite and slender, letting her silky black hair fall well below her shoulders. A graduate of the Philippine Women's University in Manila, she was working for the provincial government when Jenson first met her. Before the war Lydia's father had been treasurer of Cebu. When the Japanese came, he evacuated his wife and seven children to the relative safety of neighboring Negros. Don Pedro was considered by many to be the most honest man in the Visayas. Known to have a fiery temper, he had many quarrels with local politicians over the misuse of USAFFE funds.[21] Lydia's brother, Pedro Jr., had been a second lieutenant in the guerrillas, but later took a job as field auditor for the province. Even the rebel government of Free Negros maintained the traditions of bureaucracy and nepotism in time of war. On Sunday, 19 March 1944, Dick and Lydia were married at San Carlos, Negros Occidental.[22]

At about the time Chrisco was wounded, Bob Young had been detailed to go south with a company of guerrillas. Their mission was to pick up arms and ammunition for the Northern Negros Sector, delivered that February by *Narwhal*. Young had missed his chance to be evacuated on the big cargo sub then because he had been too sick to travel. Two other American ex-POWs, Lieutenant James E. Halkyard and Seaman Jopaul Little, made it to the rendezvous point in time to catch a ride south. In mid-April, when Young reached Colonel Abcede's DHQ, he was advised that there would be another sub soon. Young was told to stand by for evacuation.[23]

At the end of April, while his arm was still trying to heal, Howard Tom Chrisco received orders to proceed to 7th Military District Headquarters at Tolong in southern Negros for evacuation home.

Across the island at San Carlos, Dick Jenson was also ordered out. He linked up with Chrisco near Murcia. Accompanied by Filipino guides and another American, former oilman Russell L. Forsythe, the American threesome began their march to the Sulu Sea. Jenson, though under orders to leave the country, was loath to leave behind his new bride. On the second day of the trek he decided to return to his lovely Lydia. Chrisco and Forsythe could do nothing to stop the headstrong young soldier. Now a twosome, the Americans continued through the jungles of Negros, reaching the coast at the end of April.

# CHAPTER 7

# *Planter, Soldier, Oilman, Spy*

THAT WINTER AND SPRING of 1944 the guerrillas fanned out across the length and breadth of Negros to make contact with every American in hiding—civilian and military. In all there were more than a hundred refugees. The message they carried from General MacArthur was, for most, great news. He was ordering all "nonessential" U.S. citizens to evacuate the Philippines. SWPA would provide transportation. Singly, in pairs, in caravans, the refugees started their treks south. They had lived lives of deprivation and fear for two and a half years. Now they hoped against hope that there might be a way home.

GEORGE MONTENEGRO FLEISCHER was a coconut planter. If sugarcane was king on Negros, then surely coconut was queen. Planting of coconut palms was not nearly so vast, but there was a strong export market for the nut's by-products: coir, coconut oil, and copra. Two dozen miles north of Dumaguete, along the coral-paved coastal road, lay the towns of Bias and, inland, Pamplona. There, in a great crescent-shaped bowl running from the sea to the mountains, was centered Oriental Negros's coconut industry.

Most of the coconut plantations were American-owned and -operated. George Fleischer's Bio-os was typical. Started in 1917 by his father, the property had sixty thousand palms planted in neat rows and a small but efficient processing center. Unlike the sugar industry, which was seasonal, coconuts were harvested every three months. Fleischer employed a dozen Filipinos to reap the nuts from the coconut palms, some of which were eighty feet tall. And it was at the top that the nuts grew. Getting them down required a great amount of skill and not a little daring, for the harvesters had to shinny up the tree to reach the fruit. They unceremoniously dropped them to the ground, where they were loaded into a bull cart. At the processing area, workers stripped the coconuts into their various useful components. The dried meat of the nut, called copra, was the major cash crop. Once the copra was packaged it was ready to be shipped, usually through the small port at Bias. The produce was sent mainly to the United States for use in animal feeds, cosmetics, and fertilizers.

Fleischer was born on Negros in 1904, the eldest of three sons. His father was American, his mother Spanish. In 1921 the boys were sent off to boarding school in Westchester County, New York. But when Bio-os ran into financial difficulties a few years later, George was recalled to the Philippines to help his father run the plantation. In 1933, after a three-year courtship, he married Paz Lalk, a mestiza from Cebu. By the end of the 1930s the couple had sired four children: Davis, the twins Jean and Joan, and William.[1]

The family lived near the center of the plantation in a large frame house covered with lush, flowering vines. They regularly made excursions down to Dumaguete to purchase supplies. The visits gave George a chance to catch up on island news and Paz an opportunity to visit with friends. Like so many American families living in the Philippines before the war, the Fleischers led a very comfortable life.

When the war began, George Fleischer started planning for what he believed would be the inevitable evacuation of Bio-os. Scouting for hideout locations in the jungles back of the plantation, Fleischer found an ideal site at Solboron, about twelve miles up the Amblon River. There was plenty of fresh, safe drinking water; clear plots to grow food; and abundant wild game. It seemed the perfect refuge.

In January 1942 William Leland Archer, a family friend and local representative of Caltex Oil Company, showed up at the plantation with his partly dismantled airplane. Could George hide it for him in the jungles beyond the farm? Fleischer agreed. The plane was moved inland and carefully camouflaged. Unfortunately for Archer, the USAFFE sought to commandeer the aircraft to perform reconnaissance missions over southern Cebu and Negros. After just four weeks in hiding, the plane was hauled back to Dumaguete, reassembled, and put to work. In mid-April, after the Japanese had invaded Cebu, the USAFFE destroyed Archer's pride and joy so it might not fall into enemy hands. Fleischer and Archer now redoubled their evacuation efforts, for Negros seemed to be the next target.

George sent Bio-os laborers to build a camp at Solboron. In May the family moved to the hideout. But George's mother, Carmen, refused to go. Her health was poor, and she did not think she could withstand the rigors of refugee life. She stayed behind, at the plantation.

On 25 June the Japanese occupied Bio-os. They closely questioned the workers about the Fleischers. All feigned no knowledge of their whereabouts, except that the family had fled upon the arrival of the enemy. Carmen Fleischer managed to convince the Japanese that she was in fact Spanish, not American. But over the ensuing months they continued to pay her visits. The harassment took a toll on the old woman. Nearly a year after the Fleischers had gone into hiding, George finally persuaded his mother to move to Solboron.

Life in the camp was not altogether unpleasant. Each week farm hands brought staples up from the plantation. George and Leland devised a small waterwheel turbine set over a creek to provide power for some six-volt lights (removed from an automobile) and, most important, for George's shortwave radio set. Each night the family eagerly gathered around the radio to hear the latest news from station KGEI in San Francisco. Paz grew vegetables and camotes in her garden (her husband hand-pollinated the squash to ensure that it grew properly). The men hunted for meat. The monkeys they shot were skinned, the meat sliced and salted, then left to dry in the sun. The result was a dubiously tasty treat—wild monkey jerky. The streams were teeming with small fish, eels, and delicate freshwater shrimp, which made a welcome addition to the family's diet. Healthwise, the Fleischers were on their own; there were no doctors in the jungles. When Billy fell off the porch, breaking his right collarbone, his father, with no medical experience whatsoever, set the injury and taped it. It healed perfectly. Dentalwork must have been everyone's idea of torture. There were no anesthetics; solder was used to fill cavities.

The twins, Jean and Joan, thought hiding in the jungle was an adventure, a great lark. There was swimming and fishing and playing in the woods. Joan was given a hen to look after. The little girl loved to take care of the chicks that hatched, raising them until they were ready for the table. The twins especially loved birthdays, which always brought a big celebration. Paz would make a delicious cake from cassava flour, decorated with wild begonia blossoms.[2]

Fleischer and Archer soon became aware that they were not the only Americans in the hills. They learned that a large group of Silliman University refugees, led by Dr. Arthur Carson, had set up their hideout at Malabo, a dozen miles to the southwest. Communication was soon established between the two camps. Former physics professor Henry Roy Bell, who had become deeply involved with the guerrillas, became a frequent visitor to Solboron. In mid-1943 the Japanese raided Malabo, sending the families scurrying ever deeper into the jungle. The Carsons and others set up a new camp, but the

Bells and Alvin and Marilee Scaff decided to build a separate retreat at Manalanco, four miles closer to the Fleischers.

George and Paz were startled on 23 November 1943, when two guerrilla soldiers raced into their camp shouting, "Manalanco has been attacked! The Japanese captured the Bells and the Scaffs!" It was not good news, if true. But not long after, Kenneth Bell appeared at the Fleischers' doorstep to tell them that, yes, the Scaffs had been captured, but the Bell family made it out (hotly pursued by soldiers). He said his father had been shot in the leg and was limping behind with Kenneth's mother, Edna. As darkness neared, the elder Bells arrived at Solboron. George treated the bullet wound with precious sulfa powder, imploring Roy and Edna to stay with them until the injury had healed.

Toward the end of the year the Japanese Army renewed its efforts to rid the hills of U.S. citizens. They were especially interested in locating Henry Roy Bell. The Fleischers, Archer, and the Bells decided it prudent to move even farther into the jungle. In December they built another camp, twenty-one miles west of Solboron. The new hideout was not very comfortable—seventeen people were jammed into a twelve-by-twelve stilt house.

In late January 1944, when Bell and Archer got word that American submarines were beginning to visit the island, they decided to hike to the southwestern coast of Negros, hoping to catch a boat to freedom. The Carson family joined them. Despite the orders from MacArthur, George Fleischer declined to go. He believed his frail mother could not make the several-day trip across the rugged terrain. And so the Fleischers stayed on, now more fearful than ever of being found by the Japanese. Their insecurity grew until George decided that he, too, must remove his family from danger. He made arrangements for the Bio-os headman, Flaviano Nubia, to take his mother back to Solboron and care for her until he could return after the war.

Hiring sixteen cargadores, the Fleischers set out in early May for the assembly point, thirty miles by air, but twice that through the Cordillera Central. The family was joined by former Silliman student Modesta Hughes, who had been a member of the Carson household since the beginning of the war. When the Fleischers reached the Tanjay River the family boarded bamboo rafts guided by expert watermen. The children all thought it a splendid adventure, oblivious to the risks. After five days of trekking, the Fleischers reached the safety of Colonel Salvador Abcede's 7th Military District. There they learned that the Bells, the Carsons, Leland Archer, and many others had been safely evacuated to Australia in midFebruary. And there they learned, too, that another submarine was due to rendezvous within just a few days. Their relief was palpable.

ON THAT TERRIBLE DAY—Monday, 8 December 1941—Modesta Hughes found herself among the throng of panicky Silliman students trying to find steamship passage home to Mindanao. By the end of the day, news came that Davao City had already been invaded by the Japanese. There was now no safe route home for the twenty-year-old first-year Sillimanian. She walked back up the long stone jetty, across the now deserted quadrangle, to the offices of the school president, Dr. Arthur Carson. There Modesta Hughes pleaded for help. Carson had his hands full with school business, but out of sympathy and compassion he told the girl she could stay with his family until something could be sorted out.

Modesta Hughes was the fourth of six children born to Orville and Theresa Hughes. Her father had fought in the Spanish-American War, found he loved the Philippines, and decided (like so many others) to stay on. The West Virginian leased some land in the hills behind Davao, where he began cultivating coconuts and raising cattle. Wanting the best for his children, he made sure all got at least a high school education. Orville Jr. went on to Los Baños College, majoring in animal husbandry. It was Junior who encouraged Modesta to seek a degree. She applied to Silliman University, planning to train as a home economics teacher. She was accepted for the new term beginning in July 1941.

Upon arrival in Dumaguete, Modesta was assigned to dorm at Oriental Hall. For those first few months she was terribly homesick, and despite making a few friends among the other Davaoan students, she remained lonely. The freshman kept her mind off her troubles by working hard at her studies and playing intramural sports.

Toward evening on that first day of war, Modesta Hughes gathered up her few belongings and crossed the campus to the president's residence, there to be warmly greeted by Edith Carson. Buckwheating was on everyone's mind. For now, Dr. Carson elected to stay at Dumaguete as a show of unity with the local population, but his wife and two teenage sons had begun to make plans to move to a camp high in the mountains behind the city, in the shadow of Cuernos de Negros. Henry Roy Bell had found a fine site two and a half hours' hike above the tiny barrio of Malabo, near the shores of Lake Balinsasayao. Filipinos began building nipa huts, while others cleared land for gardening.

The first two years in the hills were relatively peaceful. Dr. Carson often traveled around Oriental Negros to stay in touch with other Americans. Bell traveled extensively around all of Negros, despite the substantial bounty on his head. He even made a dangerous excursion across Tañon Strait to meet with Cebu's guerrilla leaders, Harry Fenton and James Cushing.

Modesta Hughes did what she could to be helpful in camp—cooking, laundering, tending the garden, watching the children. Dr. Carson's sixteen-year-old son Bob developed a crush on the pretty young woman. Though he thought Modesta quite outgoing, he could not help but notice she remained sad about not being able to get home to Mindanao. During their months in hiding the pair became close friends.[3]

In late 1943, as the Japanese widened their searches for Americans living in the mountains, Modesta was faced with a difficult choice. The Carsons and the Bells had decided to leave Negros. Modesta, an American citizen, could have gone with them, could have gotten passage on the submarine to Australia. But she knew no one in Australia, had no idea how to contact her relatives in West Virginia. Still hoping to rejoin her family, Modesta wanted to stay in the islands. When the Sillimanians began their trip to the Sulu Sea, the young woman hiked over the hills to the hideout of Major Ben Viloria, a Silliman teacher and now a guerrilla leader. His wife, Flora, took in the abandoned student and made her part of the family. In an April 1944 visit home, Ben told the young woman there would be another submarine in May. He urged her to be on it. Modesta unenthusiastically joined the Fleischer family's caravan on the journey to Basay.[4]

THERE WERE TWO MORE families on the move that second week of May: the Macasas and the Jabonetas.

Ricardo Macasa was born and raised in Kabankalan, a thriving sugar town on the southwestern edge of the great flat, fertile plain that surrounded much of Negros. At age seventeen, having graduated from high school, Ricardo ventured to the United States to join one of his eleven brothers in the Midwest. Demitrio Macasa was studying medicine at the University of Nebraska in Lincoln. The younger brother enrolled at the university in the chemical engineering program. While attending school Macasa met a local nursing student named Viola Knox. They were soon married, deciding to settle in Lincoln. To make ends meet, Ricardo gave up his studies to work as a "man Friday" for a local doctor. In 1928 Viola gave birth to Virginia and, two years later, to Ricardo Jr. Though he was certainly eligible, Ricardo Sr. never applied for American citizenship.

After living in the United States for seventeen years, in 1935 Ricardo returned to the Philippines for a visit. Several months later he wired Viola and the children to book passage to the islands, ostensibly for a vacation. Upon arrival his wife was more than a little surprised to learn that her husband intended to stay in the islands, to settle in his old hometown, Kabankalan. There Ricardo Sr. opened a restaurant. Unfortunately the enterprise did not fare well, possibly because all his relatives took advantage of the restaurateur's hospitality, expecting free meals any time they dropped in. The place closed after a few months. Ricardo was nothing if not resilient. He found a good job as chief timekeeper at the sugar central in Binalbagan, an otherwise sleepy coastal town on the Panay Gulf a few miles north of Kabankalan. Like the Ossorios and the Reals, the Macasas lived in comfortable company housing, enjoying the many perks the position brought with it.

The first the children heard about the Japanese attacks on Luzon and Mindanao was when their parents told them to pack their things, they were moving back to Kabankalan, where Ricardo's brother Demitrio had built a thriving medical practice. The sibling put them up for a few days, then offered the use of his summer house in the hills a few miles south of town.

It was a rustic home, overlooking the wide and swift Ilog River. The Macasas settled in quickly. And like so many others, they expected their army to trounce the Japanese in a trice. But when they heard about the landings at Bacolod in May, Ricardo Sr. decided his brother's house was no longer safe, that the family must push on into the jungles and build a new hideout.

The Macasas found a haven some dozen miles farther south. For the next six months the family stayed at this shelter. Dr. Macasa brought them food and medical supplies regularly; otherwise they fended for themselves. It was a relatively quiet period until a runner from Kabankalan came with news that the Japanese were about to begin a campaign to hunt down stray Americans. It was time to move yet again.

In the process of relocating, the Macasas learned that another family of Americans, the Jabonetas, had set up camp some miles away, deep in the forest. Ricardo decided to join them there.[5]

IN 1916 ERNESTO JABONETA left Negros to join the U.S. Navy. The only position then open to Filipinos was as mess steward aboard ship. He served on the battleship USS *Connecticut* for three years, until just after the end of World War I. When he was discharged, he decided to settle in the United States.

There he met a young nurse, Ada Carson. The pair soon fell deeply in love. They planned an autumn wedding, but when Ada's father learned of the romance he disinherited his daughter, banishing her from his household. Undaunted, the couple married in Hamburg, Pennsylvania, in October 1923. Ernesto had little trouble persuading his bride, devasted by her father's rejection, to return with him to the Philippines. The couple settled in Manila. And Ada Carson Jaboneta never again saw or heard from her family.

Ernesto Jr. was born in 1925. But tragedy descended upon the Jabonetas two years later when Ernesto Sr. died after a long illness. Ada was left to support herself and her son on her husband's navy pension. They were able to stay on in Manila for a few years, taking advantage of the U.S. Navy's commissary and health facilities. But as costs in the big city rose, she decided to move down to Negros, where Ernesto had been born and still had family. They found a home in Kabankalan, living a spartan life.

In 1937 a friend of Ada's died shortly after giving birth to a girl. The American decided to adopt the child, to whom she gave the name Elizabeth. At the time, adoption laws in the Philippines were quite lax. Ada never made the adoption legal. Then it did not seem much of an issue. As far as she and everybody else were concerned, Betty was hers. Eight years later the lack of proper papers would have tragic consequences.

Ernesto Jr. (Ernie to his mother) attended the local public schools, transferring to Silliman in his junior year. He joined the ROTC there, under the direction of Salvador Abcede. Mostly the cadets marched and did close-order drills using "rifles" carved from wood. In November 1941 the unit was looking forward to a regional ROTC competition in Bacolod when the school suddenly sent all the high school students home. The political situation between the United States and Japan was rapidly deteriorating; the school did not want the younger children caught in Dumaguete should war break out. Ernie, then fourteen, rejoined his mother in Kabankalan.

One morning Ada was listening to her radio set when the news blared, "Japan has attacked Pearl Harbor and Luzon!" Alarmed, she called a family friend (and cousin to Ernesto Sr.), twenty-five-year-old Peping Jaboneta. "What should we do?" she asked. "Head for the hills" was the reply. In short order Peping had organized a small caravan to carry the family to a hiding place a few miles from town. They loaded a carabao-drawn wagon with personal belongings, food, and cooking utensils. It struck Ernie that the situation must be pretty serious—the road was already clogged with other buckwheating families.

On the way out of town, the column of refugees halted. The managers of the Kabankalan sugar central were imploring people to help burn hundreds of tons of raw sugar stored in the bodega before the Japanese could capture it. A large crowd went to help. But they soon learned sugar that does not burn easily. "Pour it in the river!" Peping exclaimed. So swarms of men hauled the fifty-kilo sacks of brown sugar out of the storehouse and loaded it onto a train. In the process Ernie and Peping liberated a couple of sacks for their own needs. "We don't know how long the war will last," they reasoned as they moved the staple to their wagon. The train rumbled out toward the trestle over the Ilog. Thousands of sugar sacks were unceremoniously dumped.

That job done, the Jabonetas returned to their cart to continue their journey south. Peping had located a fine hiding place, or so he thought, and proceeded to construct a bamboo-and-nipa hut. The spot was near the crest of a small mountain that provided a sweeping view of the Ilog far below.

For the first few months life was quite amenable, until the day the Japanese began to shell the hills indiscriminately. Pamphlets were dropped by plane stating quite clearly that any person found outside a twelve-mile radius of Kabankalan would be shot. Many of the locals were alarmed enough by the warning to pack up and return to town. But the news only served to strengthen the Jaboneta boys' resolve to stay out of Japanese hands. It was time to move on.

Ada, however, decided to stay put. "It's too hard," she told the boys. It took them hours to convince her to go along. To make the trip easier for her, they let her ride the carabao. The four marched through dense jungle, cutting vines and creepers, getting cut and scratched in the process. After five days of hacking through the woods the family found an isolated spot in which to build camp. This was home until the autumn of 1942, when word came that the Japanese were intensifying their patrols. Once again, it was time to move on.

They loaded their dwindling supplies and set out along a mountain ridge. At that altitude there was little jungle for the family to hack through. In fact, the trip became almost pleasurable. On the trail Ernie occasionally caught glimpses of Mount Canlaon far to the north, volcanic steam spewing from its twin peaks. It was a majestic sight, one he never forgot.

THE NEW CAMP WAS THE best yet. And shortly after arriving, the Jabonetas were surprised to see the Macasa family walk out of the jungle. The two families decided to share the refuge and began to make it habitable. Substantial huts were built, gardens were planted, daily chores were shared by all. Ernie and Dick Macasa, though three years apart in age, became good friends, spending most of the day together working or exploring the surrounding jungle. Their American mothers, on the other hand, spent their days feuding, or just ignoring one another.

Here they stayed until October 1943, when the Japanese Army made yet another push into the mountains. Stakes were pulled, and the two families took to the road again. They hiked until they came upon the Tablas. Under a canopy of trees at the edge of the plain they built what would be their last hideout.

One day in early 1944 some guerrilla soldiers came by the camp to check on the Americans. They carried the now ubiquitous recent editions of *Life* and chewing gum wrappers emblazoned with "I Shall Return." How did these things come to be in one of the remotest parts of all Negros? "By submarine," came the reply. The rebels told the families that not only were the subs bringing in supplies, they were also taking passengers out, to Australia.

In May the guerrillas returned with news that another submarine was due to rendezvous off Balatong Point in a few days. With no time to spare, the Jabonetas and the Macasas packed their belongings and hit the trail.[6]

FROM THE NORTH, from the south, from the east and the west, more than three dozen American citizens were making their way across the interior of Negros that first week of May. Twenty-eight had preceded them in February, safely evacuated to Australia. Many more would follow in the coming months.

# CHAPTER 8

# *The Samurai's Story*

TWO THOUSAND MILES EAST of Negros lies an island group called Truk. It is an otherwise unremarkable place save for one strategically significant quirk of geography: The lagoon enclosed by its thirty-mile-wide reef is the finest deep-water anchorage in the central Pacific. There the Japanese constructed an important—indeed, legendary—naval base.

Truk was important because from this base the Imperial Japanese Navy commanded both the sea lanes and the airways across a million square miles of ocean.

Truk was legendary because the Japanese had closed the islands to out-siders since well before Pearl Harbor, presumably to fortify them, shrouding the atoll in mystery. For years the United States had speculated about Truk's offensive and defensive might, imagining it as fearsomely powerful, essentially impregnable. American military planners even dubbed it the "Gibraltar of the Pacific."

Despite its formidable reputation, Truk had actually been something of a backwater until Allied forces invaded the Solomon Islands in the summer of 1942. Those events provoked the commander in chief (CinC) of the Imperial Japanese Navy's Combined Fleet (and architect of the surprise attack on Pearl Harbor), Admiral Yamamoto Isoroku, to base his mighty striking force at the atoll's splendid harbor. Yamamoto wanted to be close to the action, so that he might take on the American navy in the "Decisive Battle" Japan's strategists had long desired and planned. But that conclusive confrontation did not come to pass, and for months on end, as one after another of the Solomon Islands fell, the Combined Fleet lay anchored at Truk, making only an occasional sor-tie in hopes of engaging the U.S. fleet.

On 18 April 1943, tragedy struck the Japanese Navy. While on an inspec-tion tour of eastern Bougainville, Yamamoto Isoroku was assassinated by the

U.S. Army Air Force. American fliers had been tipped off to the CinC's itinerary by codebreakers who had been reading Japanese radio messages for much of the war. With this information in hand, four Lockheed P-38 interceptors pounced on the admiral's transport, shooting it out of the sky over Buin.

Five days after the disaster, Admiral Koga Mineichi was named Yamamoto's successor. Koga, too, kept his fleet at Truk, and his flagship, the superbattleship *Musashi,* became a familiar sight in the anchorage between Eten and Dublon islands at the center of the atoll. The presence of the Combined Fleet brought an expansion of Truk's naval facilities—floating drydocks, new airstrips, beefed-up artillery. Nonetheless, Truk's defenses remained weak. There was only one permanent radar station. Most of the antiaircraft guns were aboard whatever ships happened to be in port. There were no troops to repel a landing, just a navy battalion of fewer than a thousand men. Koga's chief of staff, Rear Admiral Fukudome Shigeru, worried that the enemy would eventually find out just how poorly defended Truk really was and would then mount a successful assault. His fears were well founded. In the winter of 1944 the Americans first pierced Truk's veil, then tore it to shreds.

AT NINE O'CLOCK on the morning of 4 February a lone aircraft appeared over Truk. Flying at twenty-five thousand feet, the four-engined bomber was a mere gray speck against the azure tropical sky.

In the lagoon below, *Musashi* swung at anchor in the calm waters off Dublon. Her radar operators were the first to detect the intruder. And her anti-aircraft batteries were the first to open fire. Up on the flag bridge Admiral Koga Mineichi watched the plane through his binoculars, and when his aides proffered an identification, he was not surprised. It was an American PB4Y (a navy version of the B-24 Liberator), they told their admiral. Koga knew immediately, knew instinctively, that the intruder was not there to bomb. He knew, too, that its presence foreshadowed the ruin of Truk, that its mission that day was simply reconnaissance, but that on another day, soon, many others like it would fly out of the east, heavily laden with explosives.

Koga watched as the plane made a slow beeline across the atoll, neatly ducking the fierce fire now being thrown up by guns ashore and afloat. As the B-24 withdrew to the south, a second plane was spotted. After half an hour this Liberator, too, departed, disappearing into a storm front.[1]

The admiral called his staff together in *Musashi*'s cramped flag plot, the operational nerve center of Combined Fleet headquarters. Around a map-covered table there ensued a discussion about the enemy's intentions. Koga was well aware of the Americans' vast and rapidly growing capabilities. Just five days earlier and nine hundred miles to the east, U.S. troops opened the campaign for the Marshall Islands with landings on Kwajalein and Majuro atolls. The following day marines landed at Roi and Namur islands, securing both within twenty-four hours. Koga had been receiving reports all week that the Japanese hold on the Marshalls was fading with each passing day. As he had with the Gilbert Islands, Koga was ready to write off the Marshalls, to contract Japan's defensive perimeter still farther.

Koga soon realized he had little choice but to disperse his fleet before the Americans returned to Truk in force. He ordered his ships to flee: to Tokyo, to Singapore, to Palau. That very evening the battleships *Yamato* and *Nagato* set sail. The CinC would follow in *Musashi* the following week.

WHEN THE TWO U.S. Marine Corps Liberators touched down later that day at Bougainville in the western Solomons, technicians descended upon the planes. They quickly unloaded the bulky aerial cameras, rushing their films to the photo lab. Within hours eight-by-ten glossies were on the desks of fleet intelligence officers, who pored over every print with powerful stereo magnifiers. The analysts were astonished by what they saw: at least one superbattleship, two aircraft carriers, ten cruisers, dozens of destroyers, submarines, patrol boats, auxiliaries, tankers, freighters, and transports.[2] On the airstrips that dotted the several islands they could see nearly two hundred fighters and bombers. And in the waters off Dublon Island were more aircraft—two dozen floatplanes and six long-range flying boats. In the opinion of the intelligence staff, Truk more than lived up to its reputation. In a summary of the photo mission they wrote, "The whole picture provides factual confirmation of the importance for which this area has always been assessed."[3]

*MUSASHI* LEFT FOR JAPAN on 10 February. There Admiral Koga had scheduled meetings with the highest levels of his country's military command, with the Navy General Staff and the joint Army-Navy Imperial General Headquarters.

Koga Mineichi was not a brilliant, charismatic leader like his predecessor, Yamamoto, but he was a steady hand. He was congenial, professional, and held in high regard by his peers. Lanky and slightly balding, Koga kept his graying hair closely clipped. He wore a neatly trimmed mustache in an arch above his thin lips. He had piercing dark eyes deeply set in an otherwise unremarkable face. Koga's forty-year career was in many ways distinguished only by its plodding, logical progression to the top ranks of the Imperial Japanese Navy.

Koga was a native of Saga Prefecture on the southern island of Kyushu, born there in 1885. He was raised to revere the Bushido code of his ancestors—the Way of the Warrior—for he proudly traced his lineage back to the fabled samurai. As a schoolboy he certainly studied the famous battles of that warrior class, including Dan no Ura, fought in the Inland Sea near Saga exactly seven hundred years before his birth—a renowned, decisive sea battle that brought to a close the bloody Gempei Wars, which had raged throughout Japan in the late twelfth century.[4] Koga liked to say that a Saga samurai should pick the time and the place he would die, "the earlier in battle the better."[5] Koga entered Eta Jima, the Japanese naval academy, in 1902, graduating three years later as a "passed midshipman," fourteenth in his class. He rose slowly through the ranks of the force's junior officers until, in late 1922, he was promoted to commander and sent to the postgraduate course at the Naval Staff College. After completing the course and teaching there for a year, Koga, now a captain, joined the staff of the Combined and First Fleet.[6]

In 1926, his star still rising, Koga Mineichi went to Paris as the naval attaché for the Japanese embassy. The following year he joined his country's delegation at the Geneva Arms Conference, consulting on technical issues. During his three years in Europe, the young captain became fluent in French and picked up a smattering of English. In recognition of his work France, Greece, and Italy awarded him decorations: the Legion of Honor (2nd Class), the Phoenix (1st Class), and the Order of the Italian Crown (1st Class), medals he proudly wore throughout his career. Returning to Tokyo in 1929, Captain Koga became senior aide to the navy minister.

After this long string of administrative jobs it was time for Koga to return to sea. The year 1930 brought a tour as commanding officer of the heavy cruiser *Aoba,* and the following year as the CO of the battleship *Ise.* He was back on shore in 1932, attached to the Navy General Staff (NGS) after his promotion to rear admiral. At the "Red Bricks," the sobriquet given the Navy Ministry building in Tokyo, Koga was made a member of the Navy Technical Council, advising on military research and development. Membership on the council brought the new admiral into close touch with the latest naval aviation technologies and tactics, providing valuable insight into the role of airpower at sea. He rose to become chief of the Second Section of the NGS in 1934, as a special inspector appointed by Emperor Hirohito himself.[7]

In 1936 now Vice Admiral Koga returned to sea, commanding Cruiser Division 7. But Tokyo again beckoned. He took over as vice chief of the Navy General Staff, working with the imperial household, where he had cultivated many contacts. Here he first met and began a long friendship with then Captain Fukudome Shigeru, a man considered one of the brightest, most reliable staff officers in the navy, and destined to become the admiral's wartime chief of staff. Following a stint as commander of the Second Fleet, Koga was promoted to CinC, Japanese Naval Force in China, based in Shanghai. He commanded a small fleet—just a few cruisers, destroyers, patrol boats, and auxiliaries—but it was nevertheless a prestigious assignment. On 10 November 1942, now full Admiral Koga Mineichi became head of the Yokosuka Naval District, an important position despite its mundane-sounding title. Finally, with the death of Yamamoto, on 21 April 1943, the fifty-seven-year-old Koga was made commander in chief of the Combined Fleet—a job many in the Imperial Japanese Navy believed he had long been groomed for.[8]

After seven days at sea, Koga's flagship, *Musashi,* reached Tokyo Bay on the very day the Americans had chosen to return to Truk.

WHEN AMERICAN ANALYSTS finished their work on the Truk photos, sailors added each print to a growing mosaic of the atoll. Within days the maps, the photos, and the analysts' interpretations had reached Pearl Harbor and the office of CincPac—the U.S. Navy's Commander in Chief, Pacific—Admiral Chester William Nimitz. It was Nimitz who had directed the drive across the central Pacific, commencing in the Gilberts, moving north to the Marshalls. As he reviewed the intelligence on the enemy islands, CincPac dreaded the thought of an all-out assault on Truk. He believed the atoll was virtually unassailable, that casualties would be very high. Still smarting from the public outcry over American losses at the invasion of Tarawa the previous November, Nimitz ordered Admiral Raymond Ames Spruance, commander of the Central Pacific Force, to soften up Truk with air strikes using a new and potent weapon, the "fast carrier" task force.

When the war began the United States Navy had just seven large aircraft carriers. Since then, four had been lost. The USS *Lexington* went down at the Battle of the Coral Sea on 8 May 1942; the *Yorktown,* a month later, at the Battle of Midway. *Wasp* and *Hornet* were sunk five weeks apart during the campaign for the Solomon Islands in the fall of 1942. For an entire year Chester Nimitz did his best to hoard his remaining carriers, awaiting the arrival of a new generation of ships—the Independence-class light carriers and the Essex-class heavy carriers. Both were capable of speeds of more than thirty-three knots, able to keep up with the fastest ships in the fleet. These finally began to trickle into Pearl Harbor in the summer of 1943. Air-minded naval planners pushed their leaders to concentrate the new carriers into large, mobile strike forces. And they got their wish. The new warships, now suddenly numerous after the long drought, were organized into task groups of three carriers, usually two heavy and one light, and then into task forces of three to four groups. The combined strength of a single fast carrier task force was easily seven hundred to nine hundred aircraft, a balanced force of fighters and bombers, scouts, and torpedo planes. This gave the U.S. Navy awesome offensive power at a critical turn in the war.[9]

The fast carrier task force made its first appearance late in the summer of 1943 for a raid against enemy-held Marcus Island. Though a small target of little consequence, Marcus gave navy tacticians an opportunity to learn how a well-coordinated carrier task force might operate. Despite some mistakes, analysts considered the raid a successful experiment. The carrier groups continued to refine their techniques throughout the fall with strikes against Baker, Tarawa, Wake, and Rabaul. The trial by fire came in November with Operation Galvanic, the Gilbert Islands campaign. Following a command shakeup just after Christmas, Rear Admiral Marc Andrew "Pete" Mitscher took charge of the fast carrier fleet, now dubbed Task Force 58. Mitscher, a navy flier since before World War I, was widely respected throughout the service. The new air admiral's first assault was against the Marshalls at the end of January 1944. By mid-February, with operational and tactical problems mostly ironed out, Task Force 58 turned its might toward Truk.[10]

At dawn on 17 February Task Force 58's nine carriers began launching their planes. As the squadrons arrived over their targets, flak from enemy antiaircraft guns blackened the sky above Truk lagoon. Fortunately the Japanese gunners had had little practice on real airplanes. Most missed by a wide margin. By noon the Americans had won complete air superiority and began to concentrate their efforts on the many ships in the harbor.

The next day Task Force 58's aircraft returned to Truk to polish off the few remaining targets. By the end of the operation, called Hailstone, the Japanese had lost two hundred fifty planes and two-hundred-thousand tons of shipping.[11] Truk was finished as a front-line base. Even though the Japanese continued to reinforce the island, eventually putting thirty thousand troops on

Truk, the atoll immediately became a backwater once again, bypassed by a new American strategy that neutralized rather than invaded powerful island fortresses such as Truk and Rabaul. They were left to wither as the American juggernaut pushed on across the Pacific.

Arriving at Tokyo amid a stream of reports about the destruction of Truk, Koga began a six-day series of conferences to discuss the future conduct of the war at sea. The Combined Fleet chief sought approval from the admirals of the General Staff to modify his own battle plan—a strategy designed to draw the Americans into a conclusive fleet engagement on the high seas. Koga wanted to redistribute his forces around a revised "last line of defense," a perimeter running from north of Japan, through Saipan in the Marianas and Palau in the Carolines, all the way down to western New Guinea. The new boundary was a far cry from the original, which had extended out beyond the Marshalls, the Gilberts, and in the South Pacific, down to the Solomons and eastern New Guinea. But in the course of the past two years the Allies had put Japan on the defensive, taking island after island, whittling away at the empire. To be sure, Nippon still controlled vast territory: almost all of Southeast Asia, the Philippines, eastern China, and most of Micronesia. But by February 1944 the Japanese faced Allied drives on two fronts: MacArthur's offensive up through New Guinea and Nimitz's straight across the central Pacific. Imperial General Headquarters put its faith and its dwindling naval resources into a plan to stop the advance with a single "winner take all" engagement at sea. They called it the "Decisive Battle."

The credo of the Decisive Battle had its origins in Japanese strategic thinking following the successes during the Russo-Japanese War. Nippon's first and only Decisive Battle had been fought in the Korea Strait, just east of Tsushima Island. There, at the end of May 1905, the Russian Baltic Fleet and Japan's Combined Fleet clashed. In the two-day contest the Nipponese, led brilliantly by Admiral Togo Heihachiro, annihilated the Russians. Only four of the thirty-eight vessels comprising the Baltic Fleet survived.[12] The triumph at the Battle of Tsushima gave rise to an uncompromising Japanese naval doctrine calling for a decisive surface engagement between big-gun capital ships. The spoils of such a battle, it was believed, would be nothing less than control of the seas by the victor. Such a battle might even win the war.[13]

Ever since Tsushima, the Japanese had planned for, built for, trained for that one, single, conclusive battle. The Decisive Battle became a deeply ingrained article of faith for two generations of IJN officers. It was the reason Nippon had built the two superbattleships *Yamato* and *Musashi*—seventy-thousand-ton leviathans with eighteen-inch guns capable of outshooting any ship afloat—and planned to build even more. It was at the core of every strategy, every tactic promulgated by the Imperial Japanese Navy for nearly forty years.

Koga Mineichi's Decisive Battle strategy—he called it the Z Plan—was first issued on 25 August 1943, after three months' work by the admiral, Chief of Staff Fukudome, and the Combined Fleet's planning staff.

Like Yamamoto before him, Koga was an air-minded admiral. This was a surprise to his colleagues, for unlike his predecessor, Koga had no experience with naval aviation; he had served on battleships and cruisers his entire career. Indeed, he was a member of the navy's *teppo-ya,* the "Gun Club" of surface-force adherents. But Koga could clearly see the value of aviation in protecting his own fleet and in using aircraft to cause grievous damage to his enemy's fleet. When he stepped in to fill Yamamoto's shoes, Koga was already aware that the war he would be fighting was defensive in nature. Burdened by the dogma of the Decisive Battle, Koga decided he could achieve the desired results by employing his air forces as though they were a unit of the fleet. He oversaw creation of the carrier-centric First Mobile Fleet, organized along lines similar to the U.S. Navy's fast carrier task force.[14] Admiral Ozawa Jisaburo, an experienced carrier commander, led the new unit and was given tactical command of the big-gun ships, a departure from Japanese Navy practice. Koga also pushed the expansion of the IJN's land-based air squadrons, a move that dramatically increased the number of aircraft available to attack the enemy, for at the heart of Koga's Z Plan was the close coordination of sea power and airpower.

To facilitate annihilation of U.S. forces, the plan called for the creation of six "Belts of Preparedness," sectors where the IJN maintained relative control through an interlocking grid of land bases and predisposed fleet units. It was Koga's intent to lure the U.S. fleet into one of these zones, where he would have tactical advantage. The admiral expected that the next American assault would come in No. 3 Belt: the Marianas and the Carolines. If his enemy complied, Koga would unleash a "C-Type" operation, whereby the carriers of his First Mobile Fleet would "carry out surface strike and aerial operations" first, and "subsequent operations [would be] from base."[15] By combining the strength of his fleets at sea and in the air, Koga Mineichi planned to best his enemy or die trying.

By the end of his week in Tokyo the admiral had won from the Imperial General Staff approval to put the updated Z Plan into action. On 23 February

Koga, once again aboard flagship *Musashi,* sailed out of Tokyo Bay en route to Palau in the Western Carolines.

PALAU IS PARADISE, or about as close as anyplace can ever come. To describe Palau requires hyperbole and cliché, for it was, and is even now, one of the most beautiful places in all the Pacific—the archetypal South Seas Valhalla. The chain is comprised of more than three hundred islands lying just above the equator, six hundred miles east of the Philippines. The northernmost, Babelthaup, is the second largest in all Micronesia; only Guam is bigger. Kayangel, a low coral atoll off the tip of Babelthaup, is nothing less than a poetic idyll: unspoiled sandy beaches, tiny thatched-hut villages, coconut palms waving in gentle trade winds, transparent waters teeming with colorful sea life, dark-skinned men spearing turtles from spindly outrigger canoes.

Just below the big island lies Koror, the population and business center of Palau. In the two decades since Japan had grabbed Palau (and the rest of Micronesia) from the Germans, the Japanese had turned Koror Town into a tropical mini-Tokyo. Sixty-five hundred Japanese immigrants squeezed the native Palauans off their lands to build a town not unlike many back in the homeland. Tidy houses wore peaked roofs; shoji screens and tatami mats were ubiquitous furnishings. The winding main street was lined with shops selling rice and sake and soy sauce, and fine restaurants serving miso soup, soba noodles, even Kobe beef, all imported from Japan. A splendid Shinto shrine sat serenely on a hill just north of town. The imposing headquarters of the Nan'yo-cho—the South Seas Government—sat on another. Roads were paved, electricity was reliable, there was even a sewage system.[16] And in the public park, amused Palauans watched their colonial rulers play a strange stick-ball-glove game called *yakyu* (also known as beisu-baru).

Unlike the Marianas, where the soil was fertile and farming was the predominant occupation, agriculture did not flourish in Palau. Several attempts were made to plant marketable crops, but success was elusive. Instead, Palau turned to the sea to provide its wealth.

Just a mile beyond Koror lay Malakal and its deep-water harbor. The Japanese had begun in 1927 to create a commercial port adjacent to the small island (part of which they leveled for fill). Here, before the war, was located a thriving fishing industry, complete with a tuna cannery and ice plant. Here, too, were fuel tank farms, capacious wharves and spacious warehouses, even a few factories. Nearby, a pearl farm grew and shipped to Mikimoto in Tokyo ten thousand cultured pearls each year. Malakal became the busiest port in all Micronesia. From all over the empire, ships made their way to Palau to offload consumer goods and to fill their holds with the islands' aquatic bounty.

With the coming of the war the harbor was often filled with visiting warships and military transports. Oil depots were enlarged. More freight sheds were hurriedly constructed. Antiaircraft and shore defense batteries were installed. A second anchorage, just over the ridge from Malakal Harbor, was created for the overflow of vessels passing through Palau on their way south from Japan to New Guinea and the former Netherlands East Indies. A concrete causeway linked Malakal with Koror, and another linked the town with Arakabesan Island, just to the west across a shallow channel. By 1944 Arakabesan had become a busy naval station, home to two seaplane bases. One was for small floatplanes, the other for the big four-engined, long-range patrol bombers. The island was, by this time, completely off-limits to civilians, Japanese and Palauans alike.[17]

A couple of miles below the bustle of Malakal, paradise returned in the form of the "Rock Islands," one of the most enchanting sights in Micronesia. A hundred or more verdure-covered, mushroom-cap islets dot the bays. An impressive enough scene from a boat, from the air the view is entirely captivating: the Rock Islands appear to float above the luminous sapphire waters, surrounded by a great ring of white wavelets marking the boundary of the reef separating the shallow lagoon from the depths of the indigo sea. The Rock Islands had no military value in 1944, but they were a feast for the eyes, there simply to be enjoyed.

At the bottom of the barrier reef sits Peleliu, shaped like a finger pointing northward. This island was Palau's fortress. The Japanese had built a huge air base in the center of Peleliu, and were leveling a second on the adjoining island of Ngesebus. The craggy hills along the western coast were peppered with caves that Japanese Army troops worked at feverishly to interlink and reinforce.

Seven miles beyond Peleliu, outside the reef, lies Angaur. This small island also boasted an airstrip and a defensive garrison, as well as a large phosphate works originally built by the Germans at the turn of the century and now operated by the Japanese government.

As *Musashi* turned into the lee of Toagel Mlungui Passage, her sailors lined the rails gawking at the lush, green islands, the white beaches, the crystal waters; gawking, too, in their mind's eye, at the beautiful, compliant women said to inhabit these tropical islands. They counted their yen in anticipation of long visits to Koror Town's saloons, there to drink familiar beers: Sapporo, Asahi, Kirin. Thirsts slaked, they would move on to the geisha houses, replete with kimono-clad, geta-shod girls from back home.[18] Passions cooled and stumbling their way around town, the sailors might then spend their remaining money—if there was any—on a finely woven pandanus hat, or a Palauan storyboard carving. Until this cruise most had been stationed at Truk, that vast and dreary naval base. But Palau . . . even in the middle of the war, Palau was the stuff of dreams and legends. And the men aboard the dreadnought were eager to get ashore for a crack at liberty in paradise.

High on the mastodon's flag bridge, Admiral Koga Mineichi paid scant attention to the ship's arrival in this beautiful place, catching up instead on overnight radio traffic from his far-flung fleet. The messages on this late February morning continued to be discouraging. Task Force 58 had bombed the Marianas—Guam and Saipan, Rota and Tinian—a thousand miles to the north. American destroyers had bombarded Japanese positions at Kavieng and the great base at Rabaul, fifteen hundred miles to the southeast. Casualties had been relatively light, but matériel losses, particularly of precious aircraft, had been worrisomely heavy. Without those planes, the Z Plan might be doomed to failure. Koga took little comfort in a report that his own forces had damaged two enemy destroyers at New Britain.[19]

For the next month *Musashi* lay quietly at anchor off Malakal. Koga went ashore occasionally, staying at the governor's residence on a hill overlooking Koror Town. He and his staff worked to refine the Z Plan, issuing a final draft version to the fleet on 8 March. Two weeks later a staff white paper titled "A Study of the Main Features of Decisive Air Operations in the Central Pacific" was completed.[20] This document suggested aerial tactics that might be used during the great Decisive Battle to come. Koga hoped the lull would continue so that his seriously depleted air forces could replace lost aircraft and train replacement pilots. All the while, the admiral kept a wary eye on the movements of the American carriers. But following the destruction of Truk and the raid on the Marianas, Task Force 58 had retired. Spruance and Mitscher returned to Majuro to plan their next foray.

SHORTLY AFTER TEN on the morning of Tuesday, 28 March 1944, Admiral Koga's communications officer, Commander Nakajima Chikataka, handed him an urgent radio message. A patrol plane from Woleai reported sighting an American fleet a thousand miles east of Palau. The commander in chief immediately called his staff together. In the confines of the plotting room the group considered the report's implications. Warnings had come in over the weekend that the Americans were at sea, but Tokyo had said only that New Guinea or the Marianas might be the target. Now it seemed clear that the enemy was sailing toward the western Carolines, and that meant Palau. The discussion centered on how best to meet the threat. One officer argued for ordering all merchant shipping in the Malakal roadstead to put to sea. Another urged an increase in air reconnaissance. However, most of the staff agreed that Admiral Kurita Takeo's Second Fleet should sortie immediately in anticipation of a fleet engagement. Koga decided to wait until more information about the enemy fleet was ascertained. His only action was to order stepped-up patrols. He had meager scouting resources at his disposal—just four long-range Mitsubishi G6M1 Bettys—barely sufficient to patrol an arc of ninety degrees, leaving uncovered three-quarters of the ocean surrounding Palau. Throughout that day worried Combined Fleet staffers awaited developments.

Further word did not come until Wednesday noon. A patrol bomber from Truk's 761 Air Group reported seeing the American task force, still steaming steadily southwest. The plane was able to get off only that one message. It was shot down soon after by the USS *Enterprise*'s combat air patrol as it penetrated the fleet's outer screen. A hasty conference aboard *Musashi* brought a flurry of orders from the CinC. Koga was now convinced the Americans would strike Palau the next day, and knew he had little time to prepare. With some reluctance the admiral moved Combined Fleet headquarters ashore, directing his flagship to join the cruisers and destroyers of Kurita's fleet. He knew this little armada was no match for the enemy, especially without carriers to provide some semblance of air protection. But he sent them just the same. Koga also tried to get the dozens of merchant ships in the harbor out into the open sea. He directed the commander of Base Force 30 at Koror to issue evacuation orders to the freighters and tankers. Despite the emergency, more than thirty vessels never weighed anchor. Finally, he ordered fighters flown in from Yap, Guam, and Saipan.

It must have been a sad moment when Koga Mineichi transferred his flag ashore. He reminded Fukudome that this move to a land-based headquarters was in keeping with his plan to make the Marianas-Carolines the last line of defense. In the event the enemy struck to the north, the plan was to move Combined Fleet headquarters to Saipan; if to the south, to Davao in southern Mindanao—wherever the CinC would be closer to the action. While Koga conferred with Admiral Kurita, Koga's staff hastily packed personal belongings and official Combined Fleet documents, Fukudome taking charge of the leather pouch containing the secret Z Plan. With little pomp, the CinC took leave of his flagship, boarding a barge for the short ride to the pier at Malakal.[21]

Late in the afternoon of the twenty-ninth the Second Fleet slipped its moorings at the Malakal anchorage, sailing through the reef at Toagel Mlungui Pass just west of Koror. The ships were under orders to head northwest of the Palaus to await news of the enemy.[22]

*Musashi* cleared the tricky passage just before sundown. At 5:40 P.M., as she entered the Pacific proper, her consorts, the destroyers *Urakase* and *Isokase,* spotted torpedo wakes heading directly for the leviathan. They flashed a warning; *Musashi* began an emergency turn, but it was too late. Two of the six torpedoes fired by the USS *Tunny* holed the battleship's bow. While the two escorts charged the American submarine, driving her deep and holding her there, *Musashi*'s captain assessed the damage to his ship. The sea streamed into forward compartments, the center anchor capstan had flooded, seven men were killed. Damage was otherwise light, and the huge vessel could still make nearly twenty knots. But while the ship was in no danger of sinking, neither was she in condition to fight a battle. That evening the captain notified Admiral Koga on Palau, and the Navy General Staff in Tokyo, that he was heading for the naval base at Kure in southern Japan for inspection and repairs. *Tunny* had just knocked out of action a major threat to the U.S. Fleet. *Musashi* would reach Kure on 3 April and spend a full month in drydock.[23]

At Koror, Koga was in the midst of planning a night air strike against the U.S. fleet. Another Betty patrol plane had provided a fix on the task force's position late in the afternoon before being shot down by American fighters. Though he had few attack planes at his disposal, the commander in chief nevertheless launched a nine-aircraft raid timed to reach the enemy at dusk. All were shot down before reaching Task Force 58. Well into the night, small groups of Japanese planes made attacks on the fleet. Scout planes snooped the task force, dropping colored flares and floating lanterns to illuminate the way for the bombers. At times, tracers from the dozens of ships in the force lit up the sky. Every few minutes a bright orange ball erupted in the darkness and fell toward the sea, quickly disappearing beneath the waves. One Judy dive bomber managed to penetrate the fierce wall of antiaircraft fire to make a drop on the cruiser *San Francisco.* The bomb fell harmlessly close aboard, and the attacker was quickly dispatched. Another plane strafed the USS *Portland,* injuring four sailors, one critically. Otherwise the effort by the Japanese was for naught. Late in the evening they withdrew, leaving Task Force 58 alone on the ocean, bearing down on Palau at twenty-two knots. Admiral Koga could now only wait.

OPERATION DESECRATE ONE BEGAN in earnest at dawn on Thursday, 30 March. Admiral Raymond Spruance passed tactical control of the Central Pacific Force to his air admiral, Marc Mitscher. With the fleet seventy-five miles southwest of Palau, the first fighter sweep of Koror, Babelthaup, Peleliu, and Angaur islands was launched from the *Enterprise* at 4:35 A.M. More than seventy Grumman F6F Hellcats wheeled in, machine-gunning and rocketing Japanese aircraft and installations on the ground and dogfighting enemy Zeros in the air, clearing the path for the lumbering bombers and torpedo planes to follow. In this initial sweep scores of enemy planes were destroyed or damaged.

As the Hellcats were finishing their assignment, the "Flying Miners" appeared low on the horizon. In the only operation of its kind during the Pacific war, carrier-based Avengers—aircraft normally used to launch torpedoes—laid seventy-eight mines throughout the two anchorages. Mining was not a popular mission among hotshot pilots; there was much grumbling before and after the drops. But later analysis proved the tactic worthwhile. One maru was sunk when she hit a mine, and many other merchantmen were bottled up in port, hoping it was safer to stay put than to run the gauntlet of magnetic mines sitting on the harbor bottom.[24]

With these ships immobilized inside the lagoon, the Curtiss Helldiver and Douglas Dauntless dive bombers had a field day, destroying the enemy vessels one by one in almost methodic fashion. More Avengers entered the fray, carrying conventional munitions. Eight of the planes, known affectionately as "turkeys" for their bulging bellies and slow speed, ganged up on the hapless *Wakatake* as she charged north along the coast of Babelthaup Island. Bombed twice earlier in the day, the old destroyer was hit by no less than four torpedoes, sinking instantly when her boilers exploded, breaking her in two.[25]

Admiral Koga Mineichi spent that first day of Operation Desecrate One in a bunker near Koror. Commander Nakajima's communications unit managed to get a few radio messages out that morning, informing the High Command in Tokyo that Palau was under air attack. Throughout that long day reports came in from the various commands around the islands, outlining the damage done. The 26th Air Flotilla on Peleliu reported multiple strikes by fighters and bombers, destroying several Bettys and Zeros on the ground, setting fire to hangars, and cratering the main runway. Angaur reported attacks against the phosphate works. Up on Babelthaup, the Toagel Mlungui lighthouse was shattered by strafing Hellcats. Much of Koror Town was set afire. Army and navy ammunition and supply dumps were destroyed on Malakal. The two seaplane bases on neighboring Arakabesan Island were shot up, their hangars bombed. Nakajima reported watching an enterprising American fighter pilot locate a gasoline storage depot in a cave across the harbor. The pilot made numerous strafing runs low and slow over the bay until he set fire to the hundreds of drums hidden from view. When the dump exploded it shot flames high into the air, spewing thick, black smoke for hours. Nakajima was impressed by the American pilot's remarkable persistence and skill.[26]

The Japanese, unable to mount an effective defense, were at the mercy of Task Force 58's aircraft. A few of their Zero fighters managed to shoot down some attackers, and antiaircraft fire accounted for several more. Twelve of the speedy Mitsubishis jumped a flight of Hellcats near Anguar, knocking one out of the sky. The defenders quickly learned that the American dive bombers were vulnerable to AA fire as they drew out of their steep dives. Over Peleliu a Helldiver was brought down as it pulled out at fifteen hundred feet. The plane was engulfed in flames; the crew bailed out but was never seen again. Similar successes were few. Usually it was the Japanese on the receiving end. An army pilot from Peleliu, flying an old and slow Nakajima Ki-27b Nate fighter, was caught on the edge of a rain squall by three *Enterprise* Hellcats. The pilot was obviously a skilled flier who knew his airplane well. Though the bigger, faster, better-armed and -armored Grummans had the edge, the little Nate had one significant advantage: It was vastly more maneuverable. Just as the F6Fs would come in for the kill, their competitor would put his craft into some radical aerobatic gyration that put him out of reach for the moment. This game of aerial "cat and mouse" went on for some forty-five minutes as the Japanese pilot expertly weaved in and out of the clouds, evading his tormentors. When the Nate ran low on fuel, the pilot decided to make a run for it. He dived out of the clouds, only to be jumped by the American fighters. He did his best to evade their attack, but it was not long before the obsolete craft was hit and smoking. The navy pilots were relieved when they saw their worthy adversary pull back the canopy and start to bail out. They were then horrified when the enemy flier's parachute entangled in the Nate's tail, dragging him down to his death.[27]

Toward the end of the first day, Koga received a report of an American transport group heading westward from the Admiralty Islands. The news caused much concern, for it seemed to suggest that an invasion of Palau might be imminent.[28] Koga's position now seemed untenable, his ability to implement the Z Plan impaired. Isolated on the archipelago, the commander in chief had no way to direct the Combined Fleet. After a brief discussion with his officers, he decided to withdraw the next night to Davao, six hundred miles to the west. Fukudome instructed Nakajima to order three flying boats to transport the CinC and his staff. That evening the officer got a radio message through to Admiral Shiro Takasu, the commander of the Southwest Area Fleet in Surabaya:

```
851st FORCE WILL IMMEDIATELY HAVE THREE TYPE 2 LARGE FLYING
BOATS STAND BY TO MOVE UP TO DAVAO.[29]
```

Overnight the Japanese again made attacks on the American fleet, now steaming northeast of Palau. And again, the Japanese effort failed miserably; their losses were high, the damage to their enemy nil.

Before the sun rose on the thirty-first of March, Task Force 58 launched a second day of fighter sweeps, followed by a second day of bombing and torpedo attacks. Photo analysts had spent the night poring over reconnaissance pictures, sorting out the merely damaged from the totally destroyed, making target lists for Friday's raids. The strike was a repeat of the first, lasting only until noon, for there were far fewer objectives to hit.

In the bunker on Koror, word came back from Surabaya that the 851st could supply only two seaplanes. Another radio message was sent out, this time by Fukudome:

```
1. HEADQUARTERS COMBINED FLEET WILL DEPART PALAU TONIGHT
   31ST (OR EARLY APRIL 1) AND PROCEED TO SAIPAN VIA DAVAO.

2. DESIRE AIR GROUP 851 DESPATCH TWO FLYING BOATS AND AIR
   GROUP 802 DESPATCH ONE FLYING BOAT TO PROVIDE
   TRANSPORTATION FOR ABOVE MOVE.[30]
```

By midday Friday the American attacks had slackened noticeably. The Japanese now believed the enemy fleet was retiring. This estimate made Koga waver in his decision to leave that evening. He now considered waiting until the morning of the first, when it would be safer than flying at night. But that afternoon a patrol plane reported sighting Task Force 58 just east of Palau. The report convinced Koga to leave that evening. Days later, Commander Nakajima learned that the reconnaissance pilot had not spotted the U.S. fleet, but rather mistook whitecaps breaking over reefs and rocks for enemy ships. It was a fateful error.[31]

In fact the U.S. fleet had indeed retired at high speed to the north, its two-day strike against the Palaus successfully completed. Against the loss of twenty-five aircraft in combat, Task Force 58 claimed more than a hundred Japanese planes destroyed and many dozens more damaged. Thirty-six vessels, most of them merchantmen, were sunk or severely damaged. As it had at Truk, the lightning raid on Palau left the Japanese reeling and left paradise a shambles.

AT EIGHT O'CLOCK on the night of the thirty-first the big Kawanishi H8K2 flying boats from Saipan settled on the calm waters off the still-smoldering seaplane base. They approached the long concrete ramp, mooring in the shallow bay. These aircraft, code-named Emily by the Allies, were acknowledged to be the finest flying boats in the world. They handled superbly in all weather conditions. They were heavily armed (with five powerful 20mm cannons and six 7.7mm machine guns). With a top speed of nearly 300 mph, they were fast for large seaplanes. And the Type 2, as the Japanese called it, had an astonishing cruising range of more than forty-four hundred miles. American pilots held the Emily in high esteem, considering it the hardest Japanese aircraft to knock out of the sky.

An hour after the planes came in, Admiral Koga and most of his staff arrived at the base—forced to cross the channel by boat after the enemy destroyed the narrow causeway between Koror and Arakabesan. For security reasons, Koga and his chief of staff would fly in separate aircraft. The CinC would ride in the first plane, the #1 Boat, flown by the 851 Air Group's senior pilot, Lieutenant Namba. Fukudome (and the Z Plan) would fly in #2 Boat, supplied by the 802 Air Group, with his aide Captain Yamamoto Yuji and other officers. #3 Boat, its arrival at Palau delayed, would fly out the communications and clerical staff with their top-secret codes. In answer to a radio query about the safety of landing the Kawanishis at night, a notice addressed to the Davao and Saipan seaplane bases read:

IT APPEARS WATER LANDINGS CAN BE MADE AFTER SUNSET.

This message put most of the staff's minds at ease, though Nakajima remained troubled about the night flight.

An air raid siren pierced the darkness as the passengers were ferried out to the flying boats. Boarding the capacious Emily, Admiral Koga turned to Fukudome and said, inexplicably, "Yamamoto died at exactly the right time." He envied his predecessor that fact, he told his old friend, then added somberly,

"Let us go out and die together."[32] Koga knew that Japan was losing the war, knew, too, that there was little he could do to turn the tide. A historian once wrote of the samurai, "The sincerity of his intentions mingles with the purity of his mission, which requires from him an unflinching devotion to a seemingly hopeless cause."[33] This well described the "Way of the Warrior." And Koga Mineichi as well. The two comrades shook hands, bade farewell. The doors were sealed, the engines started, and at ten sharp #1 Boat taxied out to Koror Harbor, pointed its nose due west, and took to the air for the three-hour flight to the Philippines. #2 followed moments later. The sirens' wail ceased as the planes disappeared into the darkness—there would be no further attacks that night. No one on Palau then knew that Task Force 58 had moved on, was hundreds of miles away, steaming toward another island target.

FOR A KAWANISHI, the six-hundred-mile journey from Palau to Davao was a mere hop. At least it should have been. An hour and a half out of Arakabesan, Koga's plane ran into an enormous storm front. It will never be known what evasive actions Lieutenant Namba may have taken to avoid the weather. But sometime that night the plane carrying Admiral Koga Mineichi, commander in chief, Imperial Japanese Navy Combined Fleet, vanished without a trace. The samurai from Saga had met his death.

# CHAPTER 9

---

## *The Seventh Son*

THERE ARE TIMES WHEN the Pacific refuses to live up to its name. The last day of March 1944 was one of those. An anonymous tropical storm swept furiously across the western Pacific that night, carrying with it raging winds, spears of lightning, torrents of rain. And in its midst the #2 Boat carrying Rear Admiral Fukudome Shigeru, Z Plan, and most of Koga's staff bucked and yawed. The Kawanishi's pilot tried to work his way around the gale. He took the plane down, he took her up, but he found no relief from the tempest. With the storm virtually impenetrable, Davao now seemed an unreachable destination. Out of frustration the pilot pointed his plane northward in an attempt to avoid the storm altogether. Strong headwinds slowed the craft. The flier throttled up his engines to compensate, increasing consumption of fuel. Fukudome, himself an aviator, suggested that the plane be flown to Manila. There they could wait out the furor. After skirting the storm's edge for three hours, the Emily finally broke into the clear. She was so low on fuel that reaching even Luzon was now out of the question. The pilot looked down and saw the silvery waters of Bohol Strait outlining the long, thin shape of Cebu Island. It was a recognizable landmark, a place he thought he could set his plane down safely. He told his passengers to brace themselves for an emergency landing. Fukudome immediately rose from his seat, heading for the cockpit. He told the pilot this could not be Cebu, for he had been there before. The pilot insisted this was Cebu. As the two officers argued, the moon dropped below the horizon and Cebu disappeared into the darkness. Now disoriented, and perhaps a little groggy from flying for too long at high altitude without oxygen, the pilot put the plane into a dangerously steep approach. The dive startled Fukudome; he feared they would crash. At an altitude of fewer than two hundred feet the admiral grabbed the controls from the pilot, yanking back hard on the column, trying desperately to gain some height. But the #2 Boat overresponded, her nose rose slightly in the air, her right wing dipped, and within seconds the Kawanishi hit the water.[1]

Fukudome was thrown forward by the impact, injuring his leg. What fuel remained in the Kawanishi's wing tanks exploded. Flaming aviation gas spread across the sea, encircling the wreckage. The ruggedly built Emily did not break up on impact but was rapidly shipping water. As Fukudome felt the plane being dragged below the surface, he somehow freed himself from the wreckage. He popped to the surface just out of reach of the flames. Grabbing a seat cushion as a float he slowly, painfully kicked his way around the wreck into the open waters.[2] Even in the darkness he must have been aware that there were other men around him. In fact, thirteen had survived the disaster, including the admiral's aide, Commander Yamamoto Yuji. Another dozen perished: from the impact, from drowning, from being burned alive when they surfaced into blazing fuel. As for the Z Plan, Fukudome believed it had gone down with the airplane, lost forever in the depths of Bohol Strait. He did not know then, perhaps never knew, that the plan, lying within a leather portfolio inside a small box, had also popped to the surface and was even then drifting toward Cebu.

Moments before the crash, the noise of the struggling flying boat had caught the attention of Ricardo Bolo, barrio chief of Magtalisay, a small village near the town of San Fernando. Bolo not only worked for the government, he was also in the employ of the guerrillas. For the former he administered the tiny village. For the latter he scrounged food, as well as information that might be of importance to Colonel Cushing's Cebu Area Command. There should not be a plane out this late, Bolo thought. He propped open the cloth window for a look at the sea, listening to the distressed sounds of the Emily's whining engines. His eyes scanned the sky, then the dim horizon. There was nothing to see but distant sheets of lightning illuminating bulbous gray clouds. Suddenly a bright red and orange flash lit up the horizon, then faded away. Seconds later, the noise stopped. Bolo thought this would be just the sort of important news Cushing wanted. But he also figured delivering it could wait until daylight. The chief tumbled back into bed and went to sleep.[3]

For eight hours Fukudome paddled his way toward the shoreline he could make out faintly in the distance. He later calculated that the plane had crashed some two and a half miles offshore, but a strong current slowed his progress. When the sun began to rise he could perceive a beach, a line of coconut palms, a few scattered nipa huts. To the north he could discern the tall chimney of the Asano Cement Plant. It was a landmark familiar to the admiral; he had seen it on previous visits and knew the plant was located just a few miles south of Cebu City. The sight made him feel he might now be in safe territory, where the guerrilla "bandits" dared not operate.[4]

As dawn arrived, Ricardo Bolo heard singing coming from the direction of the sea. It was an odd noise, perhaps more news for Colonel Cushing. He hurriedly dressed and dashed down to the beach, astonished to see a group of men swimming slowly toward the shore, chanting what sounded to him like "hon cha, hon cha, hon cha." Ricardo and his brother Edilberto climbed into their banca and, joined by Valeriano Paradero in his boat, paddled through the light surf toward the men.[5]

Admiral Fukudome saw the two bancas approaching him. His strength waning from the long ordeal, he was not certain he wanted to be rescued. What if the men were unfriendly, were of the resistance? He feared he might fall into the hands of his enemy, might be tortured and forced to reveal the existence of Z Plan. The prospects were chilling. Those concerns and more flooded his mind as he saw the boats draw near. But when they came alongside, his hesitancy, tempered by fatigue, receded. Admiral Fukudome Shigeru decided to take the risk. He let himself be saved.[6]

The Bolo brothers and their friend Paradero began picking up the swimmers. In deference to their admiral, the sailors persuaded the natives to take Fukudome to the beach in the first load. Volunteer Guard (VG) Feliciano Hermosa noticed two men huddled on the reef about a quarter of a mile out. Deciding to help them (he did not know about the other crewmen), Hermosa paddled his banca through the lagoon, toward the reef. But as he neared, he realized they were Japanese. Now fearing for his life, the erstwhile VG jumped into the water, pushed his boat in the direction of the men, then swam— sprinted really—back to the beach. The aviators climbed into his boat and paddled away to the north.[7]

Quite a crowd had gathered on the beach by the time all the Japanese were ashore. The Filipinos surrounded the strangers—eleven wet, exhausted men, the majority visibly injured. Ricardo Bolo pulled aside the VG officers to discuss what to do with the survivors. The soldiers knew the men were Japanese, probably figuring they came from the plane that had crashed earlier that morning. Filipinos sympathetic to the Japanese cause, believers in the Greater East Asia Coprosperity Sphere, would have immediately taken the eleven to the nearest friendly outpost. But Bolo and his colleagues hated the Japanese, hated their occupation, considered the Japanese—*Hapon* in the local dialect—their sworn enemy. Some of the VG must have suggested they shoot the men right there, right on the beach. But reason, tempered by fear of the Japanese, prevailed. Bolo decided to take the men captive. Perhaps they would provide Cushing with all sorts of important information. Concerned that the two men seen escaping in Feliciano Hermosa's banca would report the incident, Bolo ordered the Volunteer Guards to get the captives off the beach, to move them toward the nearby hills as quickly as possible.

The prisoners were ordered to walk, but it soon became apparent that not all were able. One man especially—the one to whom all the others showed considerable obeisance—had an injured leg, so the VG made a bamboo litter on which to carry Admiral Fukudome. The party left the beach, marching slowly through Barrio Balud and on to Barrio Basak. At midmorning a Japanese float-plane buzzed the villages, forcing the VG and their captives to duck for cover among the bushes. The plane circled several times, evidently not spotting the band, then flew off. It was now apparent that the enemy knew about the crash and about the survivors making it to shore.

The two Japanese in the banca had indeed sounded in the alarm. When they left the reef, the pair had paddled to Barrio Sangat, beached their canoe, and headed for the municipal building. They told their story to Vicente Rabor, the "puppet mayor of San Fernando."[8] He, in turn, took the men to the Japanese Army garrison at nearby Tina-an. Almost before Bolo had his prisoners off the beach, the Hapon were organizing a search for Admiral Fukudome and his party.

Tragedy struck the band at Basak. As the group traversed the barrio, one of the younger prisoners tried to escape, in the process attacking VG Roque Bacla-an. The Filipino soldier loathed the Japanese. Early in the occupation they had beaten and tortured him. As the two men struggled, rage surged within Roque. Using his hands to express his wrath, the Filipino throttled his captive.[9] Now there were ten.

All that day the Volunteer Guards and their prisoners hiked inland. At noon they halted for a simple lunch of bananas and coconuts. In the afternoon Ricardo Bolo returned home. Gregorio Tangub, commander of the San Fernando VGs, took over the lead. Each time the group reached a settlement, more men joined the caravan. By nightfall the growing party was several miles from the beach, but the guerrillas knew they could not let down their guard. Reports had reached them that the enemy had hundreds of troops out looking for the missing men.

Just before midnight the first Japanese radio message concerning the loss of the two Kawanishis hit the airwaves:

> A FLYING BOAT OF AIR GROUP #802 EN ROUTE FROM PP (PALAU) TO
> DAVAO MADE A FORCED LANDING IN THE SEA SOUTHWEST OF CEBU. IT
> WAS HEAVILY DAMAGED AND SANK. THE AIR GROUP #851 FLYING BOAT
> DID NOT ARRIVE AT DAVAO BY 0955 AND IT IS GREATLY FEARED
> THAT IT MAY HAVE MET THE SAME FATE. PLEASE INSTITUTE A
> SEARCH.[10]

The dispatch was sent to recipients around the empire. Just an hour later, a precautionary message, probably from Tokyo, was sent to Palau:

> FOR THE TIME BEING, DESIRE THAT 3RD COMMUNICATIONS UNIT
> ORIGINATE DUMMY TRAFFIC SUCH AS TO INDICATE THE COMBINED
> FLEET HEADQUARTERS IS AT PALAU.[11]

A great deception had begun. The Japanese knew that American intelligence employed a technique known as "radio traffic analysis." Indeed, the IJN were masters of the technique themselves. Even though your enemy cannot decrypt your messages, he can draw important and useful information from the frequency, length, and transmission point of such messages. Both sides had played the game long enough to know how much traffic a given unit generated during both normal and abnormal operations.[12] What Tokyo asked Palau to do was transmit a normal flow of Combined Fleet signals, so the Americans would continue to believe Admiral Koga was alive and well and still operating from his base on Koror. Fleet communications officer Nakajima, who had remained on Palau, directed his radio operators to generate messages of the variety and density commonly associated with fleet headquarters. The Japanese Navy High Command, already fearing the loss of the Combined Fleet commander, desired to hide any suspicion of that fact from their enemy.

By midday on 2 April a massive search for Admiral Koga's flying boat, utilizing "all available strength,"[13] was under way. Aircraft squadrons from Davao and other bases combed the southern Mindanao area. At first the search was concentrated on the mountains to the west of Davao City. The Japanese evidently had some information that the flying boat had crashed on land. By that evening a report was made to the navy minister citing the progress thus far:

> SINCE THIS MORNING, ENTIRE AIR STRENGTH IN THIS AREA HAS
> BEEN UTILIZED IN CONTINUING SEARCH FOR #1 BOAT [Koga's
> plane]. COVERING COASTAL AND SURFACE AREAS OF PHILIPPINES

INNER SEAS, SOUTH OF ROTAKUBAN, EAST OF DAVAO, AND EAST OF
CEBU.[14]

A search for Fukudome had also begun on Cebu. And though the Navy
General Staff may have been sympathetic to the admiral's plight, they had
more pressing matters on their minds:

ALTHOUGH WE HAVE BEEN CONTINUING THE SEARCH IN THE VICINITY
OF #2 BOAT DISASTER [Fukudome's plane], USING TWO FLOAT
RECONNAISSANCE PLANES FROM CEBU AND OVER 10 VESSELS, WE HAVE
FOUND NOTHING AS YET. ALTHOUGH THE GREATER PART OF CODES
WERE ON [the much-delayed] #3 BOAT, RULES FOR USE, PLACE
NAME ABBREVIATION LIST, ETC., WERE ON #2 BOAT. WITH THE
COOPERATION OF ARMY FORCES WE ARE CONTINUING THE SEARCH FOR
*IMPORTANT DOCUMENTS* WHICH MAY HAVE DRIFTED ASHORE[15] [emphasis
added].

Already the Japanese were well aware that top-secret materials may have gone
down with the Kawanishi and, if not found quickly by friendly forces, might
soon be in the hands of the guerrillas. At this early stage of the search, however,
they may not have realized that the most important document of all—Koga's
personal copy of the Z Plan—was among those missing.

SOME MILES FARTHER DOWN the beach from Barrio Magtalisay, there lived a
shopkeeper named Pedro Gantuangko. He had had a bad night, for the gout
had returned to his left foot, and the pain would not let him sleep. As dawn
broke to the east, Gantuangko spied a dark object floating just offshore. He
sent his neighbor Opoy Wamar to fetch whatever it was.

In his small banca, Wamar paddled into the shallows. He retrieved a box,
slimy with black oil. Opening it without difficulty, the fisherman discovered
inside a fancy, red leather portfolio. Opoy thought it looked important; perhaps it had some value. He laid the box down in his boat, covering it to keep
prying eyes at bay. Wamar anchored two dozen yards off the beach, then
waded ashore to tell Gantuangko the news. The merchant was curious about
the find, but cautious. He instructed Opoy to take the box home after dark, so
as not to arouse the suspicions of his neighbors.

Gantuangko must have had an unsettling day. Before the sun was at its
zenith, the beach was swarming with Japanese troops looking for the survivors
and for any flotsam that may have floated ashore from the crash. Watching all
the activity, the two conspirators grew worried. But throughout the ordeal
Wamar's banca bobbed unmolested.

That night Opoy returned to his boat to retrieve the box, wary lest he be seen. He sneaked back to his house, met there by Pedro. They nervously pulled the case from the box. The moist, shiny leather glistened like dew in the faint light of their kerosene lantern. Eager fingers stabbed at the clasp. When the men first opened the portfolio they were singularly disappointed, for all they saw were half a dozen packets of wet papers, some quite thick, most with odd characters imprinted upon them—probably Japanese, thought Gantuangko. One packet was, of course, Z Plan. Leafing through the damp documents, they came across a blank batch. Ah-ha! they agreed, surely these must have secret writing on them. They gave thought to burning a candle beneath the papers, to see if perchance a message might appear. As they finished with each bundle they carefully laid the papers on the split-bamboo floor to dry. To the pair's delight the portfolio yielded still more artifacts. Out came a long, thin silk sack with a gold drawstring. It looked as if it might have been a sheath for an officer's samurai sword. Out came a cloth sack filled with condoms. This discovery made them chuckle. Finally, they discovered a pouch of red silk. The shopkeeper was amazed as he poured the contents into the palm of his hand. Small nuggets of gold![16] This, then, was Pedro Gantuangko's booty. But what to do with it all?

The next morning he took the still-damp leather portfolio to his mother's home. And after letting the documents dry for yet another day, he placed the packets and the little sacks into a large bag, put that into the box, and put that into a hole that he filled with dirt and covered with a layer of dried fronds.[17] Pedro Gantuangko then crossed his fingers, hoping the Japanese would soon end their search, leaving him alone with his treasure.

Fukudome's party had by now climbed deep into the hills above San Fernando, heading nearly due north toward Barrio Tabunan, Cushing's CAC headquarters. Injuries to the admiral and the other sailors slowed the group considerably; that and having to make long detours around areas under increasingly vicious sweeps by Japanese Army search patrols. Two days out, the column, led by Lieutenant Salvador Varga, stopped to rest near Caloctogan at a mountainside home, now a guerrilla aid station. There the wounds were tended by Cushing's personal doctor, Major Ramon S. Torralba. The physician was worried, for Fukudome's injuries had festered and the officer was running a high fever.[18] Torralba had few medicines at hand, but did manage to clean and dress the wounds, reducing the risk of further infection.

In Tokyo the Japanese High Command was growing frantic. On the day the medic treated the admiral, this dispatch was sent by the navy minister and the vice chief of the Navy General Staff:

```
THIS MESSAGE IS NOT TO BE DECRYPTED BY ANYONE EXCEPT ACTION
ADDRESSEES (AND IS TO BE REGARDED AS ABSOLUTELY SECRET).

ON MARCH 31 THE COMMANDER IN CHIEF COMBINED FLEET WITH A
CONSIDERABLE PORTION OF THE HEADQUARTERS STAFF LEFT PALAU BY
AIR; THEY WERE PROCEEDING TO DAVAO AND ARE MISSING; WE ARE
MAKING INVESTIGATIONS. IN ORDER TO INSURE THAT THIS AFFAIR
IS KEPT SECRET AND TO LIMIT THE NUMBER OF THOSE WHO KNOW IT
WE HAVE DECIDED TO WITHHOLD FULL DETAILS. THIS INCIDENT WILL
BE REFERRED TO AS THE "OTSU" INCIDENT.[19]
```

Not everyone who heard the secret communication heeded its warnings. Unbeknownst to the Japanese, the Americans had gone far beyond mere radio traffic analysis to gather information about enemy operations. Since before the war, Allied intelligence services had been decrypting and reading enemy messages regularly. Within hours of its transmission, a mostly complete decoding and translation of the OTSU signal sat at the Far East desk of the Office of Naval Intelligence in Washington, D.C. It was among dozens of messages intercepted that day by listening posts around the world. Indeed, this one bulletin was considered simply routine, at least at first. But as it wended its way through the intelligence chain, an officer at MacArthur's GHQ in Brisbane thought it important enough to provoke a query to guerrilla leaders in the Philippines.

On 5 April 1944, the Philippine Regional Section (PRS) of the Allied Intelligence Bureau asked for specific information about an enemy plane crash.[20] The message was in a sense a wish list of things pertaining mainly to the design and characteristics of whatever type of aircraft might have crashed. GHQ wanted five rounds of ammunition from each gun and all easily removable name plates. As a sort of afterthought the sender added, "And all documents on plane."

The Americans knew a plane had crashed, should have known a VIP was aboard, but early on failed to realize the import of the information they had snatched from their enemy.

The Japanese were wasting no time reorganizing in the wake of Koga's disappearance. On 4 April Admiral Shiro Takasu, CinC, Southwestern Area Fleet based on Singapore, signaled various units that he had orders to assume the duties of commander, Combined Fleet.[21] It was a temporary assignment for

Shiro, but the NGS was frantic to fill the void left by the disappearance of Koga Mineichi until either the admiral was found or a permanent successor could be named. Another message from Shiro soon followed, requesting Combined Fleet officers to proceed to Saipan immediately. Shiro wanted to meet with Koga's few surviving headquarters staff, to draw upon their experience as he moved forward with his new command.[22]

The pressure from on high quickly filtered down to the lowliest soldier on Cebu. Desperate to find Koga or Fukudome or, most especially, the missing Z Plan, the Japanese began a ruthless campaign to uncover information—*any* information—about the flying boat disasters. They turned their troops loose on the civilian population of eastern Cebu.

Reports of the brutal treatment soon reached CAC headquarters. People were being tortured. There was a rumor that a baby was bayoneted in front of its parents. An army unit, the Ohnisi Butai, under the command of Colonel Ohnisi Seiito, attacked guerrilla strongholds in the mountainous interior, in the process razing villages and killing hundreds of innocent Cebuanos.[23]

The Hapon made a concerted search in Pedro Gantuangko's barrio. Two hundred troops combed the beaches, the mangrove swamps, and the village. They called all the town's residents together at the chapel. While officers looked on, an interpreter asked the gathering if they had "seen a box."[24] All answered in the negative. The interpreter explained that the soldiers would search their houses. Then the army ransacked homes and shops but, of course, they found nothing. But the Japanese were certain the documents were in the vicinity. Experts from the navy had studied the tides and the currents. They even took boxes, similar to the one Pedro and Opoy had found, out to the crash site and let them float to shore. Always, the boxes floated to Barrio Perilos. The next day the soldiers returned and again searched the village.

Gantuangko grew gravely concerned. He wondered what the Hapon would do to him if they found the box buried by his house. The shopkeeper decided to rid himself of his burden. He contacted a local guerrilla. "I have something extremely important for you," he told the soldier, and handed him the bag containing the documents and the rest of the loot, including the gold. Pedro wanted to wash his hands of this frightening affair, which was rapidly escalating out of his control.[25]

The next morning the Hapon returned. They forced everyone to march back to the chapel. As the interrogations began, the soldiers let the people walk past a truckload of rice and cloth. They said this would be the reward to the villager who provided information about the missing box. But no one moved, no one said a word.

By now Gantuangko was fearful Opoy might crack under the pressure. Pedro gave his accomplice money, told him to flee from Cebu. Opoy left immediately, in such an agitated state that he did not take his family with him. Pedro still felt plagued. What if Opoy's wife or daughter talked, telling the Japanese what they knew or what they suspected? Desperately afraid, the merchant finally decided to flee, too.

He put his family into a banca and set sail for Bohol, just across the strait. Less than a mile out, Gantuangko was overtaken by a Japanese patrol boat. They hailed him, ordered him to drop sail, then pulled alongside. By now the man was completely terrified, for he had heard the Hapon had killed civilians trying to cross between the islands. Soldiers searched the family's meager baggage, then asked Pedro where he was going. "To Cebu City," he lied. "Why?" they asked. "We live there," he lied. To his relief they seemed satisfied with his answers and let him go. While hoisting the sail he turned to see Barrio Perilos aflame. As soon as the patrol boat was out of sight, Gantuangko made a beeline toward Bohol and, he hoped, sanctuary.[26]

BY MIDWEEK FUKUDOME'S caravan was well into the mountains of Cebu. The island was much different from its neighbor across Tañon Strait. Whereas Negros had vast forests, Cebu was essentially bare. Whereas Negros had broad alluvial planes, Cebu had narrow coastal margins. Whereas Negros had fields of rice, Cebu grew mostly corn. Both islands had mountainous spines, though the bigger island's were nearly twice as high as Cebu's. At its widest, cigar-shaped Cebu was barely twenty miles across, but averaged only ten miles. It was at the thickest part of the island, in the mountains directly behind Cebu City, that the Cebu Area Command had established its headquarters. There, from a tree-lined river valley, Lieutenant Colonel James M. Cushing commanded a force of several thousand underarmed but fiercely patriotic irregulars.

Cushing was known throughout the Philippines as a fearless fighter and an extraordinary leader of men. He was no prima donna. Jim Cushing ate with his men, slept with his men, fought side by side with them. His humble ways endeared him to the people of Cebu. To them he was a hero. Cushing gave Cebuanos hope at a time when all the world seemed hopeless.

How had this frail, slight man from New Mexico achieved such reverence? James M. Cushing liked to tell people that he was the seventh son of a seventh son, and by Irish tradition, he would tell them, that made him a lucky man.

His father, George Cushing, was born in Ireland, but immigrated to Canada in 1887 at age fifteen. Finding little work or opportunity north of the border, the elder Cushing headed for America's Wild West, where he heard it was possible to make a fortune mining for gold and silver. George worked hard, learned quickly, and after a few years became a successful mining engineer in northern Mexico. There he met a beautiful Spanish Mexican woman. They were married and soon settled down just outside El Paso, Texas.[27]

In the first decade of the century the Cushings sired nine children. Born about 1908, Jim was last. Growing up in the Southwest was a great adventure for the Cushing boys. When he was five, Jimmy sat with his father and brothers on a hill overlooking Juárez, Mexico, watching with fascination as the revolutionary Pancho Villa laid siege to the town. It was 25 November 1913, and the battle they witnessed was considered the most brutal of Villa's three attempts to take the city. A few years later, while Jimmy and his brother Walter were riding on a train near Chihuahua, gunmen attacked, forcing the boys to take cover. For three hours the Cushings sat beneath the wheels of a coach while a pitched battle between *federales* and *banditos* raged around them. It was the first time Jimmy had ever felt trapped in a situation over which he had no control. He found the experience unsettling, later saying that it "naturally left a lasting impression."[28]

When Jimmy was twelve, his father moved the family to Los Angeles. Southern California was booming in the early twenties, and George Cushing prospered. So did the boys. Walter excelled in sports at high school, winning a football scholarship to Notre Dame, there to play under Knute Rockne. In 1927 George Jr., the oldest son and also a mining engineer, headed for the Philippines, hoping to strike it rich. Brother Charles joined George two years later, taking a job as an engineer with the North Camarinas Mining Company. And Walter, failing as both a college student and an army flier, joined his brothers in 1932, just in time for the mining boom in northern Luzon.

The exotic tales of the three wandering siblings caught Jimmy's imagination. He did not want to follow in the footsteps of his brother Frank, who lived a placid life as a mine equipment salesman in Colorado. Jim wanted adventure, and he wanted to make his fortune in that wonderful place called the Philippines. In 1936 he finally made it, with help from Charles and Walter (George had died suddenly the year before). They found their youngest brother a job—

in mining, of course. Over the next few years Jim worked for various companies, mostly on Mindanao. He occasionally crossed paths with Courtney Whitney, a prominent Manila attorney who owned interests in several mines. Cushing was hardly a great success. "I was not setting the world on fire," he later wrote. But he loved the Philippines, loved its people, and felt at home, especially in the Visayas. In 1940 Jim married a Filipina from Baybay on Leyte, Wilfreda Tabando—known to all as "Fritzi."

When the war started, Cushing joined the army. He was assigned as a demolition engineer, leading the drive to destroy Cebu City before the Japanese invasion in April 1942. Following the fall of Bataan and discouraged about his military prospects on Cebu, Cushing was granted permission to transfer to Mindanao, where the fighting was still fierce. But with General Jonathon Wainwright's surrender of all USFIP forces on 9 May, Cushing decided to go into hiding, to wait for the return of the Americans. "That they wouldn't be back had never entered any of our thoughts for a minute. Being an American, one of the few remaining on the Island of Cebu, fate had decreed a different path for me."[29]

Almost immediately after the Japanese occupied Cebu, the guerrilla movement sprang up. It was not then an organized resistance, for there were far too many groups, far too many would-be leaders with diverging agendas. And some greedy Cebuanos saw guerrilladom as a way to profit from their fellow islanders. They called themselves guerrillas, but all they were were thugs and bandits, terrorizing the countryside. Early that summer local leaders, tired of the depredations, came to Cushing, begging him to get involved with the resistance. Cushing was, at first, reluctant. But the mayors and barrio chiefs pressed their point. Cushing gave in. He went to southern Cebu to attempt to organize disparate units into a cohesive resistance force, the Cebu Patriots. By the end of August Cushing had been largely successful. It was now time to join forces with the guerrillas in the North.

On 8 September 1942, Captain James M. Cushing arrived in the camp of Captain Harry Fenton, leader of the northern resistance. Fenton noted in his diary that Jim was a "sight for sore eyes. Had a nice talk."[30] Cushing and Fenton took an immediate liking to one another, though their personalities could not have been more different. After three days of conferences, the rebel leaders agreed to jointly govern a unified force, the Cebu Area Command. Cushing would handle military affairs: the fighting. Fenton would administrate the command: the red tape.

It was the ideal role for Harry Fenton. He had never been cut out to be a guerrilla. Born Aaron Feinstein in Schenectady, New York, he came to the Philippines with the U.S. Army's medical corps in 1938. He worked a stint at Sternberg General Hospital in Manila but, like Cushing and so many other Americans, was captivated by the Philippines. Feinstein purchased his discharge and moved to Cebu. There he adopted the name Fenton and went to work as a radio announcer for KZRC in Cebu City. His *Amateur Hour* became one of the most popular shows on the air in the months before Pearl Harbor. When war came the army pulled Fenton back into the service, commissioned him a first lieutenant, this time making him a censor. That duty did not last long. Fenton was innately suspicious of everything and everybody. Letters he censored tended to look like blobs of black ink with miserly few words in between. He was so painstaking in his efforts that it snarled the entire army censoring apparatus. He was soon returned to the air.[31]

Fenton's fame grew during the early days of the war because, day in, day out, Harry Fenton laid into the Japanese with lengthy diatribes. The people loved him. The enemy hated him. They swore to hunt him down and cut out his tongue.[32] They even put a price on his head. But that did not stop his vehemently anti-Japanese broadcasts. Only with the fall of Cebu was Harry Fenton knocked off the air. That day, 9 May, General Chynoweth, commander of the now much depleted Visaya Force, ordered Fenton not to surrender, knowing the Japanese would surely torture and kill the radio man. Fenton fled into the hills.

After packing up his headquarters in the South, Cushing moved into Fenton's camp near Tabunan on 15 September 1942. To celebrate, the pair promoted themselves to the rank of major. Within days Cushing was out in the field, leading the guerrillas in small skirmishes against the Japanese Army and usually winning. The new major's irregulars took on five truckloads of Japanese and Malayans at Balamban. The results were "quite satisfactory:" thirteen Hapon killed, three wounded, and a machine gun, a mortar, and some rifles captured.[33] It seemed an auspicious start to the rebel partnership.

But back at headquarters, Harry Fenton had started to go crazy.

Ten months of war had taken a toll on Fenton's mental health. His suspicious nature was changing to out-and-out paranoia. Anyone he suspected of having dealings with the Japanese became a target of his fears. On 21 September he wrote in his diary, "One Cebu Police executed after court martial." It was the first of hundreds of hangings he would order. The next day there was another, noted by a chilling entry: "One more Cebu Police executed. (Crawled 10 yards into bushes after thought to be dead.)" On the twenty-third, "1 more

Cebu Police executed." And on the twenty-fourth, "Rafael Labrador (spy) executed." Four days before Christmas 1942, Harry Fenton confided to his journal, "No. 66 hung. He was the chief of police of Liloan."[34]

Despite the calming influence of Jim Cushing, Harry Fenton's phobias began to take over his life. He trusted no one outside his immediate circle of officers and bodyguards. It became impossible for a mere Cebuano even to approach him. Fenton lived in constant fear of assassination (though in the early days there was never a serious threat); he even believed people had tried to poison him.[35] When the Silliman University physics professor Henry Roy Bell arrived on a fact-finding mission from Major Villamor in early 1943, Bell was disarmed by Fenton's men and treated with great suspicion. The professor was horrified when he saw a well-constructed gallows at the center of the compound. Bell was told that the CAC had "already finished most of the mayors."[36] Lieutenant James Halkyard met with Fenton shortly after Bell's visit. The cocommander showed him a list of four hundred persons he had blacklisted. Halkyard noted that Fenton had already checked off—executed—more than half the names. And so the hangings continued. A teacher. A cook. A truck driver. A legislator. A "lady spy."

Cushing missed most of the internecine bloodbath. He was off fighting the Japanese in daring raids, like the one in late November 1942 against the Japanese garrison at Toledo on the island's western coast. The rebels planned only to harass the hundred or so troops dug in at the Central School. Cushing had hoped to spring a surprise attack, but as his men moved up the trails in the predawn darkness, dogs alerted the enemy to their presence. In response, the Japanese sent out patrols. When dawn broke there was a brief, bloody firefight between the Hapon and C Company. The enemy began to use mortars in an attempt to punch holes in the rebels' lines. Jim Cushing, watching the progress of the attack beside a large mango tree, suddenly moved forward to a closer vantage point. No sooner had he settled than a mortar shell exploded in the very foxhole he had just occupied, killing two guerrillas.[37] The luck of the seventh son had held again. After several hours of sporadic shooting, Cushing withdrew his men, claiming victory in this nameless little battle. Back in the safety of the hills, the commander uncharacteristically saluted his men with a brief but rousing speech.[38] The harassment of the Toledo garrison was one of many skirmishes that first autumn of war—clashes that for days at a time kept Major Cushing away from Major Fenton's wanton ruthlessness.

Jim Cushing was certainly aware of Fenton's executions and, early on, even condoned them. But there was a rising feeling among Cebuanos that Harry Fenton had become evil incarnate. As Fenton's favor fell, Cushing's soared. His soldiers considered him a great leader, his people considered him a savior. His own status began to approach myth. He routed corruption in the ranks of the guerrillas, he led his ragtag bands against superior Japanese forces, he found ways and means to feed the people. Through all this, curiously, James Cushing found himself able to overlook the excesses of his cocommander. After all, hadn't he left administration to Fenton, and weren't courts-martial an administrative function? Cushing later wrote, "Harry Fenton was a peculiar fellow in many ways. [He] did not have the happy faculty of being able to vent his spleen with a gun against the Japs. He did not care for combat. The disappointments of the first year of war, his naturally suspicious nature, plus the constant moving about and never knowing from one day to the next when he would be shot from ambush, all combined to impair his mind to such an extent that he was considered dangerous to the [guerrilla] movement."[39] Nevertheless, Jim Cushing had the blood of Cebu on his hands, too. When Roy Bell departed from Tabunan, cocommander Cushing left him with these words: "We've been rather rough in our dealings with many people, but Villamor must try to understand why." Rather than explain himself, Cushing poked his glasses and whispered to the professor with a hint of guilt in his soft voice, "But I cannot go on like this much longer."[40]

Just weeks later, a rift developed between the commanders. They argued about printing emergency money to pay for food and supplies for their troops. Cushing voted in favor, Fenton against. Cushing wanted closer ties with resistance movements on other islands; Fenton did not. Once Fenton pulled a gun on Cushing and put it to his neck, threatening to pull the trigger. The threat arose over the promotion of both men to lieutenant colonel, an otherwise auspicious event. Not long after, the Japanese made a "punitive expedition" against CAC headquarters at Barrio Tabunan in the hills above Cebu City. The cocommanders decided then to separate. Fenton took his men to Maslog, Cushing seven miles distant, to Masurela. Fenton's reign of terror continued unchecked. He had by now alienated most of the civilians on Cebu, and his misdeeds were beginning to erode the support of his officers and men.[41]

In late June 1943 a Japanese patrol surprised Fenton's camp. He barely escaped, but his Filipina wife, Betty, and his youngest son, David, were captured. On 17 July the Japanese-controlled newspaper in Cebu City published a "plea" from Mrs. Fenton for her husband to surrender.[42] The taking of his family seemed to push Fenton over the edge. He was angry that the enemy would use his wife to force his capitulation. He grew even more bitter and began to act even more irrationally. The number of executions rose. But the act that precipitated Fenton's demise was his rape of a young housemaid—an act that horrified even his most loyal supporters.

Some weeks later, after Cushing had left for the conference with Major Villamor on Negros, two groups of guerrillas went searching for Fenton, now in hiding. With the help of a former bodyguard, they found him in an isolated nipa hut and arrested him.[43]

The guerrillas were shocked by what they found inside his shack. Lying on the bed was a fourteen-year-old girl, ordered by Fenton to sleep with him. And on the floor was a suitcase stuffed with more than a hundred thousand dollars. The men turned to Fenton, anger welling deep within them. One set the American's beard aflame. Another kicked Fenton in the face until the prisoner was covered in blood.

Lieutenant Colonel Ricaredo Estrella, Cushing's chief of staff and hand-picked successor, took charge of the captive. Estrella despised Fenton, suspecting him of raping his wife. He gathered together all the battalion commanders. In their presence he charged Harry Fenton with violating the Articles of War. A kangaroo-style court-martial followed, there in the jungles of Cebu. And Aaron Feinstein, a.k.a. Harry Fenton, was found guilty as charged and sentenced to death by firing squad.

The condemned asked that a note be passed to his cocommander: "I am sure this is all a misunderstanding. Good luck to you. Harry."

On 1 September 1943, Fenton was led before his executioners. "What is your last wish?" asked Captain Pedro Lopez, commander of the squad. "I'd like to die with a cigar in my mouth." The request was granted. "Give me a handkerchief to cover my eyes." And it was so. "And hit me right here," said Fenton, motioning to his left breast. Lopez nodded, then called out, "Ready . . . aim . . ."[44]

DURING THE MUTINY ON CEBU, Jim Cushing had been on neighboring Negros meeting with Villamor, pleading for official recognition of the Cebu Area Command by General MacArthur. Cushing and the young Filipino war hero became great friends in the weeks they spent together.

While awaiting word from GHQ, Cushing told Villamor a little about his life. His brother Walter also had been a guerrilla leader—up north, on Luzon.

Jim knew little about his brother's exploits, only that he had been killed in an ambush in September 1942. His brother Charley . . . he was not cut from the same cloth as Walter. Charley had done some fighting on Luzon, but when his wife was captured by the Japanese and threatened with death, he turned himself in. Charley shared ink with Betty Fenton in the 17 July issue of the Cebu newspaper. The dutiful brother, like the dutiful wife, pleaded for the men to surrender, to come down out of the hills and live a peaceful life. Jim Cushing was amused by the enemy's effort. "My brother does not mean what he writes. He always called me Jimmy—here he writes Dear James. And he was always Charley to us—here he signs Charles."[45]

Villamor believed in what Jim Cushing was trying to accomplish on Cebu— uniting disparate rebel groups and harassing the enemy at the same time. Villamor did his best to present Cushing's case to GHQ, but he was never able to get a commitment from Brisbane. It was frustrating for both men. When Cushing returned to Cebu in early October, three American ex-POWs in tow (Russell Snell, Jim Dyer, and Irving Joseph), he discovered what had happened to Fenton in his absence. And he was furious. The now sole commander of the Cebu Area Command ordered the arrest of Lieutenant Colonel Ricaredo Estrella. While it is true that before Cushing went to Negros he had given his chief of staff verbal orders to arrest Fenton if conditions warranted, the leader never intended that his former partner be tried or executed in his absence. Cushing had further reason to deal quickly with Estrella, for there was evidence that the guerrilla had made a pact to deliver his commanding officer to the Japanese Army for thirty thousand dollars.[46] After a brief but official court-martial, the rogue officer was found guilty. A firing squad, led by Cushing himself, carried out the sentence.[47]

Jim Cushing was now on his own. Shaken by the events of that autumn, he was seriously ill for two months, confined to quarters by Dr. Torralba. Cushing's staff officers were puzzled by their leader's erratic behavior; it worried them deeply.[48] He was once a vital man, but the thirty-six-year-old's health had deteriorated after two years in the hills. At various times Cushing had been felled by malaria, dysentery, and other tropical diseases. And all the fighting and infighting had taken a toll on his psyche. In a desultory funk, the colonel stayed in his hut for days on end. But as Thanksgiving rolled around, Jim Cushing seemed to have recovered his old exuberant self. His body had healed, his mind too. It was now time, he thought, to find out just where he stood with this guerrilla force. He boldly called a conference of all his battalion commanders. They met the first week of December 1943, at Tabunan.

As the first order of business, Cushing reported on his mission to Villamor. Cushing told the assembly that differences with other island commands had been "straightened out." He told them he had tried to win recognition for the CAC but succeeded only in getting Cebu's position "definitely understood" by SWPA GHQ. The CO enumerated CAC's new and officially approved duties: "Carry out Intelligence Operations; carry out Passive Resistance against the enemy; protect the civilians in Cebu." Some officers grumbled, for the directive did not sound like a charge to battle the Hapon. But all conferees were delighted to hear that Villamor had given the Cebu guerrillas a portable radio transmitter that would enable them to communicate with other rebel groups. And finally, Cushing announced that he had been confirmed by Villamor as the CAC commander. The eighteen officers present "were enthusiastically unanimous" in approving Cushing's leadership.

The mutiny was, as expected, a touchy point. The secretary's report of the three-day meeting euphemistically summarized: "Several irregularities have been committed by some of our good officers during the last four months. With the arrest of some of our ranking officers, the smooth course of administration has been quite disturbed."[49]

When the meeting ended on 4 December, Lieutenant Colonel James M. Cushing was the undisputed leader of the Cebu Area Command. He now had a mandate to clear the decks. In the final month of the year the colonel worked tirelessly at reorganizing the resistance, always with the aim of winning recognition from MacArthur—for that meant more arms, more money, more medicine for the people. It meant, in the long run, a far, far better chance of defeating the Hapon.

By the beginning of 1944 Cushing had consolidated the resistance forces on the island and was on the verge of official approval. Jim Cushing did not know it then, but he had an ardent supporter at GHQ in Brisbane—Colonel Courtney Whitney, the chief of the Philippine Regional Section of the Allied Intelligence Bureau. A former Manila lawyer, friend, and business associate of MacArthur and now a full colonel, Whitney was close to the general, who had an abiding interest in all activities in the islands. It was Whitney's job to keep his boss thoroughly informed through the intermediary of MacArthur's longtime chief of staff, Lieutenant General Richard K. Sutherland.

Before MacArthur could approve recognition of the Cebu Area Command, he needed assurances that Jim Cushing was the right man to lead the unit, especially after the bloody reputation Fenton had earned the Cebu guerrillas. The PRS put together an assessment of Cushing from comments made by men who had worked or fought with him. From Jesus Villamor came this appraisal:

[He possesses] a dual personality—one cold, hard and unforgiving; the other, soft, sentimental, almost childish. Easily blows up but just as quickly repents. Cusses hard but is fond of quoting the "Good Book." Speaks English with a slight accent. Pronounces the suffix "ed" distinctly, as "attack-ed." Hates the Japs as much as he loves his "Cebu patriots" of whom he refers with tear filled eyes. Courageous. Leads men in combat. All Cebu is behind him. All the Japs are after him.[50]

Others had glowing remarks: "They can't make a medal big enough to fit Cushing." "Practically worshiped by the soldiers." "Too brave for his own good." Jim Cushing was not without his detractors. One American officer who had known him for years said "he was little more than a beachcomber in prewar days."[51]

Colonel Whitney then added his own estimate. Whitney had known Cushing and his brothers, Walter and Charles, before the war. He wrote of James:

Cushing is an unusual study in himself. Showing little strength in civil life, now badly crippled by arthritis and committed to the use of crutches most of the time, his fighting spirit has dominated Cebu resistance since the surrender and his leadership over a following badly harassed by consistently superior enemy forces is remarkable. I believe he and his followers merit all assistance reasonably possible.[52]

Whitney's view prevailed. In a radio message to Cebu on 22 January 1944, General MacArthur said:

```
WITH PROFOUND SATISFACTION I HAVE NOTED THE GALLANT STRUGGLE
OF THE OFFICERS AND MEN UNDER YOUR LEADERSHIP WHO, REFUSING
TO SURRENDER, HAVE SUSTAINED A RESOLUTE AND DETERMINED
RESISTANCE AGAINST SUPERIOR ENEMY FORCES ON THE ISLAND OF
CEBU. DESIRING TO RECOGNIZE THAT RESISTANCE AND GIVE IT SUCH
SUPPORT AS IS NOW WITHIN MY POWER, I HAVE CREATED THE CEBU
AREA COMMAND AND HAVE APPOINTED YOU AS THE COMMANDER.[53]
```

Cushing and his followers were overjoyed—indeed, inspired—by the news. When the USS *Narwhal* called at Balatong Point in southwestern Negros in

February, a portion of her cargo of ammunition, money, medicine, and radios was destined for the CAC. Cushing had received a small ATR-4A teleradio from Villamor in mid-1943. The breadbox-size set was only capable of reaching surrounding islands, so when Cushing needed to communicate with MacArthur, Abcede or Andrews on Negros, or Fertig on Mindanao, had to relay his messages. Part of *Narwhal's* cargo was a powerful radio that would enable Cushing to reach Australia directly, and a set of codes with which to communicate securely.

The first CAC radio transmission to Australia was on 28 March. It was a mundane composition about encoding/decoding procedures. On the day the flying boats crashed, Cushing sent out two dispatches. One complained about items missing from his *Narwhal* shipment and requested direct submarine landings on Cebu in the future. The other was a report about a skirmish between CAC troops and the Philippine Bureau of Constabulary in Cebu City.[54] It was sleepy stuff, just the sort of information MacArthur's GHQ was accustomed to receiving.

But that all changed on 8 April.

# CHAPTER 10

## *Terms of Exchange*

RUNNERS CAME INTO Cushing's camp that day with the electrifying news that the Volunteer Guards had captives from a crashed seaplane in tow and would arrive with them shortly. An excited Cushing composed a message to SWPA:

```
NR 7                                    8 APRIL 1944
WE HAVE TEN JAPANESE PRISONERS NOW EN ROUTE TO OUR
HEADQUARTERS. PLEASE ADVISE ACTION TO BE TAKEN. CONSTANT
ENEMY PRESSURE MAKES THIS SITUATION VERY PRECARIOUS. FURTHER
INFORMATION FROM PRISONERS WILL FOLLOW.
```

Reaction at the PRS was subdued when the dispatch was delivered early on the ninth. Ten prisoners seemed no big deal; they were probably just privates and corporals and maybe a sergeant or two. When Colonel Whitney received Cushing's NR7 he wrote a memo for the high command:

Any of our other guerrilla leaders would have decided this problem with 10 bullets without reference to this Headquarters. CUSHING has, however, before demonstrated a more disciplined regard for the will of higher authority. I believe you will find in CUSHING an able but still subordinate fighter and leader in whom you can fully depend to discharge his mission. At the crucial time this is what you will require.[1]

Whitney then sent a message back to Cebu, telling the guerrilla chief that the "disposition of prisoners must be in accord with our rules of land warfare," and offering to facilitate the removal of the captives to another island if necessary.[2]

As usual, Whitney signed the message "MacArthur."

Before the PRS response reached Cushing, Admiral Fukudome's party reached the rebel camp. Because of the Japanese Army's drive to locate the missing men, the CAC's regular headquarters at Barrio Tabunan had been abandoned, and a new one established near Kamungayan, just over Tupas Ridge. The two injured senior officers, Fukudome and Yamamoto, and one of the enlisted men were immediately admitted to the primitive base hospital under the care of Dr. Torralba.

Some hours later Cushing arrived at the new camp with his staff. His men brought all ten prisoners to a thatched hut for the colonel's inspection. Dropping to their knees, the Japanese lined themselves up in descending rank. Two badly burned men crawled to their positions.

The CAC commander eyed his captives for a few moments. Jim Cushing hated the Japanese. He knew what the Hapon soldiers were doing to the civilians he was sworn to protect. But he nevertheless treated his prisoners with respect. He turned to his own men. "Anybody here speak Japanese?" Salvador "Boy" Segura stepped forward. "Tell them to sit down," said the guerrilla. Boy gave the order, and all the prisoners shifted.[3]

In a quiet manner Cushing began to ask questions of the men before him. He knew they came from the crashed seaplane. He wanted to know who they were and what their business was. The spokesman for the Japanese was Commander Yamamoto Yuji, who spoke passable English. Yamamoto answered Cushing's questions evasively and none too accurately. The guerrilla chief was astonished to learn that one of his prisoners—the fat, bald one who reminded his men of the Buddha statues they used to see for sale at the department store in Cebu City—was no mere Japanese soldier, but a man admitting to be a flag officer.[4] Cushing knew this news would delight Brisbane. From the information he gathered, the colonel composed a message to MacArthur:

```
NR8                                   9 APRIL 1944
REFERENCE TEN PRISONERS—THEY CAME FROM FOUR-MOTORED PLANE
WHICH CRASHED OFF SAN FERNANDO AT TWO O'CLOCK IN THE MORNING
1ST APRIL. THEIR NAMES:
GENERAL TWANI FUROMEI,    COMMANDING OFFICER OF LAND
                          AND SEA FORCES IN MACASSAR
YOJI YAMAMOTO, MARINE OFFICER BOUND FOR MACASSAR
YASUKI YAMAGATA
MATSUTARE OKANURA, AVIATOR
USHIKISA HMANISHI
KEIS OKUJESIMI, AERONAUTICAL ENGINEER
TOMIDO OLASOGI, OPERATOR
TUSHIDO OKADA, ENGINEER
MASATUSI YUSITU, OPERATOR
TAKASHI TANIKA, ENGINEER.
```

Cushing's dispatch continued with a list of items removed from the prisoners—nothing of import—and concluded with a warning that due to the injuries of some of the captives and to the uncertain situation in the hills, additional information might be delayed.[5]

All four parts of Cushing's NR8 were received by SWPA at six o'clock on the morning of 10 April. Brisbane was indeed delighted. In fact, as the news spread, terrific excitement coursed through the corridors at the PRS, AIB, and upward to GHQ. Capturing Japanese general officers was not a common occurrence. GHQ decided it must act quickly to get the prisoners off Cebu and down to Australia. Colonel Whitney's recommendation to MacArthur is a model of restraint: "In view of the nature of the prisoners, does the C in C desire any special dispositions made?"

Yes indeed! So Army consulted Navy about a means of transporting the now important prisoners. The Seventh Fleet's intelligence officer, Captain Arthur H. McCollum, was queried about a submarine pickup on Cebu. He memoed back the next day, 11 April, that the navy was checking with Admiral Ralph Waldo Christie, commander of submarines, Seventh Fleet, about the availability of a sub. His response noted that navigational hazards would make a pickup on Cebu "extremely doubtful." He suggested that Cushing transfer his prisoners to guerrillas on neighboring Bohol, where an evacuation would be safer.[6]

When Admiral Christie received McCollum's cable he asked his staff to pinpoint the American submarine nearest Cebu. He was pleased with the name they gave him. It seemed that the USS *Haddo* was on patrol near the Japanese-held island of Tawi-Tawi at the very southern tip of the Philippine archipelago. That put the sub just a few hundred miles south of Cushing. Christie was delighted that it was *Haddo,* for the boat was captained by Lieutenant Commander Chester William Nimitz Jr., son of CincPac. What a publicity coup to have Admiral Nimitz's son bring in a high-ranking Japanese officer—perhaps even Admiral Koga himself!

Late on 11 April, Christie sent Nimitz Jr. an order to head north toward the Visayas, there to stand by for a special mission.[7]

While preparations were being made to pick up the VIPs, Brisbane received a message from a desperate Cushing, a relay by Andrews on Negros of a *two-day-old* dispatch:

```
NR11                                    9 APRIL 1944
JAP CAPTIVES FROM PALAU. ENEMY AWARE THEIR PRESENCE HERE. WE
ARE CATCHING HELL. WE ARE STAGING FAKE REMOVAL FROM THIS
```

```
ISLAND TO WITHDRAW PRESSURE, WHILE AWAITING YOUR FURTHER
ORDERS. WE WILL MAKE EVERY ATTEMPT TO HOLD THE JAPANESE
GENERAL AND NEXT RANKING OFFICER.8
```

Whitney could see that the situation on Cebu was rapidly deteriorating. He worked at top speed to send a reply to Cushing's NR11. He had his communications staff hold open the circuit to Fertig, ready to relay an urgent message to Cebu. At two o'clock in the afternoon Whitney wired:

```
[SWPA] NR5                              11 APRIL 1944
DESIRE IF POSSIBLE EVACUATION TO THIS HEADQUARTERS AT
EARLIEST OPPORTUNITY OF THE SENIOR PRISONERS, SELECTED IN
ACCORD WITH RELATIVE IMPORTANCE. NORTHEAST COAST OF CEBU IS
NAVIGATIONALLY IMPOSSIBLE. CAN YOU SEND THEM UNDER SAFE
CONDUCT TO A RENDEZVOUS SITE SOUTHERN BOHOL OR SOUTHERN
NEGROS. HOW SOON COULD PARTY BE AT SITE. PARTY BELIEVED OF
UTMOST IMPORTANCE BE ALERT TO USE OF ASSUMED NAMES AND RANKS
UNDER WHICH SENIOR PRISONER MAY POSE AS JUNIOR. DO ALL
POSSIBLE TO KEEP THEM SAFE FOR EVACUATION AND PREVENT
RECAPTURE9 [underscoring in original].
```

Throughout the remainder of the eleventh and into the twelvth SWPA GHQ was on pins and needles awaiting further word from Colonel Cushing. They could not have imagined what was taking place—what *had already* taken place—on Cebu. At six-thirty on the evening of the twelfth of April an urgent message from Jim Cushing was delivered to Colonel Whitney. The PRS chief scanned it quickly. It was brief, to the point, and it carried devastating news:

```
NR12                                    9 APRIL 1944
JAP PRISONERS TOO HOT FOR US TO HOLD. DUE TO NUMBER OF
CIVILIANS BEING KILLED, I MADE TERMS THAT CIVILIANS ARE NOT
TO BE MOLESTED IN FUTURE, IN EXCHANGE FOR THE PRISONERS.10
```

In exchange for the prisoners? Cushing made terms with the enemy and exchanged his prisoners! Whitney was crushed. He reread the signal, trying to understand why the guerrilla felt compelled to release his captives. Whitney could only guess what drove Cushing to this desperate measure. Early the next morning, 13 April, with a heavy heart and with some trepidation, Colonel Courtney Whitney sent the cable to Chief of Staff Sutherland.

Sutherland first read Whitney's memo accompanying the dispatch, "I regret the result reflected in attached message, but feel that CUSHING did all he could in the circumstances."[11] And when the chief of staff read Cebu's NR12, he exploded. How could an officer of the United States Army do such a thing, make terms with the enemy? In the heat of the moment he of course forgot his own role in the abandonment of USAFFE troops on Bataan and Corregidor and other unvalorous acts committed by MacArthur's command in the first months of the war. No, in Sutherland's eyes Lieutenant Colonel James M. Cushing was now nothing less than a traitor.

BUT SUTHERLAND WAS NOT then aware that four days had passed since James Cushing was forced to make his own decision about how to handle the crisis on Cebu. Colonel Ohnisi's troops were on a rampage. Every hour runners came into camp with news about new attacks, new atrocities. Every hour reports put the Hapon closer to Tupas Ridge and the makeshift prison.

The evening the prisoners arrived—the evening of Saturday, the eighth—had been an almost pleasant interlude for Cushing and his captives. The guerrilla spent some time chatting with "General Furomei." At first Commander Yamamoto translated, but soon the "general" joined the conversation, speaking fluent English. Fukudome never told Cushing who he really was; throughout their ordeal the colonel referred to him as the "general." But Cushing suspected his prisoner was not who he said he was. The two men enjoyed talking about things other than war. Cushing had been to Japan several times, had Japanese friends, so they talked about that. Jim introduced Fritzi to the "general." She offered him some wafers, made him some coffee. Fukudome was much touched by her kindness. Jim even introduced his two dogs, the little mutt USAFFE and Senta, the Great Dane. The Japanese were fed rice from the CAC's small stocks, and Dr. Torralba hovered, tending the injured.

Things got really hot on the ninth of April, which was to become a very long day on Cebu. Troops were closing in on the headquarters, with certain knowledge that Cushing held the prisoners. That is when he radioed his NR11, announcing the "fake removal." But, of course, the guerrilla colonel had no idea it would not reach GHQ for two days. For reasons that would never be clear, Fertig's station on Mindanao held up relaying transmission of this and other crucial signals until the twelfth.

At about midday Cushing ordered his camp abandoned. Guerrillas pulled up telephone wires, gathered papers, then swept the ground with palm leaves in an effort to hide their tracks. The base hospital was evacuated across the broad ravine to Kamungayan, and with it the ten prisoners. Fritzi Cushing and the camp cook were sent off to a secure cave hideout. Late that afternoon two columns of enemy troops—hundreds of Hapon—approached the ridges. Cushing had only twenty-five soldiers. He deployed them carefully. Suddenly firing rang out, echoing across the hills. The colonel withdrew most of his men, then he and the Dane Senta led them through a valley trail in full view of the Japanese. Machine-gun fire felled two, including a nurse. Cushing returned fire with his submachine gun, but the bullets were wasted. Another rebel fell, hit in the head.

Overhead a Japanese floatplane circled slowly, looking for the guerrillas. When the pilot spotted movement, he strafed and dropped antipersonnel bombs. When the missiles detonated they spewed molten metal. At that moment Jim Cushing somehow mustered the courage to overcome his fear of attacking planes, his fear of losing control. For once he was able to carry on as if being bombed and strafed were all in a day's work. Late in the day the Cebuano rebels regrouped beneath a cool waterfall near Met-ul. After a brief rest, Cushing led his soldiers up a steep rock face toward Masurela, then down the other side of the ridge to Kamungayan. Here the beleaguered guerrilla established his final line of defense, knowing it would be impossible to hold.[12]

At Kamungayan they found their prisoners, closely guarded in a nipa hut. There, too, Cushing was handed a report that Colonel Ohnisi's men had rounded up more than a hundred Filipinos at gunpoint. These people they intended to use as hostages to force the return of the ten captives. Cushing was unsure what to do. He kept asking his radioman if he had heard from GHQ. "Was General MacArthur too busy to reply?" he asked plaintively. He was not aware that his messages lay unrelayed by Fertig, that it would be days before SWPA received them. Another report came in— five more columns of Japanese soldiers were marching toward Tupas. It was grim news. As they marched they left behind burned houses and dead Cebuanos. Cushing could take it no longer. He could not stand by idly while his people were slaughtered. No prisoners were worth the life of a single civilian.[13]

As evening fell on the ninth, the guerrilla leader went to Fukudome. He told the "general" he planned to make terms with Colonel Ohnisi. Jim Cushing had never had to make a tougher decision in his life. Doing it made him feel sick, tied knots in his stomach, and he knew GHQ would condemn him for the choice he made. But Cushing felt he now had no option.

It was a simple offer: If Ohnisi would stop harming the islanders, he could have the missing airmen.

Fukudome offered to write to the army leader. A note was drafted:

1. For your information we have in custody from a fallen plane Marine General FUROMEI, Lieut. YAMAMOTO, Lt. OKAMRA, Lt. YAMANATA, and six (6) sailors.

2. It is our desire to return to you General FUROMEI on condition that your soldiers will stop the killing of innocent civilians. Our civilian population is innocent of any crime and must be given consideration.

> JAMES M. CUSHING
> Lieut-Colonel, Inf.
> Commanding[14]

Captain Manuel Segura wrote out a fair copy, then Commander Yamamoto translated a Japanese version. Cushing asked for volunteers to take the messages to the Japanese. Corporals Herminio Cerna and Numeriano Padayao Teves stepped forward. Carrying a white flag, the Filipinos, accompanied by two of their prisoners, marched to the enemy's front lines. A couple of hours later the men returned, answer in hand:

I understand what you meant in your letter. Our porpose [sic] of operation this time is to rescue the Japanese Navy Officers that had crashed.

I hereby promise you that our Japanese Forces will guarantee without fail that lives and properities [sic] of your men and civilians in case you will set them free to our hand.

> Sincerely Yours,
> Seiiti Ohnisi
> Lt. Col. Japanese Forces[15]

Still hoping to get some reply from MacArthur, Cushing decided to try a stalling tactic. He sent his emissaries back to the Japanese with modified terms: he would turn over four of the prisoners now; the others in a few days, arguing that they were too injured to travel.

Ohnisi's reply was curt: "All or no one at all."[16]

Cushing went to Fukudome. He wanted "General Furomei" to give his personal assurance that the killing and pillaging would stop. The veteran officer agreed. The American sent one last note to his enemy counterpart:

In keeping with our agreement we are sending the Japanese Navy Officers and other sailors which crashed and are now in our hands.

They will leave here at daylight as it is too difficult for them to travel at night.[17]

And his adversary replied:

I have received your letter. The measure taken by you is a warrior like and an admirable action.

I expect to see you again in the battle field some day.

Your friend
Seiiti Ohnisi[18]

That night, his spirit quashed by the day's events, Cushing wired his NR12 to GHQ, "JAP PRISONERS TOO HOT FOR US TO HOLD.... I MADE TERMS..."

At noon the next day, Monday, 10 April 1944, Lieutenant Pedro Villareal led a small party down a dry riverbed toward the Japanese. Fukudome was carried in a chair upon the shoulders of guerrillas. The nine others walked. When the band reached a mango tree, standing prominent and alone on an otherwise bare slope, they stopped. A group of about fifty Japanese soldiers cautiously approached. Cushing watched the event through binoculars, watched as the soldiers bowed low in the presence of Fukudome, shook hands with Villareal, then turned to climb the ridges and return toward Cebu City.

When Villareal returned to Cushing, he brought two messages. One, from Colonel Ohnisi, offered thanks for treating the prisoners "kindly." The second was from the "general." "He extended his best regards to you and men." And so the affair came to a close.

When Cushing got back to his own camp he learned there still had been no reply to any of his transmissions from the day before. But the next day, the eleventh, came a dispatch that reduced him to despair. It was SWPA NR5, and it closed:

Letter from Cushing to Lieutenant Colonel Seiiti Onishi regarding the return of the Japanese prisoners held by the Cebu guerrillas.
(Manuel Segura Collection)

"DO ALL POSSIBLE TO KEEP [PRISONERS] SAFE FOR EVACUATION AND PRE-VENT RECAPTURE."

He had tried. God knows he had tried. But those enemy sailors were nobodies. It was his people who mattered. Jim Cushing cried that night.

CHIEF OF STAFF SUTHERLAND was oblivious to all that had transpired in the mountains of Cebu when he read Cushing's NR11 on the morning of 13 April and he would not be consoled. Sutherland directed Whitney to send this message to the beleaguered colonel:

> Your action in releasing important prisoners after negotiation with the enemy is most reprehensible and leads me to doubt your judgment and efficiency. You are hereby discharged from your functions as Commander of the 7th [*sic*] Military District.

Then, to rub salt in the wound, Sutherland asked that a second signal be sent as a warning to the other guerrilla commanders in the Philippines:

> The Commander of the 7th Military District [*sic, CAC*] captured a number of important prisoners and was directed to make every effort to remove them to a place of safety. Captain [*sic*] Cushing, however, after negotiation with the enemy, released the prisoners. He has therefore been discharged from his functions as commander of the 7th Military District [*sic*].[19]

Lieutenant Colonel James M. Cushing was about to be fired by a toady general. And like all other radio dispatches sent to the islands, both of these would carry the weighty signature "MacArthur."

Back at his office, Whitney screeched at his staff, "Cushing couldn't *help* it! He couldn't help it! It meant the blood of thousands of helpless Filipinos on his hands." The PRS chief marched off to see General Sutherland. He returned within the hour, announcing to his staff that Sutherland had given him "twenty-four hours to prepare a defense" for the hapless Cushing. He ordered everyone out, then spent the night working on his brief.[20]

While Whitney labored, the USS *Haddo* continued to loiter in the Sulu Sea, awaiting further instructions. Late that evening Comsubs radioed a message releasing the boat from her special mission, directing her to return home to Fremantle. Lieutenant Commander Nimitz remained clueless about the diversion; he was never told why his boat had been ordered north.

The next morning, the fourteenth, Colonel Courtney Whitney presented Lieutenant General Richard Sutherland with a two-page memo outlining the entire Cushing situation as he had reconstructed it.

The attorney summarized all the radio messages at hand, including another that had come in overnight. He told the chief of staff that the "release was effected on 9 April or two days before our message of instructions re prisoners disposition. This action was, as a consequence, not in disregard of specific instructions."[21] Here was Whitney at his lawyerly best, arguing that his client had not yet received orders to hold the prisoners, so had disobeyed nothing.

Whitney took pains to point out that Fertig's WAT had delayed retransmission of the crucial messages from Cebu to Brisbane. He told Sutherland he was having the reasons for the holdup investigated.[22]

The colonel concluded:

> CUSHING's action was taken in the interest of the people. It will probably draw them closer to his leadership. If he is discharged as Area Commander he would revert to the position previously held (guerrilla chieftain) and it would be impossible for this Headquarters to exercise any measure of control over him or coordinate his actions or those of other forces. It would be impossible furthermore to establish any other leadership over the people, who would look upon CUSHING's discharge as a penalty for serving their immediate interests.[23]

Whitney closed his argument: "I strongly recommend that no action be taken."

Counselor Whitney's plea won the day. Sutherland relented. The matter was dropped. As far as the PRS and GHQ were concerned, the "Koga Affair" was closed. But U.S. intelligence analysts had missed telltale signs that something even bigger loomed just ahead.

Cushing's next message, arriving early on the fourteenth, piqued Brisbane's interest, though not as much as it should have. NR13 ended with this:

> FROM PRISONERS WE STILL HAVE PAPERS AND FIELD ORDERS WHICH
> WE ARE SENDING TO COL. ANDREWS' HEADQUARTERS SOUTHERN NEGROS
> AND SHOULD ARRIVE THERE IN APPROXIMATELY TWO WEEKS.[24]

Whitney's memo simply noted that the "documents in question will be available for dispatch by ABCEDE on supply trip of NARWHAL about the end of May unless desired earlier by G-2." MacArthur's G-2 (chief of the intelligence section), General Charles A. Willoughby, added a note as the memorandum crossed his desk the next day: "Description of documents indicates they . . . may be of extreme value. Suggest they be brought here at earliest opportunity."[25]

But then nothing happened for three weeks.

IT HAS NEVER BEEN CLEAR exactly when Colonel Cushing received Pedro Gantuangko's sack filled with the Z Plan. It might have arrived by runner, reaching headquarters even before the prisoners. In that case, Cushing never revealed its presence to Fukudome, and it is likely that Fukudome never realized the guerrillas had it. Because of all the confusion around the ninth of April, Cushing may not have received the sack until after the captives were exchanged. Whatever the case, by 13 April Cushing had the documents and was very curious about them.

One of his men was able to read Chinese characters. He took a shot at reading the Japanese variants but could decipher nothing. From the layout of the papers, Cushing deduced that at least one packet contained orders of some kind. They were certainly unlike any captured papers he had ever seen. Because of their fancy packaging—in the red leather portfolio embossed with an elaborate emblem—and the fact that all the packets were stamped with inked seals, Cushing rightly believed these documents were somehow extraordinary. He had the packets rolled tightly and placed inside empty mortar shells to protect them from the elements. The colonel then summoned Russ Snell and Jimmy Dyer. He knew that MacArthur had ordered the repatriation of all Americans stranded in the Philippines; knew, too, that submarines were now visiting Negros regularly. He told the ex-POWs that they were going home. Their colonel gave them a bodyguard of soldiers and the two mortar shells. He carefully impressed upon them the importance of safely reaching Colonel Edwin Andrews's headquarters. On the fifteenth of April 1944 the two Americans began the long journey across Cebu, down the west coast to Santander, across Tañon Strait in a banca, and up through the hills to the great Tablas Plateau.[26] That same day, Admiral Fukudome Shigeru, now a free man, was flown from Cebu to Manila for a few days' hospitalization before being repatriated himself.

Japanese forces were by now winding up their frantic search for Admiral Koga and his plans. Shiro Takasu, acting CinC of the Combined Fleet, sent a long radio report to the Navy General Staff in Tokyo outlining the search thus far. Dozens of planes and ships had explored a huge area of ocean between

Palau and Cebu but found no trace. On 17 April the investigation was discontinued. The OTSU Incident was closed.[27]

At about the same time, in response to a query from SWPA, Cushing sent a long message of his own, detailing what the CAC then knew about the crash of Fukudome's seaplane. He followed that eleven days later with another signal saying that "THROUGH THE HELP OF FISHERMEN WE HAVE RECOVERED A LARGE QUANTITY OF DOCUMENTS FROM THE CRASHED SEAPLANE OFF SAN FERNANDO. ALL NOW EN ROUTE TO ANDREWS HEADQUARTERS." The Kawanishi was turning into a veritable cornucopia of papers and artifacts.

Cushing, still reeling from his brushes with oblivion, also asked Brisbane to pass along a particularly heartfelt message to his mother. He wrote, "I AM IN BEST HEALTH, SENDING LOVE TO YOU ALL. YOU WILL BE PROUD TO KNOW CHARLIE AND WALTER ALSO IN ARMY HERE. CHARLIE NOW PRISONER WAR, WALTER UNCONTACTED FOR EIGHTEEN MONTHS." Jim, of course, was ill. Charlie had not been captured, but turned himself into the Japanese. And Walter was dead and had been for all those eighteen months. Hardly a word of truth, but Jimmy did not want to worry his mother.[28]

Major Ismael P. Ingeniero, guerrilla commander on the island of Bohol, radioed SWPA (through WAT) on 25 April:

```
ON 1 APRIL JAP TRANSPORT PLANE CRASHED NEAR SAN FERNANDO,
CEBU COMING FROM SOUTH. TEN SURVIVORS WITH PORTFOLIO
CONTAINING SECRET PAPERS ARE REPORTED IN CUSHING'S HANDS.
JAPS WILL PAY 50,000 PESOS FOR RETURN OF PORTFOLIO AND
PAPERS.[29] [emphasis added]
```

It is odd that Ingeniero knew that the survivors had a "portfolio" and that it passed to Cushing. The word "portfolio" was never used by Cebu or SWPA during their radio exchanges. The only possibility is that Pedro Gantuangko had talked with the Bohol rebels, had told them about his discovery. The consequences of his talking were dire. The Japanese learned that Bohol was somehow connected to the missing documents. They sent troops to the island to search and destroy. They found nothing, but they may have killed as many as seventy civilians.[30]

Brisbane's reaction to Ingeniero's news was lethargic. Whitney asked Andrews to let GHQ know when the documents arrived at his Culipapa headquarters. He then added, "Thereafter may be determined the advisability of regular pickup with supply mission or special pickup. Documents may be of considerable value."[31] The PRS chief recommended no further action.

The reward offered by the Japanese—about $25,000 (a lot of money in the Philippines then and even now)—got intelligence chief General Willoughby thinking. He suggested the enemy's offer be matched by the Americans. General Sutherland, however, coolly noted that matching the reward was not necessary: "the documents are already in our hands." And so things sat.

On the last day of April Colonel Salvador Abcede signaled GHQ that his command had twenty-two American refugees ready for evacuation. Abcede knew there were plans for a late-spring pickup by one of the cargo submarines, either the USS *Nautilus* or the USS *Narwhal.* He did not then know about the Z Plan.

On 2 May Cushing notified GHQ that Snell and Dyer and the "most important enemy documents" had made it to Andrews.[32] Whitney commented to Chief of Staff Sutherland that the documents could not be picked up by a cargo sub until the middle of May. "Do you desire that I endeavor to arrange earlier pickup by operational sub?"

But nothing happened. And so things still sat.

On 3 May American intelligence decrypted a message to high-level officers confirming the death of Admiral Koga Mineichi while "in performance of his duties," and appointing Admiral Toyoda Soemu to fill the role of commander in chief, Combined Fleet. The signal stressed the need to keep the news secret until a public announcement was made.[33]

And that announcement came on Friday, 5 May, when Tokyo radio told the world about Koga's demise and Toyoda's rise.

Only then did SWPA GHQ wake up.

On Saturday morning Colonel Whitney memoed Sutherland. He had finally connected the public announcement of Koga's loss with Cushing's past radio messages and the intercepts regarding the OTSU Incident. Now it all made sense! Whitney urged the chief of staff to act immediately. "It may be that the documents in reference now with Andrews may be of such great importance that you will want a special pickup effected."

Once again Army hastily consulted Navy. Where was the nearest submarine? Admiral Christie checked his charts. He wired back that the USS *Crevalle* was off the coast of northern Borneo, less than two days' sailing from Negros. Orders were issued at 11:00 P.M. on 7 May terminating the boat's third war patrol and sending her north on a special mission. Someone, probably Colonel Whitney, decided to use the evacuation of American refugees as a cover for the submarine's real mission: picking up the Z Plan. When further instructions were radioed to *Crevalle* late on the afternoon of the eighth, they simply stated she was to pick up "twenty-five passengers and important documents." To keep the entire matter secret, to keep those in the know to the barest few, SWPA never told Captain Frank Walker just how urgently important those documents were. And that proved a near-fatal decision.

The seventh of May was a busy day in Brisbane. Whitney worked hard to make sure every loose end was tied up. He sent a signal to Abcede:

```
DOCUMENTS DESIRED THIS HEADQUARTERS EARLIEST DATE POSSIBLE.
ADVISE SITE AT WHICH DOCUMENTS AND EVACUEES CAN BE PICKED UP
ON ELEVENTH THIS MONTH. EXERCISE GREATEST CAUTION IN THE
EXECUTION OF THIS MISSION. PRESERVE UTMOST SECRECY
CONCERNING DOCUMENTS.[34]
```

Whitney wanted to make sure Abcede fully understood the plan. Two days later GHQ sent this to Negros:

```
HAVE ARRANGED FOR SUB TO RENDEZVOUS ELEVENTH SUNSET OFF
BALATONG POINT UPON SIGHTING SECURITY SIGNALS TWO WHITE
PANELS FIFTY YARDS APART. CONFIRM IMMEDIATELY THAT SITE IS
SECURE AND AVAILABLE TO YOU FOR DISPATCHING DOCUMENTS AND
EVACUEES.[35]
```

Abcede radioed back:

```
ARRANGEMENTS OKAY REFERENCE CONTACT ELEVENTH SUNSET. I
GUARANTEE SAFETY OF MISSION AND EVACUEES.
```

Whitney would not let up. The next day, the tenth, Abcede received even more minute instructions:

```
WHEN VESSEL SURFACES BE PREPARED SEND DOCUMENTS AND EVACUEES
ALONGSIDE IMMEDIATELY TO PERMIT VESSEL TO CLEAR WITHIN
THIRTY MINUTES IF POSSIBLE. IF VESSEL DOES NOT ARRIVE ON
ELEVENTH CONTINUE SIGNALS AND VIGILANCE UNTIL CONTACT MADE.
WHEN MISSION COMPLETE ADVISE AT ONCE.[36]
```

By now the suspense must have been killing Courtney Whitney. Only two radio messages regarding the mission were sent to the *Crevalle*. And because the boat was maintaining radio silence, she never acknowledged them. He had to assume the submarine was on course and would be on time. Waiting was always the hardest part.

On Thursday, 11 May 1944, Whitney sent one last message to Abcede, just to make crystal clear the importance of this mission, as if it were not already obvious to the guerrilla commander:

IMPERATIVE THAT POSITIVE OR NEGATIVE REPORT ON RENDEZVOUS BE
RECEIVED HERE BY FOURTEEN HUNDRED ELEVEN MAY. [Station] KAZ
WILL GUARD YOUR REGULAR FREQUENCY UNTIL REPLY. KAZ WILL
STAND BY UNTIL MISSION ACCOMPLISHED.[37]

And so Courtney Whitney and Richard Sutherland and even Douglas MacArthur waited to hear back from Negros, waited for word that the rendezvous had gone smoothly and successfully and that the documents were now on their way down to Australia.

On Cebu, the seventh son of a seventh son was back in his element, fighting the Japanese. Following the handover of the prisoners, Colonel Ohnisi observed a three-day cease-fire with the guerrillas, and even after conflict renewed, his troops avoided attacking civilians. The respite gave Jim Cushing the chance to reestablish his headquarters at Tabunan, catch up on the administrative work he hated so much, and perhaps even play his guitar, his favorite way to relax.

Cushing was never able to learn exactly why his most urgent radio dispatches were held up by Fertig. When Whitney investigated the delay he was told by WAT that Mindanao had not received them until 10:35 A.M. on 12 April, and had relayed them within four hours.[38] WAT offered no further explanation, instead shifting blame to Cebu. Cushing and his staff believed that Fertig had intentionally withheld the messages—why else would Brisbane have received Colonel Andrews's relay of the critical NR11 more than twenty-four hours before Fertig's relay? There was another possibility. When Irving Joseph was evacuated from Negros in June he told interrogators that "each time the Cebu operator contacted Fertig's headquarters, he was told to stand by. For four days an effort was made to make contact and each time the result was the same."[39] Joseph added, "Cushing has his radio log to prove how Fertig gave him the runaround." Relations between the two guerrilla leaders, already strained, only worsened after the "Koga Affair."

Admiral Fukudome Shigeru was flown from Manila to Tokyo on 20 April. After submitting a report on the seaplane crash and his imprisonment, Fukudome was taken to a secluded rest house near the Togo Shrine. There he spent three weeks recuperating, three weeks when he had no contact with the outside world. His superiors kept him isolated, so he could tell no one of his experiences—of what had happened at Palau and in the air over the Sulu Sea and in the mountains of Cebu.[40]

# CHAPTER 11

# *Converging Paths*

FOR A FULL WEEK AFTER LEAVING the submarine base at Fremantle on 4 April, USS *Crevalle* had skirted Australia, pushing two hundred miles northward with each passing day. Lieutenant Commander Francis David Walker Jr. used this time to good advantage. To mold his crew of old hands and newcomers into a finely oiled battle machine, the young captain ran drills every day, at all hours. There were diving drills, surfacing drills, torpedo drills, gun drills, radar drills, sonar drills, tracking drills, and emergency drills. By 11 April, when the submarine put in at Darwin on the continent's far northern coast, Walker had the semblance of an ace crew. After topping off her diesel fuel and freshwater tanks, *Crevalle* set course for the Japanese-controlled waters above the Malay Barrier. More drills ensued until the captain was satisfied that every man aboard could perform his assigned task with masterful precision and utterly precise teamwork. On 14 April the sub began her transit through the heavily patrolled Molukka and Sibutu passages, into the fertile hunting grounds of the South China Sea.

Eight days out of Darwin, *Crevalle* reached her assigned station, the approaches to the Balabac Strait off the northern tip of Borneo, there to search for and destroy Japanese shipping. Day in, day out the submarine patrolled the channel entrances. But contacts were few. No attacks developed. For officers and men alike it became a drudge, a routine of boredom tinged with anticipation. Adrenaline flowed for exactly forty-four minutes on 23 April when radar picked up a fast-moving target. After a brief chase Captain Walker concluded that his quarry was another American submarine on her way home to Fremantle. *Crevalle* settled back into her routine. Despite the lack of activity, the captain knew that sooner or later his ship would sight an enemy vessel.

TO HELP HER CREW find targets, *Crevalle* carried three sets of eyes. Her periscopes, two forty-footers, were manned continuously on a sea and air

*187*

search. Her radar, a revolutionary new tool, provided an electronic eye capable of piercing the darkest night to reveal on a glowing screen the enemy's position. Her lookouts, a ship's eyes since time immemorial, were still relied upon to locate incoming aircraft or to sight a potential target.

Two or three lookouts hung, sometimes precariously, from small platforms welded to the periscope supports—the *shears*—which rose like spikes above the conning tower superstructure. One sailor swept his 7 × 50 binoculars to starboard. One did the same to port. Another, on the cigarette deck aft of the bridge, scanned the rear quarter. And during daylight hours one lookout, using specially filtered lenses, peered directly into the sun, hunting for enemy planes hiding in the specular brightness. Up on the bridge, an Officer of the Deck (OOD) and a quartermaster stood watch, searching far ahead. All compass points were well and regularly covered.

On a clear day a good lookout in the shears could spot a ship at a range of thirty thousand yards—fifteen nautical miles. He searched for any little phenomenon that seemed dissimilar, in any way, from the rest of the sea and sky. Often the first indication of a ship was a very slight atmospheric disturbance, perhaps an insignificant discoloration, sighted on the far horizon. This might very well be smoke from an otherwise invisible enemy merchantman. The captain usually tracked this ephemeral image until it either vanished or revealed itself as a genuine target. As the submarine closed the range, the view through the binoculars would begin to include tiny nubbins of masts. A single mast usually indicated trouble—a warship. Closely grouped masts hinted at a freighter or a bigger prize, a tanker. Widely spaced masts suggested a convoy, a really meaty target for a hungry undersea warship.

Like all fleet submarines, *Crevalle* carried two sets of radar. The SD was used to detect aircraft, the SJ, surface contacts. At regular intervals Walker's radarman, Henry Tudor Biehl, fired up the SJ search set for a few sweeps across the horizon. When it was working well, the SJ could reach out thirty-five thousand yards, about seventeen miles, and on a really good day could detect land at eighty thousand yards. *Crevalle* had a spanking new Plan Position Indicator (PPI) display, a large round screen that swept a three-hundred-sixty-degree circle around the ship. Pips on the screen revealed the range and bearing of potential targets in relation to the sub's own position. Because of its ability to project an accurate tactical picture day or night, the SJ radar became a favored tool in the hands of aggressive captains.

The SD air search radar was considered less useful and less reliable. Walker, like many submarine commanders, believed the Japanese could pinpoint his position by picking up his SD transmissions. To cut down the risk of detection by the enemy, Biehl keyed the radar for just a few seconds every minute. When it was working properly the SD might pick up an airplane contact at eighteen miles. Then again, it might not. On at least two occasions that week the SD failed to warn the sub of incoming aircraft.

Aircraft sightings were taken very seriously. Walker usually kept *Crevalle* on the surface until a plane got within ten miles. Then he took no chances: he dived the boat. One April morning, with a Japanese floatplane eight miles out and closing, Walker took his ship *down express*. "Clear the bridge! Dive! Dive!" and the Klaxons rang throughout the narrow steel hull. The lookouts leaped from the shears and down the hatch, followed by the captain himself. The quartermaster yanked the hatch shut just as the sea foamed around the bridge decking, dogging it into place. "Three hundred feet, right full rudder, course two-seven-zero." The ship was completely under within forty seconds. A few minutes later a bomb exploded close aboard, surprising everybody. For nearly two hours the attacking plane, soon joined by another, circled above the spot where the submarine had dived. At noon two more planes entered the hunt for the Americans. They didn't give up until midafternoon, leaving Walker impressed that the enemy would concentrate so many aircraft on searching for a single submarine.

MIDMORNING ON 25 APRIL the lookouts sighted wisps of smoke to the southeast. Walker changed course, and the sub quickly built up flank speed. Now the hard work began. The tracking party huddled over the tiny chart table in the conning tower. The target was hugging the coast of Balambangan Island, well inside the twenty-fathom curve (one hundred twenty feet). Working in water that shallow would provide no margin of safety for *Crevalle*. The better strategy, the *end around*, was to sprint ahead of the enemy and wait for him at a point where he had to cross into deeper water. Charts were closely inspected. A few calculations were made. Experience was factored in. The answer to the puzzle: catch him between Kalutan Point and Sampanmangio Point, where the water deepened to a roomier thirty fathoms (one hundred eighty feet).

The enemy was still ten thousand yards distant when the submarine dived and went to battle stations. Within half an hour the target was positively identified as a large freighter similar in appearance to *Lima Maru*. This identification came from successive looks at the ship's characteristics—type of bow, type of stern, deck arrangement, mast arrangement—compared to photos, drawings, and other data in a comprehensive catalog of Japanese merchant vessels compiled by the Office of Naval Intelligence and known simply by its serial number, 208J. With the periscope at high power, Walker could see two aircraft lashed to the main deck. He now also saw two small cargo ships in line behind the maru, and a yachtlike patrol escort. Flat, calm seas made his raised scope with its foamy white feather easy for the enemy to spot. He kept his frequent looks short, just a few seconds each.

At 12:45 P.M., at a range of twenty-two hundred yards, Walker pressed home his attack, firing a spread of six torpedoes from his bow tubes. A minute later the first missile struck the enemy amidships. A tremendous explosion followed, lifting the ship upward, flinging debris high into the air. Ten seconds later the second torpedo hit, breaking off the bow. Smoke completely enveloped the target. And when the smoke cleared, the target was gone. So were the three little ships, who sped for the protection of Balambangan Island's shallows. It was Frank Walker's first sinking as captain of his own ship.

He ordered the sub to surface, his gun crews to stand by for action. For twenty minutes the submarine cruised through the wreckage of the merchantman. About fifty survivors were discovered swimming in the water, but Captain Walker decided against picking up prisoners in such a vulnerable spot. At 1:15 P.M., three hours after sighting smoke on the horizon, the USS *Crevalle* came to course three-zero-zero and steamed back to her patrol station.[1]

Twenty minutes later, the SD radar picked up an incoming plane. The sub quickly dived to avoid. Over the next hour the soundman heard five bomb explosions on the passive sonar; none seemed closer than two thousand yards. As a precaution the sub stayed submerged until dark, the crew taking turns listening to the sea.

IF RADAR AND PERISCOPES and lookouts were the eyes of *Crevalle,* sonar was her ears. An acronym for *sound navigation ranging,* sonar came in two forms: passive and active. Passive sonar was first developed by the British in the late nineteenth century as a method for listening to underwater sounds. To pick them up, a special microphone, a *hydrophone,* was attached to the hull. A listener could hear the most wonderful things: the sea lapping gently against a reef, the song of the whales, the screws of a ship moving through the water. The latter had important military implications, for if a submarine could hear a ship moving, it could also determine its position and its speed. *Crevalle* used her passive sonar almost continuously to listen to the sounds of the sea. Her soundman extracted useful tactical information about the situation around the submarine just from what he could hear. By counting the turns of a ship's propellers, he could estimate her speed. High-speed screws shouted *Danger, escort!* Low-speed usually meant a fat freighter or a tanker. Torpedoes produced a high-pitched whine. The sound of a splash meant trouble—it meant a depth charge had been dropped into the water. Even the low rumble of a bilge pump could give away a ship's position to a good listener.

Active sonar was an entirely different creature. An audible *ping* was transmitted through the water. When it struck something reflective—such as a ship—the ping returned to the sender. The time it took for the round-trip, halved, very accurately measured the distance to the object. Prior to World War II, standard U.S. Navy doctrine directed submarine commanders to use the *single-ping* technique to determine the range to a target. Practical experience during the war showed this doctrine dangerous, for if the transmitting ship could hear the ping, so, too, could the reflecting ship. The mere presence of the sound gave away all element of surprise. Submarine captains preferred not to use active sonar during attacks for fear of broadcasting their proximity to the enemy.[2]

Radarman Biehl and Radio Technician 2nd Class Albert Francis Bower maintained and operated the sound equipment aboard *Crevalle*. When the boat was not at battle stations, other seamen pitched in to listen to the deep, usually Yeoman Al Dempster and Chief Pharmacist's Mate Fred Loos. During a submerged attack Biehl stayed on the sonar gear in the conning tower, while Bower went to the forward torpedo room to listen on the JP set.

The Japanese Navy had very good passive sonar, manned by highly trained listeners. Their hydrophones could pick up the sounds of a ship or a submarine moving at a speed of just five knots over a range of five thousand yards. Because the enemy on the surface was always listening, deadly games of cat and mouse were played by escorts and submarines. Usually the sub managed to wriggle safely away. But a dozen American boats were lost to enemy detection during the war.[3]

JUST BEFORE SUNDOWN on 3 May, while patrolling the Miri-Pulau Condore Line off the coast of Borneo, masts were sighted to the north. With the range to the target sixteen thousand yards, Captain Walker sounded battle stations. When the range halved, the tracking party had sufficient information for a visual identification: medium-size tanker similar to *Syoyo Maru*. Moments later a second ship, a small vessel, perhaps a tanker, was spotted well aft of the first; then a third appeared, a PC-type escort.

At 7:10 P.M. the targets suddenly disappeared from view in an increasingly thick haze. The captain ordered a quick sweep on the SJ radar. The electronic eye cut through the mist to see what human eyes could not: enemy ships at six thousand yards, glowing brightly as pips on the PPI. Walker was cautious. He did not want to betray his position by overusing his radar. Over the next hour occasional short sweeps revealed that the targets were opening the range—to seventeen thousand yards by eight o'clock. The time had come for another end around.

The captain rang up three engines and put the fourth to work charging the sub's massive batteries. Just out of sight over the horizon, the submarine sped on a great arc through increasingly turbulent seas. Two and a half hours later, at 10:27 P.M., *Crevalle* was dead ahead of the targets, now fourteen thousand yards and closing. The sky was bright from an almost full moon. Natural pyrotechnics compounded the radiance. Lightning from a huge rain squall at the submarine's back fleetingly turned night into day. Walker prudently dived the boat to avoid being spotted. By 10:58 P.M. the range was down to four thousand yards as the boat swung to fire its stern tubes. Shortly after eleven o'clock the tanker disappeared from periscope view as the squall thundered through. Walker immediately ordered radar depth. The SJ radar showed that his target was now just twenty-seven hundred yards off the aft beam. Though the big tanker could not be seen, the firing solution generated by the Torpedo Data Computer (TDC) checked perfectly with the radar range. At 11:14 P.M. *Crevalle* let loose a salvo of four Mark 14 torpedoes. Two minutes later, two explosions rocked the submarine. Three minutes later, another rumbling blast was heard. And finally, at 11:42 P.M., a tremendous explosion pierced the night. The rain was so heavy that nothing could be seen through the periscope. A radar sweep showed only two ships out in the darkness, where once there had been three.

Walker steered his ship, now on the surface, in the direction of the second vessel. At midnight the aggressive young captain began another end around. This one took just an hour. At a range of seventeen hundred yards, *Crevalle* fired four torpedoes from the bow tubes. Three missed ahead. The fourth ran erratic. The enemy ship steamed away at top speed, eight knots. For the submarine's crew it was the ultimate frustration. At fourteen hundred yards the ship was identified as a small engines-aft cargo vessel. As Walker prepared for a second attack the frightened freighter crossed Champion Bank into eighteen-fathom water and the safety of a minefield. *Crevalle* dared not follow. She would not get a second ship that night.

For the next two days the submarine continued her patrol. A six-ship convoy was spotted late on the fourth. Walker tried to get into position for an attack, but nothing developed. The ship's luck changed on 6 May. At 5:54 A.M. the high periscope watch sighted smoke on the horizon. Within fifteen minutes three of the eight ships in the convoy could be typed. The second in line was an odd-looking auxiliary. The fifth was a large freighter. The last was a huge converted tanker.

Peering through the scope, considering his options, Walker knew that conditions for an attack were not ideal. He counted three escorts, all destroyers, all alert, all very dangerous. In the air above the convoy he spotted a Sally, a twin-engine Mitsubishi Ki-21 bomber, circling vigilantly. The glassy-calm sea gave him pause for concern, for it made successful concealment difficult at best. Still, Frank Walker had enemy ships bearing down on him, and he had the means to destroy them. At six twenty-two that Saturday morning Walker sent *Crevalle* to battle stations.

He gave brief thought to firing on the nearest destroyer, but instead dropped to one hundred feet to let the warship pass over him. Seven minutes later *Crevalle* was back at periscope depth. Surveying the scene, the captain decided to go after the largest ship in the convoy, the big tanker. Tracking identified it as the 16,800-ton *Tonan Maru #2*, a converted whale factory.[4] "We have a firing solution," the TDC operator called out. "Open the outer doors. Make ready tubes one, two, four, and five." The captain took a quick look through the periscope. "Target is giving us seventy-five degrees angle on the bow, range four thousand. He has to zig or he'll run aground on the reef," Walker said calmly.[5]

It was a tense time in the crowded conning tower. The hardened steel cylinder was only twelve feet long, eight feet wide. Inside were crammed two periscopes, the slim attack scope, and the fatter search scope. At the bow bulkhead the helmsman steered the boat, while an intercom *talker* stood by, ready to pass on orders and information to the rest of the ship. The five-foot-high TDC stood along the aft port side, its dials revealing to operator Dick Bowe the relative positions of both target and stalker. On the starboard side opposite, Henry Biehl, his radar equipment unusable underwater, hunched over the sonar console, listening critically to every sound in the ocean. Al Dempster sat near the chart table, recording all that transpired—his notes later to be incorporated into the ship's log and interpreted by the captain for his patrol report. The executive officer, Bill Ruhe, stood by, awaiting a signal from the captain. And commanding officer Walker just stood waiting, his eyes darting about the small chamber, checking his bearings, checking his speed, checking his depth, and in his own mind checking and rechecking his attack plan.

Four minutes after the last look the *Tonan Maru #2* zigged back. "Up scope! Target zigging toward us, angle on the bow fifty-five port, range twenty-eight hundred."[6] After checking Dick Bowe's solution, Walker took another short look. "Angle on the bow sixty port, range fourteen hundred." Walker said they would fire when the ship was a thousand yards distant. And so they waited. Ruhe, his hand on the firing panel, watched his captain intently. Walker watched the attack develop on the whirring dials of the TDC, then took one last look. "Target looks as big as an island!"[7] He pulled his head back from the eyepiece. "Fire!" At 7:01 A.M., with the target just nine hundred yards away, Ruhe punched the red plunger four times at ten-second intervals.

The first torpedo whooshed from its tube, driven into the sea by six hundred pounds of compressed air. Within seconds the missile would reach a speed of forty-six knots. The second was unleashed. The third. Finally, the fourth. With each discharge *Crevalle* bucked upward from the loss of thirty-four hundred pounds of deadly weight. With each discharge the air pressure in the hull increased, popping men's ears. The soundman listened intently on the JP sonar to the high-pitched whine of the torpedoes driving their way to the target. "All hot, straight and normal." The Yeo watched intently as the sweep hand on his stopwatch came around. "Number one ought to hit in ten seconds, Skipper."[8]

"Up scope." Walker grabbed the handles as they rose. He wanted to watch his torpedoes strike this monster ship. In his patrol report the captain later wrote:

Observed first torpedo to hit amidships with tremendous explosion seeming to lift entire mid-ship goal post into the air. Second torpedo hit seven seconds later directly under the bridge. This hit seemed to blow the bow completely off. Simultaneously with second hit two aircraft bombs landed between us and target straddling torpedo tracks. Lowered scope. As we were in 24 fathoms began evasive action immediately. A third explosion was heard which is believed to be the fourth torpedo hitting. As we turned away breaking up noises of target were very loudly heard through the hull and it sounded as if he might be falling on top of us.[9]

That's when things got really interesting on *Crevalle*.

Knowing the destroyers would be on him quickly, the captain ordered his ship deep. "Take her down to one hundred forty feet. Right full rudder. All ahead full." As he watched the dial on the depth gauge plot their slow descent, Walker took no comfort in the fact that the now-aroused Sally bomber probably had several more depth bombs in her bay. It worried him more, though, that he had only one hundred forty-four feet of water in which to evade three angry escorts.

At 7:06, the first depth charges came, all close, all three of them.

At 7:07, ten depth charges exploded, also close, causing minor damage.

At 7:09, two more came, then seven more right behind them.

For twenty minutes depth charges rained down upon *Crevalle*, sixty-one in all. When the soundman heard the splashes he removed his headphones to protect his ears from the shock of the discharging canisters. The rest of the crew waited for the ominous *click* that preceded the *wham* of the explosion. They knew that if they heard the click, the wham had little chance of killing them. If all they heard was the wham, they knew the charges were very close and very lethal. That morning there were few clicks, lots of whams.

Walker was wary. He thought his ship might be maneuvering so close to the bottom that she was stirring up mud, telegraphing her location to the enemy ships above. At 7:33 A.M. he let *Crevalle* settle on the bottom, now one hundred seventy-four feet, with a slight down angle. The boat was rigged for absolute silence. All men not on duty—now the majority of the crew—were ordered to their bunks. Every single piece of machinery in the boat was secured except a small generator needed to power the JP sonar. People walked on tiptoes if they walked at all. And if they spoke, it was in whispers. The silence was so profound, the mere act of pouring water into a glass sounded to Walker like Niagara Falls. On the surface the three destroyers worked back and forth, methodically searching. The sounds of their screws could be heard clearly through the hull. By the captain's choice, *Crevalle* and her crew were now helpless at the bottom of the sea. All they could do was wait.

A DEPTH CHARGING WAS ONE of the occupational hazards of submarining in wartime. It was an experience no one enjoyed, and no sailor ever got used to, however often he was attacked, however loud he boasted it did not scare him.

Depth charges resemble a 55-gallon drum, but smaller. The Japanese began the war with the Type 95, which was only three feet long and eighteen inches in diameter. It carried two hundred forty pounds of TNT set off by a hydrostatic (water pressure) detonator. Before being dropped from the attacking vessel, the ordnance crew would manually set the firing mechanism for thirty, sixty, or ninety meters (one hundred, two hundred, or three hundred feet).

Depth charges destroyed submarines not by ripping great holes into their skins with high explosives but by the concussion of a tremendous blast wave that could burst seams, unseat tightly dogged hatches, and rupture valves from pipes large and small. The resulting leaks might quickly or slowly flood the ship, sinking her or forcing her to the surface, there to be destroyed by waiting enemy guns. Depth charges were dumb weapons. Usually rolled off the back of moving escorts, the canisters just bored through the sea until they reached detonation depth. They could not be placed with any accuracy. If they happened to explode within fifty feet of a submarine, they could cause considerable damage. And if they exploded within twenty-five feet they would probably sink her.

Throughout much of the war the Japanese greatly underestimated the capabilities of American fleet-type submarines. Captains returning from patrol boasted to journalists that they were not afraid of enemy depth charges because "they weren't set deep enough to reach us and weren't powerful enough to hurt us." The U.S. Navy was mortified when this secret information showed up in print. However, the Imperial Navy was delighted to learn why their antisubmarine efforts were failing. As a result, the Japanese developed a new, more powerful, deeper-detonating depth charge, the Type 2. Instead of a maximum of ninety meters, the new weapon could be set to one hundred fifty (five hundred feet). Within months ten American submarines were lost with all hands due to improved Japanese weapons and tactics. The United States countered with thicker-hulled, deeper-diving vessels, such as *Crevalle*. The new boats, the Balao class, had a test depth of four hundred fifty feet, one hundred more than the earlier Gatos. But the hull strength of these ships permitted them to go considerably deeper without undue risk. During one of her shakedown cruises, USS *Tang* pegged the depth gauge at six hundred feet and kept going—intentionally.[10] Her captain, Commander Richard O'Kane, just wanted to know how deep he could take his ship without imploding her.

Incrementally more terrifying than a depth charging was being shelled or torpedoed. A well-placed shell of almost any caliber could hole the pressure hull, making control of the ship difficult at best, fatal at worst. And a torpedoing was always fatal. Japanese Long Lance torpedoes were considered the best, the fastest, the deadliest in the world. Their one thousand eighty pounds of high explosives would blow a hole in a sub the size of a bus, sinking her in seconds, taking her entire crew to the bottom with no chance of escape, no hope of rescue.

AN HOUR AND A HALF after sinking *Tonan Maru #2*, an hour after the last of the sixty-one charges had fallen and *Crevalle* had settled silently on the shallow seabed, everyone aboard was shaken when they heard an eerie, ungodly noise. It sounded like a fearsome, slithering clanking. If ever there was a time to be afraid, this might be it. In the darkened hull the crew sat stock still, sweat pouring off their bodies as the temperature rose above one hundred twenty degrees. Throats dry, hands clenched, hearts racing, the men listened as the noise outside persisted. They could hear it moving toward them. Then it was upon them, a thunderous noise rattling across the hull. It quickly faded away, only to return time and time again. All heads were turned upward, following its progress. It was as though they could see through the thick steel hull and through one hundred seventy feet of murky water. A chain! The enemy was dragging a chain through the sea, seeking to uncover its prey. Men could see it hooking the periscope shears, dragging the submarine through the water, through the water and up toward the surface, where they would all be killed. They could imagine, too, their enemy sliding a string of fat depth charges down that chain until they exploded right there on *Crevalle*'s deck.[11] Terrible thoughts raced through the boat, but not a man cracked under the pressure. For nearly two hours the clanking continued. Finally, Francis David Walker Jr. had had enough. "Okay, that's it! Let's get out of here. Ahead two-thirds."[12] Quietly the crew went to work as the submarine awakened from her coma. It took five long minutes for *Crevalle* to break free from the mud.[13] Just before 10:00 A.M. she began to move slowly away while the enemy searched frantically, futilely for their prey.

An hour later, at periscope depth, Walker could see just the tops of one escort, about eight thousand yards distant. Another check, at 1:43 P.M., showed all three escorts still methodically searching back and forth, sixteen thousand yards astern. When *Crevalle* surfaced just after sunset she was the only vessel on the sea—at least within the range of her lookouts and her radar.[14]

That Saturday evening Walker transmitted Serial #1, his first radio message back to Australia. He briefly outlined the attacks on the marus. And according to custom, he requested permission to return to Fremantle now that *Crevalle* had expended most of her offensive might—all but five torpedoes.[15] Transmission was completed at 9:03 P.M. Walker cruised north toward the shoals of Dangerous Ground, awaiting a reply. In the crew's quarters twenty-year-old motormac John Maille sat on his bunk writing his daily letter home to his wife, Vivian. He couldn't even hint at the events he and his ship had just been through. Instead he opened with "Today I became a Christian. . . ."[16]

AT 11:00 P.M. ON SUNDAY, MAY 7, twenty-two hours after sending her Serial #1, *Crevalle* got a response from Rear Admiral Ralph Waldo Christie, Commander Submarines Southwest Pacific (ComSubSoWesPac). The urgent message was received by Radioman First Class Gerald Stutzman. He pecked furiously at his typewriter, recording the five-letter code groups as they beeped faintly through his headsets. Yanking the paper from the machine, he hightailed it for the officers' wardroom, where he found Dick Bowe, the junior officer aboard, detailed that night to decipher incoming messages. Bowe pulled out his secret pad and quickly got to work. When he finished he took the now readable message up to Captain Walker on the bridge:

```
TOP SECRET. YOUR PATROL TERMINATED. PROCEED EASTERN PART
SULU SEA. BE PREPARED SPECIAL MISSION ABOUT ELEVEN MAY.
```

Walker was not pleased. He wanted to expend his last torpedoes and go back to Australia for more—he had a war to fight. Special mission? The vague message gave no hint about what kind of mission Comsubs had in mind. Eastern Sulu Sea? That probably meant the Philippines. He called for his navigator, Bill Ruhe. Together they huddled over the charts. From their current position along the northern coast of Borneo, *Crevalle* would have to transit Balabac Strait to enter the Sulu Sea. A quick plot showed that the ship could easily be in the eastern part of the Sea by 10 May. "Set course zero-nine-zero."

The sleek fleet boat swung around, pointing her bullnose due east. At seventeen knots, she cut through the moderate seas with ease. All night and all the next day the submarine cruised on the surface, lookouts and radar steadily scanning the skies for enemy aircraft that might force the boat to dive and slow her progress.

Late in the afternoon of Monday, 8 May, another urgent message, clear and specific, came in from Comsubs ordering *Crevalle* to rendezvous three days hence off Balatong Point, on the southwestern coast of Negros Island. The mission: to pick up passengers and documents.

The die was cast.

SAM REAL WAS IN A HURRY when he trotted into his family's camp near the mouth of the Pagatban River. It was Tuesday, 9 May 1944, and he had wonderful news to share—Abcede had received word just that morning that a submarine would arrive in two days. What a thrill those words bred! Rose and the children had been prepared to wait months. Now the sub was actually on its way, and they would be leaving Negros soon. But Rose was circumspect. After all that had happened to her and her family, she could take only one day at a time. The future . . . for so long there had been no future . . . was quite simply an intangible, gossamer concept. As they had for thirty months, the family scooped up their belongings for yet another move. Before they could board the sub they had to get themselves to the rendezvous point at the mouth of the Tyabanan River, seven miles up the coast. Sam told them a banca would pick them up after dark, that it would be an all-night voyage.

That evening the family waited on the beach. Sam had collected some green drinking coconuts for the trip. Rose had cooked some beans and rice, which she put into a pandanus basket. Billy cradled his carbine and rooster, all the while keeping a wary eye on his dog, Thunderbolt. His greatest fear was being made to leave the pup behind. The banca was not long in coming. It was of good size and carried a crew of three. The family quickly settled into the long, thin hull. Rose sat in the middle, keeping Nan and Berna close. The boys went to the prow, to act as "lookouts." Sam stayed with the skipper. The sailors paddled the boat to deeper water, raised the sail, and soon caught the wind. The calm night promised a smooth voyage—it proved an absolute delight. As the outrigger slipped across the Sulu Sea, the family reveled in the feelings of freedom this adventure held forth.

The Ossorios were also on the move. After Loretta's tearful parting from her housegirl Consuelo, George had shifted his family down to the beach near Pagatban to await their boat. But because of the distance from the hill house to the ocean, the trek took longer than he anticipated—the three did not arrive until after dark. They spent the night on the beach, eating cold food for fear an open fire would attract enemy attention. Just before dawn on Thursday, 11

May, the family set off again on the final leg to the rendezvous point, arriving at the Tyabanan midmorning.

As the banca slid into the warm sand, Kenneth could see Billy and John Real playing with other children, lots of other children, farther down the beach. He quickly counted more than a dozen, from toddlers to teenagers. Beneath the shade of the coconut palms he could see groups of adults—a few women, many men; some standing, most sitting. The scene reminded the young man of a big party. He dragged his document-laden suitcases across the beach to a large, open house. There he deposited them with his mother, who had stopped to talk to Rose Real. Kenneth then ran off to join his sugar central friends.

On Wednesday, 10 May, Colonel Placido Ausejo, Abcede's second in command, stopped by the Lindholms' house. They had been staying near Tolong, in a small hut hidden on the farm of Silliman University's treasurer, Manuel Utzurrum. Ausejo told Paul that the submarine was due the next evening. "Tomorrow walk to the mouth of the Pagatban, there a banca will be waiting." It took two hours to hike down to the sea through the season's first heavy rain. They climbed into the small outrigger and made good time up to the Tyabanan, reaching there in midafternoon.[17] The Lindholms found that Viola Winn and her children had already arrived; the kids were already hard at work playing.

Russell Snell and Jimmy Dyer had left Cebu with the Koga Papers on 14 April. After a slow and perilous crossing of Cebu and then of Tañon Strait, they went straight to the headquarters of Lieutenant Colonel Edwin Andrews in the hills behind the small coastal village of Culipapa. Andrews, a mestizo, had replaced Major Jesus Villamor as the key Allied Intelligence Bureau operative in the Philippines, charged with funneling intelligence down to SWPA GHQ at Brisbane. The ex-POWs arrived on 28 April and there turned over to Andrews the precious captured documents, still sealed in their mortar shell cases. They stayed on at Culipapa while the colonel tried to sort out their future. Ten days later, much to their surprise, Howard Chrisco walked into their camp. The trio pressed Andrews for news of their disposition. It was forthcoming on 9 May, when a messenger from Colonel Abcede handed them sealed orders. The soldiers were to proceed the following night to a beach above Basay, about five miles south of Andrews's headquarters, for immediate evacuation. It was joyous news indeed. Around the campfire that night they amused one another with stories of their adventures. Snell told how Irving

Joseph had taken a German POW named Retter down to Mindanao to hand over to Colonel Fertig. Dyer told about the capture of the ten Japanese prisoners on Cebu and all the hullabaloo that had caused. Chrisco told the astonished pair about Dick Jenson's marriage to Don Pedro Elizalde's daughter. What had become, they all wondered, of Ramon Corona and Gavin White back at Bacolod? The three members of the Lucky Seven slept soundly, knowing they would soon be going home.

As dark descended on the tenth, the trio left Colonel Andrews's camp for the short march down to the evacuation point. Just after midnight they reached Basay and there settled in a large bamboo hut for the rest of the night.[18] When they awoke they could see they were quite near the sea. While looking for food that morning Chrisco and Snell ran into Bob Young, whom they had not seen since September. They all returned to Dyer, back in the shack, with a bucket of rice given to them by a friendly Filipino. As they ate, Young told them about missing out on the sub pickup in February. At first he was despondent about it, he said, but when he arrived at Abcede's District Headquarters in mid-April the colonel had assured him another vessel would be along soon.

SALVADOR ABCEDE, ACCOMPANIED BY his adjutant, Ben Viloria, rode through the night from CP Deuce, his headquarters six miles up the Pagatban. The party arrived very early Thursday morning at the evacuation command post— code-named Shangri-la, after the Tibetan utopia of James Hilton's 1933 novel *Lost Horizon.* The place was nothing more than a few bamboo huts scattered along the banks of the Tyabanan River, a mile up the coast from Barrio Basay. The CP was under the supervision of Colonel Ausejo.[19] Twenty years older than Abcede and a onetime rival for leadership of the guerrillas on Negros, Ausejo nevertheless accepted the subordinate position, performing his duties loyally and well.[20] When Abcede arrived in the camp he met with his officers about the impending special mission. Major Enrique L. Torres Sr. assured his commander that his troops had secured the entire evacuation area. All people now within the perimeter were known to the guerrilla forces; all others had been moved. The man in charge of the boats that would take the passengers out to the submarine, Ramon Monsale, assured Abcede he had sufficient craft for any situation and that all were ready to sail on a moment's notice. The doctors, José Garcia and Gregorio Venturanza,[21] assured the colonel that all the passengers were healthy and able to travel. Ausejo made an unsettling report. The guerrillas had told Brisbane there would be twenty-five people to evacuate, but already the count was nearing thirty, and more people were arriving hourly. Abcede probably frowned at that news. He had no idea what type of submarine would surface that evening off Balatong Point. If it was one of the cargo subs, he felt certain she could handle that many passengers. But if it was one of the smaller fleet submarines, he had concerns. The colonel decided to split the group, putting twenty-five in one banca, the others in a second boat. When the sub surfaced he would argue with the captain, if necessary, to get all his refugees on board. Having determined that the situation was well in hand, the young officer ordered his men to raise the security signal—two white cloth squares—high into the palms. This would tell the submarine—if it was out there—that beach and bay were secure.

Oblivious to all the preparations, sixteen-year-old Kenneth Ossorio and some of his new friends went swimming. After having spent two years in the jungles leading a seriously dangerous life, to frolic and play was a rare treat for all the children. They were not aware at the time, but crocodiles were known to live in the river and to take an occasional human, especially a child. That fact might not have stayed the children from their romp—the chances of being eaten by a croc in the river certainly seemed less than being captured in the forest by the Japanese.

Throughout the day evacuees converged upon Shangri-la. They arrived by boat, on foot, on horseback. All were anxious to be among the twenty-five chosen to leave that night on the submarine. About the only thing they had in common was American citizenship. Some, such as Howard Chrisco and Russell Snell, were native-born. Others, such as mestizos Sam and Rose Real, acquired citizenship through a native-born parent. Though many of the children had been born overseas, their parents' status passed to them as well. Gathered under the shade of the coconut grove, all they could do was wait.

# CHAPTER 12

## *The Rescue*

UNBEKNOWNST TO THE REFUGEES and to Salvador Abcede, *Crevalle* was even then patrolling a few thousand yards offshore, looking for any signs of life on the beach. At 8:55 A.M., just a few minutes after John Maille began his periscope watch, he suddenly pulled away from the eyepiece. With urgency in his voice he called out, "Mr. Ruhe? Is this what you're looking for?" Ruhe took a quick look. Smiling at the motormac, he said, "Well done, Maille. Captain to the conning tower!"[1] Walker rushed up the ladder and grabbed the scope from Ruhe. He carefully scanned the shoreline. Two white squares hanging from coconut palms caught his eye. "Looks right." Still, there were no people, no boats, just the panels. "Let's move in for a closer look. All ahead slow, course one-two-zero." When the submarine was a mile off the beach, Walker reexamined the area, turning over in his mind the chances of this whole thing being a ruse to destroy or capture his ship. The sailboat he had seen earlier had tacked to the south and was now headed in his direction. He felt a vague uneasiness. "Take some pictures," he ordered. A call went out for the ship's photographer. While the sailor rigged the 35mm Kodak to the main periscope, Walker asked him to shoot the signals on the beach. "And grab a shot of the little boat while you're at it."[2]

For the rest of the day, submerged and undetected, *Crevalle* cruised warily off Negros. That afternoon Walker returned to his stateroom, there to devise plans for the rendezvous.

The captain had to work out how he was going to get the passengers aboard without putting his ship in danger. While he wanted to have as few of his people on deck as possible, he also wanted to be able to defend *Crevalle* from Japanese attack. He resolved to use his gunners to assist the refugees as they came aboard. If trouble developed, they could immediately jump on the four-inch gun, ready to fire on the beach or to seaward at his command. Their ammunition would come from the ready lockers below the bridge. The 20mm crews were to load their weapons, then join Lieutenant (jg) Walt Mazzone's special security detail patrolling the deck. *Crevalle* would have to depend upon them to repel any attempt to take the ship. Walker would post a continuous watch on radar and both scopes, a duty that would fall to the junior officers, Lieutenant (jg) Jim Blind and Ensign Howard Geer. Ensign Richard Bowe would man the TDC if a threat from the sea developed. The assistant diving officer, Lieutenant (jg) T. W. E. "Luke" Bowdler, would stay below in the control room, ready to take the boat down in a hurry if there was any trouble. Bill Ruhe would assist the deck operations on the bridge.

The captain also had to consider how his submarine, already crowded with eighty men, was going to sleep and feed another twenty-five. He could put the majority of passengers up in the forward torpedo room, the rest aft. Because *Crevalle* had expended most of her torpedoes, there was extra space in each room. The torpedo support racks—the *skids*—normally crowded with deadly missiles, could be turned into beds; hard, uncomfortable, cold steel beds. The passengers would have to make do with a blanket or two. The object was to get the boarders out of the way of the crew as much as possible. As for meals, the cooks would have to be in the galley around the clock, the number of mess seatings doubled.

Walker had concerns about provisions, too. During the depth charging five days earlier, the freezers below the crew's mess had been shut down so enemy listeners would not pick up the sound of their compressors. Hundreds of pounds of spoiled meat had been tossed overboard afterward. He checked with his commissary officer, who reassured him there would still be plenty of food to make it down to Darwin. Confident that all was ready for the rendezvous, that all the bases were covered, Walker relaxed in his cabin.

BY MIDAFTERNOON THE BOATMEN had hidden their craft upriver under the cover of overhanging trees. Upon Ramon Monsale's signal they were ready to slip their moorings, drift downstream to the pickup point, load, and head out to sea. Toward late afternoon Colonel Ausejo and others fanned out across the groves to tell the evacuees it was nearing time to depart. They made it clear to all that only one small suitcase and nothing more would be permitted aboard. Many people had no belongings at all. But the news upset Kenneth Ossorio— he had two bags stuffed with classified papers. When he realized that Ausejo was deadly serious, he crammed as many papers as he could into one valise, leaving the other in the care of his father.

Colonel Salvador Abcede (third from left) reviewing the ROTC cadet corps
at Silliman University one month before the war began. (Rustico Paralejas Collection)

At four-thirty precisely, Colonel Abcede called for the boats. One by one they emerged from hiding, sliding into the river's current. As they approached the mouth of the Tyabanan, their crews skillfully steered them to the shallows. Shouting through a megaphone from a sandbar across the river, Abcede told the group that there were now many more passengers for the submarine than the twenty-five he had radioed MacArthur about. He assured them he would do his best to get them all aboard. When he called their names, he said, each person must hurry to the big banca, the *Susing.* When that one was full, he told them to move on to the next boat. One by one, Abcede began to read the names in a booming voice: "Viola Schuldt Winn . . . Rodger Lewis Winn . . . Norman . . . and shortly, "Sergeant Howard Tom Chrisco." Chrisco was surprised to be called so quickly, perhaps surprised to be called at all. There were officers and ladies ahead of him. "Howard Chrisco," came an impatient second call. The weary sergeant climbed into the boat and moved up to the bow. No sooner had he settled than Jamie Lindholm jumped into his arms. The boy looked up, a great big smile on his face. The battle-hardened former prisoner of war was charmed, and moved, by this simple familial act.[3] Chrisco was soon joined by Snell, Dyer, and Young. After a long wait Kenneth Ossorio heard his name called. He and his parents boarded a small banca next to another boat filling up with the seven Reals.

For Bill Real, the dreaded moment had come. It was time to say good-bye to Thunderbolt. The two had shared great adventures. More than once the dog had alerted the boy to danger, had probably saved his life. He knelt beside the rangy mongrel, knowing in his heart he would never see the dog again. He gently rubbed its belly and scratched behind its ears—just the way Bill knew Thunderbolt liked. He told the dog he would never forget him. The creature was very subdued, almost as if he understood what was about to happen. To Bill, this was the most difficult thing he had ever had to do. After a final hug and with a tear in his eye, the boy joined his family in the outrigger. "Hurry now!" the colonel implored. "We haven't much time."[4]

When the four boats were loaded Abcede, with Viloria and a radioman, climbed into a small banca carrying an American flag atop its mast. With a wave of his arm, all the boats slipped into the stream. Prows pointed seaward, the little convoy sailed toward the rendezvous a mile off Balatong Point.

ABOARD *CREVALLE* A ROUTINE periscope sweep finally showed activity on the beach. "Captain to the conning tower," blared the speaker. Walker hurried out of his cabin. Through the scope he could see there were now boats on the beach, and a large number of people were gathered around them. Thereafter Walker took more frequent looks. At 5:00 P.M. he saw two large boats and other, smaller outriggers stand out from the beach. "This is it."

For the next half hour the commander watched the progress of the little banca convoy as it slowly made its way out to the meeting point, looking like a bunch of ants coming out of an anthill.[5] *Crevalle* circled, submerged, at two knots, staying close to the rendezvous coordinates. Wanting to remain concealed as long as possible, Walker kept his looks through the scope brief—just a few seconds each. Aboard ship the tension was palpable. Orders were orders, but these orders did not sit well with some old hands. To veteran submariners, surfacing the ship a mile off enemy territory to pick up passengers seemed totally unnatural, if not downright suicidal. On the other hand, because they did not know any better, newcomers such as Ensign Bowe thought that being pinned to the bottom by raining depth charges and picking up refugees under the nose of the Japanese were standard submarine operating procedures.[6] By 5:30 P.M. the bancas and boats were just a few hundred yards off the submarine's starboard beam.

"Security and gun details, stand by. Lookouts to the conning tower. Prepare for surfacing." Men scurried through the narrow passageway. Rifles and submachine guns were issued from the small-arms locker. Drums of 20mm ammunition were broken out from the belowdecks magazine. Pharmacist's Mate Fred Loos stood by with his medical kit. Over the intercom the captain announced, "If something comes over, you close the topside hatch and jump over the side. We'll come back to pick you up."[7] No one relished such a circumstance. But from bow to stern, the crew was at action stations. Walker returned to the scope.

WHEN ABCEDE'S ARMADA reached the rendezvous point, the boats dropped sail. And they waited. Bobbing in the water, in the stillness of early evening, they waited. Forty-one pairs of eyes strained to see any sign of a submarine. More than once someone shouted, "Look, the periscope!" All eyes would shift to the spot, but there was nothing to be seen. Kenneth quickly grew discouraged, convinced there was no submarine out there, that it was all a great hoax.[8]

At 5:46 P.M. the wait ended. Two hundred yards ahead of the lead boat, *Crevalle*'s great black nose suddenly broke the surface. Everyone gaped as the ship slowly revealed herself—first the foredeck, then the conning tower, then the afterdeck, finally the stern. Men appeared on the bridge while the decks were still awash. When they hoisted the American flag above the cigarette deck, a huge cheer went up from everyone in every boat. Some of *Susing*'s passengers began to sing "The Star Spangled Banner." Loretta Ossorio began to cry. By the time the song was finished there was not a dry eye on any boat. To Howard Chrisco it all felt like being a kid at Christmas.[9] It *was* Christmas— Christmas in May.

SUDDENLY THE DECK WAS swarming with men. The armed ones were the security detail. The others were the gun crews. Still dripping, the deck gun was quickly unlimbered. The 20mm cannons were loaded and cocked and ready to fire. Walker ordered all four engines started—two for propulsion, two for battery charge. The big diesels coughed to life, white smoke pouring from exhausts along both sides of the submarine's afterdeck. "Come about to course two-nine-zero, all ahead standard."

As his ship turned toward the boats, Walker turned his attention to the task of getting the refugees aboard. "Open the after battery hatch." He looked aft to see a horizontal black wheel spinning amidships. A round door swung upward. Out crawled Chief Petty Officer Fred "Hook" Sutter, who would assist the passengers down the tricky ladder into the crew's mess. Everyone was alert as *Crevalle* approached the bancas. "All back full. All stop."

One of the boats, flying a small American flag, came alongside the submarine as she churned to a halt. "Dayon! Welcome to Negros!" hailed a man standing in the prow of the banca. After exchanging passwords, he introduced himself as Lieutenant Colonel Salvador Abcede, commander of the 7th Military

District of U.S. Armed Forces in the Far East. He asked permission to come aboard.[10]

"Come ahead!" shouted Walker.

Colonel Abcede leaped onto the hull, then scampered up the superstructure toward the bridge fairwater. He was followed by Ben Viloria and a young soldier with a spanking-new U.S. Army radio strapped to his back. The Filipino commander climbed up the ladder to the cigarette deck, met there by the American captain. As they shook hands, Walker thought him a striking figure. Abcede looked nothing like the tatty, dirty guerrilla warrior he had imagined. The young colonel—he was only thirty-one—was dressed in crisp, clean khakis and carried himself with a decidedly military swagger. Pointing to the big boat seaward, Abcede informed Walker that he had not twenty-five passengers for *Crevalle,* but forty-one. The soldier motioned to a second banca as he continued what had become a plea. "Can you take that many? Twenty-one are children, eight are women."[11] They were all American citizens.

Walker thought for a moment. He knew that life aboard his ship was going to be uncomfortable no matter how many boarded. But he also knew that there were no insurmountable problems in feeding and bedding all of the refugees. He turned back to Abcede. "Sure. We'll take them all. Just hurry them aboard."[12]

The evacuees watched as the guerrilla negotiated with the captain. The boats bobbed in the water for an interminable time. People began to wonder why it was taking so long. No sooner had distress overcome them than a signal was flashed, telling the boats to approach the submarine. Another loud cheer came when word was passed that *Crevalle* would take not twenty-five, but all forty-one. Everybody was going to go home. The tiny flotilla converged on the submarine. It was three minutes to six.

When *Susing* was made fast, sailors, dressed mostly in shorts and sandals and reeking of diesel fumes, began pulling passengers out of the boat, passing them to other men on the deck, who pushed them down the open hatch. When the big banca was empty the second took its place and the operation was repeated.

From Abcede's boat a small wooden box was carried up to the deck by another guerrilla officer. The soldier told Walker that the box contained extremely important documents, captured from the Japanese on Cebu by Jim Cushing's patriots. He added that MacArthur was most anxious to see them. A sailor picked up the box, lugged it to the bridge, passing it down through the conning tower. From there it was handed to diving officer Luke Bowdler in the control room with orders to stow it in the captain's cabin.[13]

As the sun began to drop across the Sulu Sea, *Crevalle* bustled with activity. While Walt Mazzone stood by the after hatch, the guerrilla commander approached and introduced himself. "I am Colonel Abcede," he said, then added with a mirthful grin, "That's spelled A-B-C, E-D-E."[14] Abcede walked on, toward the stern, where he had posted his own guard. He had another man on the bow. Abcede seemed very much in control of the situation. Using radios just arrived from America, he communicated with his boats, with his command post on the beach, even with his lookouts in the hills. If they saw an enemy airplane approaching they would transmit a warning in time for the submarine to submerge.

Salvador Abcede had a lot at stake ensuring that *Crevalle*'s brief call was trouble-free. The aftermath of *Narwhal*'s previous visit had caused concern at GHQ in Brisbane about sending another submarine to Basay. Off Balatong Point on 7 February *Narwhal* had successfully unloaded a shipment of supplies badly needed by the guerrillas. She then evacuated two dozen refugees, most of them civilians. But within hours the Japanese had learned, in detail, of her exploit. Five days later the enemy launched a punitive expedition against Abcede's district. They swept through villages, burning and looting as they went. They destroyed crops and livestock. They killed men and women, and children, too—eighty-nine people in all.[15] And then they left. Brisbane was dismayed by the breach of security. To overcome their apprehensions, Abcede had personally guaranteed the safety of this operation to General MacArthur.[16]

THE STILLNESS OF THE EVENING was broken by the clamor of children, a strange and disturbing sound to men at war. It caught Walker off guard. He turned from Abcede to look for the source of the noise. In the fading twilight he watched as ragtag kids clambered up the side of the submarine, looking not unlike pirates boarding a prize vessel. The children ranged from small to large, and there seemed to be many of them. Indeed, half his passengers were under seventeen years of age—the youngest, Janet Lindholm, born the day the war began two and a half years before. A couple of children were in tears, fearful of boarding the black sea monster. Mothers and sailors did their best to reassure them.

One by one the children went down the ladder to the crew's mess. Some climbed down. Others, the small ones, were dropped down the hatch by

"Gooberhead" Johnson, a seventeen-year-old gunner's mate. Seven mothers followed. But only four fathers boarded *Crevalle* that Thursday evening. Three—Ricardo Macasa, Paul Lindholm, and George Ossorio—did not intend to leave Negros. Macasa was not an American citizen. Even though he had lived in the States for seventeen years, he had never applied for citizenship. Lindholm and his family had talked about his staying behind for weeks, but only at this moment, on the deck of the submarine, had he finally made up his mind. He helped his children below, giving each a quick peck on tear-streaked cheeks. Then he bade his wife farewell. Their parting was brief, hardly tender. In her heart Clara had known he would stay, but to hear his words just now, to realize she alone would have to care for her family for the duration of the war, still came as a shock. In disbelief, Clara Lindholm descended into the boat, hearing her husband say to Bill Ruhe, "I think I'll stay up here for a little while."[17]

Paul Lindholm had come to believe that staying behind to continue his ministry was the right and proper and Christian thing for him to do. For days he had wrestled with that weighty issue; it troubled him greatly. His decision came slowly, painfully, then firmly and resolutely. He would endure the hardships of living in the mountains of Negros, a hunted man, so the men and women and children who had come to depend upon his caring and wisdom these past thirty months would not be disappointed. But he would do so only if he truly believed his family would be safe aboard the submarine. Earlier in the week Lindholm had gone to Abcede with his quandary. The guerrilla leader tried to persuade the missionary to leave; he may even have believed he had succeeded.

"Aren't you going down, Mr. Lindholm?" Abcede asked sternly, now knowing full well he would have one more passenger on the banca back to Basay. The minister replied simply that his job on Negros was unfinished. Walt Mazzone, standing nearby, was deeply moved by the words of the missionary. "Here's a guy," he thought, "who has freedom in the palm of his hand and he walks away from it to carry on his work." It was a very meaningful moment in Mazzone's life.[18] But Abcede was not pleased that his earlier arguments to persuade the missionary to leave had failed. "I have orders from MacArthur to send you to Australia." The Reverend Lindholm quietly replied, "Sir, I have orders from headquarters higher than MacArthur's to remain here with your people." Abcede shook his head and smiled. Turning to his adjutant he said, "Ben, these are the kind of people worth fighting for."[19]

On *Crevalle*'s deck Kenneth and Loretta said their brief good-byes to George. There was no big scene in the short time the family had together. It was all rather matter-of-fact. Mother and son felt secure that father would be safe. Father felt the same about wife and son. Fleeting hugs, fleeting kisses, down the hatch they went, leaving George very alone on the deck.

When he climbed from *Susing*, Howard Chrisco looked up into the faces of the palest men he'd ever seen. Even in the dead of winter nobody could be that colorless. Deeply tanned himself, he was puzzled until someone explained, "No sun. Most of us have been cooped up inside the hull for five weeks." A seaman stretched out a hand and pulled the sergeant up to the deck. "Where you from, soldier?" asked Gooberhead the gunner. "Missouri," drawled Chrisco. "Me, too! Welcome home!" the young sailor replied as he helped the sergeant, whose still painful arm hung loosely in its sling, negotiate the steep ladder down. At the bottom another sailor greeted him cheerfully, then pointed him in the direction of the forward torpedo room.[20]

For Russ Snell, leaving the Philippines was bittersweet. Before the war, before 8 December 1941, he had resolved to reenlist, to stay in the islands he had grown so fond of. But after what he had gone through since, he was now very glad to be getting out.[21] He took one last look at Negros, one last gulp of warm Philippine air, then disappeared down the hatch.

As the evacuees went down into the brightly lit crew's mess they were assaulted by a noxious combination of smells: rancid frying grease, cigarette smoke, diesel fumes, and the unmistakable odor of unwashed bodies. To their left, through a narrow doorway, they could see the crew's quarters, a darkened Quonset-shaped room crowded with triple bunks. Men not on duty peered out from under their bedding, astonished to see women and children. Looking around the mess, the passengers could see it was rather basic. Four metal tables affixed to the deck provided seating for meals and for recreation. The top of each table was covered in linoleum and inset with red and black checkers and acey-deucey boards. Beyond the tables was the tiny galley, where the ship's three cooks slaved over their hot griddle. In one corner a fancy radio sat on a recessed shelf, blaring forth music from some far distant station. Across from the galley a huge stainless steel coffee urn, percolating away, was bolted to the wall. A jungle-weary mother asked if the coffee was "real." "You bet. Help yourself," a sailor replied.[22]

From the crew's mess the evacuees were marched forward through the busy control room into officers' country and on to the forward torpedo room. The control room was bathed in eerie red light, which greatly impressed the children. On their way through, some slowed to "ooh" and "ahh" at all the gauges and wheels and multicolored lights. "Don't touch," cautioned Luke Bowdler.

When they got to the torpedo room, the refugees were asked to find a place to sit. Though there was only one torpedo in the racks, it still quite awed the children. Little hands pawed cautiously at the giant missile. Small eyes turned curiously toward the bow and the six gleaming bronze torpedo tubes festooned with numerous pipes and dials and valves. This looked like a grand jungle gym. As they approached the tubes they were summarily shooed away by torpedoman Francis Thomas MacGowan, although with a smile he told the children to call him "Mac." Unhappy at not being permitted to climb about, they settled on the empty skids.

Up on deck, the evacuees' baggage was being brought down the hatch. While supervising the guerrilla stevedores, a thirsty Major Ben Viloria was handed a jug of ice water from the galley—his first cold drink after nearly three years in the jungle.[23] He was delighted by the refreshing treat. From the bridge Colonel Abcede viewed the quieting scene with satisfaction. He was pleased with the speedy progress his men had made getting the passengers out to the submarine and safely on board. Walker, too, was pleased with the short turnaround. The young colonel descended to his banca, there joining Paul Lindholm for the trip back to the beach. As the boat pushed off, a voice shrieked out of the darkness.

"Hey! Wait for us!"

Startled, Abcede spun around to see one last banca pull alongside. "The Reals!" Hands reached out to pull five children and two parents aboard, then hustled them belowdecks—Rose shaking and sobbing as she climbed down the narrow ladder.[24] "My God, I thought we were going to be left behind."

The Reals' banca had been loitering two hundred yards off the submarine's bow, waiting its turn to approach the big ship. As the empty *Susing* pulled past the outrigger, a man shouted to Sam, "The sub is full! There's no more room. You better turn back now."

That news practically sank the little boat. Rose burst in to tears. Bill and John were ashen. Sam grew sullen. Disappointed, restrained, he told the boatman to head for shore. The bow swung around and began to gain speed, when all of a sudden a voice called out, "Ahoy, small boat—return to disembark your passengers!" The relief was immense and immediate. In Visayan, Sam urged the boatman to turn the boat. The banca spun a quick half circle and tacked back to *Crevalle,* where sailors were waiting to haul the family aboard. Nancy, Berna, and Fritz were passed up in the arms of submariners. John and Bill climbed up the steep sides themselves. Rose enjoyed flirting with the men who helped her to the deck. Sam, scowling, followed behind. The family was the last to board.[25] When the family was safely below, Abcede finally took his leave.

When the colonel's banca had cleared *Crevalle,* Walker issued orders to get his ship under way. "Secure the deck. Steer course two-one-six. Standard speed." He then went below to sort things out. The time was 6:37 P.M., just thirty-eight minutes after the first passenger came over the side.

LIEUTENANT GEORGE MORIN led Viola Winn and her children to the officers' wardroom in the forward battery compartment. There, in the center of the table, was a pile of candy. Viola pulled a chocolate bar from the stack. She slowly unwrapped it, snapped off a corner, laid it on her tongue. Tears rolled down her cheeks as she savored the sweetness. Memories of chocolate bars past flashed through her mind. It was the best she had ever tasted.[26] The Lindholm children joined their friends in the wardroom. Eleven-year-old Beverly's eyes lit up when she saw the treasures on the table. She eagerly grabbed a candy bar, practically devouring it in one bite. Then she grabbed another, and another, until she began to feel quite queasy. She would not touch chocolate again for years to come.[27]

On her way through the galley Loretta Ossorio stopped to ask the cook if she could have a piece of "real bread." He gave her a quizzical look. In the jungle, she told him, "we didn't have real bread—wheat bread." Wheat flour had run out years before. Cassava bread made a poor substitute. "I don't ever remember having any in the hills,"[28] she said wistfully as she took her first, happy bite of American white bread.

Twelve-year-old Bill Real stopped dead in his tracks when his family passed through the control room. He had never seen such an array of lights and dials, knobs and wheels, switches and gauges. The machinery at sugar central had nothing on this submarine. He approached a small metal table near the center of the room and peered down at a large circular dial. "What's this?" he asked. "How's it work?" All he got for his curiosity was a stern look. He turned to rejoin his family, but his considerable curiosity about how this great vessel functioned had been thoroughly piqued.[29]

Major Edward Franklin McClenahan was quite happy to be aboard *Crevalle.* He had spent, by his own account, two and a half miserable years in the jungles of northern Negros. Passing Walt Mazzone in the passageway, McClenahan said, "Do you know what I had for breakfast the other day?" Mazzone gave the army man a quizzical look. "I had Japanese liver!" The diving officer decided then and there to steer clear of the major. McClenahan was not happy with his bunking arrangements in the after torpedo room, so he sought out Frank Walker. "You know, you're a lieutenant commander and I'm a major. Where do I really sleep?" Annoyed, Walker replied, "In the bunk you've been assigned." "Well," said the major, "what do I call you?" More annoyed, Walker curtly replied, "Captain!"[30]

As things began to settle, Chief Yeoman Al Dempster moved through each compartment recording the names of his passengers.

In the forward torpedo room Dempster encountered the apparition that was Howard Tom Chrisco. "I was a prisoner of war on Bataan." The Yeo, startled to hear the word "Bataan," stopped writing. Before him stood a thin, dirty, barefoot man in tattered fatigues, his right arm in a sling. The soldier was deeply tanned. His eyes, deeply set in a hollow face beneath a horizontal wave of brown hair, darted constantly, warily, full of suspicion. His voice was tired as he spoke slowly in an Ozark drawl. "We was prisoners for fifteen months. Drove trucks for the Japanese. We escaped last Fourth of July—seven of us. Spent ten months in the jungle with the guerrillas. I got wounded on an ambush, bullet tore right through my elbow. My arm's pretty bad. You got a doctor?"[31]

Dempster knew the story of the terrible Death March on Bataan, knew that Chrisco had been lucky to survive. "You must've been through hell," he said, shaking his head slowly. "There's no doc, but we got a pharmacist's mate. Loos. We call him 'Pinky.' I'll send him up."

In the forward torpedo room Dempster found the sixteen-year-old Ossorio boy, looking for a place to put his suitcase. Kenneth did not tell the sailor it was stuffed with secret guerrilla maps and papers he had collected while working for the resistance on Negros. "Where do I put it?" the boy asked.[32] The chief looked down at the battered bag. "Well, kid, we'll stow it below the torpedo tubes. It should be safe there." The teenager seemed relieved. He climbed into his bunk, the first real bed he had seen since leaving the house on the tree-lined street. He was disappointed to find it hard and uncomfortable. Nevertheless, he was thrilled to be aboard.

In his travels around the boat the Yeo came across two civilians turned soldier, one soldier turned recluse, an ailing Filipino guerrilla who had been on a secret mission for General MacArthur, and three more ex-POWs. A trio of comely young women gave Dempster cause for concern—sailors were already eyeing them. In all, the chief recorded the names of forty people.

As he returned to the control room he passed a shaken Clara Lindholm moving toward the comfort of her children.

Their mother found them on a skid near the torpedo tubes, playing with a tiny chick one of the other children had brought on board. Clara gathered them around. The children asked about their father's decision. "We have to learn to take whatever comes and try not to question it," their mother whispered above the steady drone of the motors and the pumps and the sea rushing by outside.[33] The five Lindholms then bowed their heads in silent prayer.

AT DINNER THAT NIGHT sixteen children and mothers squeezed around the wardroom table to give thanks for their deliverance. Stewards Willie Gregory and Waymon Davis then delivered a feast the likes of which no diner had ever seen. Out came heaping plates of meat, potatoes, vegetables, pitchers full to the brim with milk, bowls of canned peaches, fresh bread, real butter, and more. It was a dazzling array of food. The adults filled their plates, ate ravenously, relished every bite. The children, many of whom had no memory of food such as this, were certain it was no good. One of the boys held up a slice of bread and asked, "What's this?"[34] The meat was not to their liking, and the milk was not right either—it did not taste at all like carabao milk. Howard Chrisco was amazed at the quantity of food given him in the crew's mess. But after the second bite he knew he could not finish it. "Pardon me," he said as he rose, "I've got to go feed the fish."[35] It would be months before he could eat normally again.

That first night aboard was a restless one for many of the passengers. For their benefit George Morin played Brahms' "Lullaby" (sung by Bing Crosby) on the wardroom phonograph.[36] The soothing tones were carried over the intercom throughout the ship, gently encouraging the smaller children to sleep. Older ones, such as Kenneth Ossorio, found that sleep did not come so easily. He went back to the crew's mess to grab a cup of cocoa and swap stories with the sailors. Chrisco made friends with some of the motormacs in the engine room. He spent most of the night amid the deafening roar of the diesels, losing his voice telling his own tales of war. One submariner gave him a pair of black dress shoes to cover his bare feet. The shoes barely fit, and were certainly uncomfortable to a soldier who had spent most of the past two years unshod. But he appreciated the gift nevertheless.

In the captain's cabin, hidden beneath his bunk, sat the sealed wooden box that Abcede had sent aboard. It would sit undisturbed—indeed, mostly forgotten—during the long voyage south.

BY DAWN THE NEXT DAY *Crevalle* was nearly two hundred miles from Balatong Point, cruising south-southeast at fourteen knots. Walker intended to stay on the surface as long as possible, to increase the distance between his ship and Negros. At 2:35 P.M. lookouts spotted two bancas at a range of eight thousand yards. The captain worried that these boats were coast watchers, that they might spot *Crevalle* and report her position to the Japanese. He decided to annihilate them.

Frank Walker felt he had good cause to sink the little boats. On the evening of 9 May, while transiting the dangerous Balabac Strait, en route to his special mission, the big ship spotted a small sailing banca with three men aboard apparently heading for Comiran Island. The captain concluded that the banca was harmless, that it did not harbor watchers. *Crevalle* steamed right past the little boat. When it was well astern of the sub its crew fired two green flares high into the sky. Walker was furious—at himself for being duped by the innocent-looking boat. Next time, he had decided, he would just shoot up little boats like that. And now he had his chance.[37]

The submarine closed the bancas at high speed. As they dropped their sails and paddled furiously for Pearl Bank Island, Walker ordered the gun crew to fire ahead of the boats with the forward 20mm machine gun. The shells only incited the outriggers' crews to paddle harder. "Empty the pan," the captain told Morin, his gunnery officer.[38] As the shells pumped into the wooden boats, the four Filipinos jumped into the sea. The ship circled the hulks, then closed for a closer inspection. The larger of the two bancas contained nothing but a straw hat, a few dried fish, and a basket. There was no evidence of a radio or of flares. Walker called the guerrilla officer, Captain Emilio Quinto, to the bridge to interrogate the men. Quinto questioned the bobbing sailors. They told him they were Moro fishermen. Walker decided to believe them. He would not take them prisoner (where would he find room for them?), nor would he kill them. He let them go, knowing they could still sail the small boat to Pearl Bank. Crevalle returned to her original course, heading for Sibutu Passage.

The second night out, while the boat was entering Sibutu, *Crevalle* celebrated Dean Lindholm's birthday. One of the cooks, Ship's Cook 3rd Class Frank "Mother" Stokes, had baked him a cake, topped with mounds of icing and nine flickering candles. After a hearty round of "Happy Birthday," passengers and crew hungrily devoured the fancy confection.

By the third day, life aboard the submarine had grown routine. The five bunks in chiefs' quarters, a small compartment abutting the wardroom, had been turned over to the ladies, including—especially including—the comely Modesta Hughes. Mothers with small children slept alongside their kids on the decks of the forward torpedo room. Most of the men were quartered in the after torpedo room, though Howard Chrisco and Kenneth Ossorio got bunks forward. *Crevalle*'s crew resorted to hot bunking: one bunk served two or three men sleeping in shifts, an unpopular but at the time quite necessary practice. The use of the toilet—the "head"—was a problem that plagued the ship. More was involved than simply flipping the flush lever. Indeed, the instructions on the use of the head listed eighteen separate steps: "See that bowl flapper valve A is closed, gate valve C in discharge line is open, valve D in water supply line is open. Then open valve E to admit necessary water. Close valves D and E." A missed step or a step in the wrong order would have (and did have) grave consequences. The problems (and mess) grew so serious and the complaints from the stewards, who had to clean up, so numerous that Captain Walker had to order his passengers not to attempt to flush the head on their own, but to let the crew do it for them.

The young children spent most of their day in the wardroom, where their mothers read to them or helped them play games such Monopoly, Parcheesi, and dominoes. The rest of the refugees, basically confined to the torpedo rooms, stayed in their bunks, read, wrote letters, or chatted with the crew. A favorite pastime was catching up with current events in the many recent copies of *Life* magazine carried by *Crevalle*. A reader might learn that *A Tree Grows in Brooklyn* was a national best-seller; that German prisoners of war in the United States were well treated, well fed, and generally happy; that young Red Skelton was one of the country's favorite comedians; or that ten Americans escaped from a Japanese prison camp in Mindanao and lived to tell their story.[39] While the picture magazines entranced Bill Real, he really preferred to wander about the boat, trying to figure out how things worked. He was not above cranking a knob, yanking a lever, or throwing a switch. One of the chiefs, wise to Billy's ways, put up a sign: "Any children found in the control room without their parents will be shot."[40] The message was ineffective. Having spent the past two years being pursued by the Japanese, Bill was not about to be intimidated by a bunch of sailors.

Radioman Jerry Stutzman let the kids come into the radio shack for a few minutes every day. They delighted in pecking at the telegraph key and spinning the dials on the radios. In the evening he let them put on the headset to listen to the dits and dahs of Morse as they danced through the air.[41] Walt Mazzone quickly made friends with four-year-old Nancy Real. He had grown a particularly spectacular beard accented by a fine handlebar mustache. Nancy was greatly amused by tugging on Mazzone's face. When he was on watch, she would take him a cup of coffee. The situation with the passengers was so chaotic that Mazzone thought Nancy was an orphan. He had two god-children her age back in the States; it grieved him to think she might be alone in the world.[42]

The crew enjoyed ribbing Chrisco, Snell, and the other soldiers despite the horrible experiences they had lived through. The sailors learned, for example, that if they dropped a metal platter on the mess deck their guests would jump out of their seats.[43] Navy thought it very funny. Army was unamused. But the crew members were genuinely interested in the amazing stories the soldiers had to tell: about the Bataan Death March, about the atrocities they had witnessed, about their escape from the Japanese, about fighting with the guerrillas.

Each evening, when the submarine was running on the surface, Captain Walker would order the hatches opened to ventilate the ship. Fetid air, built up during the day-long submergence, was quickly purged by fresh sea air, which cleansed the ship, the lungs, and the soul. Loretta Ossorio stood beneath the circular opening in the forward torpedo room, watching intently the small patch of star-speckled sky above. It was her favorite time of the day, for it hinted at the freedoms soon to come.

The submarine steamed across a vacant Celebes Sea. Soon she would have to transit Bangka Strait, then weave her way around the island-dotted, enemy-patrolled inner seas of the Dutch Indies. Australia was still twelve hundred miles to the south.

Three days after receiving orders for the special mission, Captain Frank Walker had effected the rescue of forty passengers, not twenty-five. To everyone's amazement—crew, guerrillas, and passengers—the rescue had been perfectly executed. The entire operation, from surfacing to departure, had taken only fifty-one minutes—a far cry from the five days it took *Searaven* to rescue the thirty-three Australians in 1942. Walker was pleased. As *Crevalle* cruised easily toward Darwin, spirits were high. Everyone aboard felt safe and secure.

# CHAPTER 13

# *Precious Cargo*

JUST PAST MIDNIGHT on Sunday, 14 May, *Crevalle* was nearing Bangka Passage at the northernmost finger of Celebes Island. While most aboard slept, Chief Yeoman Al Dempster was busy in his tiny office typing up *domain Neptunus Rex* cards. It was the crew's idea to pass these out to their passengers as mementos of crossing the equator, scheduled for the next day. In the galley, Mother Stokes was busy with prebreakfast chores, baking a batch of bread and rehydrating the powdered eggs. Up on the bridge, Captain Walker took over the con as his ship began the tricky transit through Bangka. Two and a half hours later he went below to catch some sleep after *Crevalle* had crossed into the Molucca Sea. As dawn overtook the boat Luke Bowdler relieved Jim Blind on the bridge, assuming the duties of Officer of the Deck (OOD). For the next four hours the boat would be his. As he looped his binoculars around his neck, Bowdler noted the low-hanging cumulus clouds. These, he thought, would give the submarine some protection from being spotted from the air. At 5:55 A.M. he was proved dead wrong.

A twin-engine Betty bomber dropped out of the clouds just a few hundred yards off the port beam, intent on sinking *Crevalle*. Bowdler instantly hit the diving alarm. As the Klaxons rang throughout the boat he yelled, "Clear the bridge! Dive! Dive!" The lookouts were dropping from the periscope shears before he finished shouting. Within seconds the bow was covered by the sea. Luke, the last down the hatch, saw the plane drop a bomb, noting with some relief that it would fall astern of his plunging ship.[1]

The crash dive and the bomb explosion woke the entire boat. Captain Walker raced from his stateroom on hearing the alarm. Billy Real, sound asleep on a skid in the forward torpedo room, was jolted awake. Howard Chrisco rose with such a start he banged his head on an overhead pipe. But the crew seemed barely excited by the incident, which many of the passengers found reassuring.

*Crevalle* remained submerged for more than an hour. Before giving the order to surface, Frank Walker called Bowdler into his cabin for a dressing down. What happened? the skipper wanted to know. As his OOD explained the situation in detail, Walker's ire dissipated. With a word of caution, he sent the young jg back to his post. "Surface. Surface," Bowdler called from the conning tower, and at two minutes after seven that gray morning *Crevalle* emerged from the depths. Within half an hour another Betty was sighted, eight miles distant. Again Bowdler dived the boat. Again the plane swooped in and dropped a bomb. And again it was not close. But just two minutes later, a third bomb suddenly exploded directly above the ship, jarring her from bow to stern. Walker decided to stay down to give things time to cool off.

Later that morning, at nine-forty, the high periscope watch sighted the smoke of six ships passing west of Tifore Island, a small atoll midway between Celebes and Halmahera, the vigilant Betty circling above the convoy. *Crevalle* still had four torpedoes in her stern tubes and one forward, and Frank Walker wanted to use them up. Despite the special mission, the secret papers, and the forty passengers aboard, Comsubs had never rescinded the ship's original orders to "wage unrestricted submarine warfare against the enemy." Walker, ever aggressive, decided to attack the enemy ships. At 10:05 A.M. he sent his crew to battle stations.

The tracking party began its work. By ten-eighteen they had identified six marus, two destroyers of the Shinonome class, two destroyer escorts of the Chidori class, and a fifth escort, a converted minesweeper. It took twenty minutes more to determine the enemy ships' precise course and range. Then came discouraging news. The TDC operator, Dick Bowe, said his calculations showed *Crevalle* could not get into position to launch her torpedoes. "The closest we could get would be seven thousand yards from the sternmost ship."[2] Walker scowled. Seven thousand yards—three and a half nautical miles—put the convoy out of range. The captain asked Ruhe to release the men from battle stations. Disappointment showed on his face as Walker dropped down the control room ladder, heading to the wardroom for a fresh cup of coffee. But five minutes later the scenario unexpectedly changed. "Captain to the conning tower!" He was told that the convoy had just changed course, zigging right toward the submarine. Walker had not expected this favorable turn of events but was glad of it. The gongs rang out as the ship returned to battle stations. The flurry of alarms wrought confusion and concern among the passengers in the forward torpedo room. The crew told them only the basics: "The captain's going after an enemy convoy." Those words were not comforting, especially after having already been thrice bombed. In the wardroom Viola Winn, oblivious to the commotion, had gathered the small children, as she did every morning, for reading and playing games. Dean and Jamie Lindholm took a pile of dominoes from a box and began another elaborate construction, while the Real boys serenely played cards.

Things were anything but serene in the tense conning tower as the pursuit continued. Crowded into the tight chamber, seven sweaty men concentrated upon waging war. By ten fifty-five the distance to the convoy had closed to twenty-eight hundred yards. Captain Walker picked his target, the third ship in the line. He would shoot when the range dropped below two thousand yards—a nautical mile. Peering at the fat freighter through the attack scope with just moments to go, Walker heard Bill Ruhe ask, "Frank, did you do a sweep? Do you know where the escorts are?" The captain grumbled at his exec's criticism but followed the suggestion. As he spun the periscope, Walker suddenly pulled his eye from the finder, shouting, "Get me down! Get me down! Flood negative!"[3]

For all his submarine experience, the captain had made a textbook error: he failed to search a three-hundred-sixty-degree arc. The skipper never spotted the smoke bomb the Japanese aircraft had dropped above him, signaling his presence to the convoy. Nor had he seen one of the deadly Chidoris break rank and turn toward him, belching thick black smoke behind a fearsome bow wake. One hundred twenty men, women, and children were about to pay for Frank Walker's mistake. As *Crevalle* plunged toward the safety of the deep, everybody aboard heard the loud, whining screws of the high-speed sub killer bearing down on them, passing directly overhead, steaming away. Only sonarman Grandma Biehl heard the telltale splashes.

As THE SUBMARINE PASSED through one hundred ninety feet, the first depth charge exploded just forward of the conning tower. The boat shook violently. And then hell broke loose. There were no clicks. Only whams. Seven more gigantic whams in rapid order. *Crevalle* was tossed about in the incompressible deep like a mere toy. She pitched, she rocked, she rolled, she swayed, groaning all the while. Crew and passengers were thrown to the deck, against bulkheads, out of bunks, under tables. The concussion caused many to see a bright flash of red and to set off loud ringing in their ears. Throughout the ship light bulbs shattered, fittings snapped, cork insulation showered down like tiny snowflakes. The thick bronze locking rings on the torpedo tube doors started to rotate open. Amid the bedlam the crew managed to close and dog all the intercompartment watertight doors.

In the first seconds of the attack all manner of things took to the air. Loose wrenches flew through the engine rooms. A two-hundred-pound tool locker levitated and spun completely around in the forward torpedo room.[4] The steel bowl in the officers' head blew off its stanchions. The blinker gun in the conning tower sailed out of its holder, smashing into Captain Walker's head. The ship's library cascaded down upon the children playing in the wardroom. Dean Lindholm's domino edifice careened deckward.

The sea streamed in through the steering wheel, soaking the helmsman and the talker. "Clear the conning tower!" Al Dempster, who had been sitting in the hatchway recording the attack approach, jumped to the control room deck, followed rapidly by others. Things were bad there, too. Water poured down from the conning tower, drenching the electronic bays full of delicate radar and sonar equipment. The emergency alarm from the master gyro compass blared. The mercury from the auxiliary compass had been blown out. Their failure meant shifting to an army tank compass bolted to the forward bulkhead. Two ominous green lights glowed on the otherwise all-red Christmas tree, the panel that showed any open hatches. Diving officer Walt Mazzone struggled to keep *Crevalle* under control as the flooding shifted the balance of the submarine in devilish ways.

The walls in the officers' quarters broke loose when their fasteners sheared. A light bulb had exploded directly above Rodger Winn's head. The shards showered down around him, but none hit him. From beneath the table scared eyes peered out. Eight-year-old Berna Real, claustrophobic and trembling with fear, watched sailors stuff mattresses around leaking pipes.[5] "Gulp air!" Mrs. Winn told the children. "Otherwise your ears will hurt from the pressure." Two young ones grabbed the legs of electrician's mate Jack William Singer as he came to check on them. Looking down into their frightened faces, he gave them a paternal pat on their heads, struck by the fact that though obviously terrified, the children did not panic. "Be as quiet as you can. If you talk or make any sound at all they can get our exact position," he told them. "You don't want the Japanese to hear us, do you?" Little heads shook no.[6]

The situation in the forward torpedo room, where most of the passengers were quartered, was alarming. Water poured in through myriad fractured vents, flanges, and gaskets. The sonar head connection leaked. The pitometer connection leaked. The starboard vent riser leaked. All the sea valves leaked. The space below the deck plates filled with water, submerging the two lower torpedo tubes. And if that was not enough, the torpedo room's heater burst into flames.

The sledgehammer blows against the hull quickly became too much for one woman. When she became hysterical, torpedoman "Rocky" Langfeldt seized her hard by the arms, shook the panic out of her, and told her to keep quiet.[7] Howard Chrisco was awed when the two cast steel dogs sealing the lower escape trunk hatch suddenly sheared off during the explosions. The oblong door flopped open, swinging crazily on a single hinge, as water trickled in.[8] Chief Torpedoman Jim Howard calmly peered into the passage. He shouted to his men that the gasket on the upper hatch had blown, ordering them to rig a chain fall to close it up. Men raced for the block and tackle. They hooked one end to the hull, the other to the lower hatch, then quickly hauled the fall tight. They knew that if the outer hatch failed, the chain would not hold the lower door, nor stop the sea from pouring in. In the middle of it all, Loretta Ossorio wrapped her arms around torpedoman Mac MacGowan. "I'm sacred," she told him. "So am I, ma'am." Kenneth jumped down from his bunk to join them. The pair felt safer clinging to the veteran submariner as the blasts continued to rock the ship.[9]

On the torpedo room deck Clara Lindholm worked at keeping her daughters calm. They had been through many scary times in the mountains, but this was downright terrifying. Here they had no control over anything. They were now truly in God's hands. Beverly asked gravely if the ship was sinking, asked if they would all die. "I don't know," Clara told her honestly. Silently she prayed her husband would not lose his family aboard *Crevalle*. When toddler Janet began to cry, a sailor gave the girl a piece of a candy bar to quiet her.[10]

THE BARRAGE WAS OVER in less than a minute, leaving behind a cyclonelike trail of destruction. In the stillness of the deep, all eyes instinctively strained upward, hoping to see through the thick steel hull, hoping to see that their enemy had broken off his attack, moved on, and would not return. A spooky silence spread throughout the boat, punctuated only by the sound of leaking water. After some moments all eyes leveled on their neighbors as if to check them out, as if to make sure everyone was all right. Clara Lindholm could clearly see terror in the eyes of her fellow refugees, perhaps, too, in the eyes of the crew. Kenneth Ossorio watched in horror as his suitcase full of secret guerrilla documents floated in the flooded bilges. Russ Snell, lying in his bunk, looked around at the mess in the torpedo room. He thought about the danger he was now in, comparing it to past perils. Fighting as a guerrilla was certainly dangerous, too, but in the jungles he could always get up and run away. "In this damn submarine there ain't no place to run!"[11]

People moved slowly and quietly around the crippled submarine. "Is it over?" they whispered among themselves. "Is it done?" Through the hull they could still hear the faint sounds of propellers and the distinct and dreaded sound of sonar actively pinging for the ship. *Crevalle* was deeper now, and depth meant safety. At four hundred feet, the sub crawled along at two-thirds speed. With his own sonar knocked out, Captain Walker had no way of determining the position of the enemy above. Suddenly the screws of the Chidori grew louder. "He's shifting to short scale. He's making a run!" "Steady as she goes," replied the skipper. All eyes again soared toward the surface. No splashes. No clicks. Only whams. Without warning a string of eight more charges exploded close aboard. The shock waves slammed against the hull with the roar of a freight train. Then the sea went silent again.

The second attack unnerved some of those who had weathered the first. Now fear gnawed at their insides, churned their stomachs, and constricted their throats. There was nothing to do but sit it out. Billy Real, dangling his feet over the edge of a top bunk, thought the whole thing was fun until he saw a sailor crying. Then he got worried. Some crewmen, such as motormac William John Curran, were more circumspect about their condition. He truly did believe this was the end, that he was about to die. But he would not give himself over to his fears. A mate asked, "How can you be so calm?" Curran looked at the man closely. "What the hell good is it to get excited?"[12] Loretta Ossorio had felt strangely composed after the first attack. A devout Catholic, she prayed silently to herself as the explosions rocked the boat. When the second attack came she felt strong enough to tell her son, "Don't ask me how I know, but everything will be all right."

*CREVALLE* CREPT SILENTLY AWAY from her pursuers—undetected, or so Captain Walker hoped. Though he never gave the order for "silent running," his crew had spontaneously shut down all noise-generating systems that might give away her location, in particular the ventilation. Within minutes the temperature inside had reached one hundred twenty degrees. With the humidity nearly one hundred percent, the air was suffocating. Sweat poured off people in rivulets, saturating the decks, while beads of condensation covered the hull walls. Dean Lindholm, sitting in the dimness of the wardroom, grew concerned that water from burst pipes was drenching him. He looked around the room to find the source until he realized he was being soaked by his own perspiration.[13] Doc Loos cruised the passageway, passing out salt tablets. When he reached the wardroom, he fetched some cool water for the children. He cautioned them to stay put while the captain evaded the enemy. Walker himself stopped by, too, telling Viola Winn and her wards they were doing just fine. When he left, Rodger Winn asked his mother to say a prayer. "Dear Heavenly Father, we thank you that you took care of us in the mountains and on the trip to this submarine. Watch over us now and keep us safe."[14] Twelve hushed voices finished the prayer, "Amen."

As minutes became hours the air inside *Crevalle* grew foul; the finite amount of oxygen within the pressure hull was slowly being replaced by carbon dioxide. To preserve precious air, Walker ordered the crew not to smoke. By then the oxygen was so depleted a match would not have stayed lit. He also ordered $CO_2$ absorbent to be spread around the compartments. The white powder soaked up carbon dioxide, prolonging the atmosphere a little longer. In the wardroom the kids began to fall asleep. "Blessed is the sleep of little children," thought Viola Winn, not perceiving the danger. Breathing became difficult, and with the suffocating heat came enervation. Those who could, lay in their bunks. Few men were on their feet. Walt Mazzone was one of them. He fought to keep the boat level and neutrally buoyant. Knowing how critical his job was to the survival of the submarine, he steadied himself with one arm wrapped around the control room ladder, his eyes constantly scanning the depth gauges, woozily alert for even minute variations in pitch or depth.

Forty minutes after the second attack Grandma Biehl managed to get the passive sonar working. He huddled in the damp conning tower, straining to hear the noises of the sea. The first pattern had knocked out the sound training motors; it was necessary for radioman Albert Bower to move the sonar heads manually up in the forward torpedo room. Biehl and Bower communicated via talkers. "Give me another two degrees right," Biehl would ask. "Two degrees right," would come back the response. It was slow going, but eventually Biehl provided his captain with an accurate tactical picture of the enemy's activities. As the noon hour approached, the captain knew there were three ships circling and pinging. Biehl whispered some good news to Walker: the enemy could not find the submarine. At 12:02 P.M. Walker ordered the boat's speed cut from two-thirds to one-third to conserve the battery. He then concentrated upon lightening the ship—there were twenty-two tons of water in the forward bilges, making control precarious. Any slight change in the sub's angle sloshed thousands of gallons of water, shifting the boat's balance. At her last refit in Fremantle, *Crevalle* had been given a powerful new centrifugal trim pump for an occasion such as this. In short order tons of water were forced back into the sea. Walker was very pleased with the new pump. It was, he wrote in his report, "wonderful and pumped quickly and quietly."[15] For the next hour and a half, while the pump ticked silently away, the Japanese continued their sweep for the submarine. Many times they passed directly overhead *Crevalle* without picking her up. At 1:29 P.M. Biehl could no longer hear screws, only pinging. At 3:00 P.M. he could hear nothing but the Molucca Sea. The talker in the forward torpedo room passed on the news. Everyone was thrilled that their five-hour ordeal was over.

People finally began to relax. Compartments filled with the sound of chatter as crew and passengers compared their experiences. "They're all severe," said Jack Singer to one of the civilians. "Most of the crew take it matter-of-factly. But you gotta have confidence that everything's gonna be okay. When you've made a few runs you get used to it—to a degree. Well, you're never totally used to it, but after you settle down, it's mind over matter. You say a silent prayer and you go through it."[16]

At five-thirty that afternoon Walker ordered Mazzone to take the ship up to sixty-six feet—periscope depth. Hoping against hopes, he ordered the main scope raised. When he peered through the eyepiece he could see nothing. "Down scope." Walker moved to the attack scope and tried again. "Down scope." They were both smashed, and *Crevalle* was blind. Walker ordered the boat down to one hundred fifty feet, the course held at three-one-zero.[17]

An hour later Walker ordered the ship up to radar depth, forty-five feet. Radar operator Biehl had already warmed up the SJ search set when the captain gave the signal to start the motor that would rotate the parabolic dish. He flipped the switch and waited. He flipped it again. And waited. A frustrated Biehl told him the set was dead. Frank Walker now faced a dilemma. He believed that if he surfaced there would not be any ships in sight. But he was not sure. Japanese escort captains had more than once caught an unwary submarine in just such a predicament. The sub killers would shut down their engines and drift, while their sonarmen listened very, very carefully. He mulled the risks over in his mind. "Lookouts to the conning tower. Surface! Surface!"

The Klaxons rang out three times as *Crevalle* rose from the depths.

All hands were alert to the dangers as *Crevalle* slowly rose to the surface. Decks awash, lookouts and captain raced up the ladder to the bridge. A quick scan across the horizon revealed nothing. A relief. A more leisurely survey also revealed nothing. Greater relief. Once Walker was satisfied there was no enemy threat, he ordered the hatch in the forward torpedo room opened to ventilate the submarine. The room immediately became a maelstrom as fresh air was sucked the length of the boat, feeding the four hungry diesels near the stern and rapidly replacing the dank, lifeless atmosphere within the hull. Dean Lindholm was drawn like a magnet to the opening, there gulping down great lungfuls of ocean air.[18] Up on the main deck, repair parties surveyed the damage in the waning light. The first depth charging had smashed the breech cover off the four-inch gun. The forward bridge fairwater was dimpled and the ammunition ready locker blown open. All running lights and the searchlight were smashed. The 20mm gun mounts had been torn loose. Most serious of all, the bow planes would not rig in, which would make running on the surface difficult. After reviewing the list, Captain Walker counted his blessings, for he knew the damage might have been much worse, even fatal. His ship was less crippled than she was hobbled. But she was out of commission as an offensive weapon. She had lost two of her eyes—the radar and periscopes. And her hearing—the sonar—was impaired. But she was still afloat, she could still dive, and though it would take a little longer, she could still get safely down to Australia.

Throughout the night of 14 May *Crevalle* cruised southward on the surface at sixteen knots. Belowdecks the mood was subdued. Sailors worked through the night trying to fix the long list of damaged equipment. Radarman Biehl sat on the deck of the conning tower, patiently disassembling the electronics bay. Albert Bower carefully dried each component as Biehl pried it out of the rack, fragile tubes and condensers spread at his feet. With the radar out, Captain Walker cautioned his lookouts to be extra alert. He did not want the enemy springing out of the pitch-black night. The passengers slept fitfully, fearing another attack might come. But many took comfort in the fact that familiar routines had not changed. Mother Stokes still baked his bread. Al Dempster still typed his reports in his tiny office. Captain Walker still strolled through the boat, making sure everybody was okay.

On Monday morning Clara Lindholm woke up feeling paralyzed. The intensity of events the day before had drained away all her strength. Doc Loos came to check on her. He took her pulse. He listened to her lungs. He looked at her throat. Then he asked her a few questions. After mulling over the symptoms he announced that she was suffering from "battle fatigue." Clara was amused by the diagnosis. Loos gave her some tranquilizers and within a few hours she was her normal, cheerful self again.[19]

Midmorning, sonar picked up distant pinging. A sense of fear instantly permeated the boat. *Crevalle* was in no shape to go through another encounter with a determined enemy. For two hours Biehl, Bower, and Dempster tracked the active sonar. By noon they lost contact. Word was quickly passed through the boat. People relaxed again. At 4:30 P.M. the master gyro compass was restarted, and by eight-twenty that evening it was back in commission. That night, navigator Bill Ruhe went up on deck to shoot the stars with his sextant. With a good reading he was able to calculate the submarine's true position. At 9:00 P.M. on Monday Walker was able to send a radio message to Comsubs, outlining his failed attack and the resultant damage to his ship.

Shortly after midnight on Tuesday, 16 May, the submarine finally crossed the equator. Al Dempster brought cheer to his passengers by passing out the *domain Neptunus Rex* cards he had prepared before the attack, each signed by Frank Walker and Bill Ruhe. Many of the refugees had looked forward to the "crossing-the-line" party planned for the occasion, but events intruded; the cards would have to suffice. The quality and quantity of food began to change. This was not unusual at the end of a long war patrol, but was now exacerbated by the further loss of fresh meat, spoiled when the freezers were shut down during the depth charge attack in the Molucca Sea. Mother Stokes and the other cooks were forced to use more rice, a shift in diet that pleased no one but the children, who had survived on the grain in the jungles. Having toiled nearly nonstop since the attack on Sunday, early Tuesday evening Henry Biehl and Albert Bowers got the SJ search radar working. Partially. The pair had stripped every component from the radar rack, cleaned it, checked it, replaced it if they could, then reassembled the conglomeration. Next they tackled the radar projector unit. That involved removing a large flange in the conning tower, held fast by twenty long bolts. The work was slow and tedious. When they took off the cover, a circuit board fell out. Grandma said he had found the problem. "The standing wave resistance card was blocking the circular wave antenna."[20] Luke Bowdler, the OOD, looked puzzled. Biehl, waving the card in his hand, explained he was now sure he could fix the SJ. Topside, a repair crew had been working on the jammed radar mast. "Try it now!" somebody yelled down the hatch. When Biehl flipped the rotator motor switch, the dish

DOMAIN NEPTUNUS REX
(Regions of the Raging Seas)

HARKEN ALL YE!

Pay due Homage to *Ricardo C. Macasa Jr.*

for on the _____ on *14 MAY* 194*4*
He did enter my realm, — Undergoing all Maltreatment
and torture in such a manner as to prove him well worthy
of being admitted as a member of my Royal Court.
Whereunto I have signed and do set my Seal of approval.

Attest:                              NEPTUNUS REX
Davy Jones.                          Ruler of the Deep.

"Crossing the equator" card handed out to all forty passengers on *Crevalle.*
Note the name of the submarine has been cut out, and the card is
signed by Frank Walker and Bill Ruhe.
(Dick Macasa)

failed to spin. He thought for a few moments, then turned to Walker. The radar
could be turned by hand, he suggested. The captain agreed to try, and soon the
SJ hummed back to life. At first the radar could see but a mile around the boat,
but it was better than being totally blind, especially at night.

At eleven minutes past midnight on Wednesday, Captain Walker sent a second message to Comsubs, giving *Crevalle*'s estimated time of arrival at Port
Darwin. He then knuckled down to write his patrol report.

Every submarine captain was expected to submit a detailed report of all
aspects of his patrol when he returned to port. Comsubs had established an
outline that skippers were expected to follow closely. Walker, with the help of
Bill Ruhe, began writing a time line of all noteworthy events on the patrol,
based upon the ship's log, and ending each day's entry with *Crevalle*'s position, miles steamed, and fuel used. There were sections on the weather
encountered and all ship and aircraft contacts that had been made. Each attack
was covered in detail, including the serial numbers and maintenance history of
the torpedoes expended. Because of the depth chargings, the section "Major
Defects and Damage" ran six pages. When he got to "Personnel," Walker cited
Ruhe, Mazzone, and Morin for their "superb performance."[21] Because of the

top-secret nature of the special mission, Walker elected to submit a separate report for 9–11 May. Chief Yeoman Al Dempster typed up the completed report on Multilith stencils, ready for immediate duplication and distribution upon arriving back in Fremantle.

Leaks continued to plague the crew and passengers throughout the voyage. Walker's new trim pump worked overtime keeping the bilges relatively dry. And the bow planes continued to cause trouble, too. When *Crevalle* surfaced on Wednesday evening the planes, critical to depth control submerged but a hindrance to the helm on the surface, would not rig in. They had to be laboriously cranked back into position by hand. The captain urged his repair crew to concentrate on fixing the plane motors and linkage. They succeeded in restoring the bow planes to full operation by Thursday morning. And Biehl continued to work on the SJ radar—managing to increase its effective range. Late on the seventeenth it saw land at thirty-seven miles.

Just before sunrise on Friday, 19 May 1944, *Crevalle*'s radar picked up the outline of northern Australia. And at 6:29 A.M. her lookouts spotted two boats to the south. As the vessels got closer they could make out the lines of a sleek Fairmile-class Australian Navy motor launch and a dumpy motor ketch. They were heading for the American submarine. When Captain Walker rang up All Stop, his ship rapidly lost way in the slight chop. The launch approached *Crevalle*, the launch's skipper hailing through a megaphone that he was there to pick up the passengers. This was a surprise to Walker. He had always assumed he would drop them off at the boom jetty inside Darwin Harbor. Another man, in U.S. Navy khakis, called out that he was there for the "mail" Walker had brought out from Negros. The one-hundred-twelve-foot HMAS *ML815* came alongside and was tied up to the submarine. Commander X. M. Smith, who headed the American base at Darwin, clambered up the side. Walker ordered the sealed wooden box brought from his stateroom.[22] He had wondered what was in the container, what was so important that a base CO came to pick it up personally, but Walker was never to find out. Smith gave the submariner a signed receipt for the box. Sailors cautiously lifted it into the launch.

Her duty done, the Fairmile pulled away to let the sixty-ton trawler *Chinampa* nuzzle alongside.

Belowdecks in the submarine word spread quickly among the forty that they were disembarking now, not later, in Port Darwin. There was a sudden a frenzy of activity. Sailors descended into the torpedo room bilges to retrieve still-soggy suitcases. Howard Chrisco pulled on the navy-issue black dress shoes a seaman had given him. Clara Lindholm and Viola Winn donned their best dresses. Nancy Real grabbed a last kiss and hug from Walt Mazzone. In short order, everybody was ready.

Chief Hook Sutter opened the after battery hatch. One by one the evacuees climbed the steep ladder into the bright Australian sunshine. They had not seen the sun since they left Negros eight days before. It seemed brighter than they ever remembered. Captain Walker called the group together on the deck—they assembled next to the battered four-inch gun. He addressed them in his deep, rich Down East voice: "You have been our precious cargo," he began. "Your conduct aboard this ship was magnificent." He continued by apologizing for hauling his passengers into a dangerous situation; he was sorry for the inconvenience caused. He explained that *Crevalle* was a warship on a war patrol, she still had five live torpedoes. He said he had felt duty-bound to fire them if a target presented itself. He thanked his passengers for bearing with the hardships his decision entailed. And he ended by warning them "not to mention at any time the name of this ship, the locality of your embarkation, or the means by which you have been evacuated."[23] To Walker's surprise the gathering then applauded him.

The forty refugees gather on the deck of *Crevalle* just outside
Darwin Harbor, 19 May 1944.
(U.S. Navy from U.S. Naval Institute Collection)

There was just time to pose for a picture. The captain took his place next to Loretta Ossorio and Virginia Macasa in the front row. "Squeeze together a little more," cried the photographer. They squeezed. "You, in the back, with the wavy hair, stand taller!" He did. "Everybody smile!" Click. "One more, please." Click. And then it was time to leave. "Hey, 'depth-charge buddy'!" Mac MacGowan called out to Loretta. "Here's my mom's address in Los Angeles. Call her if you can, tell her I'm fine. If you get down to L.A., be sure to stop by, she'd love to see you."[24] MacGowan gave her a big hug and a peck on the cheek. Then there was a flurry of final good-byes, hugs, kisses, shaking hands, don't-forget-to-writes. And, of course, tears. Many eyes, many cheeks, were moist that morning.

Over the side they went—women first, then the small children, carefully passed from hand to hand. The caretaker of the group, Colonel George H. Yeager of the AIB, signed a receipt for his wards. By 8:45 A.M. everyone was aboard, the lines cast off. Then *Chinampa* turned from the submarine and pulled away. It was headed to a remote intelligence base on the eastern side of the harbor. Waving continued on both boats for many minutes. When Walker returned to the bridge, he snapped a series of orders to get under way. *Crevalle*, under the protection of the Fairmile, still had a two-hour cruise before she would dock in Darwin.

# CHAPTER 14

# *Freedom*

THE REFUGEES MAY HAVE expected Australia to be a land of milk and honey, but as the *Chinampa* drew nearer to shore, many began to wonder. Far to the left, far to the right, all they could see was a flat tableland stretching behind modest brown cliffs. Gray gum trees, singly and in small clumps, punctuated the stark landscape. Far in the distance they could make out the city of Darwin. All hoped it would be their destination. The harbor was busy, a little like Manila Bay before the war. They slid past a fleet of uncountable warships and auxiliaries and merchantmen—cruisers, tankers, landing barges; frigates, freighters, and submarines. The forty noted, too, a forest of forlorn masts poking out from the deeps, solemn testimony to the five dozen raids the Japanese made on Darwin. The sight of the sunken ships made a vivid impression on Kenneth Ossorio, for he had never seen such devastation.[1] The old trawler sailed on down the center of the channel, parallel to the city, making no move toward shore. Now the forty were puzzled and vaguely upset. Why weren't they headed into town? The boat kept on a steady course. Two miles farther they felt *Chinampa* lean to the left, just a thousand yards off Fort Point at Darwin's southern tip. But instead of heading for the dock, their vessel entered another, narrower channel and kept going right on past town and, as it seemed, past all civilization. Now the forty could see no towns, not even any houses. Eyes wandered across the desolate landscape. Brown. All brown and gray. Then they noticed bright patches of green off the port bow. It seemed from such a distance to be a forest. But as the ketch sailed closer, the sharper-eyed passengers noted a familiar pattern to nature's arrangement. Their disappointment was manifest when they realized the boat was heading straight for a mangrove swamp.

*Chinampa* made a hard turn to the left just before reaching a small, rocky island. The big boat's engines slowed, then stopped. She wallowed in the gentle swells as a smaller, distinctly nonmilitary-looking boat—perhaps some rich man's yacht before the war—came alongside about a half mile offshore. The passengers were told that *Chinampa* could carry them no farther, for the water was too shallow. They were asked to gather their things and climb carefully into the other vessel. Soon the boats parted and the yacht headed straight for the swamps. After just a few minutes this boat, too, slowed, then stopped. The refugees were now truly baffled. "Where are we?" Colonel Yeager remained tight-lipped. All of a sudden a fleet of rowboats sprang out of the dense mangroves, making their way toward the cruiser.[2] To many it was a mirror image of that scene off Balatong Point.

Once again the troupe clambered over the side, careful to avoid a dip in the sea. When all were embarked, the rowers pulled on their oars, heading back to the slough.

The refugees were landed at a small dock nearly hidden among the mangroves, delighted to be on land again after eight days at sea. They walked, still barefoot, up a well-trodden path to a group of tin-roofed huts. There the forty were greeted warmly by a squad of American nurses. A basket of fresh apples sat upon a veranda table. "Help yourself," said one of the nurses. Rodger Winn approached cautiously. He turned to his mother. "Have I ever eaten an apple?" Viola Winn said with a laugh, "No, none of you have. But oh, they're so good!" And she took one for herself.[3]

The women and small children were led into the first building and shown cots with clean sheets and brightly colored packages resting on top, gifts from the Red Cross. The children tore at the boxes, delighted and amazed by what they found inside: combs and real soap, playing cards, even chewing gum. The biggest hit was the most simple—a toothbrush.[4] One child, accustomed to sleeping on the ground and most recently on a torpedo skid, took one look at the bunks and with worry in his voice complained to his mother, "If I go to sleep in that bed I'll fall out."[5]

Their temporary home was called the Lugger Maintenance Section. The name was meant to divert attention from this otherwise top-secret base. Prior to the war, Darwin had been a hub for the Japanese pearling industry. The boats used by the pearlers, sampans to the Japanese, were called luggers by the Australians. In December 1942 a group of Australian and Dutch commandos had arrived to convert the abandoned government quarantine station into a base for clandestine operations. The LMS, as it became known, was operated by the Allied Intelligence Bureau.[6] It was used for training parties about to be inserted into enemy-held territory in the Netherlands East Indies, the Solomons, and the Philippines, and, more recently, for receiving Americans evacuated from the Philippines. The LMS had been a busy way station since the first group of refugees had arrived in November 1943. The evacuees, under the care of Courtney Whitney's Philippine Regional Section, were kept well away from the commando teams—even the ever-observant Kenneth Ossorio and the ever-curious Bill Real were unaware of their presence.

The newly free spent the day lounging around the camp, eating fresh fruit and vegetables, catching up on the latest newspapers and magazines. The children were amused by the antics of a kookaburra's cackling cry, and were delighted, too, to watch the colorful parrots and budgerigars roosting in the trees. U.S. Army quartermasters brought out cardboard boxes full of surplus khakis and fatigues. Ernesto Jaboneta, at the end of the line, pulled out the last pair of pants, disappointed that they were vastly oversized. That afternoon Bill Real decided to wade in the clear waters, not realizing there might be boy-eating crocodiles hidden among the gnarled swamp roots. As evening approached Kenneth and Loretta Ossorio wandered down to the small beach between the mangroves to enjoy the sunset. Within minutes they retreated in haste, pursued by hordes of pesky sandflies.[7]

After a filling dinner the forty turned in for the night, knowing they would be rousted by their guards well before dawn for the long trip to their next destination.

CREVALLE HAD FOLLOWED well astern *Chinampa*, but upon entering the harbor had headed straight for the navy base at the foot of Mitchell Street on Darwin's southern end. There she moored to the boom jetty at 10:42 A.M. Repair crews came aboard to assess the damage caused by the 14 May depth charging. It was decided that only minor repairs could be made locally. The heavy work would have to wait until the boat reached Fremantle. Except for those on official business—and except for Captain Walker, who lit out for the airfield to have a drink with flier friends—*Crevalle's* officers and men were confined to the jetty. Most did not object, for Darwin was not exactly an exciting liberty port.

Even in mid-1944 Darwin felt like a forward base. It was the largest city in northern Australia—indeed, the only place in Australia's Northern Territory, then and now, big enough and bustling enough to rightly be called a city. It is a community unique on the Australian continent, for Darwin is closer to Manila than to Sydney or Melbourne. After the Japanese made a deadly raid in

February 1942, most of the city's fifty-eight-hundred inhabitants had been evacuated to the south. That first attack, by carrierborne aircraft, sank eighteen ships in Darwin's vast harbor, killed more than two hundred people, destroyed dozens of Allied airplanes, rendering the place virtually untenable as a defensive base.[8]

In those dark days of early 1942, Darwin had practically been the front line—the enemy just a short hop across the Timor Sea. Because Allied commanders believed the Japanese were planning an invasion of Australia, Darwin's defenses were beefed up with local troops hurriedly returned from duty in the deserts of North Africa and with green but eager American soldiers. A sprawling air base was built in the savanna outside Batchelor, fifty miles south of Darwin. Among the first planes to reach the new base, in February 1942, were those long-missing Douglas A-24 attack bombers from Jimmy Dyer's beleaguered, flightless 27th Bomb Group. Originally bound for the Philippines, the planes spent their lives in the defense of Australia.

By mid-1944 the Japanese were on the run, all thoughts of invading Australia gone. As Allied troops pushed across the Bismarck barrier, Darwin's importance had begun to fade, but it nevertheless remained an important port, especially to the submarines providing supplies to the Philippines.

THE SLEEK *ML815* reached the wharf at Darwin well ahead of *Crevalle* and *Chinampa*. Commander Smith passed the wooden box containing Admiral Koga's papers to an officer courier waiting on the jetty. The officer was rushed to nearby Darwin Airport, there handing his package to an army pilot. The papers had been deemed so important, needed so urgently at GHQ, that the army air force ordered a special courier flight, probably using its fastest, longest-range fighter, the Lockheed P-38 Lightning, the same type of aircraft that hunted down Admiral Yamamoto Isoruku the year before. The plane was airborne within minutes. Some six hours and eighteen hundred miles later, the Lightning touched down at Brisbane. By mid-Friday the precious cargo was in the hands of SWPA's chief of intelligence (G-2), General Charles A. Willoughby.

Anticipation was high at GHQ. Because Willoughby and his people had known only that the package was coming, not what it contained, G-2 had arranged a diverse welcoming committee: coders in case the papers required decoding, translators and materials experts if they required special handling. He had all the bases covered.

Eager hands carefully opened the wooden box, carefully prising out its contents. They placed Pedro Gantuangko's leather portfolio on a table, noting the gold-embossed seal of the Imperial Japanese Navy. When the flap was opened, the examiners could see sheaves of paper tied together with silk ribbon, and others bound in red. High-level stuff, commented an observer—the Japanese used red covers only for the most important documents. A white-gloved hand reached into the cavity, removed a folder, and opened it with care, revealing pages imprinted with Japanese kanji characters in purple-blue ink. The analysts crowded around. "Mimeo," offered one officer. "Plain language!" announced another, clearly astonished. A communal sigh was released, for no code would have to be broken. The document would require nothing more than translating.

Colonel Sydney Forrester Mashbir stepped to the fore. A Japanese-language expert, he headed the Allied Translator and Interpreter Section (ATIS) of SWPA. With his neatly trimmed mustache and his center-parted hair, Mashbir looked a little like movie swashbuckler Douglas Fairbanks. The unit under his command provided language services to MacArthur's entire organization, interrogating captured prisoners and translating captured documents. His unit would now tackle the initial work on the Koga Papers, arguably the most important cache ever to come their way. After everyone had had a chance to see the portfolio's contents, Mashbir's men removed them to Indooroopilly, a rambling old house on the outskirts of Brisbane requisitioned by ATIS as its headquarters.

HOURS BEFORE SATURDAY'S DAWN, nurses at the LMS awakened the forty refugees, fed them a cold breakfast, and at 4:00 A.M. packed them into buses. As the convoy drove south along the Stuart Highway, Ernesto Jaboneta was surprised and delighted to see kangaroos hopping through the headlight's faint beams. He had lived all his life in the Philippines. He never thought he would ever see a live kangaroo, when all of a sudden he heard a low "whump!" The sound caught Kenneth Ossorio's attention. "What was that?" he asked the driver. "Just another wallaby," said the man. "Another wallaby? You hit many?" Ossorio asked, aghast. "Yeah, the road's sometimes littered with them."

After ninety minutes the buses passed through the wired gates of the air base at Batchelor. All eyes were glued to the flight line, where row upon row of shiny aircraft sat in the dim newness of the day. As the convoy drove down the taxiway, mouths gaped at the collection of bombers and fighters and transports. Why didn't MacArthur have these three years ago? was the question on everybody's minds. The buses pulled to a stop in front of two Douglas C-47s. As the sun peeked up from behind the distant Yambarran Range, forty weary men, women, and children climbed aboard for a flight to somewhere else.

For most, the experience of watching the sun rise from ten thousand feet above a desert was unique and quite wonderful. The beauty of the sky and of the earth below made up, in part, for the discomfort of the airplane. The unyielding steel bench seats running the length of the fuselage were quickly abandoned in favor of the hard but very cold floor. Bill Real had no idea how cold it was until he looked down at his fingertips and noticed they had turned blue. Blankets and sleeping bags had been provided by their knowing AIB minders. Howard Chrisco and Loretta Ossorio shivered together under one. When the pilots glanced back, all they could see was a pile of huddled humanity covered in olive drab wool.

By midmorning the lumbering "Gooney Birds" were well on their way south, passing high above the "land of the never never," following the narrow ribbon of tarmac that was the Stuart Highway. By lunchtime the planes touched down at Alice Springs to refuel. The passengers debarked to stretch, to warm up, and to eat a quick meal. The next hop, the long one, took the planes east across the great, trackless Simpson Desert, over the broad river valleys and rolling mountains of Queensland. It was dark when the C-47s arrived at Brisbane. Ernie Jaboneta watched from a window as the brightly lit city came into view. It was the first time he had ever seen a big city; the sight gave him goose bumps. He later wrote it was "very emotional to see such a thing."[9] A small welcoming committee greeted the refugees—some AIB people, Red Cross officials, ladies from the Brisbane Women's Club.[10] All the men and sixteen-year-old Kenneth Ossorio were told they would be taken to the army's 42nd General Hospital in Brisbane. Ten refugees were loaded onto army ambulances and driven off in the darkness. Among them was six-year-old Rodger Winn. His mother had asked Colonel Yeager if her son could get medical treatment. The boy had a series of boils on his bottom, causing him great discomfort. Yeager said yes, and when Viola and Rodger parted, she told him she would stop by that night or, at the latest, early the next morning, to see how he was doing. As the truck drove off, the other thirty refugees, the women and the other children, climbed into a bus for what Viola thought would be a short hop to their next camp.

Yeager had not told the group where they were headed. Darkness fell as the bus slowly wended its way through and out of Brisbane. The driver turned onto the Bruce Highway, headed north away from the city. Viola Winn grew alarmed. Thinking he was lost, she asked the driver if he knew where he was going. "To the Red Cross center. It's seventy-two miles out of Brisbane. We'll be there by nine."[11] Viola slumped back in her seat. "Poor Rodger!" But she took heart in the knowledge that her son would be in good hands. She resigned herself to their separation.

The bus rolled through the night, up the "Sunshine Coast," toward the small resort town of Caloundra. Sure enough they pulled in just at nine, greeted by Miss Alice Thompson, director of the rest camp, a Red Cross volunteer formerly of Penn State's Alumni Office. The refugees' new home was the Strathalan Hotel, a rambling two-story clapboard structure just up the road from the beach.

The nurses had laid out a sumptuous dinner for the weary travelers. But before the troupe could eat, Miss Thompson insisted they be sprayed for bugs, then bathed. A refreshed, sweet-smelling group of thoroughly disinfected Americans sat down for their meal. For the first time in years they were treated to green salads with all the fixings and fresh, creamy cow's milk. Household conveniences awed the Winn children. Norman had been only two when the family went into hiding, Elinor just six months. Neither had known a world with lights that went on and off with the flick of a switch, or water that flowed from a pipe controlled by a mere flip of the wrist.[12] As the two played, Viola was amused by their antics. It was after midnight before the trio settled down on stuffed mattresses, heads nestled on feather pillows, to say prayers of thanks for their safe journey.

EARLIER THAT MORNING *Crevalle* weighed anchor from her mooring to tie up alongside the Liberty ship SS *Henry Dodge* for reprovisioning. Frank Walker hated to leave Darwin. He had good friends among the Royal Australian Air Force fighter pilots based there, and he loved to spend the night carousing in their officers' club. Walker had much to celebrate, having survived the clutches of death not just once, but twice in the past month. As usual in this port, the captain staggered in rather late that Saturday morning. The boat got under way shortly after noon. By midnight *Crevalle* was one hundred sixty-six miles from Darwin, steaming west at fourteen knots. The voyage to Fremantle would take eight days and would be, all hoped after this event-filled third patrol, uneventful.

C OLONEL  M ASHBIR ASSEMBLED a team of his best ATIS men, led by his deputy, John Anderton.[13] Looking more like a fullback than a language expert, Major John E. Anderton had been a lawyer in San Francisco before the war. He turned out to possess a great facility with the language. In fact, he was called the "Kanji Kid," for his ability to recall Japanese characters."[14] Anderton had distinguished himself at the section by producing two specialized Japanese-English dictionaries: one on medical terms, the other on kanji abbreviations that ran to seven thousand characters.[15] This second work would prove invaluable in the coming days.

The first order of business was to make photostatic copies of each sheet of the Koga Papers. In this way the originals were preserved; the translators would work from the resulting photographs. The men went to work behind closely guarded doors early on Saturday morning, 20 May. They quickly identified one document to be copy number six of five hundred fifty copies of "Secret Combined Fleet Order 'Ops. No. 73.'" It had been issued, the second line indicated, on 8 March 1944, from the flagship *Musashi* at Palau. And it was signed by none other than the late commander in chief of the Combined Fleet, Koga Mineichi.

The translators labored slowly and deliberately. It was exciting, exacting work as they moved methodically from one kanji character to the next. When they came upon an ambiguity they made a note of the character at the bottom of the page, so that other linguists might see for themselves what their quandary had been. The preamble to Ops No. 73 was an outline of the plan to follow:

1. The Combined Fleet is for the time being directing its main operations to the PACIFIC Area where, in the event of an attack by an enemy Fleet Occupation Force, it will bring to bear the combined maximum strength of all our forces to meet and destroy the enemy, and to maintain our hold on vital areas.

2. These operations will be called "Z Operations."[16]

Page two revealed a table called "Classifications of Operations." This sent the team scrambling for an atlas, trying to find English place-names for "Otori" (the Japanese-held mid-Pacific island of Wake), "Minamitori" (the Marcus Islands), and "Chishima" (the Kuriles, north of Japan). Thereafter followed a dozen more pages of tables, many in excruciating-to-translate detail. Not being familiar with naval terms, the all-army team occasionally found themselves at a loss for words. They just plowed on as best they could.

All day and night Saturday, all day and night Sunday the ATIS team struggled. Slowly the Z Plan began to be revealed. The operations, painted in broad
strokes, outlined a plan capable of devastating American army, navy, and air
forces:

All forces will concentrate to attack the enemy transport convoy and
endeavor to annihilate it.

Attack and annihilate the enemy using full strength, and cooperating closely
with Base Air Forces.

By Monday the twenty-second they were ready to show their work to General Willoughby.

The G-2 was excited by the significance of the translation. Koga's papers
illuminated Japanese naval thinking in a way no one had ever imagined possible. It was as if the admiral was sitting right there at the table with them, poring over every little detail, explaining each nuance of his strategy. It was an
unprecedented intelligence find.

The next day ATIS released "Limited Distribution Translation No. 4, 'Z'
Operation Orders." Distribution of this top-secret document was indeed limited, for only twenty copies were reproduced. The first copy went by officer
courier to General George C. Marshall, army chief of staff in Washington,
D.C., and chairman of the Joint Chiefs of Staff. Douglas MacArthur was recip-
ient of the second copy.

John Anderton's team then locked themselves up again, this time to attack
a packet of papers, one with the provocative title "A Study of the Main Features
of Decisive Air Operations in the Central Pacific."[17]

SUNDAY AT THE STRATHALAN HOTEL was a busy day for the thirty refugees.
After a hearty breakfast, those who wished were permitted to attend services at
nearby churches. It was the first time Viola Winn and Clara Lindholm had sat
in cold, hard pews in more than two years. Later, army and Red Cross workers
asked everyone to fill out personnel forms. Civilian clothing was provided,
relief donations from caring Australians. Red Cross director Alice Thompson
had been through this routine several times now. She knew what the refugees
would need, what they would want. She took pains to cater to the special
requirements of the many children. A doctor gave each person a quick
checkup, promising a more thorough medical exam in the coming week. The
army briefly interrogated the adults, asking that they turn over all diaries, letters,

and photographs. "You'll get them back after the war," they were told. Army officers then made everyone take an oath of secrecy. The expatriates were to tell no one where they had been or how they got to Australia. "The safety of those still in the Philippines is at risk," they were warned. Even the smallest children took the warning to heart. If questioned by local residents the kids would simply say they had "come by bus," which was certainly true. No one in Caloundra ever learned from this bunch that it had been Frank Walker's bus.

At the beginning of the week the army began a series of intensive interrogations of all *Crevalle*'s passengers. The first officers to arrive at Caloundra were sent by Colonel Whitney's Philippine Regional Section. The G-2 men were primarily interested in the personal history of each refugee. On their tail came agents from Counterintelligence, who wanted to know more about the guerrilla movement, its leaders and operations, and the effect the resistance was having upon both Filipinos and Japanese.[18]

Interrogators also visited the refugee men and boys at the 42nd General Hospital. These ten had settled into a comfortable officers' ward the previous Friday evening. They were separated from the general patient population, and they, too, were warned about saying anything regarding their pasts. Like the group at Caloundra, the Brisbane refugees were well fed and well looked after. Rodger Winn's boils responded quickly to treatment; his doctors thought he would be able to rejoin his family in a few days.

All four of the ex-POWs were in poor shape. Howard Chrisco was diagnosed with worms. "You'd sure be a good guy to take fishing," the gastroenterologist said to the puzzled sergeant. "You've got roundworms, hookworms, and pinworms." Chrisco managed a faint smile. The Missourian was no longer able to straighten his arm. Now, nearly two months after he was wounded in the ambush near Murcia, the muscle had atrophied. Physical therapists began to work on the limb, placing it into a hot-water whirlpool that reminded Chrisco of a washing machine. After a few minutes in the bath, nurses covered the arm with cocoa butter and massaged it. Within a week the soldier had regained partial use of his arm, but was told further treatment would have to wait until he returned to the States.

Russ Snell, plagued by malaria and dysentery, looked a pitiful sight. The day the war started, the six-footer had weighed one hundred ninety-two pounds. When he stepped upon the scale in Brisbane he was shocked to see the dial register a mere ninety-five.

As they grew accustomed to freedom, the refugee children began to explore their new surroundings. The winter solstice was just a month away; Caloundra was no longer the frenetic seaside resort it had been through the summer months, December through March. It had reverted to being a sleepy village, inhabited now only by year-round residents and old-age pensioners. The refugees felt as if they had the whole place to themselves. Rose Real had been an accomplished rider in the Philippines. With the help of Miss Thompson she was able to hire horses for herself and her boys. They could often be seen galloping along the broad beaches. On his own, the adventurous Bill Real liked to sneak off with one of the Red Cross workers' bicycles. Until he got caught. He explained to the irate woman, "It was too much temptation not to run around town." She let him off with a short lecture. He never tried to borrow the bike again.[19] His brother John spent time fishing down at the town pier. One day a kindly old man helped him bait his hook with something that looked suspiciously like moss. The fish must have loved it, for in no time the boy hauled in two great perch. John carried the fish back to the hotel, proudly presenting them to the cook, who fried them up and served them for dinner. Ernie Jaboneta found it endlessly entertaining to watch the Australian Army defend Caloundra's beach from mock invaders. The teenager had never seen such well-armed men before; they made the scraggly guerrillas of Negros seem like kids at play with pop guns. And the tanks and halftracks and Long Tom guns were more impressive still.

The daily routine of life at the Strathalan was broken one day when all the small kids boarded an army bus and were driven down to Brisbane for a field trip. They were taken shopping, though there was not much to buy. But the thing the kids loved most was a visit to the city zoo. Having lived for more than two years in a jungle, most of the children had had intimate contact with a huge variety of creatures, some of them quite dangerous. But none had ever seen the likes of a live elephant or lions and tigers or giant crocodiles. To John Real, the trip to the zoo was one of the high points of his short stay in the Antipodes.

ADMIRAL CHRISTIE WAS WAITING on the dock as *Crevalle* tied up on 28 April. As soon as the gangplank was secured, he scampered up the gangway to shake hands with Frank Walker and his officers. ComSubs was very pleased with the boat's patrol. That morning he gave Walker a verbal "Well done." Later, after reading the patrol report, Christie made a strong written endorsement commending Walker's aggressiveness:

This fine war patrol was the Commanding Officer's first as such. Skillfully and intelligently fighting his ship, he inflicted severe punishment upon the enemy, thereby conforming to the impressive standards set during CREVALLE's previous patrols. The Commanding Officer's courage, and determination to get at the enemy, even under the most adverse conditions, is noted with admiration. Blanketing air coverage, shallow water, glassy seas, and the threat of mine fields failed to deter him from his will to damage the enemy.

Not everyone aboard *Crevalle* would agree with Christie's assessment. Some men felt Walker had been too bold, that he had taken too many risks with their lives. A few requested transfers to other boats.

And Christie's endorsement made only one veiled reference to the rescue: "On her return, CREVALLE successfully accomplished a Special Mission."

Christie knew when he wrote those words how important that mission had been, how important those papers were. Though not on ATIS's distribution list, he had been kept apprised of the Anderton team's progress. And he knew, of course, the whole story behind *Crevalle*'s pickup. Neither on the dock that sunny Sunday morning in Fremantle, *or ever,* did Admiral Ralph Waldo Christie tell Lieutenant Commander Francis David Walker Jr. about the contents of the precious cargo.

Repair crews were astonished by the damage *Crevalle* had suffered during her two severe depth chargings. They were especially impressed with the big dimple in the skin near the bow of the submarine, where the concussion from a single canister had dished the inch-thick steel inward. Engineers estimated that repairs to the boat would take a month, twice as long as the usual refit period. Within hours of arriving at Fremantle, *Crevalle*'s crew had disbursed to their rest camps, and a relief crew had taken their place. Her third patrol was now well and truly over.

ON 25 MAY Major Anderton sent to Colonel Mashbir his team's twenty-nine-page translation of "A Study of the Main Features of Decisive Air Operations in the Central Pacific," collateral notes, and other documents from the cache. The ATIS commander released the study as "Limited Distribution Translation No. 5," with a top-secret classification.

Colonel Willoughby thought the Z Plan and its accompanying air operations study was an intelligence coup. So, too, did the chief of staff, General

Sutherland. And when he saw it, MacArthur was pretty impressed. But what did it all mean? The LDTs were sent to Captain Arthur McCollum, the Seventh Fleet's director of Naval Intelligence and navy liaison with Courtney Whitney's Philippine Regional Section. McCollum had been in on the "snatch" from the very beginning, when it was thought Cushing might be holding Admiral Koga himself.

Early in his naval career McCollum had trained as a Japanese-language specialist. He had vast experience in the most sensitive of intelligence matters. The DNI carefully read the army's translations of the two documents. He knew at first glance that the Z Plan was "hot." And he knew it had to get to Admiral Nimitz as quickly as possible.[20] Two copies were flown by officer courier for hand delivery to the Joint Intelligence Center, Pacific Ocean Area (JICPOA) at Pearl Harbor, there to be studied by Admiral Nimitz's people, who would better understand the naval implications of Koga's last will and testament.

It was a long way from Brisbane to Pearl—nearly five thousand miles. A lumbering army bomber, routed straight through, took more than forty-eight hours to island-hop across the South Pacific. By the end of that week the courier had safely delivered his top-secret package into the hands of Nimitz's Fleet Intelligence officer, Captain Edwin T. Layton.

Layton was another Japanese-language expert, one of the few on the navy's roster before the war started. He had been Admiral Husband E. Kimmel's intelligence officer the day the Japanese attacked Pearl Harbor, and was one of the few officers Nimitz retained after he replaced the disgraced Kimmel. When Layton looked at the ATIS translation he immediately saw there were problems with it, not the least of which was a bold stamp:

```
TOP SECRET. NOT TO BE COPIED OR REPRODUCED WITHOUT
PERMISSION OF GENERAL MACARTHUR.[21]
```

Under Admiral Nimitz's signature, the captain fired off a message to SWPA GHQ asking for the general's consent to distribute the LDT. Deeply concerned about translation errors, Layton also radioed Colonel Mashbir at ATIS to ask for photostats of the *original* Japanese documents. He wanted to be absolutely certain the language was correct, for what he had before him seemed to indicate the Combined Fleet planned to mass its ships and planes in a coordinated action against the next advance in the Pacific by U.S. forces.

Layton and his admiral had to wait another two days for the copies to reach Hawaii. He then closeted himself in his office to retranslate the entire Z Plan.

The effort took Layton and his small group of navy translators all night.[22] But they were pleased with the results; Anderton had gotten it mostly right. Photostatic copies were made for distribution to task force commanders, even then steaming westward for the invasion of the Mariana Islands.

THE SAME DAY THE ATIS completed translation of the Z Plan, Jim Cushing radioed GHQ with a message reporting the Japanese had not yet given up trying to recover Koga's papers. Through informants, the enemy knew Cushing's men had found more documents. The IJN commander in Cebu dropped leaflets across the island, reading in part:

> Return unconditionally until the noon of 30th May 1944, all documents, bags and clothings either picked up from the said airplane or robbed of the passengers and crew.
>
> We notify you that in case you fail to fulfill our demand, the Imperial Japanese Navy will resort to drastically severe method against you.[23]

The note must have amused Cushing. But Colonel Courtney Whitney took it more seriously, sending a memo to General Sutherland with a copy of Cushing's radio, adding comments about ATIS's progress translating the Z Plan:

> Documents received are in process through ATIS, others from same recovery arrived in Negros too late for pick up on the 11th. Those received appear to contain a file of operational orders of the enemy combined fleet and a file of navy dispatches.
>
> Navy have decided that special pick up of remaining documents should be effected and arrangements are now being made towards that end.[24]

SWPA was most concerned about the rest of the documents recovered from the crash of Fukudome's Kawanishi on 1 April. Through radio exchanges, Whitney knew there was at least one more load of papers, but was unsure where they were or who had them. The PRS chief did not like being confused when so much was at stake. He sent this message to Cushing on 23 May:

> HAVE ALL ENEMY DOCUMENTS ARRIVED AT ANDREWS HEADQUARTERS? IF
> NOT DISPATCH REMAINDER IMMEDIATELY AND ADVISE WHEN THEY MAY
> BE EXPECTED TO ARRIVE THERE. PRESERVE UTMOST SECRECY.[25]

In response, Salvador Abcede wired back on the twenty-fifth to say that the papers had not yet arrived from Cushing. Four days later he radioed that "some documents and parts of Jap machine gun are now on hand. Cushing informs that more of his couriers are coming with documents."[26]

SWPA was busy preparing to pick up the second, and they hoped final, batch of the Koga Papers. The USS *Nautilus* was finally being readied for patrol. Whitney sent a warning to Abcede:

> EXPECT SUPPLY SHIPMENT ARRIVE YOUR AREA AROUND 20 JUNE. BE
> PREPARED TO UNLOAD FULL CARGO 100 TONS DURING ONE NIGHT.
> SHIPMENT WILL BE 4/5THS FOR YOU, 1/5TH FOR CUSHING. [PUT]
> ALL ENEMY DOCUMENTS FROM CUSHING ON THIS VESSEL.[27]

On 30 May the Japanese Army and Navy garrison commanders on Cebu dropped another leaflet to the guerrillas. They demanded nothing less than the surrender of Jim Cushing. "We have decided to resort to the firm and drastic measure against you. Our offensive, from now on, will increase extremely in its vigor and fierceness."[28]

After that, things got very hot in the already steamy Visayas.

WHEN THE REFUGEES had settled in comfortably at Caloundra, Mrs. Jean MacArthur stopped in for lunch. All of the Strathalan's residents were turned out and told to line up to greet the general's wife, who was accompanied by her son, five-year-old Arthur, and Colonel Courtney Whitney. The women found the general's wife charming. Over avocado salad they all swapped stories about their escapes from the Philippines. Everybody seemed awed by Mrs. MacArthur's tales of running from doomed Corregidor in a PT boat. Viola Winn observed that the visit helped form a close bond among the women, for they had all survived desperate times.[29]

As June approached, the families were pronounced fit by the doctors, fully debriefed by Intelligence. Kenneth Ossorio managed to wangle permission to make the trip up from Brisbane to Caloundra for a day. He arrived in town wearing a snappy U.S. Army uniform with the provisional rank of sergeant.

For some reason G-2 had overlooked Ossorio's secret treasure. His suitcase full of guerrilla documents sat on the floor of his mother's room, ignored by all. When he got to the Strathalan he was interviewed by a SWPA colonel about his activities with the resistance on Negros. The officer would ask a question, Kenneth would ponder it for a few moments, excuse himself, then disappear into the back room. There he rifled through his files for a document that would shed light upon the question, reappearing with an elucidation. This went on for some while until the colonel asked, "Where are you getting this?" The boy answered sheepishly, tentatively, "My collection." The man pressed the teenager, "Can I see it?" Kenneth winced. He had already left one box of papers behind at Basay; he did not want to lose the second one. But he realized he had little choice. "I'll get them." And so he offered up his maps and memos, propaganda and broadsheets to the astonished officer. "You know you can't keep this," said the colonel as he examined the valise. Kenneth winced again. Before his very eyes his collection was impounded. He was given receipts for it and told, "It will be returned after the war." Ossorio was angry about the confiscation, for he had spent the best part of two years amassing it. Kenneth returned to Brisbane certain he would never see a shred of his cumulus again.[30]

Ernie Jaboneta got to make the trip in the other direction. One day he and a friend took the bus down to Brisbane. Like Ossorio, he wore an army uniform. It was the first time in his life he had visited a big city and he felt, quite frankly, overwhelmed. While strolling down the street the seventeen-year-old was stopped by an American MP. "You're out of uniform," the sergeant charged. Jaboneta was at a loss to understand what the soldier was talking about. "You got on a nonregulation tie." The young man pulled a letter of identification from Colonel Whitney out of his back pocket, handing it to the MP. The sergeant read the contents slowly, carefully, then grunted, "Don't matter who you are, you're still out of uniform." The policeman ordered Jaboneta to follow him. They hiked several blocks to an American compound. As they entered, the teenager thought he was going to be arrested, but instead the MP hauled him into the post exchange. They went straight to the men's department, where the sergeant picked out a proper black tie. He made Ernie put it on. "Now you're regulation," said the soldier with satisfaction. The men went to the cashier. The MP signed a chit and as they left the PX told Jaboneta to be more careful next time. Ernesto and his friend spent a happy day in Brisbane, catching a late coach back to the safe haven of the Strathalan.[31]

A few days later Jaboneta discovered that Australian friendliness toward Americans might not be universal. He and his pal James Smith (a refugee from Panay who had come down on *Angler*) decided to attend a dance at Caloundra Town Hall. The local lasses took quite a shine to the new boys, much to the displeasure of the local lads. After Ernie and Jimmy took the girls for a few spins around the floor (to the latest swing tunes), the Australian boys confronted the two Americans. They persuaded Ernie and Jimmy that it might be best for all concerned if they left. Now. And they did, in the process learning something about the finer points of international relations. The next time a local dance came up the boys skipped it, instead preferring the company of two off-duty nurses. American nurses.

On 3 June 1944 came the news everybody was waiting for. Miss Alice announced: "Time to pack your bags, you're going home."

BACK ON THE BUSES and back to Brisbane. There Viola had an emotional reunion with Rodger. He had had a great time in the children's ward. His nurses took good care of him, he made friends among the few other kids there, he had eaten well and even gained weight. But after two weeks of separation he was thrilled to see his mother and siblings again.

The soldiers among the forty stayed behind, at least for now. Howard Chrisco, Russell Snell, Jimmy Dyer, and Floyd Reynolds were transferred out of the 42nd General Hospital to a rest camp called Ascot—a sea of tents, really—at a nearby racetrack. There the men were issued uniforms, but not *new* uniforms. Chrisco was furious with the clothing he received, for it was stained and he believed it must have come from a dead or wounded soldier. Chrisco had always been particular about the condition and appearance of his clothing. This disgusted him. He went directly to Captain Striedel, the AIB liaison officer, to complain. "Sir, I'm not a damn bit proud of this uniform." "Tell me, son." And Howard Tom Chrisco let go with a slurry of foul epithets about his experiences as a POW, as a guerrilla, as a refugee, and when he was he finished he told the captain he thought he deserved to be given a good uniform, a new one, a Class A outfit. "Come with me," said the officer. The pair went to a tent where Striedel jumped on the phone and jumped down the throat of a quartermaster sergeant at the other end of the line. After a few loud barks and grunts he put the receiver back in its cradle. "You go on down and pick out what you want. They'll take good care of you now."

Chrisco headed down to the QM tent. He found a fine pair of pants and a coat, but had trouble choosing a shirt. He had a choice of two shades of green and two finishes, one hard, one soft. As he discussed the merits of each with a clerk he felt a tap on his shoulder. He turned to face a man who looked somehow familiar. The man said, "Aren't you Howard Chrisco?" "I am," he answered, staring at the man, trying to place him. Then it hit him. "And you're from Salem. You're a Platt!" Sure enough, it was Morris Platt from Salem, Missouri, brother of one of Chrisco's longtime, hometown buddies.[32]

After that, the Ozark neighbors often went into Brisbane for a night out,

Morris appropriating transport for the pair because he was in charge of the motor pool. Chrisco thought himself bad company on their sojourns since he was still under secret orders not to say a word to anyone about any of his experiences. He just paid the bar bills and let Platt do all the talking. Forbidden to contact even his own family, Chrisco persuaded Platt to call home for him, to tell his mother and father that he was safe in Australia and hoped to be back soon.

There was no ceremony at the dock when the thirty-one civilian refugees boarded their chartered Dutch transport for the journey home. Each family was assigned a small stateroom. They carried more now than they had when they left *Crevalle*. There were new clothes, books, and a few souvenirs of their short stay in Australia.

The MS *Boschfontein* sailed with the tide in the early hours of Tuesday, 4 June 1944. The sleek, seven-thousand-ton vessel was crewed by Dutchmen, now stateless because of the German occupation of their homeland and the Japanese occupation of the Netherlands East Indies. Also aboard were more than a thousand war-weary veterans, members of the famous U.S. 1st Marines. From December 1943 to May 1944 they had fought—and won—a bitter campaign on New Britain.[33] Their losses were high, their tenacity glorious. Now the survivors were headed home. But their fame and glory did them little good on the Pacific crossing. While the refugees had cabins, the marines were jammed into racks of narrow beds in the holds below the main deck. While the unfortunate marines ate glop from tin platters, the refugees ate fine food at tables set with linens, china, and silver. At one such meal Sam Real let his ugly temper reign. Son Fritz was being bratty at lunch one day. A waiter, tired of the boy's antics, cuffed him on the back of the head. Sam saw it and the hackles rose. He jumped out of his chair, confronted the man, then knocked him halfway across the room with a mighty punch. Real was hauled up before the captain and read, essentially, the riot act. The guerrilla officer promised to rein in his anger.

The *Boschfontein* sailed alone, without escort, relying upon her speed to outrun any enemy submarines lurking in the depths. Extra cautious, the liner zigzagged across much of the Pacific to foil would-be hunters. Two days out of Brisbane a news bulletin electrified everybody aboard: ALLIES INVADE EUROPE. It was D Day, the sixth of June. Throughout the ship there were quiet celebrations, especially among the Dutch crew, for now, for the first time, there seemed to be an end to the war in sight—distant, to be sure, but certainly in sight.

There were few activities aboard ship to help the refugees while away the days. The adults often played cards or just caught up on reading. Bill and John

Real liked to roam, but found the crew unhelpful, their access to all the really interesting places (such as the engine room and the bridge) blocked. When the vessel neared the equator, many slept out on the deck to escape the cabins' stifling heat.

Ken Ossorio enjoyed talking with the marines down in the hold. He was shocked by their physical condition—gaunt bodies with hollow-eyed faces stared at him from the stacked bunks. Sweeping his arm across the ship's hold, a marine said, "We're all that's left from Guadalcanal." Ossorio had heard of that great struggle in the Solomons, knew that the 1st Marines had landed on Guadalcanal in 1942 and had held the island for four months until relief arrived. He could only shake his head at their terrible losses. Still, Kenneth felt he had something in common with these men. He was not much younger than many of them, though they nevertheless ribbed him for being "underage." "Hey, kid, ya being shipped home cuz you're too young?" they taunted him. Little did they know he could have held his own during the long bull sessions when war stories flew, could have astonished everybody with his own tales of life among the guerrillas. But like all the other refugees, Ossorio was sworn to secrecy, forbidden to even hint at his adventures on Negros or of *Crevalle*'s wild ride.

On Tuesday, 20 June 1944, *Boschfontein* sailed under the Golden Gate Bridge. Bill Real was sure the ship's 120-foot masts would hit the famous span. He was surprised when she cleared with room to spare. As the liner cruised down the channel, her thousand thrilled passengers lined the rail talking excitedly, gawking at the exotic sights spread out before them: old Fort Point, Angel Island, Alcatraz; in the distance the silver towers of the Bay Bridge, Nob Hill, Russian Hill; in the far distance Sather Tower rising thirty stories above the university campus at Berkeley. Blimps and a squadron of navy fighters escorted the ship toward Fort Mason's port of embarkation, just a few blocks from fabled Fishermen's Wharf. Tugs came alongside to nudge the ship to her dock. When the hawsers were pulled tight, gangways were passed across to the sounds of a marine band playing Sousa tunes and other patriotic music.

Army and Red Cross workers were on hand to greet the ship. The refugees were led into the warehouselike embarkation hall. Subjected to a cursory customs check, they gathered in small groups, awaiting their fate. A man in a dark suit sought out Kenneth Ossorio. He showed the boy a badge, told him he was an agent with the FBI. Somehow the bureau knew about his suitcase of secret papers (still back in Brisbane) and his experiences with the guerrillas on Negros. The agent made an appointment to talk with Ossorio at length.[34]

A smattering of relatives was on hand to greet passengers. Wesley Schuldt had received word from the Red Cross that his sister Viola would be returning from the war. He had driven down that morning from his home in Stockton to meet her and the children.

The refugees were taken by their new minders to a hotel in downtown San Francisco, there to decompress and begin what for some would be a long acclimation to life in America. One of the first orders of business for Clara Lindholm and Viola Winn was to send telegrams to the Presbyterian Board of Foreign Missions at INCULCATE NEW YORK. Viola briefly sketched for the Board her family's adventures during the previous thirty months, then asked for information about Gardner. Clara wired that she would be sending Paul's mission report for the period 1941 to 1944.[35]

The next day Viola received a response from New York informing her that another missionary, repatriated in 1943, had seen Gardner at Santo Tomas Prison in Manila. At that time he was in good health and was singing with a camp quartet (bass, no doubt). It was the first word she had had about her husband since he walked down that hill in Pacuan Valley in late July 1942. It was not much news. But those few lines on the wire filled her with hope. If he had survived this long, he would survive the rest of the war. She knew, in her heart, that was a fact. He would survive. And then Viola Schuldt Winn began to cry. It was the first time since they heard the terrible news on the radio that Pearl Harbor had been attacked that Viola had permitted herself to cry. And the tears poured forth in a torrent. Rodger and Norman wondered worriedly why their mother was sobbing. "Why are you crying?" they asked. She told them their father would soon be home, for she knew the war would soon end, that her family would soon be reunited. "I know that," said Rodger knowingly.[36] She could only smile at his innocent confidence.

Ten-year-old John Real was awestruck by San Francisco. One afternoon he escaped from his hotel room, bent on exploring The City. He was fascinated by the cable cars. He found it difficult to believe that such big buildings could be built on such steep hills. He had never seen so many people crammed into such a small space before, nor had he seen so many people so busy with so many things. Everybody looked as if they were in such a hurry! The shop windows were full of wonderful things, the likes of which he had never seen in Manapla or even Bacolod. And then John realized he was well and truly lost. The City had overwhelmed him. For some while he wandered about, trying to find familiar landmarks that might lead him back to his family. But every corner brought a new and distinctly strange vista. Eventually John screwed up the courage to ask a policeman for help. And before darkness fell, the young boy was happily back with his family.[37]

At the designated time the FBI stopped by the hotel to pick up Kenneth Ossorio. They took him to an office by the bay and spent hours questioning him about the guerrilla movement on Negros. The questions were familiar—he had heard them all before, at Caloundra, and he could not understand why he was being interrogated again. He wished he still had his suitcases full of papers, for they would have helped him immeasurably. At noon his inquisitors called a break and took him to lunch at a nearby cafeteria. It was an absolutely novel experience for Kenneth. He had never before seen so much food in one place, all there just for the taking. It was a treat. After Ossorio had sated his appetite (and then some), the FBI resumed its questioning, pumping the boy for every shred of useful information he could think to supply. When they took him back to the hotel, Kenneth hoped he had seen the last of these intelligence agents.[38]

Within days the Red Cross began to sort out the refugees' futures. Most of the refugees had families somewhere in the States—had a place to go home to. Before the week was out the Lindholms were on their way to Salem, Oregon, to live with Clara's brother. The Winns were off to Sioux City, Iowa, to stay with her brother Victor. The Macasas headed for Lincoln, Nebraska. Loretta and Kenneth Ossorio crossed the bay, to stay a few weeks with friends, then entrained for Baton Rouge, Louisiana, where her father still resided in the house in which she was raised.

Some folks decided to stay on the West Coast. Sam Real was able to secure a job with Westinghouse Corporation as a turbine engineer. He moved his family across the bay to Albany, a small town adjacent to Berkeley. There the Reals moved into a government housing project, where most of their neighbors worked building Liberty ships at the huge Calships yard in Richmond. Ernie Jaboneta's family moved into housing at Candlestick Point on the southern fringes of San Francisco. He found a job as a machinist at nearby Hunters Point Naval Shipyard. And his mother began the long fight with the Immigration and Naturalization Service over Betty's right to remain in the United States. Modesta Hughes, now alone in the world, also moved to Candlestick, and also found a job at Hunters Point, as a clerk in the Payroll Department.[39]

A FEW WEEKS AFTER the civilians had sailed, it was time for the former POWs to go home. Russell Snell and Floyd Reynolds found passage on SS *Lurline*, flagship of the Matson Line. Before the war *Lurline* was the ultimate in comfort and elegance, sailing between San Francisco and the Antipodes on a regular schedule. Now she was painted a somber gray, her staterooms crowded with returning soldiers and sixty-nine Australian war brides. After zigzagging her way across the Pacific, the liner arrived in San Francisco, not to the strains of martial music but to the lilting melody of "Here Comes the Bride." Snell flew on to the East Coast, where he was hospitalized on Staten Island, New York. The first phone call he made was to his father. The second call was to his old flame, Rose Combattelli. She was now a nurse in his hometown of Rochester; it was her "Dear John" letter that had prompted Russ to join the army.

"Hello," she answered. "Do you know who this is?" he asked. "No." "Are you sure you don't know who this is?" he asked. "Well, you do sound like a boy I used to know, but he's been dead for three years." "I'm that boy," he said, "and I'm very much alive. Are you married?" "No," she replied. "Will you marry me?" Rose was flabbergasted. But by the time the phone conversation concluded, Rose Combattelli had agreed to marry Jay Russell Snell. And so they were, a week later in Rochester.[40]

Howard Chrisco and Jim Dyer made a speedier trip across the Pacific, albeit not as comfortable as Snell's—they flew. They stopped at various tropical islands, now bustling with American military might. They went on to Hawaii and then to California. Anxious to get home, the pair was unhappy to be told their next stop was Washington, D.C. They were wanted there for more interrogations. After three days of answering questions from Army Intelligence officers, Chrisco and Dyer were free to go. They caught a train to Jefferson Barracks, Missouri, just outside St. Louis. From there, Chrisco got a cousin to drive him home to Salem.

He had not told anyone he was coming home; he wanted to surprise his family, for it was his twenty-fifth birthday. He liked to tell people that since the war began he had spent "one birthday in the American Army, one birthday in the Philippine Army, and one in the Japanese Army." Now he would spend the fourth at home.

It was midnight before they reached Salem. The car jerked to a halt in front of the familiar white bungalow. With a touch of nervousness, Howard approached the darkened house. He knocked. There was no response. He knocked again. After a bit he saw a light flicker on in the back; then his father appeared in the hallway. At first Dan Chrisco did not recognize his son; he thought it was a nephew come to visit. Staring out through the screen door, all of a sudden the father realized who was standing opposite. "Howard?" The boy nodded. "Howard!?!" "I'm home, Dad." Dan got so excited he practically tore the door off its hinges. The two embraced.

"How's Mom?" Howard asked. His father broke the sad news that during his absence she had gone blind. "She's upstairs in bed."

Chrisco entered the bedroom. Dan said softly, "Laura, I've got a surprise for you." Howard approached his mother. "Mom, I'm home." Tears began to streak her face; she could barely believe she was hearing the voice of her son. He knelt by her side to give her a hug. Running her slender fingers through his wavy hair, she whispered, "It's Howard, all right. My prayers have been answered."[41]

# CHAPTER 15

# *The Admirals*

THE PACIFIC OCEAN IS unimaginably large. Sixty-four million square miles, seven thousand times larger than *Crevalle*'s native New Hampshire. The waters of the great ocean caress five of the seven continents, cover one-third of the earth's surface, make it the most prominent feature on the planet. From east to west the Pacific stretches twelve thousand miles; from north to south, nearly ten thousand.[1] It was upon this gargantuan playing field that Japan and the United States were waging war.

Japan's opening gambit had been a series of exquisitely timed attacks concentrated, with the notable exceptions of Guam and Hawaii, along the Pacific's western rim: Singapore, Hong Kong, Thailand, Malaya, and, of course, the Philippines. In the months to follow, the war had spread south to Australia, north to Alaska, east to Midway. A Japanese submarine even managed to reach the coast of California, there provoking panic by shelling an oil refinery.

The Greater East Asia Coprosperity Sphere reached its apogee in May 1942. Japan's empire, a decade earlier limited to the homeland and the tiny islands of Micronesia, then encompassed a quarter of Oceania and hundreds of millions of people. The Battle of Midway brought an end to Japanese expansion, forcing the nation to go on the defensive, to struggle simply to contain its territorial gains. Now, in the third year of the war, the United States and her allies were pushing Japan inexorably back home.

At the beginning of 1944, American planners were advocating a drive through the central Pacific, right to Japan's doorstep. A key element in the U.S. playbook was the taking of the Marianas: the occupation of Saipan and neighboring Tinian, and the recapture of Guam. It was key because upon those islands air bases could be built that would enable the army air force to fly their new long-range Boeing B-29 Superfortress bombers directly to Japan, to begin a bombing campaign designed to cripple the enemy's industrial base. The

Joint Chiefs of Staff gave the strategy the go-ahead in March.[2] Thus was born Operation Forager.

Admiral Nimitz had set 15 June as the target date. It would be the largest invasion mounted thus far in the Pacific, eventually totaling six hundred ships and a hundred twenty thousand troops. Admiral Raymond Ames Spruance would be in overall command of the massive armada. His air admiral, Marc Andrew "Pete" Mitscher, would lead the battle groups of Task Force 58, now brimming with new, fast carriers. Vice Admiral Richmond Kelly Turner would command the invasion fleet; Lieutenant General Holland M. Smith, USMC, would direct the actual assault on the beaches. Their staffs, working out of crowded quarters along the shores of Pearl Harbor, began to hammer out the myriad details involved in such a grand undertaking. The Marianas posed new problems for the planners. All previous invasions in the central Pacific had been against coral atolls, some only a dozen feet above sea level, encompassing a few thousand square yards of land. But now they faced volcanic high islands, their areas measured in miles, and most with mountainous interiors from which the enemy could mount a formidable defense. The planners decided Saipan would be the initial objective, followed three days later by an assault on Guam. And once Saipan was in American hands, neighboring Tinian would be invaded. The smaller island of Rota, dangling between Tinian and Guam and of little military value, would be left to wither on the vine. By the middle of May 1944 the final draft of Operation Forager—the basic plan and its amendments now nearly a foot thick—was ready for distribution to the fleet.

LOCATED FIFTEEN HUNDRED miles south of Tokyo and thirteen hundred miles east of Manila, the Marianas were part of Japan's inner defense ring. Their loss would be a significant strategic and psychological blow to the ever-shrinking empire. Guam, the largest and southernmost of the group, had been American territory for four decades until invaded by Japan. A hundred twenty miles to its north lay Saipan and Tinian, separated only by a narrow channel. After three centuries of Spanish rule, the Japanese had annexed them (and all of Micronesia) from Germany at the beginning of World War I.

Saipan was the administrative center of the islands. At fourteen miles long and five wide, it was the second largest of the Marianas. The southern tip featured a broad, flat plain heavily planted with sugarcane. Rolling hills quickly gave way to a chain of thousand-foot mountains running nearly to the northern tip, before falling precipitously to a low plateau just beyond Mount Marpi.

The western side of Saipan was protected by a reef; the eastern shore faced the constant onslaught of the Pacific without benefit of any barrier.

If Palau was the jewel of Japanese Micronesia, Saipan was the cash cow. When Nippon gained control of the island in 1914 it was inhabited by two thousand Chamorro natives who subsisted by fishing and farming. In the first half decade of occupation, colonization of Saipan went very slowly as the government tried various schemes to develop the island. It took an entrepreneur named Matsue Haruji to see that Saipan was ripe for sugarcane. In 1920 Matsue spent weeks traversing the island, taking soil samples and mapping out the terrain. He returned a year later to plan the infrastructure for his enterprise, and in 1922 cane planting began in earnest. To find workers, Matsue turned to the island of Okinawa, one of Japan's poorest. His company paid all the travel expenses for the migrants, then put them to work clearing the southern end of Saipan. Each farmer would be given a stake in a small plot of land, the sugar company guaranteeing a market for the cane. As the clearing and planting went on, Matsue built a modern sugar central, connected to the fields by a network of narrow-gauge railways. The first shipment of processed sugar was sent to Japan in August 1922. As production grew, so, too, did the requirement for workers. There were five thousand Japanese on Saipan by 1925, forty-five thousand by 1941. Just as on Negroes, sugar was king in Saipan.[3]

American invasion planners assumed that Saipan was a veritable bastion, that the Japanese had spent years constructing an impregnable fortress. In fact, it had not been militarized until well after the beginning of the war. There had always been a naval presence on the island, but it was mainly to operate the airfield at Aslito and a seaplane base near Garapan Town. When Saipan's small harbor was enlarged in the late 1930s, it was to better handle sugar-laden freighters, not warships. This lack of defenses was due mainly to the fact that Japan considered the Marianas part of the homeland, and as such did not take seriously any threat against the archipelago—that is, until it was almost too late. When Task Force 58 began to roam the western Carolines at will, Japanese army and navy forces in the Marianas finally woke up and began a crash program to build fortifications, from the beaches all the way up into the mountains. Their delayed efforts would prove only partly successful.

CINCPAC HEADQUARTERS was the busy nerve center of the entire Allied effort in the Pacific. Admiral Nimitz and his small staff worked from a reinforced-concrete building that perched upon the ridge of Makalapa Hill overlooking

Pearl Harbor. Just down the hill, past the Quonset huts of the motor pool, were two innocuous-looking buildings that played a major role in the Pacific offensive. The first was a ramshackle two-story clapboard structure housing the Fleet Radio Unit, Pacific (FRUPac). The second, just completed and occupied at the end of May 1944, was for the Joint Intelligence Center, Pacific Ocean Area (JICPOA). The pair formed a high-security compound surrounded by an eight-foot Cyclone fence topped by treble strands of barbed wire. Armed guards patrolled the perimeter day and night; without the proper pass, entry was impossible. Within these buildings was closeted the Allies' most secret of all secrets—the organization that intercepted, translated, analyzed, and disseminated Japanese radio intelligence. It was this group (then called Hypo and under the command of the brilliant, if eccentric, Captain Joseph J. Rochefort) that had broken enemy naval codes before the war began and who told Nimitz in May 1942 that the Japanese were about to assault Midway Island. The United States was victorious at the Battle of Midway, sinking four enemy carriers to the loss of one American flattop. It was the turning point of the war, the point at which Japanese expansion was halted and the slow march toward Tokyo began. It was also the first of many American intelligence coups.

FRUPac listened for radio signals emanating from deep within the Japanese Empire. The unit was part of a global network of listening stations responsible for copying enemy radio transmissions. Highly trained operators sat at receiver consoles, "guarding" radio frequencies known to be used by the Japanese. It was not difficult to record such transmissions, for they were all sent using a variation of Morse code. The Japanese language is usually written in Chinese ideographs called kanji. But for purposes of transmitting messages, they used a phonetic variation called katakana, further simplified to use roman letters (fifty-one instead of the usual twenty-six). FRUPac's radiomen would copy down these romanji letters, then pass the unbroken messages on to teams of decryption and translation experts, where the really hard work began. Though American intelligence was able to read a variety of secret Japanese codes throughout the war, there were many messages that could not be fully or even partially broken. Once FRUPac had extracted what it could from the intercepts, they were sent on to JICPOA for analysis.

JICPOA, formed in late 1943, was responsible for creating strategic estimates for Nimitz's planners. The unit used a variety of sources to accomplish this: intercepted enemy radio traffic, captured documents, and interrogations of captured Japanese soldiers and sailors.[4] From the information thus gathered

JICPOA published a wide range of reports, including a daily intelligence summary that was wired each morning to fleet commanders across the theater, as well as to the chief of naval operations, Admiral Ernest J. King, at the Pentagon in Washington.

DURING THE FIRST WEEK of June 1944 American forces began to assemble for the invasion of Saipan. Many fleet units were then based on Majuro Atoll, the best anchorage in the newly captured Marshall Islands. Others were in the South Pacific. Some were still loading at Pearl Harbor. On 26 May Admiral Spruance sailed from Pearl aboard his flagship, the heavy cruiser *Indianapolis,* escorted by the destroyer *Stanly.* ComFifthFleet was headed for the Marshalls, to inspect newly developed advanced base facilities.

Spruance had been in command of the Central Pacific Force (now called the Fifth Fleet) since August 1943. Prior to that he had been chief of staff to Chester Nimitz for fourteen months, and before that he had gained renown for having led the fragile American fleet to victory against a superior Japanese force at Midway. In the course of the war Spruance had earned a reputation as a brilliant, if cautious, strategist and tactician.

An unassuming man from New Jersey, Raymond Spruance graduated from Annapolis in 1906 in the top quarter of his class. The academy yearbook said he was a "shy young thing with a rather sober, earnest face and the innocent disposition of an ingenue."[5] Spruance had spent his entire career as a member of the "Gun Club," assigned to destroyers, cruisers, and battleships. He also had spent three tours at the Naval War College, as student and then as teacher, becoming an expert in naval surface warfare.

Spruance was something of a "fitness nut." For an hour or two every day, landlocked or seabound, he walked. It was a common sight aboard the flagship to see the admiral, bare-chested, wearing a pair of gaudy shorts, hiking briskly around the forecastle, staff officers panting to keep up with his pace. Aboard ship he usually dined alone, eating exactly the same thing for breakfast every morning: toast, canned peaches, coffee. During the day it was his habit to eat raw, sliced onions, "for his health," he liked to say. Spruance often spent his days quietly reading in his cabin. After watching a movie in the evening, he usually went to bed at about eight, preferring the admiral's stateroom to his sea cabin on the flag bridge. And he hated having his rest interrupted for any reason short of a genuine crisis. Spruance's long-suffering chief of staff, Captain Carl Johnes Moore, knew his boss did not like being encumbered with the nitty-gritty of day-to-day operations.[6] But when the time came for action, the warrior in Raymond Spruance emerged to lead his forces with calm, fearless, and sometimes ruthless determination.

*Indianapolis* reached Majuro on 2 June. Spruance immediately went into conference with his task force commanders, Vice Admirals Pete Mitscher and Willis A. "Ching" Lee. Spruance left the atoll the following day for a quick tour of the island group, putting in first at Kwajalein, then Roi, and finally, on 7 June, at Eniwetok.[7] The next day a navy flying boat from Pearl Harbor alighted on the huge lagoon. The plane disembarked an officer carrying a large pouch into a waiting whaleboat, which then scurried across the water to the flagship. Up the gangway went the courier, his bag brimming with top-secret documents, among them the latest revisions to Operation Forager and, perhaps of equal importance, Captain Layton's translations of Koga Mineichi's Z Plan and Fukudome Shigeru's "A Study of the Main Features of Decisive Air Operations in the Central Pacific."

Late in the afternoon of 8 June, after meeting with Kelly Turner about the forthcoming invasion, Spruance ordered *Indianapolis* to weigh anchor for the three-day voyage to Saipan. The admiral had that evening and the morning of the ninth to digest Koga's battle plans before his flagship would rendezvous with the main body of Mitscher's Task Force 58.

The preamble of the main document set forth the Japanese mission quite clearly:

> The Combined Fleet is for the time being directing its main operations to the PACIFIC area where, in the event of an attack by an enemy Fleet Occupation Force, it will bring to bear the combined maximum strength of all our forces to meet and destroy the enemy, and to maintain our hold on vital areas.[8]

On page six was an outline showing how Koga had planned to stop the American advance. The second item, the disposition of the "Surface Battle Forces," seems to have caught Spruance's eye. It read: "The striking forces of the carrier nucleus will try to operate outside the limits of enemy bases. They will attack the enemy striking forces on the *flank* and annihilate them within the limits of our bases"[9] (emphasis added).

The word *flank* appears but twice among the twenty-two pages of Z Plan. But those two references, identically phrased, seem to have captured the full attention and vivid imagination of Raymond Ames Spruance.

Spruance had every right to worry about the Japanese splitting their fleet and coming at him from two or more directions simultaneously. There was certainly ample precedence, for the flanking move was a classic Japanese tactic. Early in the century the Japanese had used a flanking maneuver to outfox and outfight the Russian fleet at the great Battle of Tsushima—a fact that Spruance later said was never far from his thoughts.[10] More recently, the admiral had seen Yamamoto divide his forces to strike from the flanks at battles in the Coral Sea, Midway, and Guadalcanal.

Spruance had a habit of trying to put himself in the place of his opponent. "What would I do if I were a Japanese with these capabilities in this position?" he would ask himself, for he fancied that his long study of warfare and his close contact with Japanese officers before the war gave him special insight into their thinking.[11] But there may have been a flaw in Spruance's own thinking. It has long been a military maxim to ask not "What is my enemy *going* to do?" but to ask only "What is he *capable* of doing?" That night aboard *Indianapolis* Spruance made an incautious assumption, for he assumed he knew what course his opponent would take, knew that Toyoda would split the Combined Fleet and outflank him at Saipan. Spruance allowed this presumption about flanking to override other factors, to neglect the main thrust of Koga Mineichi's battle plans: the concentration of Japanese forces, in particular the concentration of land-based and carrier-based air strength. It was a thrust best met by unleashing the awesome power of Task Force 58's fifteen fast carriers and nine hundred aircraft. Spruance, a big-gun admiral with relatively little naval aviation experience and no senior naval aviators on his staff to advise him otherwise, decided he must use TF58 to protect the flanks of the Fifth Fleet should the Combined Fleet sally forth. By tying Mitscher's carriers to the defense of the Saipan beachhead, he would stifle their mobility and offensive might. But Spruance's assumption was now firmly set in his mind. It would drive his actions in the coming days.

Over at Task Force 58, the thinking would be very different.

UNDER THE OVERALL COMMAND of Vice Admiral Marc ("Pete") Mitscher, Task Force 58 was organized around fifteen fast carriers in four task groups and one group of fast battleships, a total of ninety-three men-of-war. Each of the battle groups was under the leadership of a rear admiral, who could (and often did) operate autonomously. But when the groups were concentrated the force became the scourge of the Central Pacific, able to throw hundreds of aircraft into the air, able to project its power for three hundred miles in any direction.

Pete Mitscher hardly looked the part of a swashbuckling warrior. Barely taller than a jockey and just as slight, he seemed ten years older than his fifty-seven years; he had the visage, in fact, of a wizened owl. But his slight physical stature was more than made up in fighting spirit and hard-won battle experience. He graduated from the Naval Academy in 1910, joining naval aviation just six years later to become a pioneer navy flier. In 1919 Mitscher piloted the seaplane *NC-1* in one of the first, and very nearly successful, transatlantic attempts. He had started World War II as captain of *Hornet,* the carrier that launched Jimmy Doolittle's famous raid on Tokyo. Now he commanded the most powerful fighting force yet assembled in the Pacific.

Aboard his flagship, the fast carrier *Lexington,* Admiral Mitscher and his staff worked in "flag country," a rabbit warren of rooms consuming most of the fourth level of the ship's towering island structure. At the bow end was the flag bridge, a sort of three-sided veranda from which the admiral and his staff watched flight operations. There Mitscher, wearing his trademark green baseball cap, sat in a custom-built high chair facing the rear of the ship. Why he faced rear was always a mystery to his staff. Some thought their CO just wanted a better view of the busy flight deck. Others thought it was because he simply wanted to keep the wind out of his face. Whenever they suggested he face bowward, Mitscher politely deferred. While at sea he spent most of his day in his steel-and-kapok seat—smoking, reviewing messages, debriefing his pilots, and eating ice cream out of big china bowls.[12]

Through a doorway just opposite Mitscher's perch was flag plot, the nerve center of Task Force 58. It was a sparely furnished room painted sea foam green. To starboard was a large plotting table sitting upon cabinets filled with nautical charts of the entire ocean. The front bulkhead was emblazoned with instruments that revealed the ship's heading and speed, as well as wind speed and direction for air operations. Below that stood a desk where sailors tracked ship and aircraft movements, and where a yeoman sat typing a running log of all CTF58's activities. Once-vacant walls were covered now with blackboards—neat chalk scribblings revealing the makeup of the fleet, the air groups, and the distances to various targets and way points. Along the port side of flag plot was a long brown leather sofa reserved for the senior staff. During battle Mitscher and his deputies sat here, listening to radio calls coming in over the loudspeaker hung from the ceiling. Behind flag plot was the staff's office and the admiral's sea cabin. Directly below was "radio central," the communications hub of *Lexington* and her task force. Here radio reports flowed in from other ships, from other forces, from CincPac, and even from Washington.

Shortly after lunch on 9 June Spruance's *Indianapolis,* three days out of Eniwetok, rendezvoused with Mitscher's force. For more than two hours the sleek Fifth Fleet flagship had been cruising among the fast carrier groups, now spread out over a thousand square miles. The cruiser was headed for Task Group 58.3, to take up position near Mitscher's *Lexington.* At 2:12 P.M. *Indianapolis's* consort, USS *Stanly,* sidled alongside to haul aboard an important bag of mail from Admiral Spruance for special delivery to Vice Admiral Mitscher. Just over an hour later the destroyer peeled off from *"Lady Lex,"* her mission complete.

The pouch was rushed up to flag plot. There the admiral and his chief of staff, Captain Arleigh Burke, first laid eyes upon Koga Mineichi's Z Plan. It is unlikely that Pete Mitscher had any previous knowledge of the capture and translation of the Japanese document. He had left the Marshalls before the plan was received there by Spruance. Its appearance must have been electrifying. The twenty-two-page Z Plan clearly illuminated his opponent's strategic thinking. The six-page study of "Decisive Air Operations in the Central Pacific" amplified that thinking. As the air admiral digested the plans he must have been astonished by their aptness for the forthcoming Operation Forager.[13]

Subsequent events suggest that Pete Mitscher immediately grasped the import of Koga's strategy—to combine his carrier-based and land-based aircraft into a single and very powerful attack force set upon, first and foremost, the annihilation of the American aircraft carriers. That was bluntly clear in the opening paragraph of Z Plan:

> The Combined Fleet . . . will bring to bear *the combined maximum strength of all our forces* to meet and destroy the enemy[14] [emphasis added].

Mitscher's assessment of the chart showing how Koga had planned to stop the American advance was entirely different from Spruance's. Mitscher understood why the Japanese base air forces were directed to "come to grips with the enemy as soon as possible, find out the full extent of his forces, not lose contact with him." In other words, their reconnaissance was going to discover the American fleet quickly and track it day and night. Then the land-based planes were to "assume the initiative and carry out a disorganizing attack," smashing the enemy carriers first. In the meantime, the Japanese Surface Battle Forces were to "attack and annihilate the enemy using full strength, *cooperating closely*

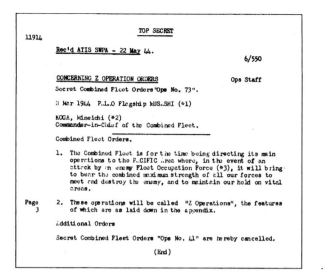

First page of Admiral Koga's Z Plan (ATIS translation). Note that this copy is number 6 of 550. (U.S. Army from the National Archives)

*with Base Air Forces*" (emphasis added). The order for the Combined Fleet's movements was telling: "The striking forces of the carrier nucleus will try to operate outside the limits of enemy bases."[15] In other words, the Japanese planned to move outside the reach of American sea and air forces—planned, in fact, to draw their enemy to an area conducive to a Japanese victory.

Mitscher was determined not to let any of that happen, flanking move or not. Unlike Spruance, whose responsibility was the security of the entire Fifth Fleet—nearly six hundred ships including and, in Spruance's mind, *especially*, the troop transports and supply vessels—Mitscher was mainly concerned with Task Force 58's carriers. But he also knew that any steps he took to neutralize enemy air power would benefit every soldier, sailor, and marine involved in Operation Forager.

Z Plan went on to reveal detailed estimates of total Japanese land and carrier air strength. Aboard nine carriers in three groups would be embarked up to four hundred fifty planes. On top of that, Koga estimated his land-based strength in the western Pacific areas to be twelve hundred fighters, bombers, and scouts. In addition, he could order another two hundred planes flown in from bases in Japan. The combined maximum strength of the Japanese air fleets was nearly twice that of Task Force 58's air groups. It looked a formidable force on paper, but as Mitscher read on, he could see it was not as potent as it first appeared. Admiral Koga was matter-of-fact in his appreciation of the quality of his carrier pilots. He noted that only half the pilots were trained well enough to take off from a carrier and carry out a striking operation. And many of those were not yet ready to land aboard the carriers after finishing their missions. Even with the additional two months of training since Z Plan was promulgated, the rookie enemy pilots would be no match for their highly trained American opponents. Of some comfort to Mitscher was the fact that since Koga's plan had been issued on 8 March, TF58 had already destroyed hundreds of Japanese aircraft during its peregrinations across the Pacific. If he could neutralize more of this force he might have, literally, half the battle won. He was willing to gamble that his pilots would prevail, and rule the skies above the Marianas. Pete Mitscher set about devising ways to keep the enemy at bay.

The original planning for Operation Forager prescribed a series of pre-invasion strikes on enemy airfields throughout Micronesia and, in particular, upon Truk and Palau. These raids would be flown mainly by B-24 bombers from MacArthur's SWPA. Indeed, the first one was in progress just as Mitscher received the Koga Papers. Locally, TF58 had been scheduled to fly missions over Guam, Rota, Tinian, and Saipan on 12 June. In light of the Combined Fleet's intentions to mass its air strength, Mitscher was not satisfied that the current blueprint would be sufficient to knock Japanese land-based air out of the contest. The admiral instructed his air operations director, Commander W. J. "Gus" Widhelm (himself a distinguished fighter ace), to tackle the problem.

Widhelm and his deputy, Lieutenant Commander John Myers, put their heads together and came up with three interrelated schemes. As was the custom in the navy, each of these was given a code name. They were, in order of precedence, the eponymous Plan Johnny and Plan Gus, and Plan Jeepers (named after the favorite saying of a fellow staff officer).

The first two plans focused upon getting a beat on the Japanese by launching the first air strikes during the afternoon of 11 June, rather than at dawn the following day. By making this change Mitscher hoped to catch the enemy off guard, for they had grown accustomed to dawn strikes. The surprise raids should allow his planes to wreak havoc upon the airfields of the Marianas. The air admiral believed that by starting early and hitting hard and often, TF58 fliers would essentially stifle Japan's ability to harm his carriers.

Widhelm and Myers's Plan Johnny was brief and to the point. It would be: "A 208-plane fighter sweep against enemy airborne and grounded planes at GUAM, ROTA, TINIAN, and SAIPAN, to launch at 1400 [11 June] from about 250 miles from objectives."[16]

Plan Gus provided for a destroyer scouting line to work ahead of the main fleet to handle direction of the airborne fighters and to rescue downed pilots.

And Jeepers called for a predawn follow-up strike on 12 June, the day the missions had originally been scheduled to begin.

After the creators had fined-tuned their plans, Mitscher sent them over to Spruance for approval.

Commander Fifth Fleet at first equivocated. He radioed Mitscher tentative approval, but *only* if Task Force 58 had not been spotted by 10 June. Mitscher was not happy. The air admiral felt so strongly about the surprise raid, felt so strongly that he had to knock Japanese land-based air out of the box before the big battle began, that he replied to Spruance, "Recommend Plan Johnny be carried out regardless contact. Enemy has assembled considerable number dive bombers and fighters on fields. Plan is to try to *prevent coordinated attack on our carriers*"[17] [emphasis added].

Spruance relented. Johnny, Gus, and Jeepers were approved late on 9 June.

U.S. RADIO INTELLIGENCE had kept JICPOA informed of the disappearance of and search for Admiral Koga Mineichi since his Emily crashed en route to the Philippines on 1 April. It was widely believed at the time, however, that Philippine guerrillas (Cushing's Cebu Area Command) had actually captured Koga, then released him. So it came as something of a surprise when, on 3 May, FRU-Pac intercepted a message to Japanese fleet commanders from the navy vice minister and vice chief of the Navy General Staff:

```
1. THE COMMANDER-IN-CHIEF OF THE COMBINED FLEET, ADMIRAL
MINEICHI KOGA, IS MISSING DUE TO AN UNDETERMINED INCIDENT
WHILE MOVING FROM PALAU TO DAVAO AND IT IS CONCLUDED THAT HE
WAS KILLED IN PERFORMANCE OF HIS DUTIES.

2. ADMIRAL SOEMU TOYODA WILL BE HIS SUCCESSOR AS OF 3 MAY.

4. ALTHOUGH THE PUBLIC ANNOUNCEMENT WILL BE MADE ON 5 MAY,
EVEN AFTER THAT DATE BE CAREFUL TO MAINTAIN SECRECY OF
PARTICULARS OTHER THAN THOSE ANNOUNCED (ESPECIALLY AS TO THE
TIME AND LOCATION).[18]
```

Who was Toyoda? The announcement sent analysts at JICPOA scurrying for information. Lieutenant John Harrison, a bright, young language officer, grabbed Layton's biographical files of Japanese officers and two days later published an intelligence bulletin called "Changes in the Japanese High Command."[19]

Harrison's appraisal of Toyoda Soemu disclosed that the admiral had been promoted above several others. Harrison said that the new CinC was "able and forceful. Extremely nationalistic and antiforeign." Like Koga, he was from a samurai family, and the two had been classmates at the Japanese Naval Academy. At the beginning of his career Toyoda had been a naval attaché in Great Britain and Germany. Over the course of twenty years he had relatively little time at sea. Once the war began he stayed ashore, in command of the Kure Naval District and then Yokosuka navy base.[20] An able administrator, Toyoda Soemu had absolutely no experience in battle.

The *U.S. Navy* chief of staff, Admiral Ernest J. King, however, warned his field commanders that he believed "Toyoda will prove to be competent, hardboiled, and influential in shaping future naval strategy."[21]

Like his predecessors, Toyoda was saddled with the onerous doctrine of the "decisive battle." It was now his turn to lure the American fleet into action (which Yamamoto and Koga both failed to do) and then, as the plan always specified, annihilate the enemy. By mid-1944 such an undertaking was probably already doomed, but the new CinC was determined to try.

Toyoda appears to have been working closely with the chief of the Navy General Staff, Admiral Shimada Shigetaro, on revising the Z Plan before he was officially promoted to command the Combined Fleet. The new plan, called A GO (literally, "A" Operation), was issued on 3 May.

There was a quandary, both at Pearl Harbor and at sea, between Spruance and Mitscher about how valid Z Plan might still be, now that Koga was two months dead. The Americans assumed his successor had revised the plan; through radio intercepts they knew of the existence of A GO. But how different was A from Z? How many changes could the new CinC Combined Fleet have made in a battle plan that had been carefully crafted over a two-year period?

Edwin Layton thought he had the answer.

On 14 June 1944, Layton included this estimate in the CincPac *Daily Intelligence Bulletin:* "I believe that the former 'Zebra Operation Order' of 8 March is in general effect with slight modifications and it is observed that the pattern of Japanese reaction thus far rather closely follows that plan." For emphasis, two days later the *Bulletin* carried this: "Evidence dated fourteenth that CinC Combined Fleet placed quote Able Operation unquote in effect with remark these operations to be decisive. CincPac estimates Able Operations generally similar to Zebra Operations, translation of which forwarded to fleet and type commanders as ATIS Limited Distribution Translation number four."[22]

Layton was not far off in his assessment. A GO was indeed very similar to the Z Plan. The defensive arena had shrunk considerably. The Japanese were now going to concentrate their forces from the Marianas to northern New Guinea, and were hopeful they could draw the American fleet into an area favorable to a Japanese victory. The new plan noted: "The battle areas have been roughly prearranged as follows: Battle Area 1.—PALAU Area. Battle Area 2.—Western CAROLINES Area."[23] Drawing their enemy into such specific locations seemed overly optimistic, even severely unrealistic. But that was precisely what the plan set forth. Otherwise, in broad strokes, the two plans were closely related, especially regarding the concentration of land-based and carrier-based air forces to smash the Americans. But, of course, the U.S. Navy could not be sure what changes the Japanese had made. Only an engagement on the high seas would reveal that.

As the Fifth Fleet steamed westward, the Japanese began preparations to implement A GO. In late May and early June, their fleet units were mainly concentrated in the Southwest Pacific. This was in large part due to an acute and worsening shortage of refined fuel oil to power the Combined Fleet.

U.S. submarines were taking a heavy toll of Japanese tankers trying to move oil from the Dutch East Indies up to the home islands. As a result, the IJN took to basing its warships closer to the oil fields—at places such as Singapore, Brunei, and the Sulu Archipelago. In the first week of June 1944 Layton's people estimated that the main body of the enemy fleet was anchored at Tawi Tawi island in the southern Philippines. A submarine sitting outside the harbor entrance reported sighting carriers, battleships, heavy cruisers, and other ships entering or leaving the isolated anchorage. This JICPOA reported in the daily CincPac *Bulletin* on 6 June.[24]

The warships at Tawi Tawi constituted the First Mobile Fleet—Japan's answer to the American fast carrier task forces. This fleet was under the tactical command of the able and very experienced carrier commander Vice Admiral Ozawa Jisaburo. And it was a powerful fleet, capable of inflicting severe, possibly mortal damage upon Spruance's forces. There were nine carriers in three groups, five fast battleships (including the behemoths *Yamato* and *Musashi*), eleven cruisers, and more than thirty destroyers.

Ozawa was a 1909 graduate of the Naval Academy. Unlike Toyoda, he had spent virtually his entire career at sea. Since the beginning of the war, he had commanded the 1st Carrier Division, the Southern Expeditionary Fleet, and now, the First Mobile Fleet. An American assessment of Ozawa noted that he was "an officer of impressive personality, dignified presence, and thoughtful habit of mind."[25] Naval historian Samuel Eliot Morison wrote that Ozawa was "a man with a scientific brain and a flair for trying new expedients. [He] was a worthy antagonist to Mitscher."[26]

Ozawa would be in tactical command of the First Mobile Fleet (just as Mitscher was of TF58), flying his flag from the new twenty-nine-thousand-ton carrier *Taiho*. When Toyoda released the A GO plan, Ozawa and other commanders flew to Tinian for four days of staff conferences. Thoroughly familiar with the plan's directives, Ozawa planned a few twists of his own. He aimed to keep his fleet out of reach of U.S. reconnaissance flights (though he was well aware that American submarines might track his movements). He intended to launch his carrier air forces out of range of American planes. And he intended to divide his carriers into three mutually supporting units.[27] Ozawa hoped that when the Americans found his forces, they would concentrate their attack upon the van, leaving the main body to strike Spruance's warships and, if they could reach the beachhead, his transports.

Tawi Tawi was not exactly an ideal fleet base. Though several hundred planes were aboard the Japanese carriers, the ships could not venture out of the harbor to continue flight training due to the constant menace of American submarines. Nor could the pilots use the airfield on the island, because it had not been completed. So Ozawa's already inexperienced air groups lost whatever edge they had whiling away their hours on this tropical isle.

Developments in the New Guinea area became distractions for the Japanese on 27 May 1944, with Douglas MacArthur's invasion of Biak, a strategically important island off the northwestern coast. Imperial Army forces fought hard to keep the Americans at bay, but it was a losing battle. Pete Mitscher would have been delighted had he known that about half the land-based aircraft in the Marianas and Palau were ordered down to New Guinea to help repel the invasion. Most of these planes were lost over Biak.[28]

On 10 June, from his flagship *Oyodo* anchored in Tokyo Bay, CinC Toyoda ordered the superbattleships *Yamato* and *Musashi* to sortie from Tawi Tawi with a convoy of reinforcements for beleaguered Biak. This force was under the command of Vice Admiral Ugaki Matome. Following reconnaissance over Majuro that revealed the presence of Task Force 58 on the fifth, and its absence on the ninth, Toyoda assumed Mitscher was on the move, and that the Southwest Pacific would now be the locus of U.S. attention. He began to make plans accordingly. Believing the Decisive Battle was near, and would occur south of the Carolines, Toyoda was ready to activate A GO. But his assessment proved to be off target. His miscalculation would cost the Japanese dearly within a week.[29]

JUST AFTER LUNCH ON 11 June the carriers of Task Force 58 turned into the wind and, in accordance with Plan Johnny, began to launch their afternoon strikes against Japanese airfields in the Marianas. Earlier that day six destroyers had been stationed twenty miles ahead of TF58 to act as radar pickets (Plan Gus). One of the carrier groups left the main formation to operate independently against targets on Guam. The other three groups remained concentrated, operating about two hundred miles east of Saipan.

The strikes were a great success. Surprise was achieved, and in the course of the afternoon an estimated one hundred nine enemy aircraft were destroyed on or above Saipan, Tinian, and Guam; another seventy were damaged. American losses were slight; eleven fighters did not come back, but five of the pilots were rescued from the sea.

At the same time, USAAF bombers pounded Truk and Palau for the third straight day. Overnight the Japanese made desultory attacks against TF58, with nothing to show for their efforts. Toyoda's land-based air force was losing a battle of attrition (but he did not know it).

In the predawn darkness of 12 June, two of the U.S. carrier groups launched Plan Jeepers attacks against the Marianas. Apparently a few enemy airplanes had been flown in during the night, but the Grumman F6F Hellcats quickly dispatched them. Northwest of Saipan TG58.4 attacked a Japanese convoy fleeing the area. They sank ten ships and damaged ten more. Once again, Mitscher's air groups ruled the skies.[30]

Back in Tokyo, Admiral Toyoda initially believed that the strikes were simply diversions for operations against Biak—raids, not preludes to invasion of the Marianas. The commander of land-based air on Tinian radioed Tokyo that his aircraft had shot down forty American planes and had suffered very little damage. It was the wrong time to distort the truth. Toyoda ordered *Yamato* and *Musashi* to continue their mission to Biak.

CincPac's *Daily Intelligence Bulletin* accurately reported: "Nil indications yet of any movements by major Jap surface forces as result Marianas attack. Up until evening twelfth all indications pointed toward Jap belief this another hit and run attack."[31]

On 13 June Ching Lee's fast battleships began a systematic (if none too accurate) bombardment of Saipan. Under the cover of the ferocious cannonade, minesweepers began to sweep the island's western coastline. This was the first clear indication of American intentions. Late that afternoon Toyoda, still a bit confused, nevertheless signaled the Combined Fleet to "stand by for Operation A."[32] Immediately the Biak-bound warships turned around and headed north. At Tawi Tawi, Admiral Ozawa's First Mobile Fleet had already weighed anchor and filed out of the harbor, their movement through the Sibutu Passage spotted by the submarine *Redfin* and duly reported to CincPac. The enemy was finally on the move.

The CincPac *Bulletin* reported as much: "CinC Combined [has] determined that present Blue [U.S.] activity Marianas was occupation and not a diversional strike. CinC Combined issued [operational orders] to 'Able' force. CinC First Mobile Fleet sortied with his striking force from Tawi Tawi." The summary concluded with: "All foregoing are deductions largely based on submarine sightings and traffic analysis with only meager amount of cryptanalysis."

With Japanese land-based air forces largely neutralized, Pete Mitscher sent two carrier task groups seven hundred miles north to the Bonin Islands on a planned strike of airfields at Iwo Jima and Chichi Jima. He hoped to knock out enemy planes flying down from Japan to reinforce the Marianas. With the knowledge that Ozawa was now at sea, but that battle could not possibly be joined prior to the seventeenth, Mitscher felt comfortable that the task groups could hit the Jimas and return in time to fight. He advised their commanders that he might recall them immediately if the situation changed. And he undoubtedly wished them "Good hunting!" The raids turned out to be a great success. Another ninety enemy planes were scratched from the Japanese Order of Battle.[33]

On the fourteenth Rear Admiral Jesse B. Oldendorf's old, slow battleships moved off the coast of Saipan to begin a systematic bombardment of the island. No longer able to keep up with the fast task forces, the veteran prewar battlewagons proved to be eminently suitable for accurately taking out enemy shore-based installations prior to invasion. Mitscher's planes continued to pound airfields on the islands, though now mostly concentrating on Saipan. And the army air force continued its strikes against Palau and Truk. At midafternoon on that same day, the First Mobile Fleet reached Guimaras Strait between Negros and Panay in the Visayas, stopping there to refuel and resupply. By this time Admiral Toyoda had decided that the Decisive Battle would commence on 19 June in an area west-southwest of the Marianas. Throughout the western Pacific the players were moving into position for the great engagement.

EARLY ON THE MORNING OF 15 June 1944, Admiral Kelly Turner bellowed the order "Land the landing force!" Heavily laden marines clambered over the sides of gray transports, inching their way down webbed cargo nets to a fleet of small landing craft bobbing on the sea. Elsewhere, landing ships opened their huge jaws and belched forth a miniarmada of troop-filled amphibious tanks. Under the watchful eyes of skilled boat directors, the little vessels churned up great arcs of white foam until every one was in position. On cue, all pointed their bows toward the island, making way quickly. Under the roar of big guns and strafing fighters, eight thousand Marines began to storm the designated invasion beaches: Red, Green, Blue, Yellow. By 10:00 A.M. all were ashore along a four-mile strip of the island's southwestern coast. By sundown another twelve thousand joined their comrades in heavy fighting.

That afternoon, after the brief stop at Guimaras, Ozawa's First Mobile Fleet was again on the move, just as orders came in from Admiral Toyoda activating operation A GO. The CinC Combined Fleet, echoing the words of Admiral Togo at the Battle of Tsushima, exhorted his men: "The fate of the empire rests on this one battle. Every man is expected to do his utmost."[34] At 7:00 P.M. Ozawa's fleet entered the Pacific through the San Bernardino Strait just north of Leyte Island. Headed almost due east at twenty knots, it was tracked for a time by the submarine *Flying Fish*. Early that evening the sub got a radio report off to Pearl Harbor, whence it was relayed to Spruance and Mitscher.

Just before midnight USS *Sea Horse* caught sight of Admiral Ugaki's battle group two hundred miles east of the Philippines and two hundred miles south of Ozawa's main body. This sighting caused a stir aboard *Indianapolis*. Spruance and his staff correctly reasoned that it could not be the First Mobile Fleet, therefore it must be an independent force. But they did not stop to consider that this new addition might join up with the main body; they continued to assume that this would be the force that would make the "end run," the flanking force. A great sea battle was now inevitable.

In light of the coming battle, Admiral Spruance decided to reorganize his own fleet. He met on the morning of the sixteenth with Admiral Turner and General Smith aboard the amphibious flagship *Rocky Mount*. Com5th postponed the invasion of Guam, scheduled for 18 June. And over the protests of Kelly Turner, Spruance reassigned seven cruisers and eleven destroyers from Turner's Task Force 51 to strengthen Mitscher's TF58. Spruance also directed all transport and supply vessels to retire two hundred miles eastward of Saipan to avoid the coming conflict.[35] At two o'clock that afternoon, Ozawa's First

Mobile Fleet rendezvoused with Admiral Ugaki's battle group to form a single, concentrated task force. It had always been Ozawa's plan to combine, not divide, his forces, as Spruance had assumed. The reasoning behind this tactic was purely practical—the Japanese did not have sufficient fuel to attempt diversionary maneuvers, only enough to bore straight in, then retire quickly.

Things were not going well for the United States on Saipan. Japanese resistance was proving fiercer than expected. JICPOA analysts had predicted that the enemy had fifteen thousand troops on the island; there were thirty thousand. That first night the Japanese Army had made at least three *banzai* charges. Though each was repelled, the toll of marines was heavy. On the second morning marines ashore were unnerved when they saw the roadstead off Saipan completely devoid of ships. The day before, the sea had been brimming with hundreds of vessels. Now there were none. Some wondered if they had been abandoned by the navy, not learning until later that Spruance had sent the supply ships away and had no plans of leaving the marines alone and stranded on the island. The fighting had grown so desperate that just before sunset on the sixteenth, General Smith committed part of his reserves to the fight, a regimental combat team from the 27th Army Division. Unable to stem the tide, more soldiers were landed the next day in an effort to resist Japanese counterattacks. By the end of 17 June, American casualties were estimated at fifteen hundred dead and four thousand wounded.[36]

At sea, the seventeenth was a day of preparation for Task Force 58. The ships reassigned from the landing force rendezvoused with their new battle groups. Floating filling stations topped off fuel tanks. Some air groups continued to fly support missions over Saipan. Long-range, radar-equipped Martin PBM flying boats, newly arrived from the Marshalls, conducted searches six hundred miles to the north and west. Meanwhile, TF58's own planes searched westward to the limits of their endurance. Nothing was spotted, making Spruance uneasy, for he knew Japanese reconnaissance planes had located and were tracking the Fifth Fleet.

Aboard *Indianapolis,* Admiral Spruance was busy considering his strategy for the coming battle. He reasoned that the Japanese intended to attack the transports off Saipan. He firmly decided that the "task of TF58 was to cover our amphibious forces and to prevent such an attack." Spruance continued to believe that the "enemy fleet might be divided, with a portion of it coming around one of our flanks." And this worried him greatly, for if he gave Pete Mitscher the freedom of movement the air admiral repeatedly asked for,

Spruance feared "such a flank attack could inflict heavy damage on our amphibious forces."[37] At 2:15 P.M., in a highly unusual move, Spruance himself wrote out his battle plan in longhand and asked Captain Moore to distribute it to the task force commanders:

```
OUR AIR WILL FIRST KNOCK OUT ENEMY CARRIERS AS OPERATING
CARRIERS, THEN WILL ATTACK ENEMY BATTLESHIPS AND CRUISERS,
TO SLOW OR DISABLE THEM. TG58.7 [Admiral Lee's fast
battleships] WILL DESTROY ENEMY FLEET EITHER BY FLEET ACTION
IF ENEMY ELECTS TO FIGHT OR BY SINKING SLOWED OR CRIPPLED
SHIPS IF ENEMY RETREATS. ACTION AGAINST THE RETREATING ENEMY
MUST BE PUSHED VIGOROUSLY BY ALL HANDS TO ENSURE COMPLETE
DESTRUCTION OF HIS FLEET.[38]
```

The battle plan prompted a quick response from Admiral Mitscher. Who, he wanted to know, was to be the Officer in Tactical Command (OTC)? It was a very basic, very important question. In all their previous missions together, Spruance had let Mitscher operate Task Force 58 pretty much the way he wanted, the senior commander rarely intruding into day-to-day tactics. The carrier admiral was not encouraged by Spruance's response: "Desire you proceed at your discretion, selecting dispositions and movements best calculated to meet the enemy under the most advantageous conditions. I shall issue general directives when necessary and leave details to you and Admiral Lee."[39] It sounded to Mitscher as if he could lead his task force, but only up to such time as Spruance deemed it prudent to take over.

Just after midnight on 18 June Spruance received a report from the submarine *Cavalla*. Earlier that night she had sighted a Japanese force of at least fifteen ships cruising due east at nineteen knots. When spotted by the sub, the First Mobile Fleet was eight hundred miles from Saipan—four hundred miles from being able to launch planes against the American invasion force. Admiral Mitscher also received *Cavalla*'s report. After some quick calculations, CTF58 realized that if he altered his present course 180 degrees, from eastbound to westbound, he might meet the enemy late on the afternoon of the eighteenth. Mitscher sent a radio message to his battleship admiral: "Do you seek night engagement? It may be we can make air contact late [in the] afternoon and attack [at] night. Otherwise we should retire eastward tonight." Ching Lee hastened to reply: "Do not, repeat, do not believe we should seek night engagement." It was a judgment with which Spruance fully concurred. Com5th radioed Pete Mitscher:

IN MY OPINION THE MAIN ATTACK WILL COME FROM THE WEST BUT
MIGHT BE DIVERTED TO COME FROM THE SOUTHWEST. DIVERSIONARY
ATTACKS COULD COME FROM EITHER FLANK OR FROM THE EMPIRE.
TASK FORCE 58 MUST COVER SAIPAN AND THE FORCES ENGAGED THERE
AND THIS CAN BE DONE BEST BY PROCEEDING WEST IN DAYLIGHT AND
TOWARDS SAIPAN AT NIGHT. CONSIDER IT UNWISE TO SEEK A NIGHT
ENGAGEMENT.[40]

Mitscher's aggressiveness was stymied once again. But he did not give up. In the comfort of *Lexington*'s flag plot, the diminutive admiral and his staff came up with an estimate that the enemy fleet could be in a position to begin launching attacks at 4:00 A.M. on 19 June. No one was comfortable allowing the Japanese to get in that close, but Spruance was adamant about tying the fast carriers to the defensive mission. Mitscher made another proposal to his commander: TF58 would "proceed during the day to the westward, the assumed direction of the enemy approach, launching searches to maximum distance during the day, reverse course toward Saipan at nightfall."[41] If reconnaissance turned up anything, the carriers would conduct night fighter and torpedo attacks against the enemy force. Com5th approved Mitscher's uncharacteristically prudent plan.

As the sun crept up over the horizon on 18 June, the Fifth Fleet knew that if Ozawa had maintained the same course and speed since last being positively spotted, day should bring at least a sighting, a report, some indication the First Mobile Fleet was coming within battle range. But Admiral Ozawa had set the date of battle for 19 June, and that was the date he intended to keep. By slowing his ships for refueling, he managed to stay on schedule and elude American reconnaissance, ensuring he would be in the desired position for a dawn attack the next morning.

Throughout the eighteenth, fighting continued to rage on Saipan, with American troops finally pushing inland despite fierce resistance. The wise Pete Mitscher gave most of his air group pilots a rest, limiting their missions to searches and combat air patrol.

At ten o'clock that evening, as TF58 steamed back toward Saipan, CincPac sent a dispatch reporting that Fleet Radio had picked up a direction finding (DF) fix on a Japanese radio transmission three hundred fifty miles west of Task Force 58. It was electrifying news, for the source was identified as the commander in chief of the First Mobile Fleet—Ozawa himself. Aboard *Lexington*, Mitscher and his staff hustled over to the circular table in flag plot. There they made some quick calculations about speed and course and distance. A lively discussion of various options available to TF58 ensued. When all opinions had been heard, Mitscher looked up at his men and said, "It might be a hell of a battle for a while, but I think we can win it."[42] Mitscher ordered one carrier group to launch a search-and-attack mission at two o'clock that morning. He then directed a message be sent to Spruance: "We propose to come to a westerly course in order to commence treatment of the enemy at 0500."

Admiral Spruance gathered in his flag plot with his staff to discuss the latest dispatch. Based upon the DF fix, several urged Com5th to turn to the west and steam toward the oncoming Japanese. Spruance was unmoved. And when Mitscher's request to "commence treatment" arrived, the senior admiral spent more than an hour considering all the strategic and tactical implications. Still fearing an enemy flanking maneuver, still concerned about the real location of the enemy fleet, Spruance turned down the proposal. He cited among other reasons that "it was of highest importance that our troops and transport forces be protected and a circling movement by enemy carriers be guarded against," and that "there is a possibility that the enemy radio transmission was a deliberate attempt to draw covering forces away from Saipan."[43] Mitscher took the news stoically, stalking silently out of flag plot, back to his sea cabin. His staff got back to work, planning for the worst—an enemy surprise attack. Arleigh Burke later said, "We knew we were going to have hell slugged out of us in the morning and we were making sure we were ready for it."[44]

Spruance felt further vindicated later that night when, at 11:46 P.M., he saw a message from Vice Admiral Charles Lockwood, commander submarines Pacific (ComSubPac) intended for submarine *Stingray*. Pearl Harbor said Japanese radio transmissions were interfering with the sub's attempts to send her report. Spruance assumed *Stingray* was trying to send a contact report and the enemy had jammed her signal. The sub's position was one hundred seventy-five miles east-southeast of the point where the First Mobile Fleet's transmission had been detected. Commander Fifth Fleet believed that this must be the enemy's flanking force. He gave more weight to the "jammed" message than to the definite DF fix. Only much later would he learn that the fix was quite real, that it was Admiral Ozawa radioing his land-based air commander on Tinian with final instructions. *Stingray*'s transmission had not been a contact report, just a routine message about a fire in the conning tower's radio antenna.[45] Spruance's decision to continue his eastward course that night would start a never-ending controversy among armchair admirals.

# CHAPTER 16

## *Decisive Battle*

THAT MORNING THE SKY above the Marianas was blanketed by high clouds. An occasional shaft of sunshine stabbed through holes punched in the vapors by lofty winds, briefly illuminating patches of the Philippine Sea like a spotlight. An occasional squall could be seen passing on the horizon, its dark, cumulonimbus form sometimes accentuated by long stabs of lightning. The slight chop on the sea would have no effect on the day's business.

Overnight the opposing fleets had set their dispositions for the battle. It was the nineteenth of June 1944.

The First Mobile Fleet had steamed eastward most of the night, to be in a favorable position by dawn. Admiral Ozawa had divided his fleet into three groups, but not for the purpose feared by his adversary. Ozawa had created a vanguard, an A Force and a B Force. His thinking was simple: the van would sail fifty to a hundred miles ahead of the main body, acting as a sort of decoy, albeit a formidably powerful one. A and B would follow behind, separated laterally by fifteen miles.

The vanguard, consisting of most of the heavy warships—four battleships, including *Yamato* and *Musashi*, nine cruisers, three light carriers, and eight destroyers—was under the tactical command of Vice Admiral Kurita Takeo, one of the Imperial Japanese Navy's most experienced flag officers. By being well in the lead, the van was expected to draw American attacks, leaving the main body hidden away to the rear. Kurita's antiaircraft batteries could throw a terrific barrage of flak into the sky. And the three light carriers could launch a combat air patrol of ninety aircraft. Ozawa believed the van could knock his enemy out of the sky. He gave Kurita orders to move no closer to the Fifth Fleet than three hundred miles. Any closer was inviting disaster.[1]

The A and B Forces were centered upon the five heavy aircraft carriers, escorted by one battleship, eight cruisers, and only fifteen destroyers. It would be from his flattops that Ozawa would launch his main attacks upon his enemy.

Ozawa Jisaburo believed he had several advantages over the Americans.

First, he knew his aircraft could outrange the enemy's fighters, dive bombers, and torpedo planes. Whereas the Americans had a combat range of some three hundred miles, Ozawa's Judys and Jills and Zeros could easily make three hundred fifty to four hundred miles. To gain this range the Japanese planes were essentially unarmored, consequently much lighter in weight. That made them easier to shoot down, but the aircraft designers and senior naval aviators had long felt it was a worthwhile trade-off.

The second advantage Ozawa had was the direction in which his ships were steaming—eastward. The prevailing winds were from out of the east, and in order for carriers to launch planes, they had to be facing into the wind. The First Mobile Fleet could continue to press its attack without having to change course. But each time Spruance and Mitscher wanted to launch or recover their planes, their carriers had to make a one-hundred-eighty-degree turn, at that point then sailing away from the Japanese.

Ozawa was counting also on shuttling his carrier planes to the two air bases on Guam to refuel and rearm. By this means he could significantly increase the range of his planes.

Last, Ozawa believed his ace in the hole was land-based air on Guam and Tinian. His base force commander on Tinian, Vice Admiral Kakuta Kakuji, kept him regularly informed of progress on the islands. Alas for Ozawa, Kakuta could not bring himself to speak the truth about Japanese aircraft losses, so throughout the run-up to the battle he had inflated his reports of damage to the Americans and deflated his own losses. Kakuta also neglected to tell his senior about the extensive damage TF58 had wrought upon the islands' airfields. On that fateful morning of 19 June 1944, Admiral Ozawa firmly believed that land-based air was mostly intact and would inflict great damage upon the enemy.[2]

If all went according to plan, this would be a great day in Japanese naval history. But for all his skill and experience, Ozawa's luck was about to abandon him absolutely.

EARLY THAT MORNING Spruance, as was his right, relieved Mitscher as OTC. He disposed Task Force 58 in five circular groups, with the big capital ships at the center of each circle. Two destroyers acting as early-warning radar picket ships sailed twenty miles ahead of Lee's battleships. The carriers followed twelve to fifteen miles behind the battle line, along a front twenty-four miles wide. At 5:00 A.M. TF58 was steaming a hundred miles northwest of Guam. Search planes had been launched as early as two in the morning but so far had turned up nothing.

The American fleet began to notice a rise in Japanese air activity at dawn. Mitscher directed his combat air patrols to head off the intruders. They gave chase, splashing several. Spruance was now aware his enemy knew exactly where TF58 was located, but he had no similar information about the First Mobile Fleet. A PBM flying boat had spotted Ozawa's ships at one-fifteen that morning, but radio failure delayed getting the report to Com5th until nine that morning, too late to be of any use.[3] The official War Diary of Com5thFleet, kept by Captain Moore, noted that the reason for the delay was being investigated, then speculated about exactly what the pilots spotted: "It may have been a concentration of one or more groups, or it may have been a single group. It did not preclude the possibility of a flanking movement." There were no further sightings. Indeed, the Japanese fleet would remain undetected throughout the long day ahead. But despite his misassumptions, Spruance was about to enjoy a remarkable run of good luck.

Suspecting that Guam was being used to stage aircraft, Mitscher sent a group of fighters to check it out. Orote Field was chock-a-block full of planes when the Hellcats arrived. Several dogfights ensued—the Americans taking the upper hand. A call for help went out to TF58. Two dozen more planes were sent to assist. When the fighting stopped just after nine, thirty-five Japanese aircraft had been destroyed.

Ozawa's vanguard, then about three hundred miles from Spruance, began launching its first raid at eight-thirty that dull morning. Sixty-nine aircraft took off for the east, soon disappearing over the horizon. A half hour later and eighty miles to the rear, a second group, with almost twice as many planes, was launched from the A Force carriers, followed by another, from the B carriers, at 10:00 A.M.[4] A fourth raid was sent airborne shortly after eleven.

At 9:57 A.M. a large bogey was picked up by Spruance's picket ships. Within minutes, dozens of glowing fluorescent blobs appeared on radar screens throughout the fleet. Mitscher knew he needed to get as many fighters into the air as quickly as possible to repel the attack, but the decks of his carriers were crowded with torpedo and dive bombers. He ordered these to launch immediately, then circle to the east of the fleet. At ten twenty-three the fighters began lifting off from the decks of the fifteen carriers. Soon there were more than two hundred Hellcats clawing through the skies, trying to gain altitude before they met the Japanese.

Rather than fly straight at TF58, Ozawa's first raid paused about seventy miles from the Americans to circle and regroup. The inexperienced pilots were being briefed by their group leader on how and what to strike. The impromptu meeting broke up after fifteen minutes; the Japanese now pressed their attack. But the delay was a huge tactical advantage to the Americans, for it gave them a priceless opportunity to get their planes and ships in position for combat.[5]

Within minutes the battle was met. And thus began the greatest aerial rout in history.

Each wave of enemy planes tried desperately to run the gauntlet of Hellcats and reach Task Force 58's carriers. Those few aircraft that did penetrate the inner screen were shot down by the massed fire of a hundred men-of-war. Few bombs or torpedoes reached their target. One smashed into the fast battleship *South Dakota* but did nothing to impede her progress.

A key to the American success was the coordination of air defenses by the fighter directors in each carrier group. These men, experienced pilots all, closeted themselves in their respective radio centrals, eyes glued to the radar screens. Using ship-to-air radio, they guided their fighters accurately and quickly toward the incoming waves of Japanese invaders.

The enemy, too, had a combat director. No doubt a battle-hardened airman, he stayed high above the fray, radioing attack instructions to his fliers. Unfortunately for the Japanese, the Americans were listening to all his conversations, translating them, then sending the information on to their own fighter directors.

During launch and landing operations, Pete Mitscher sat in his high chair, facing toward the stern as always, watching the comings and going with great interest. Spruance had usurped his role as OTC so, in a sense, the carrier admiral was just another spectator. Once the fighting began, he retired to flag plot, plunked himself down in the comfy brown sofa, and chain-smoked his way through the battle. The squawk box on the wall was never silent. When a squadron sighted the enemy, an excited "Tallyho!" would echo through the room. There would follow vivid, often profane, descriptions of the action as the pursued ran from the pursuers. "Scratch one Zeke!" "Look out, Jimmy, you got two on your tail!" "There goes another one." "Jeez, this is just like an old-time turkey shoot!" For the men confined to flag plot, this was as close to the action as they could get, but it was exhilarating stuff.

Early in the afternoon Mitscher sent his circling bombers and torpedo planes over to Guam to attempt to neutralize the airstrips there. They caught a number of enemy planes on the ground, refueling and rearming for a second attack. Bombing and strafing took out the majority. The day's count climbed still higher.

Ozawa had sent three hundred seventy-four aircraft against the Americans in four separate raids—three-quarters of his carrier air strength. By the end of the day only one hundred thirty made it back to their ships.[6] And before the end of the day, Ozawa's luck plummeted still farther.

ComSubPac had deployed more than a dozen submarines along the routes the Japanese must sail to reach the Marianas. Perhaps prescient, Lockwood had moved a group of four boats a hundred miles south of their original stations just the day before. At about 8:00 A.M. on the nineteenth, James William Blanchard, commanding USS *Albacore,* found himself in the middle of Ozawa's A Force. He gave thought to attacking the first carrier he saw, but decided to let it pass and take on the second. As Blanchard was setting up his shot, the TDC failed. Flying by the seat of his pants, at nine-ten he fired a salvo of six torpedoes from his bow tubes. He was quickly spotted by at least three escorts. He took *Albacore* deep and rigged for silent running.

As he was diving, the captain heard a large explosion, followed shortly by two others. He believed he had hit his target with at least one fish.

The target turned out to be *Taiho,* Ozawa's proud flagship. The first explosion Blanchard heard was indeed a hit on the starboard side of the carrier. The others resulted from quick action taken by a *Taiho* airman just as he lifted off from the flight deck. The alert pilot saw a torpedo wake and dived his plane into it. The torpedo exploded, taking the heroic pilot with it. The damage from *Albacore's* hit was minimal, or so it seemed at the time. The flattop was able to continue flight operations throughout the day. But fumes from a volatile mixture of petroleum leaking into the damaged forward elevator began to circulate throughout the ship. An inexperienced damage control officer decided to open all the ship's vents, which only served to spread the dangerous gases further. At about 3:30 P.M. a huge explosion ripped through *Taiho.* Officers and crew tried to save their ship, but just before sundown she rolled over and sank. Ozawa told his staff he would go down with the ship, but they persuaded him otherwise. Reluctantly he transferred his flag to the cruiser *Haguro.*[7]

*Taiho* was not the only carrier to be lost that day. At 12:15 P.M. *Shokaku* was hit by four torpedoes from USS *Cavalla.* The Japanese escorts quickly jumped on the sub, subjecting her to a brutal three-hour depth charging. The initial damage to *Shokaku* was more serious. She began to take on water, but damage control was ineffective. At 3:00 P.M. an ammunition magazine exploded, ripping the ship apart. *Shokaku* plunged beneath the waves. Two of the Imperial Japanese Navy's finest warships went to the bottom that day, along with twenty-two precious aircraft.

*Cavalla's* captain, Herman Joseph Kossler, knew that when his torpedoes hit *Shokaku* he had seriously damaged her. That evening he sent his report to ComSubs, who relayed it to Spruance. It was a simple message: "AT 2005 CAVALLA REPORTED THAT AT 1215 19 JUNE SHE OBTAINED THREE TORPEDO HITS IN A SHOKAKU CLASS CARRIER."[8] Within days radio intelligence would confirm that the great ship—the last remaining from the fleet that had struck Pearl Harbor—had been sunk. But Jim Blanchard had to wait weeks to learn what damage his torpedoes had inflicted upon *Taiho.* No reports of her sinking that day were forthcoming. He assumed she had escaped to fight another day. Only much later, when JICPOA was interrogating a captured Japanese sailor, was it learned that the carrier had indeed been sent to the bottom.

Throughout the slaughter, CinC Combined Fleet Toyoda was aboard his flagship far to the north, in Tokyo Bay. Reports from the Marianas trickled in, but communications failures left him in the dark about what was really happening in the Philippine Sea. There was little he could do to assist or advise. Toyoda just had to wait it out.

When the last stragglers reached the First Mobile Fleet, the enemy's losses totaled three hundred fifteen sure kills, to American losses of just twenty-five aircraft. Though the action would officially be named "the Battle of the Philippine Sea," that day in June 1944 became known to all as "the Great Marianas Turkey Shoot."

AS AIR ACTIVITY SLACKENED over Task Force 58, Admiral Spruance gave orders at 3:00 P.M. to change course to the west in an effort to chase the Japanese fleet. Now less concerned about a flanking maneuver, Spruance hoped to be in a position by dawn to launch a massed attack against Ozawa. At 3:00 P.M. he handed tactical control back to Mitscher.[9] Unfortunately, it took Mitscher's carriers nearly five hours to recover all the air groups, so the force was not able to begin the pursuit until nearly eight o'clock that night. Later Spruance radioed his air admiral:

> DESIRE TO ATTACK ENEMY TOMORROW IF WE KNOW HIS POSITION WITH
> SUFFICIENT ACCURACY. IF OUR PATROL PLANES GIVE US REQUIRED
> INFORMATION TONIGHT NO SEARCHES SHOULD BE NECESSARY. IF NOT,
> WE MUST CONTINUE SEARCHES TOMORROW TO ENSURE ADEQUATE
> PROTECTION OF SAIPAN.[10]

The chase was on. Once again, Ching Lee's battleships were in the vanguard, followed by three carrier groups (one stayed behind to keep Guam's airfields neutralized). But while TF58 sailed due west, Ozawa's force was steaming northwest. It was his plan to refuel on the twentieth and resume battle on the twenty-first.

Throughout the morning and early afternoon of the twentieth the Americans searched desperately for their opponent. Finally, at twenty minutes to four, a torpedo plane spotted the enemy fleet about two hundred seventy-five miles from Task Force 58.

Pete Mitscher now faced an epic dilemma. If he launched an attack at this late hour his planes would have only fifteen minutes over the target and would have to be recovered in total darkness. The potential for losses appalled the veteran airman. One of the reasons TF58's pilots so revered their admiral was because they knew he would take care of them, knew he would do everything in his power to get them back to the carriers. But they also knew that combat carried risks, and this mission would be fraught with risk. Mitscher was apprehensive, but he knew he had to take advantage of this opportunity to get at the enemy fleet before it escaped. After discussing the issue with his staff, Mitscher decided to attack. Fortunately, Spruance concurred.

At 4:25 P.M. the first planes lifted off from the twelve carriers. Two hours later, the Americans spotted the First Mobile Fleet. There were no attack coordinators this day—it was every man for himself. Some pilots singled out the oilers, figuring the enemy fleet could not function without fuel. Others went after the carriers.

The Japanese threw up a thick wall of flak, while Ozawa's few remaining planes struggled to get airborne to defend their ships. But the might of the attack was overwhelming. In short order bombs and torpedoes sank the big carrier *Zuikaku* and two oilers. Three other flattops were heavily damaged. Seventy more enemy planes were destroyed, leaving Ozawa with a pitiful thirty flyable aircraft of the four hundred seventy-three he had started with. It was not a decisive blow against the Japanese, but it was a very serious one, especially to the naval air force. The battle permanently crippled the IJN's ability to mount a meaningful carrier-based operation.

The flight home for the American pilots was one of exhilaration and fear. It was now dark; only a hint of the sun setting far to the west, to their backs, provided any illumination. The fliers knew reaching their ships would be tough and landing upon them nothing short of a miracle.[11]

When Mitscher knew his air groups were headed home, he ordered all his ships to turn on their lights. Huge searchlights were pointed straight into the sky to act as beacons. With fuel on the aircraft running low, CTF58 kept his carriers steaming westward at high speed until the very last moment, hoping to close the distance as much as possible. Pete Mitscher wanted to keep his losses to the barest minimum.

It would be a night of high drama, one unique in the annals of naval history. Mitscher watched the chaos from his seat on the flag bridge, rooting for every plane to make it home. The first landed at 8:50 P.M. Recovery operations then continued for the next two hours. Most of the aircraft made it onto the deck of a carrier. Some planes crashed on landing and were unceremoniously pushed over the side to make room for more. Those that did not reach a ship ditched at sea, their crews hoping to be picked up. Two hundred twenty-six planes had taken part in the raid. When all the losses were added up, only one hundred twenty-seven returned. Losses to flight crew were, happily, disproportionately lower. Once the seas had been scoured for stragglers, only sixteen pilots and thirty-three crewmen remained unaccounted for.[12]

Overnight a PBM flying boat reported twenty-five ships three hundred twenty-five miles northwest of Task Force 58. The plane shadowed the enemy for two hours. When Mitscher got word of the sighting he ordered full deckloads of fighters and bombers readied for a dawn launch. Throughout the daylight hours of the twenty-first, while the search continued for downed airmen, TF58 pursued what was left of Ozawa's fleet. Shortly after sundown Spruance called a halt to the chase. Ozawa sailed on to the home islands. Task Force 58 headed eastward, toward the Marianas.[13] The Battle of the Philippine Sea was over.

No sooner had the action ended than the second-guessing of Spruance's decisions started. Spruance's own task group admirals roundly faulted his leadership, believing Mitscher should have remained in tactical command throughout the entire operation and have been allowed to aggressively hunt the enemy. Spruance's decision to turn east on the night of the eighteenth, back to Saipan, rather than to pursue the First Mobile Fleet, received the harshest disapproval. Even Admiral Nimitz was initially cautious with his praise for his fleet commander's actions. In a letter to Spruance written on 20 June (Saipan time), Nimitz said:

> We share with you a feeling which I know you must have—that of frustration in our failure to bring our carrier superiority to bear on the Japanese fleet during the last few days.
>
> It now appears that the Jap fleet is retiring for replenishment, and that following a short period for this purpose we may have another chance at it. If they come back, I hope you will be able to bring them to action.[14]

Once the criticism began back at CincPac headquarters in Pearl Harbor, Nimitz stepped forward with unqualified support for Spruance's decisions, followed by Admiral Ernest King's favorable endorsement.

In the final analysis, possessing the Z Plan seems to have thrown Raymond Ames Spruance off the vital intent of the plan: the concentration of forces. His preoccupation with the flanking movement colored all his decisions that mid-June. But Marc Andrew Mitscher seems to have readily grasped the intent of the plan, and he made many aggressive suggestions to his commander to counter the threat. Some were approved. Most were not.

For the Japanese Imperial Navy, neither the Z Plan nor A-GO produced the desired results. They failed to provoke the Americans into a Decisive Battle Japan could win. As well conceived as they were, the operations were hampered by unrealistic assumptions and goals, a major flaw in many Japanese battle plans. Ozawa's vast experience was for naught, as he lost nearly all his carrier air groups, nearly all the land-based air strength in Micronesia, three impossible-to-replace heavy carriers, and two logistically critical fleet oilers. He had pressed home the attack with vigor, but luck was not on his side. It was Raymond Spruance who was blessed with a broad stroke of luck on those two days. Despite his fixation on an enemy flanking maneuver, despite his lack of experience in carrier operations, despite his overarching caution on the battlefield, he emerged victorious. But only conditionally.

For nearly sixty years naval officers, historians, and armchair admirals have debated what the outcome of the battle might have been had Spruance allowed Mitscher to steam west that night and close the range to the enemy. He might have achieved tactical surprise and sunk many more ships, though not knocking so many planes out of the sky. On the other hand, Mitscher might have seriously jeopardized Task Force 58 if his reconnaissance had not located the First Mobile Fleet (a feat the scouts were unable to achieve at any time during the first day of battle). Still, chances are that the outcome of the Battle of the Philippine Sea would have been in the Americans' favor.

While it gave the United States an intimate look into Japanese planning, the Z Plan played a lesser role in the battle than it might have, had not Spruance's fixation on one word out of thousands negated the value of Koga's legacy. In a postwar oral history, Spruance's chief of staff, Carl Moore, spoke about Z Plan and its impact upon his boss:

> Spruance's reference to an attack from either flank was something that was very much on his mind, largely because we had received a Japanese plan of action. We didn't know whether it had been received by Turner and Mitscher, but it was very significant as far as we were concerned.
>
> I think the thing encompassed heavy ships as well, with the whole idea being that if they could draw the ships to an attack in the center, and heavy ships or carriers could make an end run and get in behind, they could do the damage they wanted to do. The report indicated that this sort of action might be taken. His experience with the Japanese influenced his actions right through the operations.[15]

SAIPAN WAS FINALLY DECLARED secure on 9 July 1944. Within two weeks army units and marines stormed ashore, first at Guam, then at Tinian. On the first of August organized resistance ended on Tinian. Immediately military engineers began to level the northern half of the island to build air bases from which the United States could attack Japan with long-range B-29s. In August 1945, from one of these fields, a Superfortress took off on a top-secret mission against the city of Hiroshima—ushering in the Atomic Age and hastening the end of World War II.

The American and Japanese fleets would soon meet again in the Philippine Sea, in an even bigger battle. Shortly after the United States landed troops on Leyte in late October 1944, the Combined Fleet put to sea. The battle plan,

Sho Go, was bold and full of great risk for the Japanese. There would indeed be a flanking move—two, in fact. The main body, under the command of Vice Admiral Kurita, was to attack the beachhead with a group of heavy ships, including *Yamato* and *Musashi*. Coming up from the south, Admiral Nishimura led a small force of older battleships and cruisers. These two groups would attempt a pincer movement off Leyte, with the intention of annhilating the transports and supply vessels. Wily Admiral Ozawa would lead a force of carriers, virtually bereft of aircraft, down from the north. His job was simple—lure the American fast battleships and carriers away from protecting the landing beaches long enough to permit Kurita and Nishimura to complete their missions. The decoy worked like a charm. Fleet commander Admiral William F. "Bull" Halsey charged north, leaving only a small force of destroyers and escort carriers behind to defend the beaches. Kurita snuck in and began to pummel the outer screen of American warships. Help for the little combatants was hours away; they were sitting ducks under the barrage of the big guns. And the damage was appalling. Two escort carriers were sunk by naval gunfire and two others were damaged. Three destroyers sank, two others were damaged. Kurita had the upper hand in the battle when all of a sudden he decided to disengage and retire. Had he pressed home his attack, Kurita might very well have broken through the line and been able to sink the transports and supply ships one by one with complete impunity. Ozawa's force was decimated by American aircraft, and included the loss of four of the remaining six carriers. The three Japanese task groups limped home, never again to undertake a serious offensive.[16]

Vice Admiral Fukudome Shigeru, once Cushing's prisoner, perhaps spoke for many of his fellow officers when he told interrogators after the war, "The loss of the Marianas was a spiritual blow to me. After that loss I could see no chance for our success."[17]

# Epilogue

ON THE SECOND DAY OF September 1945 the war against Japan officially ended. After forty-five months of fighting it all came down to a ceremony on the deck of the battleship *Missouri*. There, in the middle of Tokyo Bay, a delegation of Japanese civilian and military leaders boarded to sign the instruments of surrender. To witness the historic event was gathered perhaps the largest contingent of top brass from the United States and her allies ever assembled. Indeed, the forecastle of the great battleship was sparkling with gold stars, radiant with colorful campaign ribbons. It was a memorable sight. The master of ceremonies was General Douglas MacArthur; Admiral Chester Nimitz played a subordinate role at his side. In the front row behind the two leaders stood Jonathan Wainwright, thin and frail after his years in a Japanese prison camp. Vice Admiral Charles Lockwood, leader of the submarine force that did so much to bring about this victorious day, watched the event with satisfaction. When the signing was completed MacArthur announced, "These proceedings are now closed." The world was at peace (or as peaceful as the world can ever get).

Conspicuous by their absence were Admiral Raymond Spruance and Vice Admiral Marc Mitscher. Spruance was at Okinawa, planning for the occupation of Japan. Mitscher was in Washington, D.C., hating every minute of his new deskbound job at the Navy Department.

It was just as well that Spruance missed the surrender. A shy, private man who shunned publicity for himself, he was happy to avoid the public adulation heaped upon MacArthur, Nimitz, and Halsey. Spruance just wanted to get on with his job. He replaced Nimitz as commander in chief, Pacific, in the autumn of 1945. Ten weeks later Spruance was reassigned to the billet he really cherished—the presidency of the Naval War College in Newport. In 1948 he retired to Pebble Beach, California, to the first house he and his wife had ever owned.

Duty again beckoned in the early fifties when the old warrior was appointed ambassador to the Philippines. After an eventful three-year tour, Spruance retired for good. His waning years were spent gardening, reading, and corresponding with former shipmates. Raymond Spruance died of heart failure in the spring of 1969. By his wish, he was buried next to Chester Nimitz and Kelly Turner.[1]

Pete Mitscher, utterly exhausted from four years of fighting, left Task Force 58 in the spring of 1945. His days at sea were over. He reported for duty at the Pentagon as deputy chief of naval operations for air. The position was mainly a desk job, with a healthy dollop of partisan politics thrown in for good measure. It was a move, Mitscher told reporters, that was "against my wishes and desires."[2] Fortunately he had to endure the capital for only a year. He was promoted to four-star admiral and given the helm of the Eighth Fleet, based in Norfolk, Virginia. On 26 January 1947, his sixtieth birthday, Pete Mitscher suffered a heart attack. He died in hospital eight days later.

Mitscher would have been proud to know that today's carrier task groups—they are called "battle groups" now—are still the mainstay of the U.S. Navy. The new ships dwarf the Essex-class flattops Mitscher commanded. They stretch more than eleven hundred feet in length, tipping the scales at more than eighty thousand tons. They are powered by the atom, not by bunker fuel. Their air groups are no longer confined to a three-hundred-mile combat radius. Thanks to aerial refueling, the jet-powered fighters and bombers now have almost unlimited range. And instead of just conventional bombs, the carriers' magazines stock nuclear weapons. Just as Task Force 58 did in World War II, today's carriers still project awesome power. But their mission has changed in the past half century. There are no more pitched sea battles to fight or islands to take. Now the carriers are deployed to innumerable places where small conflicts between small countries threaten the security of the United States or its NATO partners. To ensure this security, the navy plans to field a dozen carrier battle groups well into the twenty-first century.

ON THE DAY OF THE SURRENDER, a gaggle of fleet submarines was anchored within sight of the *Missouri*. USS *Crevalle* was not one of them. She was far across the Pacific, on her way home.

*Crevalle* had had a good war. She made seven patrols under three captains, each of whom received the coveted Navy Cross for each patrol he commanded. She was credited with sinking nine ships and damaging ten more.

She had sailed more than a hundred thousand miles with the loss of just one crew member. The boat herself had had numerous brushes with oblivion, notably on the fifth patrol, when a diving accident almost flooded the ship. Lieutenant (jg) Howard James Blind, the officer on the bridge at the time, was credited with saving *Crevalle* and her crew by somehow managing to close the conning tower hatch as tons of water poured through it. He was posthumously awarded the Navy Cross for his heroism.

On 23 December 1944, at Mare Island, California, Frank Walker was relieved as captain of *Crevalle* by Commander Everett Steinmetz. Two months later the sub headed back into the war. She stopped at Pearl Harbor for the installation of special mine-detecting sonar (called FMS). After a brief training period the boat sailed for the coast of China. Toward the end of this, the sixth patrol, *Crevalle* performed another special mission. Using FMS, Steinmetz was to plot the extent of the minefields planted by the Japanese at the approaches to the heavily guarded Inland Sea (sometimes called "the emperor's private pond"). It was a hairy mission, for the technology was untested. The operators had to learn how to tell a deadly mine from a friendly fish, for brushing ever so gingerly against a mine could sink the submarine in thirty seconds. But the boat got in and out safely, recording a surprisingly accurate plot of the minefields.

On her ultimate war patrol *Crevalle* joined eight other fleet boats to form a wolf pack called Hydeman's Hellcats. Their mission was to penetrate the Inland Sea—to wreak havoc upon the unescorted shipping there. The pack cautiously entered the heavily mined Tsushima Strait and began their grand adventure on 9 June 1945. A dozen days later the Hellcats transited La Pérouse Strait, the northern exit of the Inland Sea. They proudly reported back to Admiral Lockwood that the nine boats had sunk twenty-seven merchantmen and one enemy submarine. What had been called Operation Barney was a smashing success. But it was not without tragedy. Sometime during the incursion, USS *Bonefish* and all of her crew disappeared into the depths of the sea, a victim of enemy destroyers.

*Crevalle* was decommissioned at the submarine base in New London, Connecticut, on 20 July 1946. Twenty-five years later she was unceremoniously scrapped—an inglorious end to a valiant warship.[3]

AFTER FRANK WALKER WAS DETACHED from *Crevalle,* he reported to new construction. He was to put into commission and then command the submarine

USS *Odax*. But by the time *Odax* was ready for the war, the war had ended.

Walker stayed in the navy until 1965, when he was passed over for promotion to admiral. After thirty years' service, Frank Walker retired. For six years he worked for Sylvania Fleet Systems at Sands Point, New York. He now lives with his second wife in Scottsdale, Arizona.

PAUL LINDHOLM CONTINUED his evangelism on Negros until the Visayas were liberated by the U.S. Army in April 1945. He caught a troop ship back to the States, arriving in San Francisco on 26 July. The local office of the Board of Foreign Missions had arranged passage to Salem, Oregon, on an afternoon train. Paul made sure he was on that train. The office also wired ahead to Clara and the children: Your husband and father is coming home. After one year and three months of separation, the family's reunion was tearfully joyous.[4]

Paul Lindholm thrived during the war doing the job he loved most—working among the people. Clara had remained the dutiful missionary's wife, lending support to her husband, staying behind to take care of the kids. Though the challenges of life in the jungle were many and constant, she had Paul to deflect most of them. In that regard she was luckier than Viola Winn. But she had another advantage over her friend as well. Clara Malbon Lindholm was perfectly comfortable with her beliefs. Her faith in God was absolutely unshakeable. That was what carried her through months in the mountains, a dangerous undersea voyage, and life without Paul while she waited for him to come home.

After the war the Lindholms looked forward to going back to China. But the faculty of Silliman University intervened. They had sent a letter of petition to the Board requesting the Lindholms. It was signed by fifty-six teachers. The couple reluctantly agreed to return to Dumaguete, on the condition that the Board guarantee their reassignment to China. After a year at the school the Board, as promised, transferred them back to Shanghai and the East China Mission.

Paul devoted himself to the rural ministry, especially to training church leaders. But in 1949 the Communists swept through the country, forcing Western missionaries to close their missions, pack their bags, and leave the soon-to-be People's Republic of China.[5]

Just as they had five years earlier, the family fled for the sanctuary of the Philippines. Paul was undaunted by the setback. For the next thirty years he traveled the globe, visiting more than fifty countries, helping to educate thousands of ministers and laymen.

Paul and Clara Lindholm retired from missionary work in 1979. With the children grown and out of the house, they settled into a modest apartment at Westminster Gardens, a Presbyterian retirement home in southern California.

Paul's health began to deteriorate in the late 1990s. When it seemed his time to go, Clara called together family and friends to be at his bedside. Even Christian Malahay was there—he whose family had risked their lives to hide the Lindholms in the hills above Guihulngan. He later wrote, "He was in a comatose state. I pressed his right hand and whispered who I was in his ears, and he pressed my hand very strongly. I believe he still recognized me."

On the twelfth of August 1997, ten days shy of his ninety-fourth birthday, Paul Lindholm passed away. At his memorial service, a quartet—Dean, Jim, and Janet Lindholm, and Chris Malahay—sang one of Paul's favorite hymns, "Near to the Heart of God." Christian summed up what must have been in everyone's hearts: "What a great privilege it was to know a great man of God."[6]

At the turn of this century Clara Lindholm still lived at Westminster Gardens. At ninety-six she is a bit deaf, but full of vigor and love for life.

AFTER GARDNER WINN turned himself in to the Japanese, he spent his first two months locked up with other Americans in a Dumaguete schoolhouse. In September 1942 he was moved to Bacolod (where he undoubtedly came in contact with the ten POW truck drivers based in a garage just a few blocks away). Life at the Bacolod camp was not too bad. Food was reasonably plentiful, the guards rarely beat people, and there was lots of time for leisure, even an occasional baseball game. The following March Gardner and his cellmates were loaded aboard a Manila-bound freighter. Some days later they were deposited at the civilian internment camp at Santo Tomas University, smack in the heart of the capital. The deprivations were many (and grew worse as the war turned in the Allies' favor). It would be three years before American troops liberated the camp.

By the end of February 1945 Gardner Winn was on a ship heading home. Viola met her husband alone on the Union Pacific platform in Omaha. Before returning to see the children, the couple enjoyed a "two-day second honeymoon." On arriving at the Iowa home of Viola's brother, Gardner was astonished to see how Elinor had grown. He had last seen her as a year-old baby. Now she was a chattering four-year-old. The boys had changed little, he thought, though they had grown taller and huskier.[7]

Viola had grown, too—spiritually.

Before the war her life had always been placid, comfortable, and not particularly challenging. In December 1941 her closeted world was turned upside down. She was forced to face head-on an epic crisis of survival. Gardner's surrender to the enemy shook Viola to the core. She depended upon him for so much. Then he had abandoned her for principles that were well-meaning and heartfelt but that made no rational sense.

Her response to this crisis took two contrary forms. On one hand, Viola Winn retreated from the world around her. Rustico Paralejas, who would later guide the Winns and the Lindholms through the jungles to safety, visited her twice. She left him with this impression: "She was subdued, a little nervous, and looked very sad and upset over her condition. I felt my presence was not appreciated. The children, too, shared her apprehension. She never allowed her children to go play outside the house. Why? She would like them 'in' to prevent a chance passerby to see them. It would have been a different story if [Gardner] had been present."[8]

On the other hand, Viola's faith in God was strengthened. Thirty months of hiding constantly tested this faith, and in myriad ways. When Gardner left, she had no idea how she would manage three small children in the wilderness. But she did. She steeled herself to move forward, believing God was always at her side, there to comfort her in times of need. Viola Winn emerged from the war a stronger, more independent woman with an abiding confidence in the Lord.

After several months of recuperation Gardner spent a year at Cornell, then returned with his family to China. When the Communists took over, the Winns, too, were forced to flee.

Having been twice thwarted from pursuing a career as a foreign missionary, Gardner decided to call it quits. On the first of July 1949 he submitted his resignation to the Board of Foreign Missions. He now wanted to be, quite simply, a pastor at a friendly church somewhere in America. Gardner soon got his wish. He was assigned to Presbyterian churches in Iowa and later at Hillsdale, Michigan.

There Gardner Winn soared. His services, and especially his sermons (often full of surprising humor), left a lasting impression upon his parishioners. His booming bass voice reverberated off the stained-glass windows. After eighteen happy years at Hillsdale Gardner retired. Or, rather, he retired provisionally, for he spent another decade working as a "calling pastor" at various churches in western Illinois.

In a way, the Board of Foreign Missions had rightly been concerned about the difference in ages between Gardner and Viola, she ten years older. Though she lived a rich and full life, Viola Winn predeceased her husband, dying of lymphoma in 1981.

Four years later Gardner married Dora Robinson, a former Hillsdale congregant. That same year he stepped down from the pulpit for the last time.

In 1991 Gardner and Dora took up residence at Westminster Gardens. By the end of the decade Gardner had lost his eyesight and was unable to move around unassisted. He died on the twenty-third of June 1999 at age eighty-eight.[9] True to his beliefs, Gardner Winn remained a pacifist to the end of his life. And every year he sent a small donation to the Fellowship of Reconciliation.

FOLLOWING THEIR RESCUE, the sugar families took diverging paths.

George Ossorio had not gone to Australia with his family. Colonel Abcede had asked the engineer to remain behind. But all that changed when the Japanese mounted a devastating raid on southwestern Negros at the end of May 1944, a reprisal for *Crevalle*'s visit. The enemy knew the sub had taken off Americans and perhaps, they suspected, had carried away Admiral Koga's Z Plan, as well.

Ossorio asked his CO if he could be evacuated on the next supply run. Abcede did not want to lose George, but fully understood his reasons for wanting to leave. The colonel assented.

On 21 June *Narwhal* surfaced off Balatong Point. She brought in ninety tons of supplies for the guerrillas, and a four-man weather team that would send daily reports back to SWPA GHQ. George was one of fourteen Americans evacuated that evening.

The voyage down to Darwin was uneventful (Ossorio knew nothing of the experience his wife and son had been through a month earlier). Once on Australian soil he went through the usual drill of medical examinations and long interrogations by intelligence officers. He learned that Loretta and Kenneth had sailed home from Brisbane just three days before. George could have gone home, too, but he decided he wanted to continue making a contribution to the war effort. He was not "regular army," so SWPA had no place for him. Instead, he volunteered to join the American Red Cross. His offer was readily accepted.

When Loretta returned to Baton Rouge in the summer of 1944, she took a job with a local oil company. But it was not a job she found rewarding. She had admired the Red Cross workers she met in Darwin and Caloundra. Loretta Ossorio, too, joined the service for the duration of the war.

After the surrender George Ossorio went to occupied Japan as an agricultural consultant to help Japanese farmers replant war-ravaged fields. In 1946 he was joined there by Loretta. It had been nearly two years since they had seen one another.

Kenneth did his part by signing up with the navy. While at boot camp in San Diego, the war with Japan ended. But Ossorio was not off the hook. The navy deployed the seventeen-year-old sailor to Nagoya, Japan, as part of a relief crew on USS *Luzon*, a repair ship. After a few weeks the vessel was ordered to sail to Texas, there to go into mothballs. Once that task was completed Kenneth was discharged, after only thirteen months in the service.

George and Loretta came home to the States in 1948. He went to work as an engineer for Lockheed when that company bought and reopened the huge aircraft factory at Marietta, Georgia. It was a far cry from sugarmaking in Manapla. There he stayed until his retirement to Florida in 1965.

While his parents were still overseas, Kenneth finished high school and began working on an engineering degree at the University of Florida. He later did postgraduate studies at Georgia Tech and the University of Central Florida. Like his father, Kenneth went to work at Lockheed. Seven years later he took a position with Martin Marietta in Orlando, Florida. He was eventually promoted to program director, managing the development of weapons systems such as the Pershing and Hellfire missiles. Ossorio spent the rest of his career—thirty-three years—with the defense contractor. He retired in 1992.

His father had died four years earlier, having lived a fascinating, almost exotic life. Loretta is now in her midnineties, her voice still vibrant and youthful.

Kenneth's collection of secret guerrilla documents was never returned to him. He did get a handful back. But the U.S. government has held on to the rest of the contents of the battered suitcase Ossorio had lugged around for so long.

SHORTLY AFTER THE REAL FAMILY landed in San Francisco, the Red Cross found housing for them across the bay in Albany, a small coastal town just a couple of miles north of Berkeley. Because of his expertise in turbines, Sam soon found work at Westinghouse in nearby Emeryville.

One day Sam was sent to the navy base at Mare Island to meet an incoming submarine. To Real's utter surprise that boat turned out to be *Crevalle*. She had sailed from Fremantle for a complete overhaul after her fifth war patrol. Some of the crew remembered Sam. They enjoyed a brief reunion, then got down to the business of repairing the war-weary ship.

When the war was over Sam accepted a job with Bechtel Corporation that took him back to the Philippines to help restore the country's devastated industrial base. Just a few years later, Real was diagnosed with leukemia. He carried on as best he could, but as the disease advanced, he grew weaker and weaker. In 1955 the family returned to the States, where better medical care was available, but it was to no avail. Sam Real died on the fourteenth of August 1956.

After Sam passed away, Rose remarried three times. Now nearing ninety, she lives with her youngest daughter, Nancy, in southern California.[10]

It had been a heart-wrenching experience for Bill Real to leave his dog Thunderbolt on the beach at Basay. Before boarding the banca the boy had entrusted the mongrel to one of the family's housegirls, Tonia. She tried her best to look after the pet. Food was so scarce at the time, feeding soldiers and civilians taxed Colonel Abcede's resources. The dog, now growing scrawny, took to scrounging food from the guerrilla kitchens. The cooks took a dim view of the animal's activities. One day they poured boiling water on him. Thunderbolt did not survive. When Bill heard about the fate of his dog, and the manner of his death, he was moved to tears. Even today it remains an emotional memory for him.[11]

ALL TEN OF THE POW truck drivers survived the war.

Irving Joseph, Frank Reynolds, and Dick Jenson were evacuated from Negros in June 1944, on the same submarine that took George Ossorio out. All have since passed away.

After Jay Russell Snell married Rose Combattelli in Rochester, he was sent by the army to a rest camp at Lake Placid, New York. A great hullabaloo broke out over whether his promotion from sergeant to lieutenant, made by Colonel Cushing when Snell first arrived on Cebu, was valid. At one point he was demoted, then soon after re-promoted. One officer took exception to the whole issue, insisting Snell be discharged as an officer, then reenlisted as a tech sergeant. Snell was disgusted by the politics. He asked for and got a medical discharge.

The ex-POW kicked around at various jobs for years, never seeming able to make a career out of one. Looking back now, he says, "I had a lot of problems, and drank too much." Eventually Snell found a job he liked, working as a sales rep for a steel company. He kept at it until he retired to Florida. Rose Snell now suffers from Alzheimer's disease and lives in a nursing home. Three times each day Russ visits her. Some days are worse than others, for sometimes she cannot recall who he is. Those times are growing more frequent—that's the heartbreak of Alzheimer's. "It's a bitch," he says.[12]

Howard Chrisco's homecoming proved to be too much for him to bear. Too many people crowded into and around the bungalow to greet him and pepper him with questions about his time in the Philippines. The day after he arrived, he returned hastily to the solitude of Jefferson Barracks. He went home for two quieter weeks before shipping out for William Beaumont Army Hospital in El Paso, Texas. There Chrisco underwent several weeks of physical therapy on his wounded arm. Chrisco did not know what the army wanted from him for the remainder of the war, but he knew what he wanted from the army: a discharge. It was granted in November 1944.

Back in Salem, Howard Chrisco's life was very busy indeed. He worked at a number of jobs, bought and sold (at a tidy profit) a grocery and feed store, watched his mother succumb to cancer, met and married Elsie Haas. He was then twenty-seven; time to settle down, he thought.

The newlyweds rented a farm outside town, and Howard Chrisco began a new career. Things went well at first. He was able to buy his own farm a year later. In the midfifties, though, things turned sour. A three-year drought crippled the farm. A fire destroyed the barn and outbuildings. While they rebuilt their lives, the couple took day jobs—Elsie at the bank, Howard at the Missouri State Employment Security Office.

After his retirement from the state in 1979, Chrisco devoted himself to cattle farming. He gave that up in 1999, at age eighty. But Howard quickly grew bored with full retirement. By the end of the year he had bought another herd. "I had to have something to do," he said.

When the Lucky Seven escaped from Bacolod, Ramon Corona and Gavin White were down in Murcia. Throughout the war their fates were unknown, though SWPA Intelligence received reports that the men had been executed by the Japanese. In fact, after some rough treatment by their captors, the pair was sent to a work camp in Japan. They were liberated in 1945. Howard Chrisco learned shortly after the war that Corona had survived, but the two never made contact. Until 1988. On his way home from vacation, Howard detoured to Albuquerque to pay a surprise visit to his former comrade. When Ramon got the call he shot out of his house and raced to Chrisco's hotel. They had a lot to talk about. The tables were turned in the autumn of 1999 when Howard got a call he never expected: from Gavin White. White's wife had seen a story about Howard in the local newspaper. She put the two in touch for the first time in fifty-five years.[13]

OF THE FORTY PASSENGERS on *Crevalle,* perhaps Betty Jaboneta has fared worst.

Ada Jaboneta had adopted her as an infant in 1937. But the adoption was never formalized. This was not a problem when the family lived in Kabankalan. And it certainly was not a problem in the mountains. But when *Crevalle* landed in Australia, the trouble about Betty's background began. For a time it looked as though the girl would not be able to go on to America with her family. Finally, officials in Australia decided to let officials in the States deal with the sticky issue.

In mid-June the three Jabonetas were able to join other refugees on SS *Boschfontein,* bound for the West Coast. Upon arrival in San Francisco immigration officers closely questioned Ada. Why, they wanted to know, were there no papers for the little girl? The mother did her best to explain the situation, to explain that she herself was a native-born American, and that her son Ernie could rightfully claim citizenship, too. About the daughter, though, the authorities were unmoved. They did make one concession: Betty could stay in the States until the end of the war; then she must go back to the Philippines to get matters straightened out. If all the documents were properly stamped and signed, if everything was truly in order, Betty would be readmitted to the United States.

At the end of 1946, mother and daughter returned to the islands. It took months to sort things out with the Filipino and American governments. At about that time Ada received a message from Ernie in San Francisco. He and his wife had just had a baby. "Come back to see your grandson," he implored.

Ada arranged for Betty to stay behind with her husband's relatives. She then sailed home. It was the last Betty would ever see of her.

Her guardians cared little for this interloper. They bullied her, wouldn't let her finish her studies, treated her as nothing more than a servant. In the first week of May 1949 Betty received shocking news: her mother had died in San Francisco after a brief illness. The thirteen-year-old had never felt so alone. It slowly dawned on Betty Jaboneta that she would not be returning to the States, that she was fated to remain in the Philippines. For weeks she cried herself to sleep.

Betty was forced to work for her guardians for another two years. At age fifteen they married her off without her consent. Her life only got worse after that. Her husband maltreated her. The marriage did not last. After eight years he left his wife and family. In a strange way, Betty was now free.

But she would have to support her two children by herself. Without much of an education, the young woman's options were few. She ended up taking a job as a laundress.

Elizabeth Jaboneta Peralta is now in her midsixties, living with a friend in Bacolod. She has no property. She has no money. And she still takes in laundry.[14]

ON THE TWENTIETH OF OCTOBER 1944, General Douglas MacArthur made good his promise to the people of the Philippines. He returned.

He brought with him an invasion force of one hundred seventy thousand. They landed on Leyte, the most eastward of the Visayas. It was only the beginning of a long campaign to wrest control of the islands from the Japanese.

SWPA's careful development of and support for the resistance movement had already paid big dividends by providing the general with a constant flow of valuable information. Soon the guerrillas would be able to turn their attention toward battling their hated enemy, the Hapon. Guerrilla rosters overflowed with men willing and able to fight for their country—more than two hundred thousand in the ten military districts. On Negros Colonel Salvador Abcede commanded twelve thousand of those patriots.

When liberation came, the colonel and his guerrillas were there to assist.

On 29 March 1945, troops of the U.S. Army's 40th Division crossed the Guimaras Strait to assault Negros. They landed at Pulupandan, south of the capital, Bacolod, encountering little resistance from the Japanese. But as the Americans pushed inland the enemy began to fight back from defensive positions in the foothills. Abcede's men quickly proved their value, for they knew the terrain like the backs of their hands. There was nowhere the Japanese could hide without the guerrillas knowing where they were and how to get at them.

Fierce fighting continued throughout the spring. In early June, in an ironic turnabout, it was the Japanese who fled for the protection of the mountains, hotly pursued by the rebels.[15]

Once the war was won, most resistance fighters simply went home to resume their lives. But the colonel stayed in the Philippine Army. His own government awarded him two medals; the United States honored him with three, including the Distinguished Service Cross. At the end of 1945 his superiors thought enough of Abcede to send him to the prestigious Command and General Staff School at Fort Leavenworth, Kansas. The course there was usually a stepping-stone to flag rank. Abcede graduated with distinction.

He commanded a battalion of Filipino troops during the Korean War. After that, there was not much for the veteran to do. He watched with bafflement as former subordinates (Ernesto Mata among them) were promoted ahead of him into the highest ranks of the Philippine military. Perhaps seeing the writing on the wall, Salvador Abcede resigned his commission, to become the warden of Bacolod Prison.

Always partial to the bottle, Abcede's drinking grew heavier as the years wore on. A former junior officer later noted, "[D]rinking seemed to be the 'curse' of his life. [In Bacolod] I noticed the corrosive effects of alcoholism. He had thinned and his eyes had lost [their] fire."[16]

In the early 1980s Abcede wrote about his war experiences in *Nita,* a historical novel. The colonel cast himself as the fictional hero in love with a beautiful resistance fighter. Salvador Abcede died a few years later—a real war hero nobody cared about anymore.

Jim Cushing did not even make it to the 1980s.

After the Koga affair he returned to fighting the Hapon. And he did a pretty good job of it. Throughout 1944 and into 1945, the Cebu Area Command fought a number of small, pitched skirmishes with the enemy.

The army's Americal Division, fresh from bitter fighting in Luzon, assaulted Cebu at the end of March. The unit's CO, Major General William H. Arnold, ordered Jim Cushing and his men to capture Cebu City's water supply in the hills behind the town. The CAC encountered heavy resistance from the Japanese dug in at the reservoirs. It took a combat team from the 132nd Infantry four days to overcome the enemy and make the water supply secure.

The CAC's major contribution to the invasion effort was providing intelligence that the Japanese had built minefields just inland from the landing site. The information was good. Engineers discovered an extensive and very deadly trap. Not only had the enemy buried a thick blanket of antitank mines, they also had put hundred-pound bombs beneath these mines. The combination was sufficient to blow a crater the size of a tank. To clear the field soldiers got down on their bellies, cautiously probing the earth with bayonets. It was time-consuming, but eventually safe paths were marked out for the assault troops. Had Cushing not alerted the army to the presence of the mines, a bloodbath would have ensued.

Even while the fighting continued, Cushing was nominated for the second-highest award the Army could give: the Distinguished Service Cross. The citation read:

> Lieut. Col. James Cushing, CE, is cited for extraordinary heroism in the presence of the enemy during the period from 22 January 1944 to 23 March 1945.

> This officer, as Commander, Cebu Area Command, has organized and directed the guerrilla action on Cebu and developed detailed and precise information on enemy dispositions and movement which has proved of great value to military operations.

> In the performance of his duties Lieut. Col. Cushing has displayed high qualities of leadership and exemplary courage and devotion to duty, thereby inspiring the officers and men under his command to perform services of inestimable value under most difficult and hazardous conditions.[17]

The new Philippine government decided to honor Cushing, too. They bestowed upon him a large cash bonus (the amount has never been revealed).

When hostilities ended, Cushing asked for home leave. It was his first break since the war began, and his first visit to the States since coming to the Philippines in the 1930s. Upon returning to the islands he took command of the 43rd Infantry Regiment (Philippine Army), made up of his former CAC fighters. Behind the scenes there was a move afoot to promote Cushing to full colonel. In May 1946 General Styer, commander of Armed Forces, Western Pacific, submitted a recommendation that Cushing be promoted. Cushing must have made some enemies, for Styer's endorsement was "unfavorably considered" by a disgruntled, anonymous staff officer.[18]

By 1949 Jim Cushing had left the army. That year his brother Frank arrived in Manila, wanting to sponsor a charity benefit for Boys Town. Founded in Omaha by Father Edward J. Flanagan in 1917, Boys Town helped troubled teenagers turn their lives around. The community was made famous in the 1938 Academy Award–winning film *Boys Town*, starring Spencer Tracy and Mickey Rooney. Unfortunately, Frank's carnival was a fizzle. Jim later wrote, "not being a businessman he managed to lose a good sum of his own money and plenty of mine."[19]

By this time most of his wartime bonus was gone. And so was his marriage to Fritzi. She returned to her family on Leyte. Cushing decided to get back into the mining business, moving to Palawan in the southern Philippines. He seems to have barely made a go of it. On 26 August 1963, while sailing to Luzon on the interisland steamer *Diana,* James M. Cushing suffered a fatal heart attack. He was only fifty-three.

Leading the guerrillas turned out to be the high point of Jim Cushing's life. Before and after the war his life was punctuated by failures and near misses. But during those forty months on Cebu, Cushing soared to heights few men reach. He was beloved by his people, respected by his enemy.

Admiral Fukudome Shigeru, who had always had the highest regard for the guerrilla commander, expressed "deep regret" about his former captor's untimely death.[20]

THE PHILIPPINES HAVE HARDLY fared any better than Colonels Abcede and Cushing. Due mainly to an archaic class system and rampant corruption, the potential of the land and its people has never fully been realized.

The Spanish ruled the Philippines for three centuries, followed by half a century of American rule. At the urging of the Roosevelt administration, the Philippines were granted commonwealth status in 1935, with a promise of full independence in 1946.[21]

When the war ended, much of the Philippines lay in ruins. Though some officials believed independence should be delayed until the country could get back on its feet, the handover occured as scheduled on the Fourth of July 1946. A succession of duly-elected presidents did little to reform the nation or stamp out graft.

Then Ferdinand Marcos came along in the midsixties. During his first term Marcos lived up to many of his promises for reform. Things went badly wrong during his second term. Using the excuse that a Communist insurgency in the southern islands threatened the security of the Philippines, Marcos declared martial law in 1972. Opposition newspapers were shut down. Dissident politicians were thrown in jail. Congress was dissolved. Marcos ruled his country with an iron fist.

Late in the decade serious opposition began to build. In response, Marcos lifted martial law. But the presidential-ordered 1983 murder of Benigno Aquino, a respected opposition leader, shook the nation. Support for the Marcos regime nosedived. Sensing he needed a new mandate, the president called for an election on 7 February 1986. The wily politician believed he would win easily, but he did not count on Aquino's widow, Corazon, entering the race. Cory caught the imagination of the Filipino people. They saw her as a simple housewife, living in a modest suburban home, aggrieved by the killing of her husband and the ruination of her country.

The election proved a violent one, virulent with cheating by Marcos loyalists. But Cory did well at the polls, too. Both declared victory. That is when the tide began to turn in Aquino's favor.

It was obvious to all that Corazon Aquino, though a political novice, was hugely popular. In late February 1986 the military swung over to her side, forcing Marcos to flee the country. "People Power" had succeeded in ridding the nation of a despot. Now all that remained was to pick up the pieces. Cory served her six-year term, after which the voters handed the reins over to Fidel Ramos, one of the generals instrumental in supporting People Power. Ramos worked hard to help his nation prosper, to catch up with other Asian countries whose economies were growing annually at double-digit rates. But all he could squeeze was a 1 or 2 percent increase.[22]

In the third post-Marcos presidential election a former Filipino movie star with no political experience ran for the top job against better-qualified opponents. And he won. Though Joseph Estrada remains popular with his people, he is being increasingly criticized from both within and without for allowing Marcos-style "cronyism" to creep back into politics. In the fall of 2000, Estrada was impeached by the national assembly.

It may be the destiny of the Philippines that the nation never achieves its potential.

AT THE END OF EVERY SUMMER the veterans of the "silent service" converge to celebrate their victories and mourn their losses. Formed in 1954 "to perpetuate the memory of our shipmates who gave their lives in submarine warfare," the U.S. Submarine Veterans of World War II attracted ten thousand or more to their annual conventions. In 1999 that number was below three thousand, and it will continue to drop. Seventy to eighty years old now, World War II veterans from all services are dying at the rate of a thousand a day.

Every Subvet's favorite pastime is to be with his shipmates. They gather around banquet tables in the host hotel's ballroom, one table for each boat. There the old warriors reminisce about patrols past. When they get thirsty, there is a busy cash bar in the far corner. The beers and whiskeys and mixed drinks help to soften all-too-vivid memories of the terrible events the men experienced half a century before.

*Crevalle*'s table is typical. A wooden model of the ship, with its name carved in large letters, identifies the table for all comers and passersby. The sub's battle flags, embroidered with the results of her seven war patrols, form the centerpiece. Three photo albums are spread across the white tablecloth. They were assembled by Chief Yeoman Al Dempster, who cajoled pictures from a bewildering variety of sources to put together a pictorial history of his boat, including "before"and "after" mug shots of each sailor and officer who served aboard *Crevalle* during the war.

A half dozen or more men sit around the table. Once they catch up on health, family, and retirement news, their conversation shifts to their adventures in the Pacific. "Do you remember the cook, Mother Stokes?" Heads nod. "He made the best birthday cakes I ever had on any boat." Heads nod. "He died last winter." Heads shake. The war stories have been told so many times everyone knows them by heart now. There are no untold stories left. "I'll never forget when Cap'n Munson stopped *Crevalle* in the middle of the Pacific so we could take a swim. That was on the first run. Never seen anything like it before or since." Men smile politely. "Anybody seen Steiny?" That would be Captain Everett Steinmetz, CO on *Crevalle*'s last two war patrols. The men don't call him "Captain" anymore. Everybody's equal now. They just call him Steiny. "Saw him downstairs, he just checked in."

Slightly stooped, white-haired, hard of hearing, Chief Yeoman Al Dempster is the glue holding *Crevalle*'s crew together. He works hard at it: writing a quarterly newsletter, organizing most of the recent reunions, sending condolence cards to widows. And in the mid-1990s the Yeo located many of the passengers his boat had rescued fifty years earlier. He persuaded all the surviving Reals to come to the convention in Las Vegas. Rodger Winn made it one year, Howard Chrisco another. Dick Macasa and Ernie Jaboneta are planning to go to the next meeting. By 1999, with some outside help, Dempster had tracked down the fates of all but one of the forty passengers. Nothing will probably ever be known about Mr. George Andrews.

On the final day of each yearly meeting the submariners gather for "The Tolling of the Bells," a solemn memorial service for those shipmates who and ships that never made it back from the war.

Of the two hundred eighty-eight boats that fought in World War II, nearly 20 percent were lost. Of the fifteen thousand men in the submarine service, one man in four was lost. Considering that the submarine force constituted just 2 percent of all U.S. forces afloat, those are heavy losses indeed.

But that 2 percent inflicted damage far out of proportion to its size. They sank twelve hundred Japanese merchantmen and another two hundred fourteen enemy warships. The total tonnage sent to the bottom, five hundred sixty thousand, was greater than that by all other U.S. forces combined. That includes carrier air, land-based air, surface craft, and other causes. Japan relied almost entirely upon imports of strategic raw materials such as coal and iron, and most especially oil. When the submarines closed the shipping lanes, the empire was fatally crippled. But fifty-two boats never came back. Nor did the thirty-five hundred men and officers who manned them. As the submariners say, they are "on eternal patrol."

And so on that last day the Subvets gather to remember and to pay their respects. As all stand at attention, an honor guard presents the colors. The Pledge of Allegiance is recited. A chaplain says a prayer. Then the name of each missing boat is read aloud. "The *Sealion*." A ship's bell is tolled in its memory. "The *Shark*." The bell tolls again. "The *Grayling*." And the peal reverberates across the room. "The *Wahoo*." And so it goes. And everyone still stands. When all the names have been read, all fifty-two of them, a bugler plays "Taps." As the final notes die away, tears streak many faces. The reunion is over. The submariners disperse. For some it will be the last time.

# Notes

## Chapter 1—Special Mission

1. Captain Walker's official *War Patrol Report* and *Special Mission Report* form the bases for these "sub-speak" quotes.
2. MacArthur to Abcede, radio message, May 1944 (College Park, Md.: National Archives II, RG338). (References to the National Archives II hereafter, NARA.)
3. USS *Crevalle, Report of War Patrol Number Three* (NARA, RG38), p. 31. (Hereafter, *Crevalle*/WPR.)
4. USS *Crevalle, Report of War Patrol Number Three, Enclosure A, Report of Special Mission, 9 May to 12 May 1944.* NARA, RG38, n.p. (Hereafter, *Crevalle*/WPR/SMR.)
5. Crevalle/WPR/SMR, n.p.
6. USS *Searaven, Report of Third War Patrol* (NARA, RG38).
7. Actually, a total of 119 were constructed at four yards.
8. Norman Friedman, *U.S. Submarines Through 1945: An Illustrated Design History* (Annapolis: Naval Institute Press, 1995), p. 297.
9. John D. Alden, *The Fleet Submarine in the U.S. Navy* (Annapolis: Naval Institute Press, 1979), p. 105.

## Chapter 2—The Missionaries

1. Paul Lindholm, *Shadows from the Rising Sun* (Quezon City: New Day Publishers, 1978), p. 2. (Hereafter, Lindholm.)
2. Dean Lindholm, interview with author (19 November 1998). (Hereafter, DLind.)
3. Ibid.
4. Personnel Files, Paul and Clara Lindholm, Board of Foreign Missions, Presbyterian Church in the USA, RG360 (Philadelphia: Presbyterian Historical Society). (Hereafter, PHS/Lind.)
5. Ibid., p. 11.
6. *A Brief History of Silliman University*, www.su.edu.ph/suhist.htm, p. 1.
7. Robert B. Silliman, *Pocket of Resistance* (Manila: Cesar J. Amigo, 1980), pp. 25–26.
8. Donald Bell, interview with author (January 18, 1999). (Hereafter, DBell.)
9. *United States Naval Chronology, World War II* (Washington, D.C.: U.S. Government Printing Office, 1955), pp. 1–7.
10. "Dear Friends" letter, PHS/Lind (5 November 1941).
11. Viola Winn, *The Escape* (Wheaton, Ill.: Tyndale House, 1975), p. 3. (Hereafter, Winn.)
12. Naval chronology, pp. 12–13.
13. Lindholm, p. 3.
14. James and Ethel Chapman, *Escape to the Hills* (Lancaster, Pa.: The Jaques Cattell Press, 1947), pp. 13–16 (Hereafter, Chapman.)
15. Marilee Scaff, interview with author (24 January 1999).
16. Winn, pp. 7–10.
17. Lindholm, p. 6, and Silliman University Files, Board of Foreign Missions, Presbyterian Church in the USA, RG85 (Philadelphia : Presbyterian Historical Society). (Hereafter, PHS/Silliman.)
18. Winn, pp. 11–14.
19. Chapman, pp. 16–18.
20. "Dear Friends" letter (27 July 1941), PHS/Winn.
21. Gardner Winn and Marilee Scaff to author (24 January 1999).
22. Ibid., pp. 20–24.
23. Chapman, pp. 22–23.
24. Abby R. Jacobs, *We Did Not Surrender* (Manila: n. p., 1986), p. 20. (Hereafter, Jacobs.)
25. "Wartime Chronology by Dr. Arthur Carson" (1 April 1944), PHS/Silliman, pp. 3–4.
26. Chapman, p. 24.
27. Winn, pp. 36–37, and Lindholm, p. 11.
28. Ibid., pp. 38–39, and ibid., p. 12.
29. Ibid., pp. 39–40, and ibid., p. 12.
30. Clara Lindholm to author (May 1999).
31. Wedding invitation, Paul and Clara Lindholm, PHS/Lind., RG360.
32. "Interview with Clara and Paul Lindholm by Margaret Deck" (5 July 1983), MS/C272(953) (Philadelphia: Presbyterian Historical Society), p. 5 (Hereafter, PHS/Deck.)
33. "Dear Friends of Rock River" letter (6 May 1934), PHS/Lind.
34. "Paul Lindholm Bio, Revised 1948," PHS/Lind. and PHS/Deck, pp. 4–5.
35. PHS/Deck, p. 6.
36. Ibid.
37. James M. Cushing, *Autobiographical Notes* (Carlisle Barracks, Pa.: Military History Institute, Charles T. R. Bohannon Collection, 1951), p. 3.
38. Ibid., p. 4.
39. Ibid., p. 3.
40. James Halkyard, Evacuee Report (NARA, RG338), p. 5.
41. B. G. Chynoweth, *Unabridged Draft of Out of Slavery* (unpublished MS in the collection of the Military History Institute, Carlisle Barracks, Pa., n. d.).
42. Lindholm, p. 23.
43. DLind.
44. Lindholm, pp. 26–27.

45. Winn, pp. 51–53.
46. Christian Malahay to author (4 March 1999). (Hereafter, Malahay.)
47. Lindholm, p. 29.
48. Ibid., p. 30.
49. Ibid., p. 37.

**Chapter 3—Separation**
1. Winn, p. 67.
2. Malahay.
3. Winn, p. 70.
4. Malahay.
5. Winn, pp. 67–71.
6. Winn, p. 84.
7. Ibid.
8. Ibid.
9. Winn, p. 85.
10. Winn, pp. 84–86.
11. Winn, p. 87.
12. "The First Phase of Colonialism," http://violet. berkeley.edu/~korea/colonialism.html.
13. PHS/Winn, "Lovell Report, 20 November 1930."
14. Gardner Winn to author, (24 January 1999). (Hereafter, Gardner.)
15. "Statement of Purpose," Fellowship of Reconciliation, www.nonviolence.org/for/sop.htm.
16. Gardner.
17. PHS/Winn, "Record of Candidates, Viola Winn."
18. Frederick J. Heuser Jr., *A Guide to Foreign Missionary Manuscripts in the Presbyterian Historical Society* (New York: Greenwood Press, 1988), pp. 15–16.
19. PHS/Winn, "Dear Friends Letters, 1939–1940."
20. Winn, pp. 96–97.
21. Ibid., pp. 100–103.
22. Ibid., pp. 107–110.
23. Ibid., p. 113.
24. Ibid.
25. Malahay.
26. Winn, p. 119.
27. Malahay.
28. Winn, p. 121.
29. Malahay.
30. Winn, p. 121.
31. Ibid., p. 123.
32. PHS/Winn, "Viola Winn Application Files."
33. Malahay and author interview with Carmen Utzurrum Park (13 April 1999).
34. Ibid., pp. 40–41, and p. 11.
35. Author interviews with Dean Lindholm, Constantino Bernardez, and Rodger Winn; also Lindholm, p. 44.
36. Lindholm, p. 45.
37. Ibid., p. 90, and PHS/Deck, p. 12.
38. Winn, pp. 132–133.
39. PHS/Deck, pp. 11–13.

40. Malahay.
41. Winn, pp. 157–158.
42. "Submarine Activities Connected with Guerrilla Operations" (U.S. Navy, NARA, RG38).
43. Lindholm, p. 99.
44. Ibid., pp. 99–100.
45. B. Nisce Viloria, *Escape by Submarine* (Philippines: n. p., n. d.), pp. 20–23.
46. DLind.
47. Rustico Paralejas to author (26 October 1999).
48. Lindholm, pp. 105–106, and Winn, pp. 170–173.
49. Constantino Bernardez to author (2 March 1999). (Hereafter, Bernardez.)
50. Ibid.
51. Lindholm, p. 109, and letter from Clara Lindholm (6 May 1999).
52. Letter from Clara Lindholm (6 May 1999).
53. Motion Picture of the Trek, 8mm, Rodger Winn Collection; letter from Clara Lindholm (6 May 1999).
54. Lindholm, pp. 106–111, and Winn, pp. 174–177.

**Chapter 4—The Sugar Families**
1. Loretta Ossorio, author interview (16 September 1998). (Hereafter, LorettaO.) Undated notes supplied by Mrs. Ossorio (19 October 1998).
2. T. Kawata, ed., *Glimpses of the East* (Tokyo: Nippon Yusen Kaisha Line, 1935), pp. P.I. 1–20.
3. Townsend Griffiss, *When You Go to Hawaii* (Cambridge, Mass.: Riverside Press, 1930), pp. 221–223.
4. George H. Ossorio, Philippine Evacuee Report 350 (NARA, RG338, 3 August 1944). (Hereafter, GOssorio.)
5. Calvert School, www.calvertschool.org/curr1.html and table.html (12 August 1998).
6. Rose Vail Real Howard, interview conducted for author by Thad Lemay (30 July 1998, Mission Viejo, Calif.). (Hereafter, RoseR.)
7. Samuel W. Real, Philippine Evacuee Report 319 (NARA RG338, June 14, 1944). (Hereafter, SamR.)
8. Author interview with RoseR. (15 August 1998).
9. Earl Kenneth Ossorio, author interview (February 1998). (Hereafter, EKOssorio.)
10. Author interviews with William Real and John Real (12 September 1998). (Hereafter, BillR. and JohnR.)
11. LorettaO.
12. Courtland Earl Ashton, Philippine Evacuee Report 346 (11 August 1944), MacArthur Archives, RG16.
13. Courtland Earl Ashton, Philippine Evacuee Report 105 (NARA, RG338, 25 July 1944), p. 2.
14. RoseR.
15. Author interviews, RoseR. (15 and 23 August 1998).
16. BillR.

17. RoseR.
18. Ibid.
19. Major General Charles A. Willoughby, ed., *Guerrilla Resistance Movements in the Philippines* (Brisbane: GHQ, Southwest Pacific Area, 1945), p. 70.
20. EKOssorio (August 1998).
21. *Guerrilla Resistance Movements*, p. 70.
22. GOssorio p. 5.
23. Earl Kenneth Ossorio, Military Attaché Report 49 (Fort Mason, Calif.: NARA, RG338, 5 July 1944), p. 3.
24. Earl Kenneth Ossorio, letter from personal collection.
25. Earl Kenneth Ossorio, documents cited from personal collection.
26. EKOssorio, p. 36.
27. EKOssorio, author conversations (November 1998 and June 1999).
28. Earl Kenneth Ossorio, letter from personal collection.
29. Ibid.
30. RoseR.
31. BillR.
32. Donn V. Hart, "Filipino Resistance on Negros, 1942–1945," *Journal of Southeast Asian History* 5 (1) (1964): 119.
33. BillR.
34. Order from Abcede to Ossorio (15 January 1944). From the collection of Earl Kenneth Ossorio.
35. Loretta Ossorio, letter to author (12 October 1998).
36. EKOssorio, RoseR. LorrettaO.
37. BillR.
38. EKOssorio, BillR.
39. Earl Kenneth Ossorio, author interview (29 September 1998).
40. Ibid.
41. Note from Ossorio to Abcede (29 April 1944). From the collection of Earl Kenneth Ossorio.
42. *Guerrilla Resistance Movements*, pp. 69–70.
43. EKOssorio.
44. Ibid.
45. Ibid.
46. Donn V. Hart, *Securing Aquatic Products in Siaton Municipality, Negros Oriental Province, Philippines* (Manila: Institute of Science and Technology, 1956), pp. 32–55.

**Chapter 5—The Prisoners of War**
1. Jay Russell Snell, author interview (30 May 1998). (Hereafter, Snell.) Also, Jay Russell Snell, Philippine Evacuee Report 294 (NARA, RG319, 13 June 1944). (Hereafter, SnellPER.)
2. Irving Victor Joseph, Philippine Evacuee Report 336 (7 August 1944), MacArthur Archives, RG16. (Hereafter, JosephPER.)
3. John W. Whitman, *Bataan, Our Last Ditch*

(New York: Hippocrene Books, 1990), pp. 24–25.
4. Walter D. Edmonds, *They Fought with What They Had* (Boston: Little, Brown, 1951), pp. 24–33.
5. Howard Chrisco, author interview (1 October 1999). (Hereafter, Chrisco.)
6. Howard Tom Chrisco, Philippines Evacuee Report 292 (NARA, RG319, 13 June 1944). (Hereafter, ChriscoPER.) Shari Chrisco, "Lucky 7 Man" (Ypsilanti: Eastern Michigan University, 1990), unpublished term paper. (Hereafter, Shari.)
7. Floyd Calvin Reynolds, Philippine Evacuee Report 337 (NARA, RG319, 3 August 1944). (Hereafter, ReynoldsPER.)
8. Howard Chrisco, author conversation (5 June 1998).
9. Robert Lewis Young, Philippine Evacuee Report 295 (NARA, RG319, 13 June 1944). (Hereafter, YoungPER.)
10. Joseph Richard Jenson, *Philippine Evacuee Report 335* (7 August 1944), MacArthur Archives, RG16. (Hereafter, JensonPER.)
11. James Fred Dyer, Philippine Evacuee Report 293 (NARA, RG319, 13 June 1944). (Hereafter, DyerPER.)
12. Edmonds, pp. 51–52, 72.
13. Snell.
14. Chrisco, author interview (5 June 1998).
15. Donald Knox, *Death March: The Survivors of Bataan* (New York: Harcourt Brace Jovanovich, 1981), pp. 11–18.
16. Louis Morton, *United States Army in World War II: The War in the Pacific: The Fall of the Philippines* (Washington, D.C.: U.S. Army Center of Military History, 1985), p. 42.
17. Juanita Redmond, *I Served on Bataan* (Philadelphia: J. B. Lippincott, 1943), p. 34.
18. Morton, p. 380.
19. Ibid., p. 44.
20. Ibid., pp. 250–251.
21. Ibid., p. 444.
22. Ibid., p. 567.
23. Ibid.
24. Chrisco.
25. Ibid.
26. Knox, p. 154.
27. Snell.
28. Irving Joseph, "The Imitation Heroes" (unpublished manuscript), p. 4. (Hereafter, JosephMS.)
29. ReynoldsPER and ChriscoPER.
30. Shari, n. p.; Howard Chrisco, author interview (5 June 1998).
31. JensonPER, p. 4.
32. ReynoldsPER, p. 1.
33. ReynoldsPER and ChriscoPER.
34. Celedonio A. Ancheta, *The Wainwright Papers,*

vol. 1 (Quezon City: New Day Publishers, 1980), p. 56.

35. Howard Chrisco, author interview (12 June 1999).

36. Morton, p. 581.

37. Uldarico S. Baclagon, *They Chose to Fight* (Quezon City: Capital Publishing House, 1962), pp. 8–10.

38. ReynoldsPER, p. 3.

39. JosephPER, p. 6.

40. Knox, pp. 198–199, 247.

41. JosephMS, p. 23.

42. DyerPER, p. 3.

43. JosephPER, p. 11.

44. JosephMS, p. 15.

45. Joseph Francis Boyland, *Philippine Evacuee Report 162* (30 June 1944), pp. 15–16. (Hereafter, BoylandPER.)

46. JosephPER, p. 9.

47. ReynoldsPER, p. 14.

48. BoylandPER, pp. 6–7; JosephPER, pp. 7–8.

49. BoylandPER, p. 14.

50. ReynoldsPER, p. 9.

51. JosephMS, p. 29.

52. Ibid, p. 10.

53. BoylandPER, pp. 4, 7, 12, 17.

**Chapter 6—Independence Day**

1. Joseph MS, p. 26.

2. DyerPER, p. 10; Howard Chrisco, author interview (8 June 1999).

3. Chrisco, author interview; YoungPER, pp. 8–10; DyerPER, pp. 10–11; JensonPER, p. 10; ReynoldsPER, p. 20. Complete telling of escape story.

4. Chrisco.

5. Irving Joseph and Tom Bailey, "Up from the Death March of Bataan," *True Magazine* (February 1950), p. 112.

6. Howard Chrisco, author interview (9 June 1998).

7. Chrisco, p. II–4.

8. Ibid.

9. Ibid.

10. ChriscoPER, p. 24.

11. Chrisco, p. I–29.

12. Chrisco; ReynoldsPER, p. 14; YoungPER, p. 12; DyerPER, p. 11; JosephPER, p. 2, JensonPER, p. 10.

13. Chrisco, n. p.; DyerPER, p. 11.

14. Joseph MS, p. 42.

15. DyerPER, p. 7; ChriscoPER, p. 10; ReynoldsPER, p. 11.

16. JosephPER, p. 14.

17. Jesus A. Villamor and Gerald S. Snyder, *They Never Surrendered: A True Story of Resistance in World War II* (Manila: Vera-Reyes, 1982), pp. 195–200.

18. ReynoldsPER, p. 23.

19. ChriscoPER, p. 5.

20. ChriscoPER, pp. 5–6; ShariPER, n. p.

21. John Benjamin Wooster, Philippine Evacuee Report 131 (NARA, RG338, 27 July 1944), p. 9.

22. JensonPER, pp. 1, 4–5, 8, 15.

23. YoungPER, p. 10.

**Chapter 7—Planter, Soldier, Oilman, Spy**

1. George W. Fleischer, Philippine Evacuee Report 297 (NARA, RG338, 14 June 1944).

2. Joan Fleischer Jeffery and Jean Fleischer Montenegro to author (6 June 2000).

3. Robert Carson to author (8 October 1998).

4. Modesta Hughes, author interview (1 July 1999).

5. Dick Macasa, author interviews 1999–2000.

6. Ernesto Jaboneta Jr., author interviews, 1999–2000.

**Chapter 8—The Samurai's Story**

1. John Bishop, "Photo Mission: Truk," *Naval History* (February 1999), pp. 43–46. The planes were actually navy versions of the B-24, dubbed the PB4Y.

2. Samuel Eliot Morison, *History of United States Navy Operations in World War II, vol. 7, Aleutians, Gilberts, and Marshalls* (Boston: Little, Brown, 1951), p. 319.

3. Translations of Intercepted Enemy Radio Traffic, Truk, the Truk Reconnaissance (4 February 1944). Crane Files, NARA, RG38/370/05/16/1-5/2330. (Hereafter, Crane.)

4. Stephen Turnbull, *The Samurai Sourcebook* (London: Arms & Armour Press, 1998), pp. 204–205.

5. *United States Strategic Bombing Survey (Pacific), Interrogations of Japanese Officials,* vol. 2, no. 115, Vice Admiral Fukudome Shigeru (Washington, D.C.: Government Printing Office, 1946), pp. 515–523. (Hereafter, USSBS/Fukudome.)

6. *Japanese Officer Biographies* (Washington, D.C.: Naval Historical Center, Operational Archives Branch).

7. Ibid.

8. John Prados, *Combined Fleet Decoded: The Secret History of American Intelligence and the Japanese Navy in World War II* (New York: Random House, 1995), pp. 485–489.

9. Clark G. Reynolds, *The Fast Carriers: The Forging of an Air Navy* (Annapolis: Naval Institute Press, 1962 [rev. 1992]), pp. 71–72.

10. Morison, loc. cit.

11. Reynolds, pp. 136–139.

12. David C. Evans and Mark R. Peattie, *Kaigun: Strategy, Tactics, and Technology in the Imperial Japanese Navy, 1887–1941* (Annapolis: Naval Institute Press, 1997), pp. 116–124.

13. Ibid., pp. 129–132.

14. Prados, pp. 485–489.

15. ATIS *Limited Distribution Translation 4, "Z" Operation Orders* (Washington, D.C.: Naval

Historical Center, Operational Archives Division, Japanese sources). (Hereafter, Z Plan.)

16. Mark R. Peattie, *Nanyo: The Rise and Fall of the Japanese in Micronesia, 1885–1945* (Honolulu: University of Hawaii, Press, 1988), pp. 206–207.

17. Ibid., pp. 142–143.

18. Francis X. Hezel, *Strangers in Their Own Land: A Century of Colonial Rule in the Caroline and Marshall Islands* (Honolulu: University of Hawaii Press, 1995), pp. 174–175.

19. *Naval Chronology, World War II* (Washington, D.C.: Office of the Chief of Naval Operations, Naval History Division, 1955), pp. 76–77.

20. Prados, p. 551.

21. *USSBS*/Fukudome, p. 522.

22. Crane, *Musashi* (RG38/370/03/17/4/1412, 29 March 1944).

23. Ibid.

24. Samuel Eliot Morison, *History of United States Navy Operations in World War II*, vol. 8, *New Guinea and the Marianas* (Boston: Little, Brown, 1953), pp. 27–34.

25. Klaus Lindemann, *Desecrate 1* (Belleville, Mich.: Pacific Press Publications, 1988), pp. 163–165.

26. *United States Strategic Bombing Survey (Pacific), Interrogations of Japanese Officials*, vol. 2, no. 100, Commander Nakajima Chikataka (Washington, D.C.: U.S. Government Printing Office, 1946), pp. 432–435. (Hereafter, *USSBS*/Nakajima.)

27. Ibid., pp. 169–170, 193.

28. It is unclear what transport group the Japanese saw. There were no invasions in the central or South Pacific until late April and no invasion of Palaus until 15 September 1944, when the marines assaulted Peleliu.

29. Crane, Combined Fleet (CC), (RG38/370/03/04/2/1041, 31 March 1944), 0145.

30. Ibid., 0858.

31. *USSBS*/Nakajima, pp. 432–435.

32. John Toland, *The Rising Sun: The Decline and Fall of the Japanese Empire, 1936–1945* (New York: Bantam Books, 1971), pp. 478–479.

33. Turnbull, p. 299.

**Chapter 9—The Seventh Son**

1. *USSBS*/Fukudome, p. 520. Toland, p. 479.

2. *USSBS*/Fukudome, p. 521.

3. Manuel F. Segura, *The Koga Papers: Stories of WWII* (Cebu City: MFS Publishing, 1994), pp. 3–5. (Hereafter, Segura/*Koga*.)

4. Ibid.

5. Ibid.

6. *USSBS*/Fukudome, p. 521.

7. Segura/*Koga*, pp. 4–5.

8. Ibid., p. 5.

9. Ibid., p. 7.

10. Crane, CC (RG38/370/01/01/1/#1042-1044, 1 April 1944, 2237.)

11. Crane, CC (2 April 1944), 1247.

12. Ronald Lewin, *The Other Ultra* (London: Hutchinson, 1982), p. 90. Also, John Winton, *Ultra in the Pacific* (Annapolis: Naval Institute Press, 1993), p. 67.

13. Crane, CC (2 April 1944), 1310.

14. Ibid., 2124.

15. Ibid.

16. Segura/*Koga*, pp. 10–12.

17. Ibid., p. 12.

18. Manuel F. Segura, *Tabunan: The Untold Exploits of the Famed Cebu Guerrillas in World War II* (Cebu City: MF Segura Publications, 1975), p. 232. (Hereafter, Segura/*Tabunan*.) Also, *USSBS*/Fukudome, p. 521.

19. Crane, CC (3 April 1944), 2119. The paragraph is a combination of two different decodes of the same message. One of the Japanese meanings for *otsu* is "the second." The Navy General Staff may have used this designation because this was the second time the CinC Combined Fleet had been lost under mysterious circumstances in the course of a year.

20. MacArthur to Cushing, radio message NR 2 (5 April 1944), MacArthur Archives.

21. Crane, CC (4 April 1944), 0828.

22. Ibid., 0810.

23. Segura/*Koga*, pp. 18–19.

24. Ibid., pp. 12–13.

25. Ibid.

26. Ibid., pp. 16–17.

27. James M. Cushing, "Autobiographical Notes" (1951). Unpublished manuscript in Military History Institute, Charles T. R. Bohannon Collection, Carlisle Barracks, Pa. Also, Captain M. B. Ordun and Captain W. H. Stephens, "Major Walter Cushing, Guerrilla Leader and Hero of the Ilocos Provinces," undated MS in Walter Cushing File (NARA, RG407). (Hereafter, Cushing and Ordun.)

28. Ibid.

29. Cushing, p. 5

30. Harry Fenton, "1942 Diary." Unpublished MS in Military History Institute, Charles T. R. Bohannon Collection, Carlisle Barracks, Pa., p. 25. (Hereafter, Fenton.)

31. Charles A. Willoughby, ed., *Guerrilla Resistance Movements in the Philippines* (Brisbane: General Headquarters, Southwest Pacific Area, NARA, RG338, 31 March 1945), pp. 34–38. This is the original SWPA document, not to be confused with a compilation of these reports self-published by Willoughby in 1972 (see below). (Hereafter, SWPA/GRM.)

32. Segura/*Tabunan*, p. 189.

33. Fenton, p. 28.

34. Ibid., p. 42.

35. Halkyard, p. 5.
36. Henry Roy Bell, Personal Evacuee Report (NARA, RG338, 17 October 1944).
37. Segura/*Tabunan*, pp. 141–143.
38. Ibid., pp. 141–147.
39. Cushing, p. 6.
40. Scott A. Mills, *Stranded in the Philippines* (Quezon City: New Day Publishers, 1994), p. 71.
41. Segura/*Tabunan*, pp. 190–194.
42. "Cushing, Mrs. Fenton Urge All Guerrillas to Give Up," clipping from unknown Cebu newspaper (17 July 1943), in Charles Joseph Cushing file (NARA, RG338).
43. Segura/*Tabunan*, pp. 196–197.
44. Ibid., pp. 197–201.
45. Ibid., p. 194–195.
46. SWP/GRM, p. 37.
47. Ibid., pp. 203–204.
48. Segura/*Tabunan*, p. 84.
49. "Conference Held in Tupaz," USFIP, 8th Military District, Cebu Headquarters (NARA, RG338).
50. Major General Charles A. Willoughby, *The Guerrilla Resistance Movement in the Philipines* (New York: Vantage Press, 1972), p. 475.
51. Ibid., p. 200.
52. Villamor, p. 265.
53. MacArthur to Cushing (via Abcede-Andrews), radio message NR 44 (NARA, RG407/270/49/23/5/#271, 22 January 1944).
54. Messages from Cushing (NARA, RG33/290/44/3/3/#S184).

**Chapter 10—Terms of Exchange**
1. PRS Action Sheet No.1593 (9 April 1944), MacArthur Archives.
2. Ibid.
3. Segura/*Koga*, p. 21.
4. Segura/*Tabunan*, p. 235.
5. Cushing to MacArthur, radio message NR8 (NARA, RG338, 9 April 1944).
6. Memo to Assistant Chief of Staff, G-2, GHQ, SWPA, from A. H. McCollum (NARA, RG338/290/47/9/1/#47, 11 April 1944).
7. USS *Haddo*, Report of War Patrol Number Five, pp. 16–17, and author correspondence with Admiral Chester W. Nimitz Jr.
8. Cushing to MacArthur, NR 10, via Andrews (NR265 and via Fertig, 11 and 13 April 1944). MacArthur Archives, (RG16 and NARA, RG338).
9. PRS Check Sheet (11 April 1944), MacArthur Archives.
10. Cushing to MacArthur, NR12 (NARA, RG338, 12 April 1944).
11. PRS Check Sheet (13 April 1944), MacArthur Archives.

12. Allison Ind, *Allied Intelligence Bureau: Our Secret Weapon in the War Against Japan* (New York: David McKay Company, 1958), p. 236.
13. Segura/*Koga*, pp. 24–37.
14. Note from Cushing to Japanese (NARA, RG319, 10 April 1944).
15. Note from Ohnisi to Cushing (NARA, RG319, 10 April 1944).
16. Segura/*Koga*, p. 37.
17. Segura/*Tabunan*, p. 247.
18. Note from Ohnisi to Cushing (NARA, RG319).
19. PRS Check Sheet (13 April 1944), MacArthur Archives.
20. Ind, pp. 235–236.
21. PRS Check Sheet (14 April 1944), MacArthur Archives.
22. On 15 April Whitney reported to Sutherland that Fertig claimed he had not received the messages until the twelfth because Cushing was on the run. Fertig's relay of Cushing's NR11 was received by SWPA at 4:44 P.M. on the twelfth, thirty hours after Andrews had relayed the same message. The discrepancy has never been explained. After he was evacuated to Australia in June 1944, Irving Joseph twice told interrogators that Fertig's radio operators told Cebu to "stand by" while they handled other radio traffic. Cushing felt that Fertig had given him the "run-around" at a crucial time.
23. Ibid.
24. Cushing to MacArthur, NR13 (NARA, RG338, 14 April 1944).
25. PRS Check Sheet (14 April 1944), MacArthur Archives.
26. Segura/*Koga* and *Tabunan*, SnellPER and DyerPER, Joseph MS.
27. Crane, CC (17 April 1944), 1602.
28. Cushing to MacArthur, SVC5 (NARA RG33, 23 April 1944).
29. Fertig to MacArthur (NARA, RG338, 25 April 1944).
30. Segura/*Tabunan*, p. 232.
31. PRS Check Sheet (NARA, RG338, 26 April 1944).
32. Cushing to MacArthur, NR26 (NARA, RG338, 2 May 1944).
33. Crane, Koga (3 May 1944), 1200.
34. MacArthur to Abcede, NR69 (NARA, RG407, 7 May 1944).
35. MacArthur to Abcede, NR70 (NARA, RG407, 7 May 1944).
36. MacArthur to Abcede, NR72 (NARA, RG407, 10 May 1944).
37. MacArthur to Abcede, SVC15 (NARA, RG407, 11 May 1944).
38. Fertig to MacArthur, SVC37 (14 April 1944).
39. JosephPER (NARA, RG338), p. 3.
40. *USSBS*/Fukudome, p. 522.

## Chapter 11—Converging Paths

1. *Crevalle*/WPR, p. 11. Post war analysis revealed the target was the 976-ton *Kashiwa Maru*.
2. Alden, p. 46.
3. Norman Friedman, *U.S. Submarines through 1945: An Illustrated Design History* (Annapolis: Naval Institute Press, 1995), p. 247.
4. After the war the ship was identified as the *Nisshin Maru*. "*Crevalle* had downed the largest oil tanker (and, incidentally, the third largest merchant vessel) sunk by submarines thus far in the Pacific War." Theodore Roscoe, *United States Submarine Operations in World War II* (Annapolis: U.S. Naval Institute, 1949), p. 337.
5. *Crevalle*/WPR, p. 26.
6. Ibid.
7. Ibid.
8. Al Dempster to author (1998).
9. *Crevalle*/WPR, p. 26.
10. Richard H. O'Kane, *Clear the Bridge!* (Novato, Calif.: Presidio Press, 1977), p. 40.
11. Maurice "Rocky" Langfeldt, author interview (September 1998), p. 7.
12. William J. Ruhe, *War in the Boats: My World War II Submarine Battles* (Washington, D.C.: Brassey's, 1996), p. 214. Also *Crevalle*/WPR, p. 28.
13. Some of the crew believe the Japanese did indeed hook the sub, and that the reason it took so long to start moving was because *Crevalle* was restrained by a cable put there by a diver (from Walt Mazzone in author interview).
14. *Crevalle*/WPR, pp. 24–29.
15. There also was a torpedo on the forward room's skids. This weapon's warhead had a slight bulge that prevented it from being loaded into the tubes. *Crevalle*/WPR.
16. John Maille, author interview (September 1998), p. 6.
17. Lindholm, p. 114.
18. Howard Chrisco and Russell Snell, author interviews (1998).
19. Benjamin Nisce Viloria, *Escape by Submarine* (Philippines: n. d., n. p.), p. 24.
20. GRM, p. 74.
21. Viloria, p. 5.

## Chapter 12—The Rescue

1. John Maille, author interview (September 1998).
2. *Crevalle*/WPR/SMR, n. p.
3. Chrisco, author interview (19 September 1999).
4. Rose Real, author interviews (1998–1999).
5. Walter F. Mazzone, author interview (February 1998), p. 3. (Hereafter, Mazzone.)
6. Richard Bowe, author interview (1998).
7. Ronald Johnson, author interview (September 1998).
8. EKOssorio, p. 13.

9. Ibid.
10. Edward Dissette and H. C. Adamson, *Guerrilla Submarine* (New York: Ballantine Books, 1972), pp. 119–120. Also, information provided directly by Francis D. Walker Jr.
11. Ruhe, p. 218.
12. Ibid.
13. T. W. E. Bowdler, author interview (February 1998).
14. Mazzone (February 1998, June 1999).
15. Russell L. Forsythe, Philippine Evacuee Report 303 (NARA, RG338, 13 June 1944).
16. Abcede to MacArthur (via Andrews), NR72, radio message (NARA, RG338, 10 May 1944).
17. Mazzone.
18. Ibid.
19. Benjamin Nisce Viloria, *They Carried On* (Manila: Veterans Federation of the Philippines, 1998), pp. 190–191.
20. Howard Chrisco and Ronald Johnson, author interviews (1998).
21. Jay Russell Snell, author interview (1998), p. 22.
22. LOssorio, author interview (1998).
23. Ben Viloria to Al Dempster, letter (June 1998).
24. John Real, author interview (11 September 1998), p. 10.
25. Bill and John Real, author interviews (1998–2000).
26. Winn, p. 182.
27. Lindholm, p. 119.
28. LOssorio, p. I.14.
29. BReal, author interviews (1998–2000)
30. Walt Mazzone, author interview (I), p. 4, and (II), p. 9.
31. Chrisco, author interviews (June 1998, June 1999).
32. EKOssorio, author interview (August 1999).
33. Clara Lindholm, author interview (12 June 1999).
34. Winn, pp. 184–185.
35. Chrisco, II, p. 10.
36. Lindholm, p. 119.
37. *Crevalle*/WPR, pp. 1–20.
38. *Crevalle*/WPR, p. 32.
39. Summary of articles from the 10 January, 7 February, and 21 February 1944 issues of *Life* magazine.
40. Dissette, p120.
41. Gerald Stutzman, author interview (September 1998), p. 4.
42. Mazzone, I, p. 7.
43. Richard Bowe (June 1998), p. 5.

## Chapter 13—Precious Cargo

1. Bowdler (February 1998), p. 3.
2. *Crevalle*/WPR, p. 34.
3. Bowdler, p. 4, and Dissette, p. 121.
4. Ronald Johnson, author interview (September 1998).

5. Berna Real Catallo, letter to author (16 February 1998).
6. Jack William Singer, author interview (September 1998), p. 3; Winn, p. 187.
7. Langfeldt (September 1998), p. 3.
8. Chrisco (June 1998).
9. LOssorio (September 1998); Lindholm, p. 121.
10. Lindholm, p. 121.
11. Snell (June 1998), p. 23.
12. William John Curran, author interview (September 1998), p. 4.
13. Dean Lindholm to William J. Ruhe, (25 May 1993).
14. Winn, p. 187.
15. *Crevalle*/WPR, p. 64.
16. Singer, pp. 4, 7.
17. *Crevalle*/WPR, p. 39.
18. Lindholm to Ruhe (25 May 1973).
19. Lindholm, pp. 121-123.
20. *Crevalle*/WPR, p. 66.
21. Ibid., p. 68.
22. *Crevalle*/WPR/SMR, Annex A, p. 3.
23. Loretta Ossorio to author (November 1998).
24. Ibid.

**Chapter 14—Freedom**
1. EKOssorio (15 August 1999).
2. Ind, p. 203.
3. Winn, p. 194.
4. Lindholm, p. 122.
5. Ibid., p. 196.
6. Alan Powell, *The Shadow's Edge: Australia's Northern War* (Melbourne: Melbourne University Press, 1988), pp. 132-133.
7. EKOssorio, author interview (12 November 1998).
8. Powell, p. 45.
9. Jaboneta, author interview (1999-2000).
10. Winn, p. 197.
11. Ibid., p. 198.
12. Ibid., p. 200.
13. Prados, p. 551.
14. James C. McNaughton to author (6 March 2000).
15. Sydney Forrester Mashbir, *I Was an American Spy* (New York: Vantage Press, 1953), pp. 270-272.
16. Z Plan, p. 1
17. Prados, p. 551.
18. GRM, p. 210.
19. BReal, p. 59.
20. Arthur McCollom, Oral History, 13-618 (Annapolis: U.S. Naval Institute, 1971).
21. W. J. Holmes, *Double-Edged Secrets: U.S. Naval Intelligence Operations in the Pacific During World War II* (Annapolis: Naval Institute Press, 1979), p. 179.
22. Edwin T. Layton, Roger Pineau, and John

Costello, *And I Was There* (New York: William Morrow, 1985), p. 485.
23. Cushing to MacArthur, NR37 (NARA, RG338, 22 May 1944).
24. Whitney Memo to Sutherland (NARA, RG338, 23 May 1944).
25. Whitney to Cushing (NARA, RG338, 23 May 1944).
26. Abcede to MacArthur, NR132 (NARA, RG338, 29 May 1944).
27. MacArthur to Abcede, NR59 (NARA, RG338, 31 March 1944).
28. Segura/*Tabunan*, p. 251.
29. Winn, pp. 202-204, BReal, n. p.
30. EKOssorio (15 August 1999).
31. Jaboneta (August 1999).
32. Chrisco, author interview (4 November 1998).
33. Bernard C. Nalty, *Cape Gloucester: The Green Inferno* (Washington, D.C.: Marine Corps Historical Center, 1994), p. 32.
34. EKOssorio (26 October 1999).
35. Lindholm, p. 111; Winn, p. 206.
36. Winn, pp. 206-207
37. JReal (4 October 1999).
38. EKOssorio (October 1999).
39. Bill and John Real, Dick Macasa, Ernie Jaboneta, and Modesta Hughes, author interviews (1998-2000).
40. Snell (15 April 2000).
41. Chrisco (4 November 1998).

**Chapter 15—The Admirals**
1. "Pacific Ocean," *Encyclopædia Britannica Online*. http://members.eb.com/bol/topic?eu=11536&sctn=1&pm=1.
2. William T. Y'Blood, *Red Sun Setting: The Battle of the Philippine Sea* (Annapolis: Naval Institute Press, 1981), pp. 11-13
3. Peattie, pp. 123-130.
4. Layton, p. 471.
5. Thomas B. Buell, *The Quiet Warrior: A Biography of Admiral Raymond A. Spruance* (Annapolis: Naval Institute Press, 1987), p. 17.
6. Ibid., pp. 212-213.
7. *War Diary*, Commander, Fifth Fleet (NARA, RG38, June 1944). (Hereafter, *WD*/Com5.)
8. Z Plan, p. 1.
9. Ibid., p. 6.
10. Morison, vol. 8, p. 315.
11. Buell, p. 293.
12. Noel F. Busch, "Task Force 58," *Life* (17 July 1944), p. 19.
13. CincPac Daily Intelligence Summary (NARA RG457, 14 June 1944). (Hereafter, CincPac.)
14. Z Plan, p. 1.
15. Ibid., p. 6.
16. *WD*/Com5, p. 3.
17. Action Report, Commander Task Force 58 (NARA, RG38, June 1944).

18. Crane (NARA, RG38, 3 May 1944).
19. Holmes, pp. 178-179.
20. JICPOA Bulletin 76-44, Naval Historical Center (14 June 1944).
21. Crane (NARA, RG38, 6 May 1944).
22. CincPac (NARA, RG457, 14 June 1944).
23. U.S. Strategic Bombing Survey, *The Campaigns of the Pacific War* (Washington, D.C.: U.S. Government Printing Office, 1946), pp. 226-231. (Hereafter, USSBS/Campaigns.)
24. CincPac (NARA, RG457, 6 June 1944).
25. U.S. Strategic Bombing Survey, *Interrogations of Japanese Officials*, vol. 2 (Washington, D.C.: U.S. Government Printing Office, 1946), p. 566. (Hereafter, USSBS/2.)
26. Morison, vol. 8, p. 216.
27. James H. and William M. Belote, *Titans of the Seas* (New York: Harper & Row, 1975), pp. 236-238.
28. USSBS/2, Fuchida Mitsuo, p. 429.
29. Matome Ugaki, *Fading Victory: The Diary of Ugaki Matome, 1941-1945* (Pittsburgh: University of Pittsburgh Press, 1991), p. 378.
30. WD/Com5, p. 6.
31. CincPac (13 June 1944).
32. Ugaki, p. 397.
33. Morison, vol. 8, pp. 239-240.
34. Ibid., p. 231.
35. WD/Com5, pp. 11-12.
36. Ibid., pp. 13-14.
37. Ibid., pp. 15-16.
38. Ibid., p. 16.
39. Y'Blood, p. 79.
40. E. P. Forrestel, *Admiral Raymond A. Spruance USN: A Study in Command* (Washington, D.C.: Department of the Navy, 1966), p. 137.
41. WD/Com5, p. 18.
42. Taylor, pp. 220-221.
43. WD/Com5, pp. 19-20.
44. Taylor, p. 222.
45. Blair, p. 654.

**Chapter 16—Decisive Battle**
1. USSBS/*Campaigns*, pp. 239-240.
2. Y'Blood, p. 98.
3. Ibid., pp. 94-95.
4. Reynolds, p. 192.
5. Y'Blood, pp. 109-111.
6. Morison, vol. 8, p. 277.
7. Blair, pp. 655-657.
8. WD/Com5, p. 23.
9. Reynolds, p. 195.

10. WD/Com5, p. 24.
11. Reynolds, pp. 200-201.
12. Y'Blood, p. 193.
13. WD/Com5, pp. 30-31.
14. Reynolds, n. p.
15. John T. Mason, ed., *The Pacific War Remembered: An Oral History Collection* (Annapolis: Naval Institute Press, 1986), p. 209.
16. Naval Chronology, pp. 108-110.
17. USSBS/2, p. 522.

**Notes for the Epilogue**
1. Buell, p. 429.
2. Taylor, p. 305.
3. Bud Cunnally, *Ship's History USS Crevalle (SS291).* www.cyburban.com/~protrn/crevalle.htm (20 May 2000).
4. Lindholm, pp. 201-204.
5. PHS/Deck.
6. Christian Malahay to author (4 March 1999).
7. PHS/Winn, pastoral letter (4 May 1945).
8. Rustico Paralejas to author (26 October 1999).
9. Dora Winn, Gardner Winn, and Rodger Winn, author interviews (1998 to 2000).
10. Bill and John Real, author interviews (1998-2000).
11. Ibid.
12. Jay Russell Snell, author interviews (1998-2000).
13. Howard Tom Chrisco, author interviews (1998-2000).
14. Elizabeth Jaboneta Peralta, correspondence with author (May 2000).
15. Robert Ross Smith, *The War in the Pacific: Triumph in the Philippines* (Washington, D.C.: Department of the Army, Office of the Chief of Military History, 1963), pp. 607-608.
16. Paralejas, letter to the author (May 2000).
17. Citation to Accompany the Award of the DSC, RG16, MacArthur Archives (undated).
18. Aide-mémoire from Catlin Tyler, RG16, MacArthur Archives (27 May 1946).
19. Cushing, *Autobiographical Notes* (1951), p. 2.
20. Segura/*Tabunan*, "James Cushing Heart Attack Victim at 53," *Manila Times* (29 August 1963), n.p. (Segura also n.p).
21. Villamor, pp. 258-259.
22. Ronald E. Dolan, ed., *Philippines: A Country Study* (Washington, D.C.: Library of Congress Federal Research Division, 1991). http://lcweb.loc.gov/frd/cs/phtoc.html#ph0032 (1 June 2000).

# BIBLIOGRAPHY

## Books

Abcede, Salvador. *Salvador Abcede's Historical Novel Nita.* N. p.

Alden, John D. *The Fleet Submarine in the U.S. Navy.* Annapolis: Naval Institute Press, 1979.

———. *U.S. Submarine Attacks During World War II.* Annapolis: Naval Institute Press, 1989.

Ancheta, Celedonio A., ed. *The Wainwright Papers*, vol. 1. Quezon City, Phil.: New Day Publishers, 1980.

Baclagon, Uldarico S. *They Chose to Fight.* Quezon City, Phil.: Capital Publishing House, 1962.

Belote, James H. and William M. *Titans of the Seas: The Development and Operations of Japanese and American Carrier Task Forces in World War II.* New York: Harper & Row, 1975.

Blair, Clay Jr. *Silent Victory: The U.S. Submarine War Against Japan.* New York: Bantam, 1976.

Bryant, Alice Franklin. *The Sun Was Darkened.* Boston: Chapman & Grimes, 1947.

Buell, Thomas B. *The Quiet Warrior: A Biography of Admiral Raymond A. Spruance.* Annapolis: Naval Institute Press, 1987.

Chapman, James and Ethel. *Escape to the Hills.* Lancaster: Pa.: The Jaques Cattell Press, 1947.

Clark, J. J., and Clark G. Reynolds. *Carrier Admiral.* New York: David McKay, 1967.

De Uriarte, Higinio. *A Basque Among the Guerrillas of Negros,* trans. Soledad Lacson Locsin. Bacolod City, Phil.: n.p., 1962.

Dissette, Edward, and H. C. Adamson. *Guerrilla Submarine.* New York: Ballantine Books, 1972.

Edmonds, Walter D. *They Fought with What They Had.* Boston: Little, Brown, 1951.

Evans, David C., and Mark R. Peattie. *Kaigun: Strategy, Tactics, and Technology in the Imperial Japanese Navy, 1887–1941.* Annapolis: Naval Institute Press, 1997.

Forrestel, E. P. *Admiral Raymond A. Spruance USN: A Study in Command.* Washington, D.C.: Department of the Navy, 1966.

Friedman, Norman. *U.S. Submarines Through 1945: An Illustrated Design History.* Annapolis: Naval Institute Press, 1995.

Garratt, Colin. *Iron Dinosaurs.* Poole, U.K.: Blandford Press, 1976.

Griffiss, Townsend. *When You Go to Hawaii.* Cambridge, Mass.: Riverside Press, 1930.

Hamilton, Captain James W., and 1st Lieutenant William J. Bolce Jr. *Gateway to Victory: The Wartime Story of the San Francisco Army Port of Embarkation.* Palo Alto, Calif.: Stanford University Press, 1946.

Hart, Donn V. *Securing Aquatic Products in Siaton Municipality, Negros Oriental Province, Philippines.* Manila: Institute of Science and Technology, 1965.

Heuser, Frederick J. *A Guide to Foreign Missionary Manuscripts in the Presbyterian Historical Society.* New York: Greenwood Press, 1988.

Hezel, Francis X. *Strangers in Their Own Land: A Century of Colonial Rule in the Caroline and Marshall Islands.* Honolulu: University of Hawaii Press, 1995.

Holmes, W. J. *Double-Edged Secrets: U.S. Naval Intelligence Operations in the Pacific During World War II.* Annapolis: Naval Institute Press, 1979.

Ind, Allison. *Allied Intelligence Bureau: Our Secret Weapon in the War Against Japan.* New York: David McKay, 1958.

Ingham, Travis. *Rendezvous by Submarine: The Story of Charles Parsons and the Guerrilla-Soldiers in the Philippines.* Garden City, N.Y.: Doubleday, Doran, 1945.

Jacobs, Abby R. *We Did Not Surrender.* Manila: n. p., 1986.

Jones, Ken, and Hubert Kelley Jr. *Admiral Arleigh (31-Knot) Burke: The Story of a Fighting Sailor.* Philadelphia: Chilton Books, 1962.

Kawata, T., ed. *Glimpses of the East.* Tokyo: Nippon Yusen Kaisha Line, 1935.

Knox, Donald. *Death March: The Survivors of Bataan.* New York: Harcourt Brace Jovanovich, 1981.

Layton, Edwin T., Roger Pineau, and John Costello. *And I Was There: Pearl Harbor and Midway—Breaking the Secrets.* New York: William Morrow, 1985.

Lewin, Ronald. *The Other Ultra: Codes, Ciphers, and the Defeat of Japan.* London: Hutchinson, 1982.

Lindemann, Klaus. *Desecrate I.* Belleville, Mich.: Pacific Press Publications, 1988.

Lindholm, Paul. *Shadows from the Rising Sun.* Quezon City, Phil.: New Day Publishers, 1978.

Lockwood, Charles A., and Hans Christian Adamson. *Hellcats of the Sea*. New York: Greenberg, 1955.
Lockwood, Douglas. *Australia's Pearl Harbour: Darwin 1942*. Melbourne: Cassell Australia, 1966 (revised ed., 1967).
Masbhir, Sydney Forrester. *I Was an American Spy*. New York: Vantage Press, 1953.
Mason, John T., ed. *The Pacific War Remembered: An Oral History Collection*. Annapolis: Naval Institute Press, 1986.
Mills, Scott A. *Stranded in the Philippines*. Quezon City, Phil.: New Day Publishers, 1994.
Morison, Samuel Eliot. *History of United States Navy Operations in World War II*, vol. 7: *Aleutians, Gilberts, and Marshalls*. Boston: Little, Brown, 1951.
———. *History of United States Navy Operations in World War II*, vol. 8: *New Guinea and the Marianas*. Boston: Little, Brown, 1953.
Morton, Louis. *United States Army in World War II: The War in the Pacific: The Fall of the Philippines*. Washington, D.C.: U.S. Army, Center of Military History, 1985.
Nalty, Bernard C. *Cape Gloucester: The Green Inferno*. Washington, D.C.: Marine Corps Historical Center, 1994.
Netzorg, Morton J. *The Philippines in World War II and to Independence (December 8, 1941-July 4, 1946): An Annotated Bibliography, 2nd ed.* Detroit: Cellar Book Shop, 1995.
Norman, Elizabeth M. *We Band of Angels: The Untold Story of American Nurses Trapped on Bataan by the Japanese*. New York: Random House, 1999.
Office of the Chief of Naval Operations, Naval History Division. *U.S. Naval Chronology, World War II*. Washington, D.C.: U.S. Government Printing Office, 1955.
Office of the Chief of Naval Operations, Naval History Division. *U.S. Submarine Losses: World War II*. Washington, D.C.: U.S. Government Printing Office, 1963.
O'Kane, Richard H. *Clear the Bridge!: The War Patrols of the USS* Tang. Novato, Calif.: Presidio Press, 1977.
Peattie, Mark R. *Nanyo: The Rise and Fall of the Japanese in Micronesia, 1885-1945*. Honolulu: University of Hawaii Press, 1988.
Powell, Alan. *The Shadow's Edge: Australia's Northern War*. Melbourne: Melbourne University Press, 1988.
———. *War By Stealth: Australians and the Allied Intelligence Bureau, 1942-1945*. Melbourne: Melbourne University Press, 1996.
Prados, John. *Combined Fleet Decoded: The Secret History of American Intelligence and the Japanese Navy in World War II*. New York: Random House, 1995.
Price, Willard. *Pacific Adventure*. New York: Reynal & Hitchcock, 1936.
Redmond, Juanita. *I Served on Bataan*. Philadelphia: J. B. Lippincott, 1943.
Reynolds, Clark G. *The Fast Carriers: The Forging of an Air Navy*. Annapolis: Naval Institute Press, 1992.
Roscoe, Theodore. *United States Submarine Operations in World War II*. Annapolis: Naval Institute Press, 1949.
Ruhe, William J. *War in the Boats: My World War II Submarine Battles*. Washington, D.C.: Brassey's, 1996.
Segura, Manuel F. *The Koga Papers: Stories of WWII*. Cebu City, Phil.: MFS Publishing, 1994.
———. *Tabunan: The Untold Exploits of the Famed Cebu Guerrillas in World War II*. Cebu City, Phil.: MF Segura Publications, 1975.
Sherrod, Robert. *History of Marine Corps Aviation in World War II*. San Rafael, Calif.: Presidio Press, 1980.
Silliman, Robert B. *Pocket of Resistance*. Manila: Cesar J. Amigo, 1980.
Smith, Holland M., and Percy Finch. *Coral and Brass*. New York: Charles Scribner's Sons, 1949.
Smith, Robert Ross. *United States Army in World War II: The War in the Pacific: Triumph in the Philippines*. Washington, D.C.: U.S. Army, Center of Military History, 1963.
Spencer, Louise Reid. *Guerrilla Wife*. Chicago: Peoples Book Club, 1955.
Taylor, Theodore. *The Magnificent Mitscher*. Annapolis: Naval Institute Press, 1991.
Toland, John. *The Rising Sun: The Decline and Fall of the Japanese Empire, 1936-1945*. New York: Bantam Books, 1971.
Turnbull, Stephen. *The Samurai Sourcebook*. London: Arms & Armour Press, 1998.
Ugaki, Matome. *Fading Victory: The Diary of Ugaki Matome, 1941-1945*. Pittsburgh: University of Pittsburgh Press, 1991.
Underbrink, Robert L. *Destination Corregidor*. Annapolis: Naval Institute Press, 1971.
U.S. Army. *Guerrilla Resistance Movements in the Philippines*. Edited by Major General Charles A. Willoughby. Brisbane: GHQ, Southwest Pacific Area, 1945.

U.S. Department of Commerce. *Philippine Islands Sailing Directions, Section 3, Coasts of Panay, Negros, Cebu, and Adjacent Islands,* 2nd ed. Manila: Bureau of Public Printing, 1904.

———. *United States Coast Pilot: Philippine Islands.* Part 1, *Luzon, Mindoro, and Visayas.* Washington, D.C.: U.S. Government Printing Office, 1927.

———. *United States Coast Pilot: Philippine Islands.* Part 2, *Palawan, Mindanao, and Sulu Archipelago.* Washington, D.C.: U.S. Government Printing Office, 1931.

U.S. Navy. *Merchant Ship Recognition Manual: O.N.I. 208.* Washington, D.C.: Office of Naval Intelligence, 1942.

*U.S. Strategic Bombing Survey: The Campaigns of the Pacific War.* Washington, D.C.: U.S. Government Printing Office, 1946.

*U.S. Strategic Bombing Survey (Pacific): Interrogations of Japanese Officials,* 2 vols. Washington, D.C.: U.S. Government Printing Office, 1946.

Villamor, Jesus A., and Gerald S. Snyder. *They Never Surrendered: A True Story of Resistance in World War II.* Manila: Vera-Reyes, 1982.

Viloria, Benjamin Nisce. *Escape by Submarine: From Negros to Australia.* N. p.

———. *They Carried On: Silliman University Men and Women in the Negros Resistance Movement, 1941–1945.* Manila: Veterans Federation of the Philippines, 1998.

Whitman, John W. *Bataan: Our Last Ditch.* New York: Hippocrene Books, 1990.

Willoughby, Charles A., comp. *The Guerrilla Resistance Movement in the Philippines: 1941–1945.* New York: Vantage Press, 1972.

Winn, Viola S. *The Escape.* Wheaton, Ill.: Tyndale House, 1975.

Winter, Barbara. *The Intrigue Master: Commander Long and Naval Intelligence in Australia, 1913–1945.* Brisbane: Boolarong Press, 1995.

Winton, John. *Ultra in the Pacific: How Breaking Japanese Codes and Ciphers Affected Naval Operations Against Japan.* Annapolis: Naval Institute Press, 1993.

Y'Blood, William T. *Red Sun Setting: The Battle of the Philippine Sea.* Annapolis: Naval Institute Press, 1981.

## Periodicals

Bishop, John. "Photo Mission Truk." *Naval History* (February 1999): 43–46.

Busch, Noel. "Task Force 58." *Life* (17 July 1944): 17–23.

"Cushing, Mrs. Fenton Urge All Guerrillas to Give Up," clipping from unknown Cebu City, Philippines, newspaper (17 July 1943). Charles Joseph Cushing File, RG407, National Archives II, College Park, Md.

Hart, Donn V. "Filipino Resistance on Negros, 1942–1945." *Journal of Southeast Asian History* 5, no. 1 (1964): 101–125.

Joseph, Irving, and Tom Bailey. "Up from the Death March of Bataan." *True Magazine* (February 1950): 106–120.

Winn, Viola. "God Walks in the Jungle." *Christian Herald* (August 1946): 32–34.

## Unpublished Sources

Chrisco, Shari. "Lucky 7 Man." Term paper, Eastern Michigan University, 1990.

Chynoweth, B. G. "Unabridged Draft of Out of Slavery." Chynoweth Papers, Military History Institute, Carlisle Barracks, Pennsylvania, n.d.

Cushing, James M. "Autobiographical Notes." Charles T. R. Bohannon Collection, Military History Institute, Carlisle Barracks, Pa., 1951.

Fenton, Harry. "1942 Diary." Charles T. R. Bohannon Collection, Military History Institute, Carlisle Barracks, Pa., 1943.

Joseph, Irving. "The Imitation Heroes." N.d.

*Life.* Various headlines, 10 January, 7 February, 21 February, 1944.

Ordun, M. B., and W. H. Stephens. "Major Walter Cushing, Guerrilla Leader and Hero of the Illocos Provinces." Walter Cushing File, RG407, National Archives II, College Park, Md., n.d.

## Internet Websites

"A Brief History of Silliman University," Dumageute, Phil.: Silliman University (1 February 1999). http://www.su.edu.ph/suhist.htm.

Cunnally, Bud. "Ship's History USS *Crevalle* (SS291)." (5 May 2000). http://www.cyurban.com/~protrn/crevalle.htm.

"Curriculum." Baltimore: The Calvert School (12 August 1998). http://www.calvertschool.org/curr_1.html and /table.html.

Dolan, Ronald E., ed. "Philippines: A Country Study." Washington, D.C.: Library of Congress, Federal Research Division (1991; 1 May 2000). http://lcweb.loc.gov/frd/cs/phtoc.htm;#ph0032.

"The First Phase of Colonialism." Berkeley: University of California (11 February 1999). http://violet.berkeley/edu/~korea/colonialism.html.

"Pacific Ocean." *Encyclopædia Britannica Online* (7 January 2000). http://members.eb.com/bol/topic?eu=11536&sctn=1&pm=1.

"Statement of Purpose." Nyack, N.Y.: Fellowship of Reconciliation (15 February 1999). http://www.nonviolence.org/for/sop.htm.

## Archival Sources

MacArthur Memorial Archives, Norfolk, Virginia
RG16      Papers of Major General Courtney Whitney. These include guerrilla radio messages between the Philippines and MacArthur, personnel files on James M. Cushing, and evacuation reports (military and civilian).

Military History Institute, Carlisle Barracks, Pennsylvania
Charles T. R. Bohannon Collection.
Bradford Grethen Chynoweth Papers.
ATIS Limited Distribution Translation #5 (microfiche).

National Archives II, Modern Military Records, College Park, Maryland
RG24      Records of the Bureau of Naval Personnel. Deck Log of USS *Crevalle* (April–May 1944).
RG38      Records of the Office of the Chief of Naval Operations. These include action reports, war diaries, submarine patrol reports, files of the Seventh Fleet, translations of intercepted enemy radio traffic (Crane Files), and other files.
RG319     Records of the Army Staff: Army Intelligence Files of Philippine Guerrilla Papers. These include radio traffic, files of individual guerrilla districts, evacuation reports (military and civilian), and other files.
RG338     Records of General Headquarters, Southwest Pacific Area (SWPA GHQ). These include guerrilla radio messages between the Philippines and MacArthur, files of the Allied Intelligence Bureau, lists of personnel (201) files, G2 intelligence series, and other files.
RG407     Records of the Adjutant General's Office: Philippine Archive Collection. These include personnel files on guerrilla leaders, daily summary reports of individual guerrilla districts, unit rosters, and other files.

Operational Archives Branch, Naval Historical Center, Washington, D.C.
Japanese Sources, "ATIS Limited Distribution Translation #4."
Command File, Seventh Fleet, "Sub Activities Connected with Guerrilla Organizations."
Biographies of Japanese officers.

Presbyterian Historical Society, Philadelphia, Pennsylvania
RG360     Personnel files from the Board of Foreign Missions. These include members of the Lindholm, Winn, Carson, and Bell families.
RG85      Files of Silliman University, Dumageute, Negros, Philippines. These include the history and operation of the university, prewar and postwar status reports, letters from Dr. Arthur Carson, and other files.

U.S. Naval Institute, Annapolis, Maryland
Oral History Collection (ed. John T. Mason).

# INDEX